PRINCIPLES OF EFFECTIVE LITERACY INSTRUCTION, GRADES K–5

PRINCIPLES OF EFFECTIVE LITERACY INSTRUCTION, GRADES K–5

edited by
Seth A. Parsons
Margaret Vaughn

Foreword by Nell K. Duke

THE GUILFORD PRESS
New York   London

Copyright © 2021 The Guilford Press
A Division of Guilford Publications, Inc.
370 Seventh Avenue, Suite 1200, New York, NY 10001
www.guilford.com

Printed in the United States of America

This book is printed on acid-free paper.

Last digit is print number: 9   8   7   6   5   4   3   2   1

Library of Congress Cataloging-in-Publication data is available from
the publisher.

ISBN 978-1-4625-4604-6 (paperback)
ISBN 978-1-4625-4607-7 (hardcover)

About the Editors

Seth A. Parsons, PhD, is Professor in the School of Education and the Sturtevant Center for Literacy at George Mason University. He teaches in the elementary education, literacy, and research methods program areas. Dr. Parsons's award-winning research focuses on teacher education and development, teacher instructional adaptations, and student motivation and engagement. His work has appeared in many journals of educational research and practice.

Margaret Vaughn, PhD, is Associate Professor of Language, Literacy, and Technology in the College of Education at Washington State University. Dr. Vaughn's research explores adaptive and equitable practices to support student agency and literacy learning, including ways literacy instruction can honor and support students' cultural backgrounds and linguistic strengths. Her work has appeared in many journals of educational research and practice.

Contributors

Steve Amendum, PhD, School of Education, University of Delaware, Newark, Delaware

Julie W. Ankrum, PhD, Department of Professional Studies in Education, Indiana University of Pennsylvania, Indiana, Pennsylvania

Allison Breit, PhD, School of Education, University of Cincinnati, Cincinnati, Ohio

Cynthia H. Brock, PhD, School of Teacher Education, University of Wyoming, Laramie, Wyoming

Gerald Campano, PhD, Literacy, Culture, and International Education Division, University of Pennsylvania, Philadelphia, Pennsylvania

Sarah K. Clark, PhD, David O. McKay School of Education, Brigham Young University, Provo, Utah

Grace Enriquez, EdD, Language and Literacy Division, Lesley University, Cambridge, Massachusetts

Douglas Fisher, PhD, Department of Educational Leadership, San Diego State University, San Diego, California

Nancy Frey, PhD, Department of Educational Leadership, San Diego State University, San Diego, California

Kathy Ganske, PhD, Department of Teaching and Learning, Vanderbilt University, Nashville, Tennessee

María Paula Ghiso, EdD, Teachers College, Columbia University, New York, New York

Erika Gray, PhD, Department of Teacher Education and Higher Education, University of North Carolina at Greensboro, Greensboro, North Carolina

Ying Guo, PhD, School of Education, University of Cincinnati, Cincinnati, Ohio

Andrea Hayden, MA, Albany County School District #1, Laramie, Wyoming

Amy C. Hutchison, PhD, Sturtevant Center for Literacy, George Mason University, Fairfax, Virginia

Christy K. Irish, PhD, College of Education, University of Mary Washington, Fredericksburg, Virginia

Samantha T. Ives, MA, School of Education, George Mason University, Fairfax, Virginia

Gay Ivey, PhD, Department of Teacher Education and Higher Education, University of North Carolina at Greensboro, Greensboro, North Carolina

Kathleen Kniss, PhD, Albany County School District #1, Laramie, Wyoming

Shelly Landreth, EdD, Curriculum and Instruction Department, University of Texas–Permian Basin, Odessa, Texas

Jacquelynn A. Malloy, PhD, Teaching and Learning Department, Clemson University, Clemson, South Carolina

Dixie D. Massey, PhD, Teaching and Learning Department, University of Washington, Seattle, Washington

Mary McGriff, EdD, Department of Literacy Education, New Jersey City University, Jersey City, New Jersey

Chrystine Cooper Mitchell, PhD, Department of Education, York College of Pennsylvania, York, Pennsylvania

Joshua Montgomery, MA, School of Teacher Education, University of Wyoming, Laramie, Wyoming

Aimee L. Morewood, PhD, Department of Curriculum and Instruction/Literacy Studies, West Virginia University, Morgantown, West Virginia

Olivia Ann Murphy, MA, Department of Teaching and Learning, Policy and Leadership, University of Maryland, College Park, Maryland

Evan Ortlieb, PhD, Zucker Family School of Education, The Citadel, Charleston, South Carolina

Allison Ward Parsons, PhD, Sturtevant Center for Literacy, George Mason University, Fairfax, Virginia

Seth A. Parsons, PhD, Sturtevant Center for Literacy, George Mason University, Fairfax, Virginia

Zoi A. Philippakos, PhD, Department of Theory and Practice in Teacher Education, University of Tennessee, Knoxville, Tennessee

Timothy Rasinski, PhD, School of Teaching, Learning and Curriculum Studies, Kent State University, Kent, Ohio

D. Ray Reutzel, PhD, College of Education, University of Wyoming, Laramie, Wyoming

Leslie D. Roberts, PhD, Department of Curriculum, Foundations, and Reading, Georgia Southern University, Statesville, Georgia

Dana A. Robertson, EdD, School of Teacher Education, University of Wyoming, Laramie, Wyoming

Michelle L. Rosen, EdD, Department of Literacy Education, New Jersey City University, Jersey City, New Jersey

Rachelle Savitz, PhD, College of Education, Clemson University, Clemson, South Carolina

Roya Qualls Scales, PhD, School of Teaching and Learning, Western Carolina University, Cullowhee, North Carolina

Susan Schatz, PhD, The School of Education, St. John's University, Queens, New York

Kristin Conradi Smith, PhD, Department of Curriculum and Instruction, William & Mary School of Education, Williamsburg, Virginia

Ankhi Guha Thakurta, MA, Literacy, Culture, and International Education Division, University of Pennsylvania, Philadelphia, Pennsylvania

Jennifer Turner, PhD, Department of Teaching and Learning, Policy and Leadership, University of Maryland, College Park, Maryland

Margaret Vaughn, PhD, College of Education, Washington State University, Pullman, Washington

Madelyn Stephens Wells, MEd, School of Education, George Mason University, Fairfax, Virginia

Katherine Muir Welsh, PhD, School of Teacher Education, University of Wyoming, Laramie, Wyoming

Chase J. Young, PhD, School of Teaching and Learning, Sam Houston State University, Huntsville, Texas

Vassiliki (Vicky) I. Zygouris-Coe, PhD, Department of Teaching and Learning Principles, University of Central Florida, Orlando, Florida

Foreword

What does great elementary literacy instruction look like? No doubt one important answer to this question is that it targets certain areas that we know are important to literacy growth: phonics, vocabulary, writing, and so on. No doubt another important answer regards the specific instructional techniques used—techniques that research has shown to be effective at fostering word reading, vocabulary, and writing development, for example. But another important answer to this question is that great elementary literacy instruction puts these instructional targets and techniques together in just the right way.

Consider a great chef: Their work is more than just the ingredients they select or the technique they use to whisk the batter. It's also the way they put those together: the timing, the coordination, and the respect for each component of the process. Similarly, great elementary literacy instruction is not just about what we teach or the techniques we use to teach it; it's also about the timing, the coordination, and the respect for students that underlies it.

These elusive but impactful aspects of effective literacy instruction are a central emphasis in this book. The chapters offer information about timing, coordination, and respect for students that enables us to maximize the effectiveness of instructional techniques and address specific aspects of literacy development. For the sake of parsimony, I'll point to examples from only a subset of the chapters in the paragraphs that follow.

"Not enough time" is the number one concern I hear from teachers. There are just not enough hours in the school day or school year to do all that we wish we could across literacy, mathematics, science, social studies, social–emotional learning, art education, physical education, music education, health education, recreational and enrichment opportunities, relationship building, and so on. Many chapters in this book offer strategies to reduce challenges related to time. For example, Philippakos's chapter on the integration of reading and writing reveals ways that our instruction can simultaneously serve two purposes—for example, how work on writing words can also support reading words and how we can engage with texts as both mentors or models for writing and to develop comprehension. The chapter by Brock, Zygouris-Coe, Hayden, Montgomery, Kniss, and Welsh offers ways in which we can "have our cake and eat it too" with respect to content-area instruction and literacy development. We can both address content-area learning, which is all too often neglected, particularly in the early elementary grades, while also developing disciplinary literacy. As you read, I encourage you to look for recommendations from chapters that would help you make the most of every minute of our precious time with students.

Reporting on a case study of a highly effective teacher of African American children (and citing Duffy & Hoffman, 2002), Turner (2005) describes the teacher as "orchestrating" instruction: attending to individual students' backgrounds, strengths, and needs; drawing on the classroom environment as an educational tool; selectively deploying curriculum materials; organizing instructional groups and activities; and so on in an "infinitely complex and dynamic" manner (p. 30). Many chapters in this volume offer insights into how to orchestrate aspects of literacy instruction, including the chapter by Turner and her coauthors Mitchell and Murphy. In the chapter "Well-Managed and Efficient Literacy Learning Environments," Reutzel and Clark underscore the importance of some aspects of orchestration not only for students but also for teachers themselves:

> A good many teachers, especially the highly academically qualified and even the morally committed, leave the profession within the first 5 years of teaching for a variety of reasons, but one is most certainly unresolved concerns and struggles in organizing and managing a classroom effectively. (Deans for Impact, 2019)

This and other chapters reveal some teacher dispositions that necessarily underlie effective orchestration, such as Vaughn's chapter discussing teacher adaptability and McGriff and Rosen's chapter highlighting the importance of teacher reflection. Throughout your reading, I encourage you to develop and elaborate your own vision of orchestrating instruction.

Approaching the process of literacy instruction with respect for students is also fundamental to effectiveness (as well as important in its own right). Several chapters in the book address how to learn about students—in terms of specific literacy knowledge and skills and students' interests, family, community, and cultural resources (see in particular the chapter by Ghiso, Campano, and Thakurta)—in the service of providing responsive and asset-oriented literacy instruction. Endeavoring to foster each student's positive engagement with literacy learning is also a form of respect for students. Several chapters take up this topic in various ways. For example, Ivey and Gray examine what "teachers can do to arrange for deep engagement and considerable amounts of reading," and Ives, Wells, and Parsons consider how to engender student autonomy. Even chapters that don't *focus* on motivation and engagement often have some content related to this topic. For example, Young, Rasinski, and Landreth high-light instructional practices to build fluency that are likely to be motivat-ing and engaging to many students, inducing students to persist even in the face of the challenges that reading fluently can pose to developing readers. As you read the book, I encourage you to attend to ways in which teachers can operate with respect for students in literacy instruction.

Not long ago, my collaborators and I had the opportunity to synthe-size a number of studies of exemplary teachers of literacy (Duke, Cer-vetti, & Wise, 2018). In our review, as in this book, it becomes clear that effective literacy instruction is more than just a collection of instructional targets and techniques—although those certainly are important. It is a highly complex venture undertaken with active application of respect for students and entailing careful timing and coordination of instruction, experiences, and environment. Principles conveyed in this book provide valuable guidance for the journey.

NELL K. DUKE, EdD
University of Michigan

REFERENCES

Duffy, G. G., & Hoffman, J. V. (2002). Beating the odds in literacy education: Not the "betting on" but the "bettering of" schools and teachers. In B. M. Taylor & P. D. Pearson (Eds.), *Teaching reading: Effective schools, accomplished teachers* (pp. 375–388). Mahwah, NJ: Erlbaum.

Duke, N. K., Cervetti, G. N., & Wise, C. N. (2018). Learning from exemplary teachers of literacy. *The Reading Teacher, 71*(4), 395–400.

Turner, J. D. (2005). Orchestrating success for African American readers: The case of an effective third-grade teacher. *Reading Research and Instruction, 44*(4), 27–48.

Preface

We—Seth and Margaret, the editors of this book—are committed teacher educators who often discuss preservice teacher preparation courses with one another. We share textbooks used, activities implemented, assignments given, successes, challenges, and so forth. Through these discussions, we agreed that there are specific instructional methods and formats that are effective for supporting students' literacy development. However, such methods cannot simply be applied year after year without modification. Students change, classroom dynamics change, classroom situations change, and thus your instruction, too, must change. This understanding led us to focus on *principles* of effective literacy instruction—principles that we believe preservice elementary teachers must learn to effectively teach literacy.

Teaching children to read requires considerable knowledge about reading processes, child development, and pedagogy (Alvermann, Unrau, Sailors, & Ruddell, 2018; Snow, Griffin, & Burns, 2005). Students' reading proficiency is predictive of their future success (Juel, 1988; Stanovich, 1986). Students' reading proficiency at grade 3, for example, is positively correlated with productive outcomes such as successful employment and negatively correlated with undesirable outcomes such as dropping out of school and imprisonment (Horning, 2007; Steinberg & Almeida, 2004).

Teaching reading, then, is an important aspect of teachers' jobs. And this job is becoming increasingly difficult because classrooms are made up of children with diverse backgrounds, experiences, language proficiencies, and needs (McFarland et al., 2019). While this diversity adds richness to the classroom and enhances the experiences of all students, such variation in reading proficiency increases the skill needed of teachers to effectively reach all students. Thus, classroom literacy instruction is incredibly complex. Students in today's classrooms are increasingly diverse and have a vast array of unique strengths and needs.

For these reasons, lessons rarely proceed exactly as planned. Effective teachers are able to modify and adapt their literacy instruction to meet students' diverse needs and to respond to unanticipated learning situations and increased standards and student literacy outcomes.

Understanding the principles of effective literacy instruction will help novice and experienced teachers effectively plan *and* adapt their literacy instruction. When making instructional plans and adaptations, teachers can turn to these principles to make sound decisions that are rooted in evidence-based practice.

Principles are fundamental knowledge and beliefs that serve as the foundation for behavior. Enhancing teachers' understanding of the principles of effective literacy instruction will help them better reach all students' needs because this understanding allows teachers to flexibly apply effective pedagogy to the diverse situations in which they find themselves. Instructional methods are only as effective as their ability to meet students' needs. And this is where this book can supplement current texts used for teacher education and professional development efforts. The book focuses explicitly on various principles of effective elementary literacy instruction that teachers can flexibly apply to the variability of classroom instruction. Exploring these principles is the purpose of this book. To do so, we have pulled together some of the best scholars and leaders in the field to write chapters on topics in their areas of expertise.

This book is organized by three sections. The first section is "Environment." These principles are organized around the importance of creating and maintaining a print-rich environment that is well organized, efficient, full of high-interest texts, and committed to equity. The second section, "Instruction," is the heart of the book. This section includes 17 chapters, each focusing on one or more research-based principles that inform literacy instruction. The final section, "Teachers," includes two chapters: one on high expectations and one on the importance of supporting teachers as lifelong learners. This text is appropriate for teachers at any level and can be used in preservice literacy courses, graduate courses for reading coaches, or in professional development.

REFERENCES

Alvermann, D. E., Unrau, N. J., Sailors, M., & Ruddell, R. B. (Eds.). (2018). *Theoretical models and processes of reading* (7th ed.). New York: Routledge.

Horning, A. S. (2007). Defining literacy and illiteracy. *Reading Matrix, 7,* 69–84.

Juel, C. (1998). Learning to read and write: A longitudinal study of 54 children from first through fourth grades. *Journal of Educational Psychology, 80,* 437–447.

McFarland, J., Hussar, B., Zhang, J., Wang, X., Wang, K., Hein, S., . . . Barmer, A. (2019). *The condition of education, 2019.* Washington, DC: Institute of Education Sciences, U.S. Department of Education.

Snow, C. E., Griffin, P., & Burns, M. S. (Eds.). (2005). *Knowledge to support the teaching of reading: Preparing teachers for a changing world.* San Francisco: Jossey-Bass.

Stanovich, K. E. (1986). Matthew effects in reading: Some consequences of individual differences in the acquisition of literacy. *Reading Research Quarterly, 21,* 360–407.

Steinberg, A., & Almeida, C. (2004). *The dropout crisis: Promising approaches in prevention and recovery.* Boston: Jobs for the Future.

Contents

PART III. TEACHERS

PART I

ENVIRONMENT

1

. . . .

Print- and Text-Rich Classroom Environments

Allison Ward Parsons and Christy K. Irish

When entering an effective elementary classroom, one of the first visible elements should be plenty of print in the room. There are many forms that this visible print can take, starting with a wide variety of books, anchor charts, word walls, student work products, class-created writing, and much more. The common thread running through each of the above examples is the purposeful use of print as a communication tool to extend student literacy learning across the school day. The print-rich classroom embodies the true purpose of writing: authentic communication with others. Through thoughtful (metacognitive) modeling, a teacher can leverage the print-rich classroom to support students' literacy development and ownership of learning. Immersion in a print-rich classroom models for students that literacy is accepted as part of the regular routine, where writing is used for multiple purposes, such as journals, reading, management, and daily practical application.

Conventional literacy is comprised of speaking, listening, reading, and writing. Students, therefore, must grasp the connection between spoken and written words as a way to share their ideas through speaking and writing, and to understand others through listening and reading. These skills are interrelated (Scarborough, 2002) and progress through predictable stages starting at birth (Tracey & Morrow, 2012). The classroom environment supports students' skill development when teachers design effective print-rich environments with appropriate scaffolding. Print- and text-rich classrooms are a vital component of developing students' literacy knowledge through reading and writing authentic and agentic student communication. Thoughtful immersion in print is an excellent (and low-cost!) way for teachers to demonstrate the practical and engaging aspects of literacy for elementary students.

For the purposes of this chapter, we define *print* as written words that are displayed and available for student reference in a variety of formats. We define *text* as connected print that students encounter during the school day (Duke, 2000). The key characteristic of a *text* is connected meaning that is encapsulated within the linguistic communication (Harris & Hodges, 1995). Examples of texts include books of all genres and formats, poems, songs, and so forth, that students must comprehend. Toward our goal of describing effective uses of classroom print, we separate meaning-based, comprehensible texts and "displayed print" (Duke, 2000, p. 209), which includes word walls, lists, charts, and labels to help students connect printed letters and word labels with classroom objects or curricular content. Both are important to include in classrooms and are used with different purposes.

Theoretical Orientation

Two theories guide this chapter. The first is automaticity theory (LaBerge & Samuels, 1974), which states that there is limited cognitive attention for any given task. In the case of reading, decoding print is laborious and reduces time for the reader to comprehend the text. By thoughtfully immersing students in print that is purposefully used for regular instruction and reinforcement of learning, teachers build student awareness of classroom print, supporting automatic recognition of letters and words.

The second guiding theory is transactional theory (Rosenblatt, 2013), which states that reading is dependent upon an individual's interaction and interpretation of text to derive meaning, most often for learning or enjoyment. Following this theory, each student–print interaction is a chance for learning and reinforcement of knowledge that aids deeper understanding. Especially when considering the needs of students who are not yet fluent readers, Bruner (1966) reminds us that the teacher is irrevocably connected to what and how students learn since they act as intermediaries between written language and spoken language. In this perspective, the teacher provides instruction and opportunities for students to interact with print, thereby making sense of the written words. The teacher guides transactions between students and texts, helping students gain meaning. When students can take advantage of print interactions throughout the day, they learn to automatically recognize and read displayed print, and that words convey useful information to communicate with others. Thus, reading and writing development becomes more appealing and valuable to them.

Creating a Print-Rich Classroom

To provide a print-rich classroom environment, teachers must have a clear understanding of student prior knowledge, language development, and curricular needs. Print and texts available within classrooms should vary according to grade and age levels, and should evolve throughout the school year as students develop literacy knowledge. By considering what students know about print and text, and then planning a variety of purposeful print interaction opportunities for students, teachers can better use classroom space to scaffold student learning.

Students should be involved in the co-creation of most classroom print for two reasons: (1) to learn the conventions and purposes of print and (2) to develop student agency and ownership to build ongoing engagement in learning and literacy. This sense of agency gives students the confidence to take control of their own learning and act strategically and metacognitively (Johnston, 2004).

In the following sections we will describe how a variety of techniques can be thoughtfully and flexibly incorporated into elementary classrooms to enhance students' awareness of and engagement with print in order to enhance literacy development. Each section is organized to aid adaptability between the needs of students in lower (kindergarten through Grade 2) and upper (Grades 3–5) elementary. We urge teachers to be metacognitive about the applications, adapting use for their students as they see fit.

Effective Implementation of Print- and Text-Rich Classrooms

Research supports blending print exposure with explicit instruction (see Chapter 11) to provide younger students and emerging readers with foundational development for concepts of print, vocabulary, and oral language skills (National Early Literacy Panel, 2008; Whitehurst & Lonigan, 1998). More recently, O'Leary and Ehri (2020) demonstrated that explicit instruction is necessary for young students to connect printed letters and words with spoken words, suggesting that orthographic knowledge (correct word spellings) and systematic knowledge (letter names, letter–sound correspondence) are interconnected elements.

As students move through school, print exposure has been shown to significantly relate to students' decoding and fluency (de Jong, Bitter, van Setten, & Marinus, 2009; Ehri, 2005; Mano & Guerin, 2018; Taylor,

Pearson, Peterson, & Rodriguez, 2003) and to their vocabulary, comprehension, and content knowledge (Sparks, Patton, & Murdoch, 2014; Stanovich & Cunningham, 1993). The sophistication of print in the classroom should increase for upper elementary grades. Many students, especially English learners (ELs), will continue to rely on and make connections with the print in their environment, so adaptations to meet student needs are important. For example, while it is unlikely that a fourth-grade teacher in an fully English-speaking classroom would need to label classroom objects with English vocabulary, that same teacher with new EL students may choose to scaffold vocabulary knowledge by matching English labels with students' home language translations (e.g., a worktable could feature a label with the English word *table* and a Spanish-speaking student could translate and write the word *mesa*). Many of the same concepts of print will continue to be used, including book flooding, labels, anchor charts, and word walls (these are described below). Focusing on engaging and authentic print experiences will help establish literacy as a regular facet of the classroom routine.

Connected Texts in Classrooms

Books of all formats and genres are useful to include in classrooms. The term *book flooding* (Elley, 1989) helps teachers consider the number and types of books to have available in a classroom. Providing students with opportunities to read an extensive array of high-interest books has been connected with increased language and reading comprehension (Allington et al., 2010; Mangubhai, 2001). Students are equally likely to enjoy nonfiction and fiction genres, and broad genre exposure builds awareness of different types of books (Duke, 2000; Yopp & Yopp, 2006), further inspiring students to engage in reading.

Picture books should be shelved so that the covers are visible. Novels and other chapter books tend to be thicker and can be shelved with spines facing outward, but the slim spines of picture books mean that students cannot easily identify their favorites and are less likely to pick up and explore a good book. Organizing books by topic, genre, and series can also be helpful: A student who is interested in insects will appreciate the information books arranged according to topic. Similarly, a student who enjoyed *Don't Let the Pigeon Drive the Bus!* (Willems, 2003) may also enjoy *The Pigeon Finds a Hot Dog!* (Willems, 2004) and other books in the series.

Simply displaying books in the classroom is not enough; print must be *used* in order to affect student learning. Books should be read aloud as part of regular instruction and then integrated into other areas of the classroom to deeply connect reading and writing with content learning. For example, sharing Aliki's *Digging Up Dinosaurs* (1988), a picture information book about dinosaurs and paleontologists on a dig, can provide vocabulary and context for a fossil dig experiment. Similarly, books about plant life cycles, such as *The Amazing Life Cycle of Plants* (Barnham, 2018), can add depth of understanding to a seed-growing experiment.

Print Referencing

A text-rich lower-grades classroom also includes multiple opportunities to interactively read aloud with students in a print-referencing style (Justice, Kaderavek, Fan, Sofka, & Hunt, 2009). When print referencing, a teacher adds value to a read-aloud by drawing student attention to interesting features of print embedded in the book illustrations or text. Print referencing aids student understanding of text organization, letters, words, and general print meaning. This can be as easy as discussing a word embedded in an illustration, or inviting young students to match text letters with their initials. Helping students notice print-salient features directs their attention to the text and bridges their literacy development (Zucker, Ward, & Justice, 2009).

Text Sets

To expand older students' understanding of conceptual themes, disciplinary objectives, and student interests, text sets offer a thoughtful approach. These book collections are grouped around a specific theme and should include a variety of genres and formats. Text sets contain similar and repeated vocabulary (Paynter, Bodrova, & Doty, 2005) that reinforces student learning through topic engagement and fluency development through wide reading (Kuhn, 2005). For example, after reading a text set of seven fiction and nonfiction books about mammals, students should notice repetitive vocabulary in the books such that context helps them understand the concepts.

Co-Creating Print in Classrooms

Much of the print in classrooms should be co-created with students to reinforce how and why print is matched with spoken words. When teachers involve students in shared and interactive writing, multiple learning opportunities occur, including knowledge of letter–sound correspondences, letter formation, syntax, grammar, and writing to convey meaning. Further, when teachers encode letter sounds and discuss spelling while writing with students, orthographic and phonological knowledge combine for improved student learning (O'Leary & Ehri, 2020). Interactive writing occurs when the teacher shares the pen with students during writing and they form letters and words to boost their developing skills (McCarrier, Pinnell, & Fountas, 2000).

Labels

Printed words offer students a concrete format to anchor their spoken vocabulary and conceptual understanding. Adding simple labels to classroom objects helps younger students connect objects with their written names. This practice is also helpful for ELs as it provides a concrete connection to vocabulary (Ecchevaria, Vogt, & Short, 2013). Words are learned on an as-needed basis, meaning that a child learns a new word to better communicate with others (Carey, 1978). Noun labels are considered among the easiest to learn (Tomasello, 2003), lending support for physical labels on objects or places in a classroom (e.g., table, whiteboard, shelf).

Much as noun labels are useful for classroom objects and locations in the lower grades, expanded labels are useful for upper-grade students who have learned more about the parts of speech and are ready to expand their vocabulary use. Adding a descriptor or adjective to a simple noun label on an object can build students' awareness of detail and other parts of speech (Paynter et al., 2005). Whereas a kindergarten room may contain simple labels for "chair" and "table," an expanded label would include more information, such as "rocking chair" and "small, yellow, wooden table." A simple co-creation activity invites students to brainstorm and write as many expansions as possible for the labeled object, which expands their concept of the object as well as adjective use.

Concept Charts

Frequently displayed in the classrooms of lower grades are a variety of concept charts to match basic concepts with associated name labels. This includes colors, numbers, opposites, and shapes. Alphabet charts, or friezes, are also classroom fixtures. These often contain upper- and lowercase letters and objects that help students anchor the letter and sound, and some include word labels. Many teachers also affix individual alphabet strips to student desks or work tables to provide an easy visual reference for young students learning to write and match letters with sounds. Concept charts should be placed in a location that is visible to all students and integrated into class discussions to build awareness of print.

Student Names

Students' names are an important component of a text-rich environment because students are regularly asked to recognize their printed names on coat and backpack hooks, desks/tables, take-home folders, and student job boards. Names are words that carry significant meaning for students at an early age and therefore will also be one of their first writing attempts (Cabell, Justice, Zucker, & McGinty, 2009). Writing names should be taught explicitly; one way to do this is by having a student trace the letters in their name and then move to writing the letters. Teachers can build name recognition through print-based activities such as simple puzzles, magnetic letters to first match a name card and then freely spell, or a "name hunt" in the classroom to find their name and those of their classmates.

Word Walls

As students move toward more conventional reading (using letter-sound decoding skills), word walls can be successfully incorporated into the classroom (Neumann, Hood, Ford, & Neumann, 2011). Many teachers introduce word walls with alphabet letter headings. This practice helps students identify and use beginning letters and sounds in words, which supports letter-sound awareness (O'Leary & Ehri, 2020). Again, word walls are most effective when students co-create the print. Examples include adding students' names to the word wall in the early weeks of the school year. Later, students should initiate word entries based on their topic interest, high-frequency words they are learning, and words gleaned from books and curricular content.

An increasingly popular option is to create an interactive word wall so that students can borrow words to use in their writing. This can be as simple as locating the word wall under a whiteboard or bulletin board so it is within easy student reach. Teachers can make two copies of each word, mounting one on the wall, and affixing the second on top with Velcro, a magnet, or other repositionable adhesive. That way, a student can borrow a word to study and use in writing and then easily replace. With regular guided practice reading the word wall, students will learn the words. As that occurs, teachers can free space on the word wall by removing known words and grouping them on a binder ring according to type or content. That way, students seeking high-frequency words can locate the matching word ring and take it back to their seat for use, furthering their ownership of their word learning. By drawing student attention to word wall words and updating words throughout the school year as learning occurs, the word wall remains a dynamic reference point for students.

Word walls in upper elementary classrooms often assume a disciplinary focus to aid content vocabulary development. It is common to find a math word wall in a math center, or a science word wall in the science area. Such word walls can be used to deepen students' conceptual knowledge. For example, grouping words according to semantic clusters (Paynter et al., 2005) or hierarchical relationships (Parsons & Bryant, 2016) helps students identify meaning connections between words and recognize structures and categories. Teachers guide students to notice and label relationships between words. Then students can reference the wall when writing to express content knowledge. Regular student engagement with an upper grades word wall, with familiar words removed and placed on rings for ongoing student reference, remains an important consideration for effective print use.

Personal Dictionaries

While large word walls extend class understanding and organization of new vocabulary, some students may also create personal word walls, dictionaries, or thesauruses to organize words. Personal dictionaries should include words that students use often or are of high interest, and can include a sketch, an example, or a student-created definition to develop word knowledge (Beck, McKeown, & Kucan, 2013). Such collections offer students agentic ownership of new words, which helps develop "word consciousness," or interest and awareness of words (Graves & Watts-Taffe, 2002).

Anchor Charts

Anchor charts are a written documentation of steps, concepts, or thinking processes (Bacchioni & Kurstedt, 2019). These are frequently used to clarify classroom routines, activity instructions, and curricular content, using print to promote student independence (Martinelli & Mraz, 2012). Co-creation of anchor charts helps students understand procedures and concepts through discussion and interactive writing, which serves as a model for written language processes. Particularly for young students and ELs, pictures and words can be mixed to ensure clear comprehension.

Co-created anchor charts can provide written references that remind students of activity expectations. For example, while discussing with students how to use the classroom library (e.g., read a book independently, read to a friend, listen to an audiobook) a teacher can invite student help to write (and draw, when applicable) the shared expectations on an anchor chart and place it close to the library where students will be reminded of expectations. Student agency and engagement increases when they know how to complete their work, and anchor charts add opportunities to interact with print.

Anchor charts also serve as authentic models and mentor texts for craft writing in upper elementary classrooms. For example, after a lesson on writing a friendly letter, the class drafts a sample letter and labels the parts on a chart. They review the procedure and ensure understanding of the purpose and components of the letter-writing process. The anchor chart is then displayed for easy student reference while writing independently.

Increasing Print in Classroom Learning Activities

Print-rich activities should provide opportunities for students to create and practice authentic reading, writing, speaking, and listening. For example, the classroom library offers many opportunities for print-rich activities with connected text. Students can read independently, create a new book jacket, or use nonfiction resources to "fact-check" a fiction book. Adding graph paper and pencils to a science center for students to measure, record, and describe plant growth adds authentic purpose to their work. Similarly, adding folded cardstock and pens to a social studies center and inviting students to create a greeting card for a calendar event offers an authentic communication opportunity.

Upper elementary students often move about the classroom to engage in various activities to practice reading, writing, and oral language development. The teacher and the students can co-create clear written instructions for each workspace that provide directions and options for the center, as well as practical information such as what students do with completed work and how to clean up. For example, if the student writes a letter to a classmate, how can it be delivered? Providing clear expectations will build student agency and responsibility.

Conclusion

Print- and text-rich classrooms show that print has communicative purpose while supporting student learning throughout the school day. Automaticity theory (LaBerge & Samuels, 1974) suggests that repeated and purposeful exposure to print results in increased opportunity for comprehension as cognitive abilities are less tasked with print decoding. Transactional theory (Rosenblatt, 2013) states that all print is understood through individualized interactions between texts and readers. In both cases, thoughtful immersion in print that is co-created and used as part of regular classroom instruction is an effective literacy principle. For students learning to read in lower grades, the print-rich environment bridges students' spoken language with their developing knowledge of reading and writing for shared meaning. For students who are developing fluency in reading and writing, a print-rich environment offers referents and immersion in supportive text that students can employ in their own writing.

REFERENCES

Allington, R., McGill-Franzen, A., Camilli, G., Williams, L., Graff, J., Zeig, J., . . . Nowak, R. (2010). Addressing summer reading setback among economically disadvantaged elementary students. *Reading Psychology, 31*(5), 411–427.

Bacchioni, S., & Kurstedt, R. L. (2019). Personalized anchor charts: Bridging small-group work to independence. *The Reading Teacher, 72*(5), 652–658.

Beck, I. L., McKeown, M. G., & Kucan, L. (2013). *Bringing words to life: Robust vocabulary instruction* (2nd ed.). New York: Guilford Press.

Bruner, J. S. (1966). *Toward a theory of instruction.* Cambridge, MA: Harvard University Press.

Cabell, S. Q., Justice, L. M., Zucker, T. A., & McGinty, A. S. (2009). Emergent name writing abilities of preschool-age children with language impairment. *Language, Speech, and Hearing Services in Schools, 40*(1), 53–66.

Carey, S. (1978). The child as a word learner. In M. Halle, J. Bresnan, & G. Miller (Eds.), *Linguistic theory and psychological reality* (pp. 264–293). Cambridge, MA: MIT Press.

de Jong, P. F., Bitter, D. J. L., van Setten, M., & Marinus, E. (2009). Does phonological recoding occur during silent reading, and is it necessary for orthographic learning? *Journal of Experimental Child Psychology, 104*(3), 267–282.

Duke, N. K. (2000). 3.6 minutes per day: The scarcity of informational texts in first grade. *Reading Research Quarterly, 35,* 202–224.

Ecchevaria, J., Vogt, M., & Short, D. J. (2013). *Making content comprehensible for English learners: The SIOP model* (4th ed.). Boston: Pearson.

Ehri, L. C. (2005). Learning to read words: Theory, findings, and issues. *Scientific Studies of Reading, 9*(2), 167–188.

Elley, W. B. (1989). Vocabulary acquisition from listening to stories. *Reading Research Quarterly, 24,* 174–187.

Graves, M. F., & Watts-Taffe, S. M. (2002). The place of word consciousness in a research-based vocabulary program. In A. E. Farstrup & S. J. Samuels (Eds.), *What research has to say about reading instruction* (pp. 140–165). Newark, DE: International Reading Association.

Harris, T. L., & Hodges, R. E. (Eds.). (1995). *The literacy dictionary: The vocabulary of reading and writing.* Newark, DE: International Reading Association.

Johnston, P. H. (2004). *Choice words: How our language affects children's learning.* Portland, ME: Stenhouse.

Justice, L. M., Kaderavek, J., Fan, X., Sofka, A., & Hunt, A. (2009). Accelerating preschoolers' early literacy development through classroom-based teacher–child storybook reading and explicit print referencing. *Language, Speech, and Hearing Services in Schools, 40*(1), 67–85.

Kuhn, M. R. (2005). A comparative study of small group fluency instruction. *Reading Psychology, 26,* 127–146.

LaBerge, D., & Samuels, S. (1974). Toward a theory of automatic information processing in reading. *Cognitive Psychology, 6,* 293–323.

Mangubhai, F. (2001). Book floods and comprehensible input floods: Providing ideal conditions for second language acquisition. *International Journal of Educational Research, 35,* 147–156.

Mano, Q. R., & Guerin, J. (2018). Direct and indirect effects of print exposure on silent reading fluency. *Reading and Writing, 31,* 483–502.

Martinelli, M., & Mraz, K. (2012). *Smarter charts (K–2): Optimizing an instructional staple to create independent readers and writers.* Portsmouth, NH: Heinemann.

McCarrier, A., Pinnell, G. S., & Fountas, I. C. (2000). *Interactive writing: How language and literacy come together, K–2.* Portsmouth, NH: Heinemann.

National Early Literacy Panel. (2008). *Developing early literacy: Report of the National Early Literacy Panel.* Washington, DC: National Institute for Literacy. Retrieved from *https://lincs.ed.gov/publications/pdf/NELPReport09.pdf.*.

Neumann, M. M., Hood, M., Ford, R. M., & Neumann, D. L. (2011). The role of environmental print in emergent literacy. *Journal of Early Childhood Literacy, 12*(3), 231–258.

O'Leary, R., & Ehri, L. C. (2020). Orthography facilitates memory for proper names in emergent readers. *Reading Research Quarterly, 55*(1), 75–93.

Parsons, A. W., & Bryant, C. L. (2016). Deepening kindergarteners' science vocabulary: A design study. *Journal of Educational Research, 109*(4), 375–390.

Paynter, D. E., Bodrova, E., & Doty, J. K. (2005). *For the love of words: Vocabulary instruction that works.* San Francisco: Jossey-Bass.

Rosenblatt, L. M. (2013). The transactional theory of reading and writing. In D. E. Alvermann, N. J. Unaru, & R. B. Ruddell (Eds.), *Theoretical models and process of readings* (6th ed., pp. 923–956). Newark, DE: International Reading Association.

Scarborough, H. S. (2002). Connecting early language and literacy to later reading (dis)abilities: Evidence, theory, and practice. In S. B. Neuman & D. K. Dickinson (Eds.), *Handbook of early literacy research* (pp. 97–110). New York: Guilford Press.

Sparks, R. L., Patton, J., & Murdoch, A. (2014). Early reading success and its relationship to reading achievement and reading volume: Replication of "10 years later." *Reading and Writing, 27,* 189–211.

Stanovich, K. E., & Cunningham, A. E. (1993). Where does knowledge come from?: Specific associations between print exposure and information acquisition. *Journal of Educational Psychology, 85*(2), 211–229.

Taylor, B. M., Pearson, P. D., Peterson, D. S., & Rodriguez, M. C. (2003). Reading growth in high-poverty classrooms: The influence of teacher practices that encourage cognitive engagement in literacy learning. *The Elementary School Journal, 104*(1), 3–28.

Tomasello, M. (2003). *Constructing a language: A usage-based theory of language acquisition*. Cambridge, MA: Harvard University Press.

Tracey, D. H., & Morrow, L. M. (2012). *Lenses on reading. An introduction to theories and models*. New York: Guilford Press.

Whitehurst, G. J., & Lonigan, C. J. (1998). Child development and emergent literacy. *Child Development, 69*, 848–872.

Yopp, R. H., & Yopp, H. K. (2006). Informational texts as read-alouds at school and home. *Journal of Literacy Research, 38*, 37–51.

Zucker, T. A., Ward, A. E., & Justice, L. M. (2009). Print referencing during read-alouds: A technique for increasing emergent readers' print knowledge. *The Reading Teacher, 63*(1), 62–72.

CHILDREN'S LITERATURE

Aliki. (1988). *Digging up dinosaurs*. New York: Crowell/Harper & Row.

Barnham, K. (2018). *The amazing life cycle of plants*. Highlands Ranch, CO: Peterson's and BES.

Willems, M. (2003). *Don't let the pigeon drive the bus!* New York: Hyperion Books for Children.

Willems, M. (2004). *The pigeon finds a hot dog!* New York: Hyperion Books for Children.

2

•••••

Well-Managed and Efficient Literacy Learning Environments

D. Ray Reutzel and Sarah K. Clark

One question that teachers ask about most frequently is how to organize their classrooms to be efficient and well managed. While it may seem a trivial task, organizing the classroom literacy environment is arguably the most important place to begin preparing for rigorous and effective literacy instruction (Reutzel & Clark, 2011). Even after 30 years, the words of Chall, Jacobs, and Baldwin (1990) still ring true: "No one will debate the idea that a rich literacy environment is helpful for achievement in literacy" (p. 162). When a teacher walks into his or her classroom for the first time, myriad questions will likely emerge, such as "Where will whole-class and small-group instruction take place?"; "Will I have a classroom library? If so, where will it be?"; "Which books will I include in my library?"; "Where should I put writing supplies?"; "How will the children interact with me and peers?"; and "How will I use display areas and labels in my classroom to encourage literacy development?" These questions provide a cognitive framework to design a rich, responsive literacy classroom environment as a foundation for effective literacy instruction.

The complexities of the classroom environment have been explained from a bioecological (Brofenbrenner & Morris, 2006), from a transactional (Morrison & Connor, 2009), and from a developmental perspective (Rimm-Kaufman, La Paro, Downer, & Pianta, 2005). These perspectives, or theories, help us understand the influence the classroom environment has on students and the effectiveness of the teaching and learning that will occur there.

So then, what does an organized classroom set up to be an optimal and effective literacy classroom look like? Reutzel and Jones (2010) articulated seven important guidelines to consider:

1. Provide ample literacy materials and supplies.
2. Organize and arrange the classroom physical space as well as the literacy materials and supplies.
3. Establish effective routines and procedures that are understood and practiced by children.
4. Design strong literacy instruction that reflects an established curriculum based on the Common Core State Standards for the English Language Arts (CCSS-ELA; National Governors Association Center for Best Practices & Council of Chief State School Officers, 2010) and objectives.
5. Incorporate effective literacy instructional practices that are based on empirical evidence.
6. Incorporate effective progress monitoring practices that can inform instruction to meet the needs of all learners.
7. Establish and maintain regular communication between parents and families about each child's literacy progress.

Similar themes within research suggest that teachers consider the physical organization of the classroom itself, including the traffic flow and furniture arrangement, accessibility to and quality of materials and texts, rules and procedures governing interactions in the classroom, the role each adult plays in the classroom, the content knowledge, knowledge about literacy skill acquisition, abilities of individual students, and the opportunities for student choice and initiative to encourage student engagement (Morrow, Reutzel, & Casey, 2013).

Four Essential Literacy Components

The CCSS-ELA describe four components of effective literacy instruction: (1) reading, (2) writing, (3) listening, and (4) speaking. In what follows, we describe the literacy classroom environment from the perspective of these four essential literacy components.

Reading

In order to support foundational reading skill acquisition and comprehension, teachers have long been encouraged to provide a wide variety and types of texts for students. These include literature, poetry, informational texts, brochures, maps, recipe books, newspapers, comic books, and graphic novels. Teachers also help students to make cross-cultural connections through reading literature and informational text (Duke, Cervetti, & Wise, 2018). Texts should introduce a wide variety of genres, topics, and themes. Texts are stored in a well-organized classroom library where students have easy and frequent access (Reutzel & Clark, 2011). Texts can be organized in a variety of ways, including reading levels, themes, or topics, and by type (e.g., literature, poetry, and informational texts). The texts in the classroom library should be rotated regularly to keep it fresh and engaging for students.

To encourage reading, teachers can make the classroom library comfortable with pillows, rugs, a rocking chair, and containers that make selecting and putting texts away easy. Teachers should consider a check-out system so texts and materials do not get lost. Print may also be displayed for students to "read the room" (see Chapter 1 for extended examples).

Writing

Zhang, Hur, Diamond, and Powell (2015) have described how materials and resources in a classroom can support and enhance writing instruction. When organizing the classroom for writing instruction, teachers consider the types of writing materials that are made available to students. For example, these might include a visible alphabet frieze, word cards, writing prompts and templates, a variety of paper (e.g., lined, blank, colored, graph, notepads, sticky notes), a variety of writing tools (e.g., pens, pencils, label maker, computer/printer, stamps/pad), and examples of writing completed by teachers, others, and the students themselves. The teacher should create a designated place for writing to occur that is comfortable and where students have easy access to writing materials. Reutzel and Clark (2011) also recommend a word wall where students can add word cards as the year progresses to encourage vocabulary development or a sight word wall to encourage learning words that need to be memorized instead of decoded.

Speaking and Listening

Teachers need to be thoughtful and intentional in order to help students develop their oral language and listening skills. Teachers can stock their classrooms with whisper phones to allow students to practice speaking and hearing themselves speak (Thoermer & Williams, 2012), plastic or old/unused cell phones, menus from local restaurants, engaging read-aloud books that teachers have already shared (Lynch-Brown, Tomlinson, & Short, 2010), books that provide rich language opportunities (e.g.,

Where the Wild Things Are by Maurice Sendak and *Click, Clack, Moo: Cows That Type* by Doreen Cronin; Whorrall & Cabell, 2016), and free choice center activities such as a café, kitchen mealtime setting, a dress-up or theater area, a puppet and a puppet stage, multiple small-group settings for students to engage in conversation, non-teacher-directed activities, and natural settings and opportunities for students to use sophisticated words, repeat words, and ask questions (Dickinson & Porche, 2011; Early et al., 2010).

Teachers also ensure that children have exposure to a variety of digital texts they can listen to (Allington, 2012) using a variety of technology-based devices, such as a Kindle, an iPad, a Nook (Larson, 2007), or a Chromebook and a set of headphones. Additionally, there are a wide variety of quality apps and websites that teachers can employ to assist students in developing listening and speaking skills (e.g., see *www.storylineonline. net*). See Figure 2.1 for an example of how to set up a literacy classroom designed to help children learn to read, write, listen, and speak effectively.

One final question: How can a teacher determine whether their classroom has been designed and organized in ways that will encourage effective literacy instruction? There are three well-researched assessments teachers can use to examine the quality of literacy environments in their classrooms. These three instruments include (1) the Classroom Literacy Environmental Profile (CLEP; Wolfersberger, Reutzel, Sudweeks, & Fawson, 2004); (2) the Child/Home Early Language and Literacy Observation (CHELLO; Neuman, Dwyer, & Koh, 2007); and (3) the Early Language and Literacy Classroom Observation, Pre-K (ELLCO Pre-K; Smith, Brady, & Anastasopoulos, 2008). These instruments can assist teachers in determining how the organization and areas of their classroom can be strengthened in order to lay the foundation for effective, meaningful, and rich literacy instruction.

What Does Effective Literacy Instruction Look Like?

The elements of effective literacy instruction for young children have long been a topic of research, discussion, and argument. The findings of the National Reading Panel (NRP; National Institute of Child Health and Human Development, 2000) outlined five essential evidence-based recommendations of daily literacy instruction for teachers to implement into their daily literacy instruction: (1) phonological awareness, (2) phonics, (3) fluency, (4) comprehension, and (5) vocabulary. Yet, according to the National Assessment of Educational Progress (National Center for Education Statistics [NCES], 2019), one of the biggest educational challenges of our time is providing high-quality literacy instruction to *all* students.

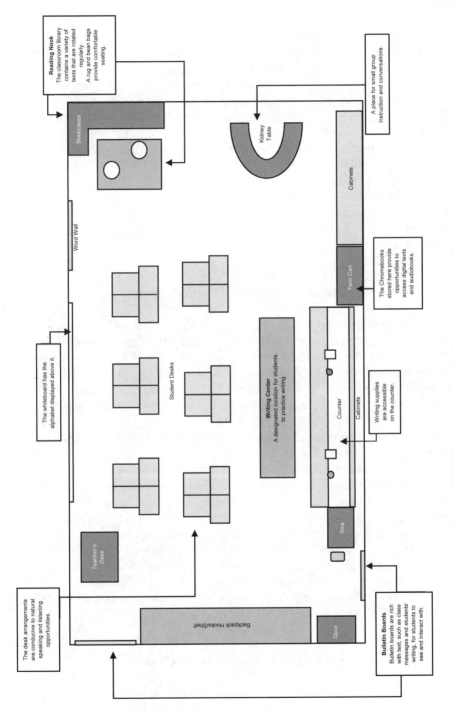

Reading Nook
The classroom library contains a variety of texts that are rotated regularly.
A rug and bean bags provide comfortable seating.

A place for small group instruction and conversations.

Kidney Table

Cabinets

Tech Cart

The Chromebooks stored here provide opportunities to access digital texts and audiobooks.

Bookcases

Word Wall

The whiteboard has the alphabet displayed above it.

Student Desks

Writing Center
A designated location for students to practice writing.

Counter

Cabinets

Writing supplies are accessible on the counter.

Sink

Teacher's Desk

The desk arrangements are conducive to natural speaking and listening opportunities.

Backpack Hooks/Shelf

Door

Bulletin Boards
Bulletin boards are rich with text, such as class messages and students' writing, for students to see and interact with.

FIGURE 2.1. Example of a literacy classroom layout.

A recent report of the National Assessment of Educational Progress (NCES, 2019) suggested that only 35% of fourth graders in the United States were reading at proficient or advanced reading levels. These results are concerning because children who do not read proficiently by the end of third grade have a greater likelihood of dropping out of school, experiencing long-term academic failure and diminished career and academic opportunities in their future (Fiester, 2010).

Many researchers have demonstrated that literacy development is initiated long before children enter school and receive formal instruction (Neuman & Dickinson, 2003). Unfortunately, most children will not naturally progress through developmental phases of emergent literacy without intentional instruction from a knowledgeable and skilled teacher along with numerous opportunities to practice literacy skills (Snow, Burns, & Griffin, 1998).

Literacy Instruction for *All* Students

Response to intervention (RTI), or a multi-tiered system of support (MTSS), is an effective approach for identifying students who need more than what the general education classroom instruction in literacy could provide (Fuchs & Fuchs, 2017). Fuchs and Fuchs (2017) recommend a three-tiered approach that offers Tier 1, Tier 2, and Tier 3 instruction. Tier 1 is described as grade-level literacy instruction and is provided to the majority of students (80%) in a classroom, and this tier is seen as preventative and proactive (Fletcher & Vaughn, 2009). Tier 2 instruction attends to the needs of approximately 15% of students who are at risk and are in need of rapid, responsive, and targeted small-group interventions. In some schools when adequate resources and personnel are available, Tier 2 instructional time has also been used to support students who benefit from instruction that is beyond grade-level instruction (see Colorado Department of Education, 2016). Tier 3 instruction employs more frequent, individual interventions that are assessment based and program driven of longer duration. Some schools employ either a pull-out approach where students leave the classroom to work with a specialist or a push-in approach with specialists coming into the classroom to work with students (Rissling & Kucan, 2018).

The Value of Explicit Instruction

In addition to RTI, researchers also recommend explicit instruction to provide intentional and purposefully instructional interactions among teachers and students. Explicit instruction has been shown to be an effective instructional model for teaching children to read (National Institute of Child Health and Human Development, 2000). While researchers have defined explicit instruction in a myriad of ways, it has commonly been described as instruction that employs teacher modeling, guided, and independent practice as key components for teaching students a wide variety of literacy skills and strategies (Archer & Hughes, 2011). Torgesen (2004) described explicit instruction as "instruction that does not leave anything to chance and does not make assumptions about skills and knowledge that children will acquire on their own" (p. 363). See Chapter 10 for an extended discussion of explicit instruction.

Because many elementary schools in the United States have adopted and rely heavily on a core literacy program to provide resources for daily literacy instruction, it is important to note that many core literacy programs do not include all components of explicit instruction (Reutzel, Child, Jones, & Clark, 2014). Consequently, teachers will need to carefully consider what resources to use and what might need to be supplemented in the core literacy programs to ensure effective explicit instruction occurs.

Instructional Time Allocation and Distribution: The Coin of the Classroom Realm

Another critical component in setting up an effective and well-managed literacy classroom is to establish a daily instructional routine that allocates sufficient time (allocated learning time) for English language arts (ELA) instruction. Not surprisingly, research has demonstrated that the more time students spend engaged in learning, the more they learn (Brophy & Good, 1986). That should almost seem to go without saying, but we believe it bears emphasis here. As a teacher, you set the stage for effective literacy instruction by how much time you allocate and how well you use the time allocated. This means that instructional factors like conceptual tempo, pacing of lessons, transitions between lessons, practice design, movement of students within and outside the classroom to different learning settings, and individual and group response rates all play an essential role in how much and how well students learn.

Time is a limited resource. Ask anyone on the street if they have enough time, and the answer is always, no! In fact, ask some people if they need more money or more time, and they would often trade money for more time. There is no time to waste when it comes to teaching and learning ELA in schools and classrooms! How well students will learn the ELA is inextricably linked to *how much time* is allocated overall in the daily classroom instructional schedule and *to which elements* of the ELA standards, concepts, and skills time is allocated.

How much time should teachers allocate in a school day to ELA instruction? There is no absolute answer to this question. However, based on the results of a yearlong naturalistic experiment in Chicago Public Schools, Shanahan (2004) found that teachers who allocated a minimum of 120 total minutes to ELA instruction each day achieved remarkable results. His research showed that 120 minutes of time allocated specifically to the daily literacy block strongly predicted school effectiveness and led to the highest level of student ELA outcomes ever recorded in the history of the Chicago school district.

In another study (see Figure 2.2), we see how allocation of time within the literacy block relates to school effectiveness (Taylor, 2011). It is clear from an examination of Figure 2.2 that the more effective schools in literacy allocated more time to small-group instruction, independent reading, and writing in response to reading, and less time to other independent activities.

Why would small-group instruction, reading independently, and writing in response to reading be so highly predictive of literacy outcomes for students? Most teachers teach these in small groups to be able to target interventions in *tiered* literacy instruction to meet students' identified ELA learning needs. Small groups are also more effective settings to ensure that students are *actually* reading and writing because teachers require students to respond to instruction and practice tasks more frequently with increased feedback (Mathes et al., 2005).

	Minutes Spent in Whole Group	Minutes Spent in Small Group	Minutes of Independent Reading	Minutes Writing in Response to Reading	Minutes in Other Independent Activities	Total Minutes in Reading
Most Effective Schools	25	60	28	14	7	134
Moderately Effective Schools	37	26	27	15	7	112
Least Effective School	30	38	19	9	17	113

FIGURE 2.2. Allocated time in reading instruction by level of school effectiveness.

Organizing time in classrooms to provide students with access to adequate time in small-group instruction is absolutely vital. But time in small-group instruction alone is insufficient to produce great learning outcomes. For example, having students participate in what some teachers call "center" activities where they might spend time cutting out words for word sorts and gluing them on a sorting sheet, listening to books read aloud on a recording device, coloring pictures on a worksheet of words representing initial consonant sounds, using book nooks to read when they cannot yet read, and so forth, have little relationship to student learning outcomes. In fact, these types of independent activities are often a waste of instructional time and effort for both teachers and students. As Diller (2003) notes in *Literacy Work Stations: Making Centers Work,* "If it takes longer to make something than it does for children to use it instructionally, then don't bother making it" (p. 10). Many teachers have been led to believe that 40 minutes in independent learning centers is a great exchange of instructional time in order to be able to support small-group, tiered ELA instruction. This is only true if the independent practice provided maximizes the number of repetitions a student is expected to perform within the time allocated.

Spaced, short practice intervals over time, versus what is called *massed* practice, is more effective for students to learn and apply essential, foundational early literacy concepts, skills, and strategies, for example, a letter a week (Jones & Reutzel, 2012). The number of required student responses or repetitions within any learning activity, including literacy center activities, is highly related to how well students will develop literacy skills, concepts, and strategies.

The concept of interleaving instruction is also vital. *Interleaving* is a process where teachers arrange practice opportunities that mix multiple ELA concepts, skills, or strategies during practice in order to improve learning. *Blocked* practice, on the other hand, involves studying a single concept, topic, skill, or strategy very thoroughly before moving to another topic. It is important that practice focuses on more than a single skill, concept, or strategy in ELA instruction (Epstein, 2019). For example, if students are practicing phonemic awareness, working on initial phoneme identification and also segmenting spoken words into phonemes is an example of interleaving practice for two phonemic awareness skills for optimal learning.

The question "To which ELA elements should practice and instructional time be allocated?" is clearly a matter of prioritization. Teachers ensure that instruction is targeted to essential elements of ELA instruction as opposed to ineffective or less effective elements of ELA instruction. Shanahan (2004) recommends that total daily ELA instructional time ($N = 120$ minutes) be divided into four 30-minute segments focused on the essential evidence-based elements of ELA instruction: foundation skills such as word work, fluency development, comprehension instruction, and writing and spelling (see Figure 2.3).

Organizing allocated ELA learning time in classrooms to provide student access to essential elements of ELA instruction will pay great dividends. After studying Figure 2.3, teachers will notice that this recommended distribution of time to essential instructional elements is directly linked to state standards and ELA Common Core Foundational, Reading, Writing, and Language standards that form the basis or backbone of many classroom, district, and state ELA standards.

Finally, we illustrate four options, ranging from simple to complex, for managing the remainder of the students during the implementation of small-group ELA instruction in the elementary school classrooms (see Figure 2.4).

In Option 1, students work independently or with a partner at their desks or tables completing *daily assigned* literacy tasks. These tasks are often displayed on a classroom list—menu style—where students complete tasks they are assigned each day. During small-group instruction time, the teacher is stationed in an area of the classroom specially prepared to offer tiered small-group instruction to students who share specific instructional needs. The teacher pulls students from the whole class into the small-group instruction, and when small-group ELA instruction is

Foundational Skills Instruction (60 Minutes) Small Groups or Whole Class	Comprehension Strategy Instruction (30 Minutes) Small Groups or Whole Class	Writing and Spelling Instruction (30 Minutes) Small Groups or Whole Class
Word Work (30 Minutes) • Print Concepts • Phonological Awareness • Phonics and Word Recognition **Fluency** (30 Minutes) Using both literature and information text . . . • Rate • Accuracy • Expression	**Literature *and* Information Text** • Key Ideas and Details • Craft and Structure • Integration of Knowledge and Ideas • Range of Reading and Level of Text Complexity **Vocabulary Acquisition and Use**	**Writing** • Text Types and Purposes • Production and Distribution of Writing • Research to Build and Present Knowledge • Range of Writing **Language** • Conventions of Standard English • Knowledge of Language

FIGURE 2.3. Allocation of 120 minutes of ELA instruction time. Adapted by permission from Reutzel and Clark (2019). Copyright © 2019 The Guilford Press.

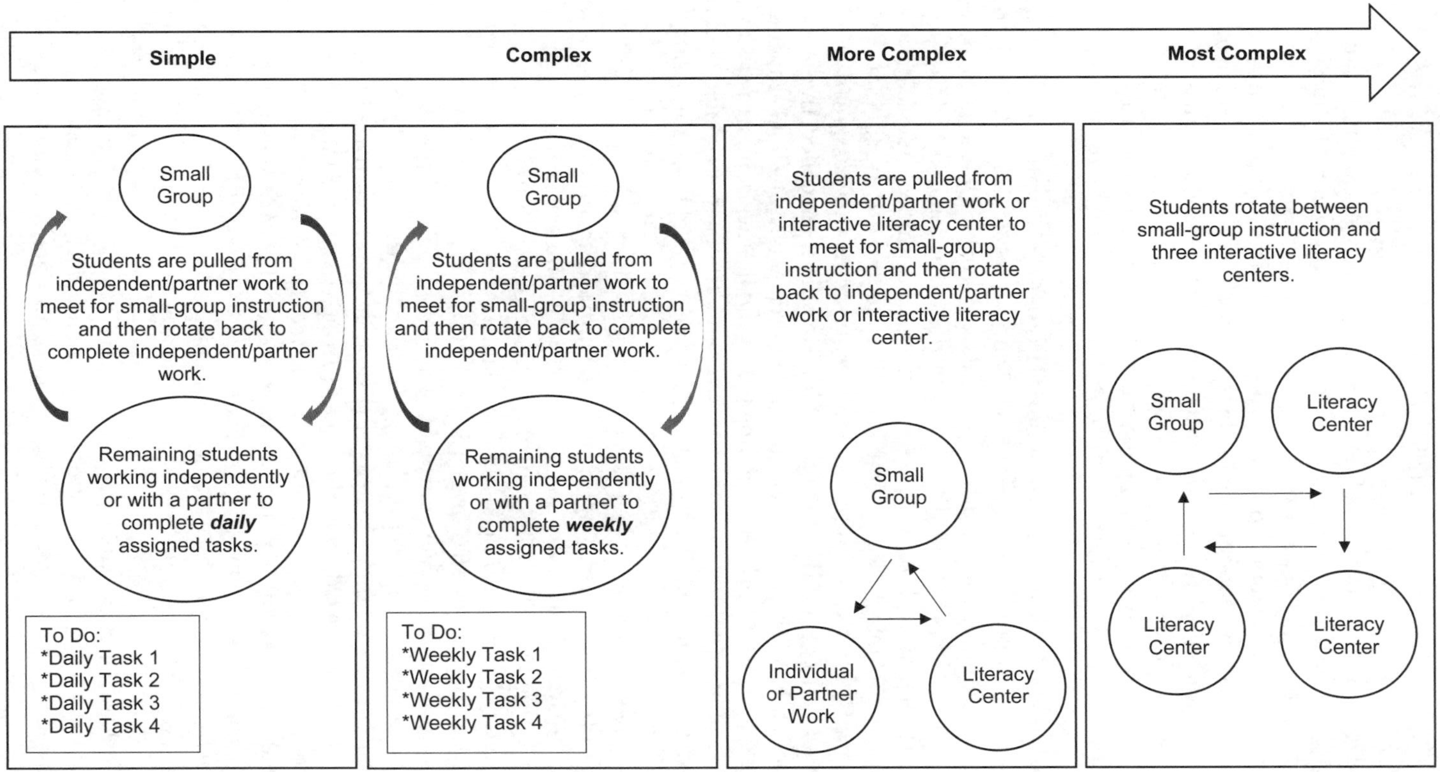

FIGURE 2.4. Options for organizing to support small-group ELA instruction. Adapted by permission from Reutzel and Clark (2019). Copyright © 2019 The Guilford Press.

concluded, students rotate back into the whole-class setting and resume their assigned tasks at their seats and the next small group of students is pulled from the whole-class to receive small-group instruction.

Option 2, the complex option, looks very similar to Option 1 except that the majority of students are working independently or with a partner at their seats, completing weekly instead of daily assigned literacy tasks. This means that assignments may spill over from one day to the next. These weekly tasks are listed menu style, where students select from the menu the order of the tasks they are assigned to complete during the week.

Option 3 is a more complex option. This option is similar to the first two options except that a single literacy center has been introduced into the menu of options. Most of the students are working either independently or with a partner at their seats on their teacher-assigned literacy tasks, or they are working with a small group at an independent literacy center. Students may be assigned a specific time to go to the literacy center or may be invited to go to a literacy center after their assigned tasks are completed for the day or week. This is sometimes called the workshop model. It is important that the teacher create a way to hold students accountable for the work to be completed in the literacy center to ensure that it is not just keeping the students quiet and otherwise occupied while the small teacher-led intervention groups are meeting but that the instructional time being spent in the literacy center is valuable and connected to the objectives to be taught that week.

Option 4, the most complex small-group instruction option, occurs when the teacher works with small, targeted ELA instruction groups and the remaining students rotate through three or more independent literacy centers. This option can also be adapted to include another small-group ELA instruction group that is staffed by a classroom aide, parent volunteer, or another teacher who is assigned to help in the classroom during small-group instruction time—this may be the special education teacher, the English language learner (ELL) teacher, or the Title I teacher or aide. Students are called to their small group (flexible, dynamic, tiered instructional ELA group) from an assigned "center rotation" group (mixed-abilities group). Literacy centers are teacher selected, designed, and provisioned. Literacy centers focus on activities and tasks that reinforce Tier 1 and Tier 2 ELA instructional skills, concepts, and elements of word work, fluency, vocabulary, comprehension instruction, and writing and spelling.

In designing effective literacy centers, it is important that tasks completed at the centers have a component of accountability and performance. We caution teachers against the creation of too many literacy learning centers. In the early part of the year, fewer literacy learning centers are easier for both teachers and students to manage. As the year progresses, adding a few new literacy learning centers, especially optional literacy learning centers, can add variety to the ELA time block. As the school year progresses and students acquire more experience with the rotation between learning centers, we have found it better to assign children a set of specific tasks to be completed among multiple literacy centers rather than a controlling rotation through various literacy centers on a timed basis. In other words, student may want to stay longer in some centers to complete the set of tasks and less time in others. Many teachers introduce or review the expected behaviors and tasks to be used in literacy learning centers at the beginning of each week, check for understanding, and then use the remaining time that day and the rest of the week to focus solely on supplementary ELA instruction.

It is important to note that the option of supplementary ELA instruction, often related to Tier 2 ELA instruction in an RTI scheme of instruction, requires upfront planning and material preparation from the teacher so that students have access to the centers and can work independently, allowing the teacher to focus time and attention on ELA small-group targeted instruction. Establishing clear procedures for this center time, teaching those expectations, and practicing them with the students initially and again whenever needed will maintain the consistent positive working tone that is needed for all students to succeed.

Organizing the ELA Classroom: Preparing Students for Success

Now that we have outlined several options for supporting small-group instruction in the ELA classroom, we discuss how to prepare the students to engage successfully within such an organizational framework. This is a procedural step that is often overlooked by teachers, which leads to disastrous outcomes—having prompted more than one teacher to say when implementing complex supports for small-group ELA instruction, "Well, that didn't work!"

At the beginning of each school year, literacy learning centers in and around the classroom may be fully furnished, have tasks designed, and be ready for the children to use, *but don't be tempted to do so just yet!* Wait until you have had a few weeks of whole-class work to build community and to train students in the expectations for using these classroom literacy learning centers optimally.

We urge teachers to spend small amounts of time each day these first few weeks, perhaps no more than 10 minutes, to explain expectations, set limits, and model appropriate procedures for using and caring for the literacy tools, materials, and tasks found in literacy learning centers. Toward the end of this introductory training period, teachers invite students to role-play how to enter and move among the literacy learning centers in the classroom, how to properly use the materials, how to clean up the literacy tools and materials within each center, and how to manage their time well to complete assigned ELA practice tasks within the time allocated. Finally, a daily schedule of literacy routines should be posted in the classroom in a conspicuous place and reviewed each day with students to help them learn the order and content of the events that will occur each day to create a predictable routine. See Figure 2.5 for an example of what a daily literacy instruction schedule might look like in a third-grade classroom. This sample daily ELA schedule incorporates the Big Five for literacy instruction, the multi-tiered approach, explicit instruction, supplements made to the core literacy program, the CCSS-ELA, and the Next Generation Science Standards (NGSS Lead States, 2013) for third grade.

Minimizing Transition Times and Maximizing Practice and Instruction Time

Training children for efficient movement between activities and into and out of various classroom literacy learning centers is essential for minimizing transition times and maximizing literacy practice and instruction time. Here again, our experience has taught us the value of using timers, stop watches, and so forth, to motivate students to accomplish tasks briskly and without dallying. A worthwhile goal is to reduce transition times between activities and movements to other classroom spaces to a single minute so that the bulk of classroom time is spent on reading and writing practice and instruction. We use three steps to make this happen. First, we use a consistent signal, such as a hotel registration bell or turning off the lights, to alert children to stop what they are doing or freeze and listen for directions. Second, we provide brief, well-sequenced, and repetitive oral directions coupled with written directions displayed on cue cards. Children must look, listen, and read to get the directions for what is to be done. Third, we use our signal device once again to alert children to follow the oral and written directions to move to the next classroom literacy. These procedures, like those procedures we have previously described, should be modeled, practiced, and role-played to ensure that classroom ELA instruction and practice time is maximized.

Third-Grade Schedule for Daily Literacy Block

8:00–8:15 Welcome, Attendance, Lunch Count

8:15–9:00 Whole-Class (Tier 1) Lesson using explicit instruction with supplements provided to the suggested lesson in the core literacy program

CCSS RL.3.1: Teaching students to answer questions referring explicitly to text

9:00–10:00 Small-Group Instruction: Tier 2 Explicit Instruction (*Designed to meet individual student needs in small groups*)

Group 1: Decoding words with vowel teams (using second-grade text)

Group 2: Decoding words with digraphs (using third-grade text)

Group 3: Decoding words with prefixes (using third-grade text)

Group 4: Decoding multisyllabic words (using fourth-grade text)

*During this time, Tier 3 instruction is being provided to one student who needs intensive intervention with instruction provided by special education teacher using a push-in approach.

*When students are not meeting with their teacher during small-group instruction, they are working on a rough draft of their opinion paper that was introduced and taught the previous day.

10:00–10:15 Break

10:15–10:45 Fluency Practice: Students meet in assigned groups to practice Readers' Theater script. The emphasis for the day is on using punctuation to aid expression.

10:45–11:15 Vocabulary Practice: Students design and create their own Word Pictures (see *www.readingrockets.org/article/sharing-wordless-picture-books*) to practice definitions of vocabulary words from text introduced during Whole-Class Tier 1 instruction.

11:15–11:30 Teacher Read-Aloud: To align with NGSS science topic on social interactions and group behavior to help animals survive, teacher reads informational text aloud to students. Book title is *Animal Groups* by Clara MacCarald (Rourke Educational Media).

FIGURE 2.5. Sample of third-grade daily literacy instruction that incorporates the Big Five, a multi-tiered approach, and explicit instruction.

Conclusion

. . . .

Classroom teachers are ordinary people who do extraordinary things (Reutzel & Clark, 2011). They are passionate, talented, and committed individuals who truly want to make a difference in the lives of their students. Many teachers enter the teaching profession filled with optimism, only to encounter the harsh realities of classroom management and organization. A good many teachers, especially the highly academically qualified and even the morally committed, leave the profession within the first 5 years of teaching for a variety of reasons, but one is most certainly unresolved concerns and struggles in organizing and managing a classroom effectively (Deans for Impact, 2019). It is our hope that this chapter has helped our readers to think more clearly, systematically, and strategically about how to organize their ELA instructional routines and classroom literacy environments so that students become avid readers and writers and teachers can enjoy the rewards that inherently come from seeing the light of literacy go on in their students' eyes.

REFERENCES

Allington, R. L. (2012). *What really matters for struggling readers: Designing research-based programs* (3rd ed.). Boston: Pearson.

Archer, A. L., & Hughes, C. A. (2011). *Explicit instruction: Effective and efficient teaching.* New York: Guilford Press.

Brofenbrenner, U., & Morris, P. A. (2006). The bioecological model of human development. In R. M. Lerner & W. Damon (Eds.), *Handbook of child psychology: Vol. 1. Theoretical models of human development* (6th ed., pp. 793–828). Hoboken, NJ: Wiley.

Brophy, J., & Good, T. (1986). Teacher behavior and student achievement. In M. Wittrock (Ed.), *Handbook of research on teaching* (3rd ed., pp. 328–375). New York: Macmillan.

Chall, J. S., Jacobs, V. A., & Baldwin, L. E. (1990). *The reading crisis: Why poor children fall behind.* Cambridge, MA: Harvard University Press.

Colorado Department of Education. (2016). *Colorado READ Act:* Tiers of reading instruction, meeting the needs of all students. Retrieved from *www.cde.state. co.us/coloradoliteracy/tiersofinstruction.*

Deans for Impact. (2019). Learning together through evidence: Insights from year 1. Retrieved from *https://deansforimpact.org/wp-content/uploads/2019/03/ Learning_Together_Through_Evidence_DFI_2019.pdf.*

Dickinson, D. K., & Porche, M. V. (2011). Relation between language experiences in preschool classrooms and children's kindergarten and fourth-grade language and reading abilities. *Child Development, 82,* 870–886.

Diller, D. (2003). *Literacy work stations: Making centers work.* Portland, ME: Stenhouse.

Duke, N. K., Cervetti, G. N., & Wise, C. N. (2018). Learning from exemplary teachers of literacy. *The Reading Teacher, 71*(4), 395–400.

Early, D. M., Iruka, I. U., Ritchie, S., Barbarin, O. A., Winn, D. C., Crawford, G. M., . . . Pianta, R. C. (2010). How do pre-kindergarteners spend their time?: Gender, ethnicity, and income as predictors of experiences in pre-kindergarten classrooms. *Early Childhood Research Quarterly, 25,* 177–193.

Epstein, D. (2019). *Range: Why generalists will triumph in a specialized world.* New York: Riverhead Books.

Fiester, L. (2010). Early warning!: Why reading by the end of third grade matters (KIDS COUNT Special Report, Annie E. Casey Foundation). Retrieved from *https://ed.psu.edu/goodling-institute/policy/special-report-executive-summary.*

Fletcher, J. M., & Vaughn, S. (2009). Response to intervention: Preventing and remediating academic difficulties. *Child Development Perspectives, 3*(1), 30–37.

Fuchs, D., & Fuchs, L. S. (2017). Critique of the national evaluation of response to intervention: A case for simpler frameworks. *Exceptional Children, 83*(3), 255–268.

Jones, C. D., & Reutzel, D. R. (2012). Enhanced alphabet knowledge instruction: Exploring a change of frequency, focus, and distributed cycles of review. *Reading Psychology, 33*(5), 448–464.

Larson, L. C. (2007). *A case study exploring the "new literacies" during a fifth-grade electronic reading workshop.* Doctoral dissertation, Kansas State University. Retrieved from *https://krex.k-state.edu/dspace/handle/2097/352.*

Lynch-Brown, C., Tomlinson, C., & Short, K. (2010). *Essentials of children's literature* (7th ed.). New York: Pearson.

Mathes, P. G., Denton, C. A., Fletcher, J. M., Anthony, J. L., Francis, D. J., & Schatschneider, C. (2005). The effects of theoretically different instruction and student characteristics on the skills of struggling readers. *Reading Research Quarterly, 40*(2), 148–183.

Morrison, F. J., & Connor, C. M. (2009). The transition to school: Child-instruction transactions in learning to read. In A. Sameroff (Ed.), *The transactional model of development: How children and contexts shape each other* (pp. 183–201). Washington DC: American Psychological Association Books.

Morrow, L. M., Reutzel, D. R., & Casey, H. (2013). Organization and management of language arts teaching: Classroom environments, grouping practices, and exemplary instruction. In C. Evertson & C. Weinstein (Eds.), *Handbook of classroom management* (pp. 569–592). New York: Routledge.

National Center for Education Statistics (NCES). (2019). *The nation's report card: A first look; 2019 mathematics and reading* (NCES 2014–451). Washington, DC: Institute of Education Sciences, U.S. Department of Education.

National Governors Association Center for Best Practices & Council of Chief State School Officers. (2010). *Common Core State Standards for English language arts and literacy in history/social studies, science, and technical subjects.* Washington, DC: Authors.

National Institute of Child Health and Human Development. (2000). *Report of the National Reading Panel. Teaching children to read: An evidence-based assessment of the scientific research literature on reading and its implications for reading instruction; Reports of the subgroups* (NIH Publication No. 00-4754). Washington, DC: U.S. Government Printing Office.

Neuman, S. B., & Dickinson, D. K. (Eds.). (2003). *Handbook of early literacy research* (Vol. 1). New York: Guilford Press.

Neuman, S. B., Dwyer, J., & Koh, S. (2007). *User's guide to the Child/Home Early Language and Literacy Observation (CHELLO) tool.* Towson, MD: Brookes.

NGSS Lead States. (2013). *Next Generation Science Standards: For states, by states.* Washington DC: National Academies Press.

Reutzel, D. R., Child, A., Jones, C. D., & Clark, S. K. (2014). Explicit instruction in core reading programs. *The Elementary School Journal, 114*(3), 406–430.

Reutzel, D. R., & Clark, S. K. (2011). Organizing the classroom for effective literacy instruction: A survival guide. *The Reading Teacher, 65*(2), 96–109.

Reutzel, D. R., & Clark, S. K. (2019). Organizing effective literacy instruction: Differentiating instruction to meet the needs of all literacy learners. In L. M. Morrow & L. B. Gambrell (Eds.), *Best practices in literacy instruction* (6th ed., pp. 359–385). New York: Guilford Press.

Reutzel, D. R., & Jones, C. D. (2010). Assessing and creating effective preschool literacy classroom environments. In M. C. McKenna, S. Walpole, & K. Conradi (Eds.), *Promoting early reading: Research, resources, and best practices* (pp. 175–198). New York: Guilford Press.

Rimm-Kaufman, S. E., La Paro, K. M., Downer, J. T., & Pianta, R. C. (2005). The contribution of classroom setting and quality of instruction to children's behavior in kindergarten classrooms. *The Elementary School Journal, 105*(4), 377–394.

Rissling, K., & Kucan, L. (2018). Negotiating practicum experiences in a reading specialist preparation program. *Reading Horizons: A Journal of Literacy and Language Arts, 57*(3), 2.

Shanahan, T. (2004, November). *How do you raise reading achievement?* Paper presented at the Utah Council of the International Reading Association, Salt Lake City, UT.

Smith, M. W., Brady, J. P., & Anastasopoulos, L. (2008). *Early Language and Literacy Classroom Observation: Pre-K tool.* Towson, MD: Brookes.

Snow, C., Burns, S., & Griffin, M. (1998). *Preventing reading difficulties in young children.* Washington, DC: National Research Council, National Academy of Sciences.

Taylor, B. M. (2011). *Catching schools: An action guide to schoolwide reading improvement.* Portsmouth, NH: Heinemann.

Thoermer, A., & Williams, L. (2012). Using digital texts to promote fluent reading. *The Reading Teacher, 65*(7), 441–445.

Torgesen, J. K. (2004). Lessons learned from research on interventions for students who have difficulty learning to read. In P. McCardle & V. Chhabra (Eds.), *The voice of evidence in reading research* (pp. 355–382). Baltimore: Brookes.

Whorrall, J., & Cabell, S. Q. (2016). Supporting children's oral language development in the preschool classroom. *Early Childhood Education Journal, 44*(4), 335–341.

Wolfersberger, M. E., Reutzel, D. R., Sudweeks, R., & Fawson, P. C. (2004).

Developing and validating the Classroom Literacy Environmental Profile (CLEP): A tool for examining the "print richness" of early childhood and elementary classrooms. *Journal of Literacy Research, 36*(2), 211–272.

Zhang, C., Hur, J., Diamond, K. E., & Powell, D. (2015). Children's early writing skills: An observational study in Head Start classrooms. *Early Childhood Education Journal, 43*(4), 307–315.

CHILDREN'S LITERATURE

Cronin, D. (2000). *Click, clack, moo: Cows that type.* New York: Simon & Schuster Books for Young Readers.

MacCarald, C. (2019). *Animal groups.* Vero Beach, FL: Rourke Educational Media.

Sendak, M. (1984). *Where the wild things are.* New York: Harper & Row.

3

· · · ·

Literacy Teaching for Equity

María Paula Ghiso, Gerald Campano, and Ankhi Guha Thakurta

Literacy teaching and learning is at the heart of long-standing debates about educational equity. The push for accountability has resulted in a focus on direct instruction and test preparation, as schools contend with pressures to show gains in student literacy proficiencies or face potential takeover, restructuring, or closure. Black, Brown, and Indigenous students disproportionately attend underresourced schools with restrictive literacy curricula. Literacy measures such as reading levels or prompt-based responses orchestrate much of children's lives in school, and students from nondominant backgrounds are too often positioned as blank slates to be filled with "the basics" through a banking model of instruction (Freire, 1970) that position students as passive recipients of knowledge.

At the same time, educators and researchers have long challenged this orientation, documenting the rich cultural, linguistic, and experiential resources of children and families from historically minoritized groups (e.g., de los Ríos, 2018; Ghiso, 2016) and seeking to build trusting relationships between schools and communities premised on intellectual respect and reciprocity (Valdés, 1996). In this chapter, we highlight two mutually informing conceptual principles that can guide a more equitable vision to literacy instruction: the epistemic privilege of nondominant identities (Campano, 2007; Moya, 2002) and the role of communities of inquiry (Cochran-Smith & Lytle, 2009) as methodological vehicles for research and practice. Both principles work together to help challenge paternalistic approaches to collaboration while helping to forge a shared vision of educational justice informed by the lived realities of teachers, students, families, and communities. We draw on our own research examples to showcase how teachers can be adaptive toward difference—differences not merely in learning styles or abilities but also in terms of the fuller epistemic resources that are embedded within the lives and experiences of the students in our classrooms, whose perspectives can help reshape literacy instruction for the better.

Epistemic Privilege and Communities of Inquiry

The epistemic privilege of minoritized identities refers to the idea that those who experience injustice are in a unique position to investigate the dynamics of power that produce inequality, and also to imagine and construct more just social arrangements (Campano, 2007; Mohanty, 1997, 2018; Moya, 2002). Such an understanding of epistemic privilege, if not named as such, has probably been around as long as people have been sorted hierarchically along identity categories. In order to navigate the social world and survive, individuals and communities need to be able to read how power operates and how systems of oppression—such as racism, patriarchy, homophobia, ableism, and class exploitation—become reproduced institutionally, including in schools, universities, and other contexts of teaching and learning.

A literacy curriculum that recognizes and draws on the epistemic privilege of students and communities shares a family resemblance with other asset orientations to instruction, including funds of knowledge, culturally relevant and sustaining pedagogies, and community cultural wealth. Each of these approaches has grown out of distinct intellectual and disciplinary lineages, and therefore may be more or less attuned to different educational dynamics and have both unique and overlapping pedagogical implications for literacy instruction. For example, the concept of funds of knowledge stems from cultural psychology and Vygotskyan perspectives on identity formation; deriving from the work of González, Moll, and Amanti (2006) on the household and classroom experiences of individuals from working-class Mexican communities in Tucson, Arizona, it operates with the view that the "historically accumulated and culturally developed bodies of knowledge and skills" found in these communal networks are "essential for household or individual functioning and well-being" (pp. 72–73).

Culturally relevant and sustaining pedagogy (Ladson-Billings, 1995, 2014; Paris & Alim, 2017), on the other hand, emerges from ethnographic approaches and critical race theory (Bell, 1992). This sociocultural view of teaching and learning, underpinned by an awareness of how formalized schooling in the United States has historically advanced the interests of White supremacy, argues for the sustainment of "linguistic, literate, and cultural pluralism" in classrooms (Alim & Paris, 2017, p. 1). Community cultural wealth has genealogical links to sociology, theories of cultural capital (Bourdieu, 1986), critical race theory, and ethnic studies. Proposed by Tara Yosso (2005), the concept operates from the premise that the cultural resources found within communities of color, often unrecognized or dismissed by "White, middle class" rubrics, are central to both the educational success of those from nondominant communities and larger processes of social transformation (p. 77). While all of these approaches have been taken up in the field of literacy studies in various ways, they share a commitment to challenging deficit framings of students and provide conceptual frameworks to honor their cultural and experiential resources in the curriculum.

Our understanding of epistemic privilege, a concept both connected to and distinguished from the ideas and perspectives described above, derives broadly from philosophy and more specifically from feminist and women of color epistemologies. Its emphasis is on understanding the relationships among identity, social location, and knowledge generation, and it presupposes that any project of progressive educational justice must grapple fundamentally with certain epistemological questions such as the following: who is or is not considered to have knowledge, and who is or is not in a position to make important claims and normative evaluations about the world? With these types of concerns, the idea of epistemic privilege shares an affinity with theories of coloniality and larger discussions arising from the Global South about the geopolitics of knowledge production (Moraña, Dussel, & Jáuregui, 2008).

All students (and educators) in the school system, by virtue of being human, are heirs to or have some relationship to these ongoing colonial histories—as perpetrators, victims, or admixtures of both. This connection to colonialism may be especially relevant to the field of literacy studies, because who has been deemed more or less literate and whose literate traditions are or are not valued as sources of knowledge are intimately entangled with histories of genocide and epistemicide, including the systematic destruction of people's languages, intellectual archives, literate practices, and knowledge systems (Mignolo, 2000; Rasmussen, 2012; Saldívar, 2004). Educators who are committed to disrupting social reproduction might begin by interrogating which traditions of intellectual and creative activity have become legitimized in schooling, and which ones are marginalized, criminalized, or rendered invisible. The pedagogical promise is that by thinking about literacy as a critical sociocultural practice (Lewis, Enciso, & Moje, 2007; Street, 1995), rather than a technology or a possession, educators may adapt the curriculum to recognize the rich literacies already present in communities while simultaneously providing a curricular platform for students to demonstrate and generate knowledge about the world.

The emphasis we place on the epistemic advantage of students' intersectional experiences—and by extension those of their families and communities—has important ethical implications for teaching and learning, when we think of ethics fundamentally as our interactions with others. Following Rancière (2004), it would entail educators beginning with the presumption of radical equality in their relationships with all members of a learning community: that everyone is an intellectual, theorist, and researcher whose ideas and capacities to produce critical thought must be taken seriously. This presumption of equality is important for all students, but in particular for those who have had aspects of their identities stigmatized in schools. It is one way to mitigate savior ideologies that too often permeate even the most progressive educational initiatives. We believe that trust cannot be cultivated in an intellectual community unless everyone genuinely feels they might learn from and have their own epistemic horizons expanded through their relationships with everyone else. In many schools and classrooms, we have argued that the most profound intellectual resources are the students' themselves.

How, then, do educators adapt their classroom practice in order to create the conditions to mobilize the epistemic privilege of students? We view this as a matter of not simply altering practice improvisationally but also realigning teaching and learning along some fundamental principles. It is here, then, that we perceive the benefits of introducing communities of inquiry into classrooms. This pluralistic approach to knowledge production stems from the tradition of practitioner research and the teacher research movement, and is characterized by participation by diverse stakeholders "who are positioned differently from one other and who bring distinctive kinds of knowledge and experience to bear" on the inquiry at hand (Cochran-Smith & Lytle, 2009, p. 142). Though educational inquiry communities typically feature researchers and educators, their fundamental approach assumes the intellectual benefits of bringing a plurality of distinct and often underrepresented perspectives into knowledge production, teaching, and learning. Further, they lay emphasis on the process of inquiry itself, that is, the relational and dialogic means through which individuals pool their collective resources "to help bring about educational and social change" (Cochran-Smith & Lytle, 2009, p. 140). We propose that communities of inquiry may prove fruitful and supportive structures for literacy learning in classrooms, as dialogic spaces in which the epistemic privilege of underrecognized students are brought to the fore.

One inspiration for how we are thinking about communities of inquiry organized around the epistemic privilege of its members is the Combahee River Collective (2015), which was formed to address the intersections of anti-Black, patriarchal, and homophobic forms of oppression. The Combahee River Collective has recently informed literacy scholars' efforts to help (re)imagine communities of inquiry to better account for the role that difference and multiplicity play in participatory research. For example, Player (2018) documents how members of a girls of color writing community, the Unnormal Sisterhood, investigate the overlap and differences between their respective experiences in schools, creating the conditions to enact a sense of solidarity and construct a shared vision of educational justice.

From our conceptual vantage point, identity is not static and there is not a deterministic relationship between one's social location and one's perspectives. Coupling epistemic privilege with communities of inquiry highlights the ways in which the construction of knowledge is a dynamic and relational learning process. Through collaborative inquiry, participants might transform nascent feelings into more developed critical discernment and analysis of their own social worlds. As educators and former school teachers committed to the ideals of public education, we also believe that the chasm between individual's experiences are not—or not always—unbridgeable; through thinking alongside others and across boundaries or race, class, generation, gender, sexuality, language, (dis) ability, and migration status, for example, everyone has the potential to expand their own epistemic horizons. This potential is only fully realized, however, if educators, first and foremost, and students cultivate the humility to decenter their own taken-for-granted worldviews to make room for those of others.

Implications for Literacy Teaching and Learning

A prevalent aspect of literacy instruction entails how to access existing texts—breaking and comprehending encoded meanings (RAND, 2002) and situating them within disciplinary histories and the norms and routines of schooling (Alvermann, 2002). Yet literacy instruction is also productive, and the emphasis on design highlights the possibility of not only accessing meaning but also constructing new and different knowledge about the world. As Luke and Freebody (1999) argue, readers must be adept text users and text analysts; they must be able to navigate the multiple social contexts in which texts are used and examine texts with a critical lens to discern how they work to construct reality. Scholars have also documented the disciplining power of literacy in school: how classroom dynamics and broader policies can position students as more and less "literate" and how these distinctions often map onto larger social stratifications. Thus, literacy educators must juggle supporting students in the varied practices of what it means to engage with and create texts while being cognizant of how reading and writing have been mechanisms that perpetuate social inequality.

The principles of epistemic privilege and communities of inquiry disrupt binaries of who counts as a knower in the classroom and underscore the co-constructive potentials in literacy instruction. Rather than viewing students as "having" literacy or not, epistemic privilege calls attention to how students may bring their own intellectual legacies that could be invited into the learning space. This shift challenges deficit ideologies that undergird much conventional schooling. From a lens of epistemic privilege and communities of inquiry, the task of the teacher is not to rank individuals on their skills and affix labels such as "struggling" or "advanced" readers or writers. Rather, under this vision teachers seek to coordinate the different skills and interests that all students bring to collaboratively create knowledge. These collective inquiries would blend access to the power codes (Delpit, 1992), mobilization of knowledges from the cultural and historical legacies of students and their families (e.g., Gutiérrez, 2008), and attention to critical issues and purposes that matter to members of the classroom community (e.g., Dutro, 2019; Vasquez, 2004).

These principles align well to the notion of adaptive teaching (e.g., Vaughn & Parsons, 2013), as teachers discern the complex interplay among their students' knowledges, their instruction, and the official curriculum and make pedagogical decisions that link micro-levels of classroom interaction with more macro-level concerns. This adaptive instruction is more than merely differentiation that seeks to address the knowledge students may lack (e.g., explicitly teaching vocabulary to students designated as English learners). Rather, it starts from the recognition of the knowledge everyone brings, so that students and teachers can learn alongside each other. Instruction animated by recognition of students' epistemic privilege and the power of the collective forces the teacher to ask different questions—for example: What cultural ways of knowing and linguistic repertoires are students drawing on that we could all learn from? What experiences and critical insights do students have that could drive the curriculum? What are students' experiences with the literacies of schooling (such as its sorting mechanisms and labeling), and how might their understandings make classroom cultures more inclusive and equitable?

Just as communities of inquiry are important among teachers and students, they are also an essential component of teachers' own reflective practices. In the moment-by-moment, educators make decisions to adapt to what they are learning from and about students. But teachers are not removed from social dynamics, and their decisions are informed by their own perspectives, identities, and experiences. What initially may seem like the "right" decision could reproduce hierarchies, dismiss students' knowledge, or forward assimilation into dominant White culture. Communities of inquiry among teachers are one mechanism for pausing the frenetic pace of classroom life and lingering on moments of discomfort, uncertainty, or tension in order to reflect on the implications of certain instructional practices and how we as educators might be complicit in the normative practices of schooling.

Mobilizing Epistemic Privilege in Communities of Inquiry: Examples from Literacy Research and Praxis

Over the years we have documented the ways in which the epistemic privilege of youth learners may be prioritized in communities of inquiry both within and beyond traditional classroom settings. For example, fifth-grade students in Gerald's class drew on the diasporic artistic and activist tradition of the Teatro Campesino to form a performative inquiry community, Dancing Across Borders (DAB; Campano, 2007). The DAB troupe not only critiqued inequities within the school system—in skits such as "What the Teacher Didn't Know"—but also enacted a collective and joyful academic space that provided an alternative to the district's emphasis on individual accountability and authorship, where students previously marginalized within traditional schooling could claim and make their intellectual voices audible to multiple audiences. Gerald and María Paula also worked with third-grade children in the postindustrial Midwest who provided incisive interpretations of young adult fiction by tapping into the Black intellectual literary legacies of self-determination and liberation through literacy that go back to the slave narratives and Frederick Douglass (Campano, Ghiso, & Sánchez, 2013). These types of opportunities are easily lost during this educational era of standardization, especially if teachers do not adapt their instruction to be sensitized to the rich epistemic resources in communities of color and of students with nondominant experiences.

On our community-based research project, for example, a nearly decade-long partnership between university researchers and families from minoritized communities in South Philadelphia dedicated to the pursuit of greater equity and access in the educational system (Campano, Ghiso, & Welch, 2016), multiple generations of university researchers and doctoral students have convened meetings, workshops, and lessons in which they foreground alternative ways of knowing and being. These collaborative community engagements have been shaped by a principle animating the larger project: the importance of learning from the knowledge and experiences of those most systematically marginalized to "raise critical questions about how the world is structured and how it may be transformed" (Campano, Ghiso, Yee, & Pantoja, 2013, p. 315). Though occurring out of school, we believe this broader philosophy as well as the pedagogy it has inspired might productively inform the literacy instruction of teachers in more traditional settings.

Throughout this university–community partnership, researchers and team members have perceived the importance of holding space for the identities and semiotic resources of youth learners in communities of inquiry. Proving central to the enactment of adaptive and socially conscious literacy instruction, the importance of this was recently made clear in the fall of 2019 when researchers and doctoral students worked alongside community youth to prepare for a roundtable presentation at the National Council of Teachers of English (NCTE) conference in Baltimore, Maryland. The presentations focused on three priorities for greater educational equity in Philadelphia public schools—increased language access in schools, Advanced Placement classes for all, and the importance of culturally relevant pedagogy—that were generated by families and youth within the larger partnership as they worked together to research issues that affected children's educational opportunities. Youth members chose the topics about which they felt the most passionate and worked in small groups to create presentations for NCTE conference attendees in order to make their inquiries public to a broader audience and in the hopes of inspiring action and change.

The facilitators of the youth program, consisting of doctoral students from the University of Pennsylvania and college-age members of the St. Thomas Aquinas community, encouraged youth to draw upon their knowledge, experiences, and communicative repertoires to support the work of their inquiry groups. They also refashioned the traditional hierarchies structuring relations between students and instructors by positioning themselves as co-investigators. These pedagogical orientations contributed to the formation of a supportive atmosphere in which youth felt comfortable sharing their personal views on the three priorities. In the language access group, for example, youth from Indonesian and Latinx communities discussed how the limited availability of translation services in schools negatively affected their learning and sense of belonging. One of the youth participants was a young man of Mexican descent. For him, a lack of adequate translation services rendered the school system inaccessible to his primarily Spanish-speaking family members. As he observed, "I picked [this topic] because I personally think it's important because I went through this type of stuff. Our parents couldn't understand—they couldn't help us. Nobody should really have to go through that." Sustained discussions in the inquiry community thus surfaced the emotional complexities and power dynamics associated with language access, allowing youth to draw attention to the linguistic traditions that existed in their communities as well as to the broader geopolitics of knowledge and expression that diminished their worth in schools.

Other youth who noted feeling silenced or marginalized in schools gained visibility and confidence through the inquiry process. Jay, for example, was a soft-spoken ninth grader of Indonesian descent who described herself as a "difficult" and "unpopular" student for always asking questions. Framing this inquisitiveness as a testament to Jay's capacity for critical thought, the facilitator of the session (a former classroom teacher) encouraged her to assume a leadership role in her group and determine how best to communicate the group's ideas to conferencegoers alongside her peers. Jay then took the lead on co-designing a poster with her peers that visually represented the impact of limited language access on youth from minoritized backgrounds across time (Figure 3.1).

Drawn on separate panels by another student in the inquiry group, the first section, on the left, depicted a distraught student in a learning

FIGURE 3.1. Panels from the group's poster on how language access affects learning.

environment with little to no linguistic resources. The second, showing the same individual after some time, included a large question mark above the child's head. For Jay, this visual captured an underacknowledged yet salient consequence of the limited linguistic access that often characterizes school instruction: the ongoing and accumulated sense of alienation experienced by speakers of multiple languages in English-dominant learning settings. Reflecting on the poster panel, she observed, "Without language access but going to school for a few years, the student will probably lose their language, so they'll lose a piece of their identity." Jay's insights, reflecting her personal experiences as a member of a minoritized linguistic community, showcased her expertise and contribution to the complex rhetorical task of representing the issue of language access at a conference.

Through the process of collective inquiry, then, the youth in the partnership connected their personal brushes with limited language access to broader matters of equity in the school system. But their work was not limited to critique; besides identifying the complex effects of these issues, they also used their communally generated knowledge to propose productive and justice-oriented solutions. These recommendations were eventually distributed to the teacher, administrator, and researcher attendees of the NCTE conference (Figure 3.2).

Youth-Generated Suggestions for Language Access for All

For teachers:

☐ Create translated scaffolds for students who don't speak English, since it is not their first language.

☐ Make students feel that their whole identity is valuable.

☐ Give assignments that will encourage students to know their home language.

☐ Include information about diverse classroom communities and cultures in lesson plans.

For administrators:

☐ Try to provide translation in as many situations as possible. For example, they could ensure school notices are translated, as are notes for parents during parent–teacher conferences.

☐ Reach out to parents who are new to the school and maybe to the country, and help them feel welcome.

FIGURE 3.2. Excerpts from youth-generated handout for NCTE 2019 roundtable presentation.

Recommendations for Literacy Instruction

. . . .

As our examples illustrate, literacy instruction that is guided by the principles of communities of inquiry and the epistemic privilege of nondominant identities brings attention to power and issues of equity, shines a critical light on the routines of schooling, and highlights the transformative potential of working together to enact change. A classroom teacher guided by these principles starts not with assessing what a student may be lacking in terms of literacy skills in order to apply necessary pedagogical supports but rather, seeks to learn from students about the often-invisible effects of schooling-as-usual and their perspectives on what would constitute effective instruction. As the youth inquiries highlighted in this chapter suggest, these insights may include the precarity experienced by families as they navigate barriers to educational access and cultural, linguistic, or racial marginalization, as well as ideas for leveraging multilingual resources to include families and strengthen community connections.

We offer the following recommendations for educators as they strive to cultivate classroom communities more attentive to students' knowledge and animated by an ethos of mutuality and interdependence.

• *Explore and celebrate the multiple literacies that students already possess.* All students bring knowledge from their community histories. As educators, it is important that we all take steps to interrupt deficit characterizations of students from historically marginalized groups. Rather than casting some students or their families as not having strong literacy backgrounds, what are ways to recognize and learn from the ways that literacies are key to social life and historical struggles within community contexts?

• *Normalize more expansive understandings of literacy in the classroom by encouraging students to use multiple semiotic modes.* Expanding beyond a print-based text allows varied knowledges to surface. Through visual or oral storytelling, students may have a platform to convey critical insights about a topic or to share *testimonios* (Saavedra, 2011) of their experiences. These literacy practices can provide access to the official curriculum and also suggest new forms of inquiry that can change what gets prioritized in classrooms.

• *Provide students with ongoing curricular opportunities to use their home languages.* A grounding in students' and families' knowledge can encourage educators to challenge the monolingual, monocultural nature of much literacy instruction, and instead look for ways to cultivate pluralistic spaces of learning energized by students' multilingual repertoires.

• *Support and encourage the formation of student-led communities of inquiry.* Literacy pedagogy need not be anchored solely to teacher-centered or policy-driven priorities. Starting from student interests and concerns is one generative pathway whereby literacy pedagogy can become central to exploring the social or communal issues that students identify as important.

• *Partner with community organizations and local leaders.* Community leaders and community-led organizations have on-the-ground knowledge of issues affecting students and their families and experience in advocating for change. Developing partnerships can strengthen relationships between home and school and lead to co-creating more culturally relevant literacy instruction.

We encourage educators to nurture a sense of wonder about the multitude of literate practices and intellectual traditions throughout the world, including those that have germinated in nonelite contexts, such as our children's neighborhoods, and ones that are passed on through their transcultural and transnational networks. As the novelist José Rizal (1884) reminds us, "Genius is like the light, the air. It is the heritage of all."

REFERENCES

Alvermann, D. (2002). Effective literacy instruction for adolescents. *Journal of Literacy Research, 34*(2), 189–208.

Bell, D. A. (1992). *Faces at the bottom of the well: The permanence of racism.* New York: Basic Books.

Bourdieu, P. (1986). The forms of capital. In J. G. Richardson (Ed.), *Handbook of theory and research for the sociology of education* (pp. 241–258). New York: Greenwood Press.

Campano, G. (2007). *Immigrant students and literacy: Reading, writing, and remembering.* New York: Teachers College Press.

Campano, G., Ghiso, M. P., & Sánchez, L. (2013). "Nobody one knows the . . . amount of a person": Elementary students critiquing dehumanization through organic critical literacies. *Research in the Teaching of English, 48*(1), 97–124.

Campano, G., Ghiso, M., & Welch, B. J. (2016). *Partnering with immigrant communities: Action through literacy.* New York: Teachers College Press.

Campano, G., Ghiso, M., Yee, M., & Pantoja, A. (2013). Toward community research and coalitional literacy practices for educational justice. *Language Arts, 90*(5), 314–326.

Cochran-Smith, M., & Lytle, S. (2009). *Inquiry as stance: Practitioner research for the next generation.* New York: Teachers College Press.

Combahee River Collective. (2015). A Black feminist statement. In C. Moraga & G. Anzaldúa (Eds.), *This bridge called my back: Writings by radical women of color* (4th ed., pp. 210–218). Albany: State University of New York Press.

de los Ríos, C. (2018). Toward a *corridista* consciousness: Learning from one transnational youth's critical reading, writing, and performance of Mexican corridos. *Reading Research Quarterly, 53*(4), 455–471.

Delpit, L. (1992). Acquisition of literate discourse: Bowing before the master? *Theory Into Practice, 31*(4), 296–302.

Dutro, E. (2019). *The vulnerable heart of literacy: Centering trauma as powerful pedagogy.* New York: Teachers College Press.

Freire, P. (1970). *Pedagogy of the oppressed.* New York: Continuum.

Ghiso, M. P. (2016). The laundromat as the transnational local: Young children's literacies of interdependence. *Teachers College Record, 118*(1), 1–46.

González, N., Moll, L. C., & Amanti, C. (Eds.). (2006). *Funds of knowledge: Theorizing practices in households, communities, and classrooms.* New York: Routledge.

Gutiérrez, K. (2008). Developing a sociocritical literacy in the third space. *Reading Research Quarterly, 43*(2), 148–164.

Ladson-Billings, G. (1995). Toward a theory of culturally relevant pedagogy. *American Educational Research Journal, 32*(3), 465–491.

Ladson-Billings, G. (2014). Culturally relevant pedagogy 2.0: A.k.a. the Remix. *Harvard Educational Review, 84*(1), 74–84.

Lewis, C., Enciso, P., & Moje, E. (Eds.). (2007). *Reframing sociocultural research on literacy: Identity, agency, and power.* New York: Routledge.

Luke, A., & Freebody, P. (1999). A map of possible practices: Further notes on the four resources model. *Practically Primary, 4*(2), 5–8.

Mignolo, W. D. (2000). The many faces of cosmo-polis: Border thinking and critical cosmopolitanism. *Public Culture, 12*(3), 721–748.

Mohanty, S. (1997). *Literary history and the claims of history: Postmodernism, objectivity, multicultural politics.* Ithaca, NY: Cornell University Press.

Mohanty, S. (2018). Social justice and culture: On identity, intersectionality, and epistemic privilege. In G. Craig (Ed.), *Handbook on global social justice* (pp. 418–427). Chelthenham, UK: Edward Elgar.

Moraña, M., Dussel, E., & Jáuregui, C. A. (Eds.). (2008). *Coloniality at large: Latin America and the postcolonial debate.* Durham, NC: Duke University Press.

Moya, P. (2002). *Learning from experience: Minority identities, multicultural struggles.* Berkeley: University of California Press.

Paris, D., & Alim, H. S. (2017). *Culturally sustaining pedagogies: Teaching and learning for justice in a changing world.* New York: Teachers College Press.

Player, G. D. (2018). *Unnormal sisterhood: Girls of color writing, reading, resisting, and being together.* Unpublished doctoral dissertation, University of Pennsylvania Graduate School of Education, Philadelphia, PA. Retrieved from *https://repository.upenn.edu/edissertations/3018.*

Rancière, J. (2004). *The philosopher and his poor.* Durham, NC: Duke University Press.

RAND Reading Study Group. (2002). Executive summary. In C. E. Snow (Ed.), *Toward an R&D program in reading comprehension* (pp. xi–xxi). Santa Monica,

CA: RAND. Retrieved from *www.rand.org/pubs/monograph_reports/2005/MR1465.pdf.*

Rasmussen, B. B. (2012). *Queequeg's coffin: Indigenous literacies and early American literature.* Durham, NC: Duke University Press.

Rizal, J. (1884). Brindis speech (E. Medina, Trans.). Retrieved from *https://vdocuments.mx/jose-rizals-brindis-speech.html.*

Saavedra, C. M. (2011). Language and literacy in the borderlands: Acting upon the world through testimonios. *Language Arts, 88*(4), 261–269.

Saldívar, J. D. (2004). Response to "devils or angels." In J. Mahiri (Ed.), *What they don't learn in school: Literacy in the lives of urban youth* (pp. 75–77). New York: Peter Lang.

Street, B. V. (1995). *Social literacies: Critical approaches to literacy in development, ethnography, and education.* London: Longman.

Valdés, G. (1996). *Con respeto: Bridging the distances between culturally diverse families and schools.* New York: Teachers College Press.

Vasquez, V. (2004). *Negotiating critical literacies with young children.* New York: Routledge.

Vaughn, M., & Parsons, S. (2013). Adaptive teachers as innovators: Instructional adaptations opening spaces for enhanced literacy learning. *Language Arts, 91*(2), 81–93.

Yosso, T. (2005) Whose culture has capital?: A critical race theory discussion of community cultural wealth. *Race, Ethnicity and Education, 8*(1), 69–91.

PART II

············

INSTRUCTION

4

• • • •

Phonemic Awareness and Phonics

Evan Ortlieb, Susan Schatz, and Kathy Ganske

As the topic that has gained more attention in the last 2 years than any other (Cassidy, Grote-Garcia, & Ortlieb, 2019), early literacy has garnered the educational, political, and social limelight across the United States. There is no greater educational need than ensuring that every child has an opportunity to achieve, and this can be accomplished through enacting principles of effective early literacy instruction. Knowledge of words (spelling, sight vocabulary, morphology, word meaning) and word parts (phonological awareness, phonemic awareness, alphabet, phonics) serve as a foundation to literacy development. While all of these components of early literacy are valuable components to literacy programs, these are building blocks to the foremost objective of literacy instruction: reading for understanding.

Principles of effective literacy instruction involving phonological awareness and phonics serve as the foci of this chapter. While debates about the science of reading, or the processes that guide the teaching of children to read, remain, what is not up for debate is that literacy skills (e.g., alphabetics, decoding, syllabication) are invaluable to all readers. High-quality reading materials provide both relevant content and experiences, and should serve as resources that promote opportunities for students to hone their skills and love for reading.

Early literacy instruction affects not only PreK–2 performance but also later reading success. In turn, educational policies about what educators teach, when they teach it, and even sometimes how they teach it is predetermined. We believe that teachers should maintain the ability to customize instruction for their diverse literacy learners using evidence and assessment data to drive their pedagogical decision making. The success of early literacy teaching and learning is determined largely by three constructs: amount of experience (time), content of the experience (curriculum), and quality of experience (teaching; Shanahan, 2019):

- *Amount of early literacy experiences* is determined by length of the school day (with full-day kindergarteners consistently outperforming their half-day peers), allocated minutes to literacy experiences in and beyond the English language arts (ELA) block (core and disciplinary literacies), and the efficiency of instruction (keeping students on task and engaged).
- *Content of the experience* is influenced by the curriculum (published or teacher made) both in print and digital realms, and supplemented through digital reading environments as well as other online resources. Culturally appropriate and relevant content should be provided to ensure seamless connections between in and outside the classroom.
- *Quality of experience* is manifest through mindful decisions regarding whole-class, small-group, and individual instructional opportunities without unnecessary repetition. For instance, we should not use individual instruction for what can be taught in a small-group setting, or use small groups for what could be learned in a whole-class environment. Being intentional is paramount to efficient, high-quality literacy instruction.

High-Quality Phonemic Awareness and Phonics Instruction

The best early childhood and elementary teachers make it look easy; they are seamless in their transitions, their classrooms run like clockwork, and the innumerable moving parts work together in harmony. These educators were not born with an innate ability to teach; rather, they have achieved mastery from understanding what comprises highly effective early literacy instruction, including attention to phonemic awareness and phonics.

Phonological awareness instruction involves teaching children how to recognize patterns in spoken words (rhyme, alliteration), gain an awareness of phonemes and syllables within words, and hear multiple phonemes within words. It should be noted that *phonemic awareness* consists of a subset of phonological skills involving the manipulation of sounds and is recommended for children in preschool through kindergarten (National

Early Literacy Panel [NELP], 2008). For instance, kindergarten teachers provide hands-on activities where children can sort pictures by initial sound (e.g., students sort pictures like a bird, bat, ball vs. cat, car, cage), or task students with discriminating words orally that do not belong (teacher says "cat," "mat," "bag"). By progressing through a scope and sequence of these skills that build upon one another, students are positioned to succeed in not only isolated skill exercises but also other literacy activities involving spelling, word recognition, fluency, and comprehension.

Phonics instruction aims to lead young children to learn the essentials of the alphabetic system of English. Moreover, it is invaluable that students learn letters and sounds in a sequence that together contribute to word identification and in turn fluency, vocabulary development, and overall reading comprehension. Such a progression begins with easier letter combinations, followed by consonant digraphs and blends, and then more difficult vowel digraphs with an initial focus on blending and segmenting simple CVC (consonant–vowel–consonant) words and then moving into letter combinations and segmenting words into onset and rime (e.g., /cl/ /ip/) (Ehri, 2003).

Culturally responsive kindergarten phonics instruction incorporates a student's background knowledge within a systematic program encompassing instruction in short vowels, consonants, blends, digraphs, and final-*e* syllables. Sound and syllable instruction continue in first grade with long vowels, *r*-controlled vowels, complex vowel patterns, and diphthongs. Second grade continues on with learning, multisyllabic words, prefixes, suffixes, and syllable types (Achievethecore.org, n.d.). Such a clear progression supports an approach for teachers to see how students progress along a developmental continuum. Although many students are at different places along these phases, teachers can adapt and differentiate their instruction depending on what their students need (Ehri, 2003). The easier students can identify words, the more they can focus their attention on understanding what they read. A less taxing experience is also one that is more engaging and rewarding (Cummins, 2011).

The many and varied relationships between sound–symbol correspondences, spelling patterns and word pronunciations, and decoding/encoding print and pronunciation require extensive planning and instruction (Ehri, 2003). Explicit and systematic phonics instruction has been found beneficial in grades K–2 (National Reading Panel [NRP], 2001), regardless of the type of phonics program (What Works Clearinghouse, 2016). Students who receive phonics instruction are also better spellers (Foorman & Torgesen, 2001), as they understand spelling patterns (graphemes) of the English language. These initial phonological learnings unlock the language that underpins content learning.

Phonemic awareness and phonics are part of a core literacy program that aims to equip students with the ability to read, spell, and understand oral and written language. While there are innumerable instructional techniques to teach these specific skills already discussed, this chapter provides a discussion of some guiding principles of effective instruction that can be flexibly applied in the early grades classroom.

Principles of Effective Early Literacy Instruction

Principle 1: Students Need Modeling (Not Just Expectations) to Learn for Transfer

Teaching phonemic awareness and phonics is akin to becoming an intuitive cook. Rather than relying on exact recipes for each meal, understanding some guiding principles about how different foods interact, key core ingredients, and a willingness to continually refine a craft permits a chef to be flexible and responsive to the season's ingredients. Systems thinking organizes phonemic awareness and phonics instruction in an integrated and flexible framework of core principles of literacy instruction. An emphasis on *modeling,* culturally relevant content, a continuum of phonemic awareness instruction, and integrated systematic phonics instruction permits each classroom to transform into a *bottega,* like a fine farm-to-table restaurant, in which a master teacher is shaping the learning of others.

Making connections among graphemes, phonemes, and meaning marks early reading acquisition. When learners see and hear a word, they segment the graphemes in the spelling, map it onto phonemes in pronunciation, and form connections. The spelling becomes bonded to pronunciations, connections in meanings are activated, and the word is retained in memory (O'Leary & Ehri, 2020). Understanding the process by which letters and sounds map onto one another and activate meaning, teachers are situated to provide students with the modeling needed to create a meaningful reading and writing connection, thus achieving the aim of phonemic awareness and phonics instruction—understanding how words work (Blevins, 2017).

Relevant Content and Transferable Skills

Research has repeatedly shown letter knowledge and phonemic segmentation as two of the strongest predictors of later reading achievement with far-reaching effects (Jones & Reutzel, 2012; O'Leary & Ehri, 2020).

Additionally, understanding literacy benchmarks improves both diagnostic and instructional efficiency. For instance, if students understand 10 or more letters at the end of preschool, they are likely to experience early literacy success in kindergarten. Meeting these benchmarks means not only ticking the completion box on skill learning but also that those skills will lead to wide success in literacy as well as other subject areas.

Explicitly teaching the names of letters and modeling the pronunciation and formation of the letter and sound is essential.

1. *Introduce the name of the letter:*
   a. "The name of the letter is _____. This is an uppercase _____. This is a lowercase _____."
   b. "Watch me as I write the letter." (Describe your motions or "letter story" as you write the letter.)
   c. "Let's practice." (Ask students to name the letter as you point to written or physical forms of the letter.)
2. *Introduce the sound of the letter:*
   a. "The letter _____ represents the sound _____. Or the name of the letter is _____; the sound that it makes is _____."
   b. Practice saying the sound (short sound for vowels), identifying key words that begin with the sound, blending, and/or segmenting.

Optimal benchmarks for letter-naming abilities include identifying 18 uppercase and 15 lowercase letters at the beginning of kindergarten. While all are important, not all letters or all phonemic awareness skills are equally useful. Some letters and sounds are more easily acquired than others; blending and segmenting transfer to reading skills far more than some other phonemic awareness activities, for instance. Just as when teaching Greek and Latin word parts, instruction must prioritize transferable reading skills that promote content learning in all disciplines.

Progression of Skills

Students advance in their reading abilities as they learn to transfer skills across multiple contexts. As such, it is beneficial for educators to spend time on the power skills of oral blending and segmenting as they move through an easier to more complex progression focusing on syllables, onset and rime, and phoneme by phoneme segmentation (Blevins, 2000).

For instance, during an interactive read-aloud of the culturally reflective text *La Oruga Muy Hambrienta,* the bilingual edition of *The Very*

Hungry Caterpillar (Carle, 2011), Ms. Joland explicitly models how to segment sounds in words for her emergent bilingual kindergarten students: "On Wednesday he ate through three . . . hmm, what's this word? Watch me as I segment the sounds in the word /p/ /l/ /u/ /m/ /s/, *plums*. On Wednesday he ate through three plums. Students, did you see how I stop and use the sounds I know to break the word into parts and then blend it back together to read the word?" Ms. Joland then continued with the read-aloud and interactive discussion. (More texts like the one used by Ms. Joland can be found online at *https://wowlit.org/links/globalizing-common-core-reading-list*).

Phonemic awareness and alphabetic activities can be paired through multimodal activities. "When written words are seen and heard, grapheme–phoneme connections are activated automatically to connect spellings to pronunciations in memory" (O'Leary & Ehri, 2020, p. 76). In oral blending (after first modeling the skill), this may involve presenting a picture of a basket with the word *basket* underneath and then orally presenting the syllables *bas* and *ket* followed by asking students to combine syllables into the word *basket*. Then, students move to smaller speech sounds and blend the onset /m/ with the rime /ap/ into word *map*. From there, students blend sound by sound as they combine /m/ . . . /a/ . . . /p/ into *map*.

Modeling

So how do phonemic awareness, alphabetics, and phonics come together in a primary classroom? A gradual release of responsibility model of literacy instruction supports students through the phases of learning, offering modeling from both teachers and peers while encouraging differentiation from day one of the school year (Ortlieb & Schatz, 2019). The "I do it, we do it, you do it together, and you do it alone" phases of gradual release of responsibility offer students various levels of scaffolded support (Pearson, McVee, & Shanahan, 2019). Recursive in nature, the gradual release of responsibility positions teachers to integrate reading and writing and vary the levels of support at any given point in time (Ortlieb & Schatz, 2019).

Picture Ms. Joland introducing concept of word through culturally relevant rhyme. Concept of word is voice-to-print matching. It is something that develops after beginning consonant knowledge before a student can recognize individual sight words. Concept of word is thought to serve as a linchpin in bridging a more primitive form of phonological awareness to more sophisticated for a final logical awareness (Flanigan, 2007).

During a mini-lesson, Ms. Joland models finger-pointing of text while reading with fluency and intonation. Students practice pointing and reading with Ms. Joland. From there students move into collaborative peer groups in which they benefit from peer modeling of reading shared texts. Understanding that a firm concept of word needs to be established before a student can read words in isolation (Ford-Connors & Paratore, 2015), Ms. Joland links her reading lesson to a shared writing activity for a group of students developing concept of word.

During this small-group strategy instruction, Ms. Joland engages students in a discussion about their favorite recess activities. Ms. Joland then models writing a line to represent each word of the sentence "I like to kick the ball" that the group created about recess. From there the students and teacher point to the lines as they say each word in the sentence until they have matched their speech to each word in the sentence. After that students use phonetic spelling to write each word. Then, students partner in groups and create their own forms of writing. Shared writing through a gradual release of responsibility supports teachers in providing a scaffold between the ability to segment and blend sounds into phonics instruction in which students attend to beginning and ending sounds in words and their use of the information to read and write words (Ehri & McCormick, 2013).

Teachers can also model other concept-of-word activities, such as by first matching pictures with words, which requires knowledge of at least the initial sounds and providing opportunities for children to make books with words in a predictable text (Gately, 2004). All the while a feedback loop is fostered through the gradual release of responsibility (see Figure 4.1). As teachers engage with students through modeling that leads its way to learning for transfer, they are able to flexibly lead and facilitate whole-group, small-group, and individual sessions.

Principle 2: Students Need to Connect Early Literacy Skills and Not Simply Learn Isolated Skill After Skill

Phonemic awareness should be combined with alphabet instruction and phonics in an explicit and systematic way in K–2 classrooms. We discussed the importance of teacher and peer modeling to ensure students learn for transfer (Frey, Fisher, & Hattie, 2017). In addition to teaching through the phases of learning, it is essential for teachers to integrate phonemic awareness, alphabetic, and phonics instruction in an explicit and systematic way (Piasta & Wagner, 2010). Just as the phonemic awareness skills of oral blending and segmenting move from easier to the more complex, learning various letters and sounds falls on a gradient of complexity.

FIGURE 4.1. Recursive writing model. Reprinted by permission from Ortlieb and Schatz (2019). Copyright © 2019 Emerald Publishing.

The enhanced alphabetic method of learning offers an opportunity for teachers to engage in effective assessment-guided, differentiated, alphabetic instruction (Piasta, 2014; see Figure 4.2). While seemingly innocuous, the nuances of how to teach letters and sounds makes a big difference in the near goal of learning letters and sounds as well as in the transfer goal of general literacy achievement (Stahl, 2014). The enhanced alphabetic knowledge (EAK) instruction involves flexible instructional cycles based on alphabet knowledge learning advantages.

Since all letters are not created equally, the EAK cycles ensure less time is spent on letters that are easy to learn and more time is spent on

LETTERS & SOUNDS IN A TYPICAL PROGRESSION OF COMPLEXITY

LETTERS

o	b	a	c	x	p	s	e
h	t	w	m	r	k	d	f
l	y	z	g	l	y	z	g
j	n	i	q	u	v		

CORE SOUNDS

c	a	b	t
p	s	k	o
j	z	f	d
m	v	e	g
l	h	n	r
q	i	w	x
u	y		

EXTENDED SOUNDS

ch	sh	th	wh
au	ng	ck	ee
ae	ie	oe	ue
oo	oo	ou	oi
aw	au	er	ir
ur	or	ar	

FIGURE 4.2. Core letters and sounds in a typical progression of complexity.

letters that are harder to learn. Adapted from Jones and Reutzel (2012), these advantages are organized into the following categories:

- *Letter-name advantage.* Any letter in the student's first name, especially the first
- *Letter-frequency advantage.* Letters from more to less frequent: consonants (*r, t, n, s, c, d, p, m, b, f, v, g, h, k, w, x, z, j, q, y*) and vowels (*i, a, e, o, u*)
- *Alphabet order.* Letters at the beginning and end of the alphabet
- *Letters that match their sound.* Easiest: The sound of the letter name comes at the first position of the letter (*b, d, j, k, p, t, v, z*)
- *Oral language.* Vowels are usually learned by 1 year of age, and these consonants are often part of a student's oral language by age 4 (*n, m, p, h, t, k, y, f, ng, b, d, g, w, s*)
- *Look alike.* Curvy letters like *a, c,* and *o* and straight letters like *A, E,* and *L*

A modified enhanced alphabetic instruction routine involves identifying the letter name and sound, recognizing the letter in text, and producing the letter form (Jones & Reutzel, 2012). In an instructional cycle, teachers complete the following routines:

- Introduce the name of the letter.
- Model the pronunciation of the letter.
- Practice recognizing the letter in text.
- Practice forming the letter from memory (not merely copying or tracing).

In a developmentally appropriate way, students can spy the letter in environmental print, shared writings, and predictable texts. Such a routine connects foundational skills in learning through connecting alphabetic, phonemic awareness, and phonics instruction to connected text in an explicit and systematic way. As a possible transition to phonics, children's invented spellings are sensitive measures of their phonemic awareness (Flanigan, 2007). Identifying and producing letters in the enhanced alphabetic instructional cycle provides opportunities for both instruction and ongoing formative assessment. Table 4.1 shows the letters and sounds of the English language from easiest to most challenging.

Connecting newly learned skills to those already mastered as well as to those that will follow ensures that children understand the purpose for their learning. Meaningful engagement in activities involving rich and culturally relevant literature that facilitates skill learning positions all learners to thrive in early childhood education.

TABLE 4.1. Elements of Alphabetics Instruction

What It Is	Letters and Sounds That Fit This Advantage	Why and How It Works
Student's own name advantage	• Any letter in the student's first name, especially the first letter of the name	• It motivates the student, because it helps the child feel important. • The student's name is used often both when speaking and in print.

Letter frequency advantage	• Letters from more to less frequent
	  ○ Consonants: *r, t, n, s, l, c, d, p, m, b, f, v, g, h, k, w, x, z, j, q, y*
	  ○ Vowels: *i, a, e, o, u*
		• The more often a letter is seen and labeled, the earlier the child begins to recognize that letter as a symbol with meaning.
		• Consider spending more time on the less frequently occurring letters, so students receive more support with the more challenging letters.

Alphabet order	• Letters at the beginning and end of the alphabet	• Just like lists, alphabet letters at the beginning and end of ABC songs are easier to remember. • Letters at the beginning or end may be a fun place to start, and move through quickly, and letters in the middle of the alphabet need more time.
Letters that match their sound	• Easiest: The sound of the letter name comes at the first position of the letter (*b, d, j, k, p, t, v, z*) • Moderate: The sound of the letter name comes at the second position (*f, l, m, n, r, s, x*) • Challenging: Letter names have no association or have confusing association with their sound (*h, w, y, c, g,* vowels)	• When the name of the letter closely connects with the sound that it makes, it is easier to remember. • If you think of it like baseball, it's easy to learn first base, because a lot happens there, then second base, and then shortstop is a bit more confusing because it is not attached to a base.
Oral language	• Vowels are usually learned by the time a child is 1 year old • Consonants often learned by 4 years of age: *n, m, p, h, t, k, y, f, ng, b, d, g, w, s* • Consonants often learned after 4 years of age: *l, r, v, z, sh, ch, j, zh, th*	• The easier it was to learn to speak the sound, the easier it is to learn the letter that matches the sound. • Special note, each child develops in his or her own unique time. These are guidelines. Honoring a child's own unique development is important. Also, early intervention with hearing and pronouncing letters and sounds is hugely effective. Don't hesitate to reach out to a speech and language pathologist for a quick screening.
Look alike	• Curvy letters (e.g., *a, c, o*) • Straight letters (e.g., uppercase *A, E, F, L*)	• Having students think about how letters are formed creates a category or storage bin in their mind for those letters.

Note. Based in part on Jones, Brown, and Sias (2015).

Principle 3: Students Need to Make Text Connections within Phonemic Awareness and Phonics Instruction, Not Just Experience Learning in Isolated/Disconnected Activities

Besides teaching children to identify sounds, letters, and words, teachers must provide ample opportunities for all learners to read and engage with text every day to support an overarching aim of reading with accuracy, fluency, and with understanding. Having students interact with a variety of texts (i.e., text sets) fosters wide word exposure, content learning, and knowledge of text structures (Neuman & Roskos, 2012). Moreover, students who are exposed to connected texts are challenged by reading words and phrases in context rather than just words in isolation (also known as contextualized linguistic effects), not to mention the value of making mental representations of text (schemas) that contribute to content knowledge acquisition. These diverse reading experiences ensure an engaging literacy block and afford teachers ample opportunities to differentiate based on assessment data of skills, experiences, and content knowledge, such as in the example of Molly, a second-grade native English speaker. Molly knows how to pronounce some single-syllable sight words but finds it challenging to decode words (e.g., *shirt, great, play*). She has exceptional listening abilities and can retell stories almost verbatim after a read-aloud, especially stories and informational texts about animals and their habitats.

Understanding Molly's literacy behaviors enables her teacher to build on her strengths of listening, retelling abilities, content knowledge, and interest in an effort to enhance her decoding abilities. Instructional recommendations may include small-group and individual instruction involving teacher modeling and decoding words (oral and written) together in isolation and then in text, since there are occasions in the following months of second grade where these skills will be stressed in the curriculum.

Nonetheless, there is an infinite number of opportunities to decode in high-quality literature, not just decodable and predictable books, and thus the quality of the literary experience should not suffer for the need of the skill. Instead, a customized plan for improvement can be crafted and delivered, and needed skills can be refined in a timely fashion to continually develop Molly's early literacy skills.

Although phonemic awareness and phonics are generally not part of the curriculum beyond second grade, it is recommended that consideration of these foundational skills be given for older students who have not mastered these skills when a lack of those skills stymie their literacy development and reading comprehension. In these instances of teaching phonemic awareness and phonics with older students, the need to make text connections cannot be stressed enough.

Advancing Children's Word Knowledge through Integration of the Three Principles

Teachers can integrate the principles of modeling, connected facets of literacy, and connected text through their word work and thereby leverage time and opportunities to teach phonological awareness and phonics skills in tandem with other needed literacy understandings. One way to do this is through whole-class interactive book reading; another is through small-group word study instruction based on the SAIL instructional framework (Ganske, 2016). Both have the added benefit of incorporating differentiation to better meet individual needs. A brief description of each follows.

Interactive Read-Alouds

Whole-class read-alouds that engage children in thinking and discussing texts are common experiences in kindergarten and first-grade classrooms. The focus is typically on comprehension, but with multiple readings of the text, these read-alouds can also be excellent springboards for talking about and reinforcing language—vocabulary, phonological awareness, and phonic understandings.

For example, consider Ms. Grayson, a kindergarten teacher. One day she reads aloud a big-book story, such as *I Looked through My Window* by Michaela Morgan, to develop children's understanding and appreciation of the story, one in which a child looks through his bedroom window several times and each time asks the reader/listener, "Guess what I saw?" In each instance a monkey, bear, or other animal greets the child with a "Hello" and the question "Any room for me in your nice warm bed?" Eventually they all pile on, leaving hardly any room for the child. Entrance of the boy's mother on the last page and her wishing him "Sweet dreams!" brings children's imaginations back to the reality of a bed full of stuffed animals.

Ms. Grayson's rereading of the text the next day focuses on expanding the children's vocabulary through discussion of *mischievous* monkey, *fluffy* bear, or *squashed*. She asks the students to tell about a time they were *mischievous* and invites them to act out the word *squashed*.

For a third reading of the story Ms. Grayson marks several words with features that characterize different children's levels of phonological awareness or knowledge of phonics. For children still learning to accurately count syllable units, she marks with highlighter tape the words *animals, listen,* and *mischievous* and asks the children to clap and count the syllables. For another group the task is pointing out rhyming words (*be/me*) on a page. In addition, she asks children beginning to associate letters and sounds to consider the highlighted word *win* and find another word that starts with the same sound (*we, we're, wasn't*), using their memory for the text to aid them in finding it. When time allows it, she asks the class to count all the *t*'s or *s*'s on a favorite page of the story. While this last activity and the read-aloud itself are carried out with the whole group, the other activities just described enable teachers to address the different understandings of children, yet do so in a whole-class setting.

Finally for all but perhaps the first reading, Ms. Grayson points to the words as she reads them, so that by a fourth or fifth reading of the story the children know what the text says and can "pretend read" along, anticipating words based on their starting letters and known sounds. This type of tracking of text helps children develop a concept of word, namely, the alphabetic principle or print to speech match discussed earlier in this chapter.

Small-Group Word Study Instruction with SAIL

SAIL (Ganske, 2016, 2018) is an acronym that stems from the words *survey, analyze, interpret,* and *link,* components of a small-group word study lesson that relies on categorization. While teachers can address decoding strategies and phonic features during read-alouds and guided reading, a dedicated word study time is another valuable way to advance children's word learning in systematic ways that build on what they already know and considers what they are ready to learn. This approach is important because these understandings develop at different rates for different children. Although small-group word study instruction has often been used to meet this need, instruction is not always optimal; rather, it can become routinized and without much talk or thought on the part of students (Ganske & Jocius, 2013). SAIL was developed in response to these issues.

Survey

Modeling plays a crucial role in SAIL, especially during the first component: survey. Teachers like Mr. Campbell check to be sure the children can identify the words or pictures being worked with and that they know what the words mean. In a word family sort with *-all* and *-ill* words, he might ask students to provide another meaning for *fall* besides "drop" and discuss the season of fall. Once word/picture recognition has been checked, Mr. Campbell sets out an exemplar for each of the categories in the sort; in our example, perhaps *ball* and *hill.* He then takes the remaining cards and begins to model the placement of several cards under their appropriate categories. To encourage attention to sound, each time he places a card he says the word and checks to see which exemplar it matches by saying the name of each category header. After modeling the process and thinking aloud to decide on the placement of the word, Mr. Campbell asks if one of the children is ready to try placing a word or picture card. He continues the process with other children until all the cards have been placed.

Analyze

Next, Mr. Campbell asks the children to determine whether the words are all accurately placed. To do so, they read aloud the words in a category and listen to see that they all have a like sound; in our example, this would be *-all* or *-ill*. Pairs of students share their thinking and then talk about it with the group. When words are used, children must also pay attention to the spelling pattern that characterizes each category, namely, consider whether all the words in a category have the same pattern as well as sound. After the children have checked one category, they move on to the next category.

Interpret

Mr. Campbell considers this the so-what part of the lesson. If the words are all placed correctly, what is there to be learned from the sort that can help the children be better readers and writers. He guides children to understandings such as "If I see *-all* in a word I'm trying to read, I'm going to think of *ball*; *t-a-l-l* would be *tall*. And if I want to write the word *tall*, I can use what I know about *fall*." There are many ways to describe takeaways for Interpret. What matters is that the concept is useable with other words and that the children have the opportunity to think and talk about it.

Link

This part of the lesson is very important, because it takes the work of exploring words in isolation back to context. During Link children apply their knowledge of the features (and perhaps vocabulary) by reading a sentence that contains other *-all* or *-ill* words, or through interactive writing of a sentence that contains words with the particular features under study. For example, Mr. Campbell might ask the children to try reading "He went down the hall to get the pill" or engage them in group-writing the sentence "We will fill the can with bills." For the latter, he models how to stretch out words so children can better catch the sounds and then with the children repeats the sentence to count the number of words. He then draws a blank for each word and engages the group in contributing to the spelling, rereading the text with the completion of each word. This part of SAIL integrates reading and writing, reviews the phonic feature being learned and requires children to apply it, and returns the learners to connected text. Link and the other parts of SAIL also emphasize student talk and cognitive engagement, two ingredients that add to student motivation and ultimately to their learning.

Conclusion

The three principles discussed in this chapter provide a framework for early literacy instruction:

- Principle 1: Students need modeling to learn for transfer.
- Principle 2: Students need to connect early literacy skills.
- Principle 3: Students need to make text connections within phonemic awareness and phonics instruction.

While most curricula emphasize segments of literacy instruction to include whole-class, small-group, and individual instruction, some fail to articulate the nuances between options for whole-class instruction, including demonstrations, read-alouds, and modeling, to name a few. Modeling is required to scaffold learners to build upon what they already know to position them to transfer those learnings and skill development to other settings. Connecting between early literacy skills is inextricably linked as an extension to teacher modeling. Once students grasp initial concepts like phoneme segmentation, they must connect other skills such as phoneme blending. After all, being able to segment sounds in a word is not fruitful without blending the sounds back together.

Making text connections focuses on meaning acquisition within phonemic awareness and phonics instruction. A focus on connecting text enables students to view "literacy" as more than just words or learning grammar rules but also an opportunity to learn about the world around them. Those natural curiosities must be cultivated continuously to maintain a love for literacy.

Integrated approaches to foundational literacy instruction provide the balance that all literacy educators seek, both with respect to connecting early literacy skills to one another and separately making text connections to those skills as they learn. Learning content does not come after learning to read; they occur in unison through opportunities to practice skills using high-quality and diverse literature. As soon as students can decode simple words, they should have opportunities to practice reading new and familiar words or word parts in connected texts. In being mindful of these three principles of early literacy instruction, teachers can lead children to engage in environments of skill development, content knowledge acquisition, and literacy learning while being poised to confront unknown words and comprehension challenges that come their way.

REFERENCES

Achievethecore.org. (n.d.). Instructional content—ELA/Literacy: Foundational skills. Retrieved February 20, 2020, from *https://achievethecore.org/category/1206/ela-literacy-foundational-skills*.

Blevins, W. (2017). *A fresh look at phonics: Common causes of failure and 7 ingredients for success.* Thousand Oaks, CA: Corwin Press.

Cassidy, J., Grote-Garcia, S., & Ortlieb, E. (2019). What's hot in 2019: Expanded and interconnected notions of literacy. *Literacy Research and Instruction, 58*(1), 1–11.

Cummins, J. (2011). Literacy engagement: Fueling academic growth for English learners. *The Reading Teacher, 65*(2), 142–146.

Ehri, L. C. (2003, March 17). *Systematic phonics instruction: Findings of the National Reading Panel.* Paper presented at the Invitational Seminar organized by the Standards and Effectiveness Unit, Department for Education and Skills, British Government, London, UK.

Ehri, L. C., & McCormick, S. (2013). Phases of word learning: Implications for instruction with delayed and disabled readers. In D. E. Alvermann, N. J. Unrau, & R. B. Ruddell (Eds.), *Theoretical models and processes of reading* (6th ed., pp. 339–361). Newark, DE: International Reading Association.

Flanigan, K. (2007). A concept of word in text: A pivotal event in early reading acquisition. *Journal of Literacy Research, 39*(1), 37–70.

Foorman, B. R., & Torgesen, J. (2001). Critical elements of classroom and small-group instruction promote reading success in all children. *Learning Disabilities Research and Practice, 16*(4), 203–212.

Ford-Connors, E., & Paratore, J. (2015). Vocabulary instruction in fifth grade and beyond: Sources of word learning and productive contexts for development. *Review of Education Research, 85*(1), 50–91.

Frey, N., Fisher, D., & Hattie, J. (2017). Surface, deep, and transfer? Considering the role of content literacy instructional strategies. *Journal of Adolescent and Adult Literacy, 60*(5), 567–575.

Ganske, K. (2016). SAIL: A framework for promoting next-generation word study. *The Reading Teacher, 70*(3), 337–346.

Ganske, K. (2018). *Word sorts and more: Sound, pattern, and meaning explorations K–3.* New York: Guilford Press.

Ganske, K., & Jocius, R. (2013). Small-group word study: Instructional conversations or mini-interrogations? *Language Arts, 91*(1), 23–40.

Gately, S. E. (2004). Developing concept of word: The work of emergent readers. *Teaching Exceptional Children, 36*(6), 16–22.

Jones, C., Brown, L., & Sias, C. (2015). *Enhancing alphabet knowledge instruction through design and curriculum planning.* Paper presented at 2015 National Title I Conference, Salt Lake City, UT.

Jones, C., & Reutzel, D. R. (2012). Enhanced alphabet knowledge instruction:

Exploring a change of frequency, focus, and distributed cycles of review. *Reading Psychology, 33*(5), 448–464.

National Early Literacy Panel. (2008). *Developing early literacy: Report of the National Early Literacy Panel: A scientific synthesis of early literacy development and implications for intervention.* Retrieved March 1, 2020, from *https://lincs. ed.gov/publications/pdf/NELPReport09.pdf.*

National Reading Panel. (2001). Teaching children to read: An evidence-based assessment of the scientific research literature on reading and its implications for reading instruction. Retrieved March 2, 2020, from *www.nichd.nih. gov/sites/default/files/publications/pubs/nrp/Documents/report.pdf.*

Neuman, S. B., & Roskos, K. (2012). Helping children become more knowledgeable through text. *The Reading Teacher, 66*(3), 207–210.

O'Leary, R., & Ehri, L. C. (2020). Orthography facilitates memory for proper names in emergent readers. *Reading Research Quarterly, 55*(1), 75–93.

Ortlieb, E., & Schatz, S. (2019). Passing the pen: A gradual release model of the recursive writing process. In M. B. McVee, E. Ortlieb, J. S. Reichenberg, & P. D. Pearson (Eds.), *The gradual release of responsibility in literacy research and practice* (pp. 205–215). Bingley, UK: Emerald.

Pearson, P. D., McVee, M. B., & Shanahan, L. E. (2019). In the beginning: The historical and conceptual genesis of the gradual release of responsibility. In M. B. McVee, E. Ortlieb, J. Reichenberg, & P. D. Pearson (Eds.), *The gradual release of responsibility in literacy research and practice* (pp. 1–22). Bingley, UK: Emerald.

Piasta, S. B. (2014). Moving to assessment-guided differentiated instruction to support young children's alphabet knowledge. *The Reading Teacher, 68*(3), 202–211.

Piasta, S. B., & Wagner, R. K. (2010). Learning letter names and sounds: Effects of instruction, letter type, and phonological processing skill. *Journal of Experimental Child Psychology, 105*(4), 324–344.

Shanahan, T. (2019). The science of reading: Improving reading achievement. Retrieved from *www.shanahanonliteracy.com.*

Stahl, K. A. D. (2014). New insights about letter learning. *The Reading Teacher, 68*(4), 261–265.

What Works Clearinghouse. (2016). *Self-study guide for implementing early literacy interventions.* Washington, DC: Institute of Education Sciences.

CHILDREN'S LITERATURE

Carle, E. (2011). *La oruga muy hambrienta/The very hungry caterpillar* (bilingual ed.). Key West, FL: World of Eric Carle.

Morgan, M. (2000). *I looked through my window.* Barrington, IL: Rigby.

5

. . . .

Reading Fluency

Chase J. Young, Timothy Rasinski, and Shelly Landreth

Reading fluency is most accurately defined by its three components: the ability to recognize words accurately, to recognize words with automaticity, and to read with expression that matches the meaning of the text (Samuels, 2002; Schreiber, 1980; Young & Rasinski, 2018). These three components of fluency come together and serve as the foundation for reading comprehension (Benjamin & Schwanenflugel, 2010; Rasinski, Rikli, & Johnston, 2009).

For years, fluency was considered a neglected reading goal because teachers rarely included in their intervention plans a focus on fluency (Allington, 1983). For example, a student identified as having difficulty with automatic word recognition might receive basic phonics instruction as remediation rather than fluency instruction. Allington argued that students who struggle with fluency should actually receive fluency instruction.

Nearly two decades later, the National Reading Panel (National Institute of Child Health and Human Development, 2000) cited reading fluency as an integral part of the reading process, bringing fluency research and instruction back to the forefront. Unfortunately, much of the reading fluency research included in the report measured only reading rate, and as a result, classroom instruction began to focus on speed rather than overall reading fluency. Subsequently, students were assessed with timers, were required to meet speed goals, and were sometimes held back when not meeting the "words read correctly per minute" grade-level expectation. Thus, educators began to view reading fluency as only reading rate, perpetuating the misconception of fluency's definition and its role in reading instruction. While is it important for students to read words automatically and at an appropriate pace (Rasinski, 2000), we need to keep in mind that the main goal of reading is comprehension, not speed. Reading fluency is often understood as the bridge between phonics and reading comprehension.

Of course, this confusion is not new. In 1991, Dowhower pointed out that reading fluency instruction and research often left out a crucial aspect of reading fluency: prosody (i.e., reading with expression). Ironically, prosody seems to be the aspect of fluency most strongly correlated with reading comprehension (Miller & Schwanenflugel, 2008). Students who read with adult-like expression are more likely to understand what they read (Benjamin & Schwanenflugel, 2010).

Thus, students who can read words accurately, at a good pace, and expressively tend to have better reading comprehension (Sabatini, Wang, & O'Reilly, 2019). LaBerge and Samuels (1974) explained this phenomenon with their theory of automaticity. They argued that readers with increased proficiency in automatic word recognition can reallocate their cognitive resources away from the lower-level word decoding task to the ultimate goal in reading: comprehension. Therefore, building fluency in reading is a necessary process for reading success (Snowling & Hulme, 2005).

What Is the Principle?

We believe the primary principle of reading fluency, as in any task that requires automatic or near automatic performance, is authentic practice. Like many other tasks in life, practice is essential in developing proficiency. Authentic practice is an effective principle of literacy instruction because it requires students to practice reading engaging texts (see Chapter 14) to develop skills and proficiency that can transfer to subsequent reading experiences.

Repeated readings is an instructional practice to support fluency. Samuels (1979) found that when readers practice reading one text several times to the point where they can read it with a degree of fluency, improvement was shown not only on the text practiced repeatedly but also on new texts never before seen by the reader. In other words, the effect of the repeated readings generalized beyond the texts that were practiced. While repeated readings has been demonstrated to be an effective approach for improving fluency, a practical (and we might argue artful) problem is how to make repeated readings an authentic and engaging experience for students. Because of the current emphasis on reading speed, students are often asked to read a text repeatedly for the purpose of reading it fast.

An authentic way of looking at repeated reading is to think of it as rehearsal. For example, actors, singers, and professional speakers all rehearse texts that they will eventually perform for an audience. The rehearsal is aimed not at reading fast but at creating a performance that is meaningful and satisfying for the audience—expression that reflects the meaning of the passage rehearsed is the goal. If we accept the premise that the goal of rehearsal is a meaningful performance, then are there texts that can be used in an expressive and meaningful manner? Of course, the answer is a resounding *yes*! Certainly stories can be performed orally (think teacher read-aloud), but so can poetry, songs, scripts from plays, speeches, monologues, dialogues, and more. We contend that these types of materials are ideal for fluency development as they require an expressive and meaningful reading to be successful.

How Can the Principle Be Applied?

This principle can be applied in many aspects of a literacy program. As we develop fluency activities and interventions, we keep the principle of practice at the forefront. Practicing reading is really the key to developing a fluent reader. With that in mind, we look to approaches that provide authentic practice in reading, such as poetry recitation, song fests, theatrical plays, rereading favorite stories, and so on. Teachers can use this principle when planning their own instruction.

When developing fluency lessons, the "north star" is authentic practice. To further illustrate how we apply this principle in varying ways and grade levels, we offer you a few research-based examples.

Fluency Development Lesson

The Fluency Development Lesson (FDL; Rasinski, 2010) was developed as a daily intervention lesson for students who struggle in fluency and whose difficulties in fluency affect their comprehension. The goal of the FDL is for the student to achieve daily success in reading by learning to read a new text fluently each day. The FDL incorporates elements of wide reading practice (each day a new text), repeated reading practice, assisted reading with partners, word study, authentic performance, and home involvement. The format for the 20-minute lesson follows a routine of the teacher taking responsibility for reading the daily passage, approximately 50–200 words, and gradually shifting responsibility for the reading to the students. The lesson begins with the teacher selecting a daily short text to be mastered by students and making two copies for each student. The texts can be poems, nursery rhymes, song lyrics, segments from stories or speeches from history, and so forth. Below is the daily lesson sequence for the FDL:

1. The teacher introduces a new, short text and reads it to the students two or three times while the students follow along silently.
2. The teacher and students discuss the content of the passage as well as the quality of teacher's reading of the passage.
3. Teacher and students read the passage chorally several times. Having different groups read different lines in the text can be used to create variety and maintain engagement.
4. The teacher organizes student into pairs or trios. Each student practices the passage three times while his or her partner listens and provides support and encouragement.
5. Individuals and groups of students perform their reading for the class or other audience, such as another class, a parent visitor, the school principal, or another teacher.
6. After the performance, the students and their teacher then choose five or more interesting words from the text to add to the individual students' word banks and/or the classroom word wall.
7. Students then engage in 5–10 minutes of word study activities (e.g., word families, word sorts with word bank words, word walls, flash card practice, defining words, word games) under the guidance of the teacher.
8. The students take one copy of the passage home to continue practicing with and receiving positive feedback from family members. The other copy of the text remains in each student's school folder for continued practice and performance in school (e.g., end-of-week poetry slam).
9. The following day students read the passage from the previous day to the teacher or a fellow student for accuracy and fluency. Words from the previous day are also read, reread, grouped, and sorted by students and groups of students. Students may also read the passage to the teacher or a partner who checks for fluency and accuracy.
10. The instructional routine then begins again with Step 1 using a new passage.

Several studies have demonstrated the effectiveness of the FDL in improving students' word recognition accuracy and automaticity, expression, and overall reading achievement (DiSalle & Rasinski, 2017; Zimmerman et al., 2019).

Readers' Theater

Readers' Theater is a tool or process used in theater for helping performers gain control over scripts they will later be performing for an audience. As an instructional practice, Readers' Theater was developed as an authentic form of repeated readings (Tyler & Chard, 2000). In the educational context, Readers' Theater is an activity that engages groups of students in rehearsals and a performance of a text. Research indicates that Readers' Theater can improve reading fluency (Griffith & Rasinski, 2004) and reading comprehension (Young, Durham, Miller, Rasinski, & Lane, 2019) as well as motivation and engagement (Clark, Morrison, & Wilcox, 2009; Rinehart, 1999; Worthy & Prater, 2002). Readers' Theater can be implemented in a variety of ways and in different contexts, although most researched approaches follow a systematic protocol.

One such protocol has been found to improve reading fluency and takes little time to implement. In 2009, we (Young & Rasinski, 2009) described a 5-day format that required only 5–10 minutes per day. On Mondays, teachers select scripts, read the texts aloud, and have students select their favorite. After considering the text as a whole, the students return to school on Tuesdays, meet with other students who chose the same text, and work to assign parts. Once parts are assigned, the students rehearse and focus on word recognition automaticity. Student group rehearsals focus on expressive reading on Wednesdays, and the students engage in final rehearsal on Thursdays. On Fridays, the students perform for an audience of classmates, teachers, school staff, parents, and others. In terms of the principle of fluency instruction, the students engaged in practice that was authentic throughout the week, which involved repeated readings of texts with a purpose.

We also spent some time further developing the Readers' Theater format to include reading comprehension and word study activities (see Young, Stokes, & Rasinski, 2017). Other fluency activities have also been adjusted to include specific reading comprehension tasks, such as the update on the neurological impress method (NIM; Heckelman, 1969) that Flood, Lapp, and Fisher (2005) called NIM Plus. They followed the same timeless NIM fluency protocol, and added a comprehension component. Keeping the principle of practice in mind, and considering comprehension goals, a teacher might target more than one competency in addition to reading fluency to achieve a more synergistic effect.

An Evolution of Reading Fluency Interventions Based on Practice and Results

This section describes how we used the principle of practice to modify and update reading fluency interventions over time. The following interventions are most often delivered one-on-one and are reserved for your most struggling readers. We first describe how we modified repeated readings, and then how we combined repeated readings with the neurological impress method, and finally how we used that combination in a more authentic way.

Repeated Readings

The method of repeated readings (Samuels, 1979) became a widely used and effective means for increasing students' reading fluency, particularly in regard to accuracy and automaticity. In the study, students read a text repeatedly until they reached a desired words read correctly per minute. More recently, we use the principle of repeated readings and made some modifications to increase motivation and authenticity as well as focus on expressive reading (Mohr, Dixon, & Young, 2012).

First, we selected texts that were high quality and appealed to the student. For example, Emilio was a third-grade boy who struggled with reading fluency. After surveying his interests, we chose to use humorous poetry as the texts for intervention. One such text, *How to Torcher Your Teacher* by Bruce Lansky, was used for Emilio's intervention as we thought he might like the poem, thereby increasing his motivation.

We asked him to read the text the first time, and recorded his words read per minute, accuracy percentage, reading comprehension, and reading prosody. For accuracy and words per minute, we timed his reading and marked his errors. In order to measure his reading comprehension, we used the retell rubric from the Developmental Reading Assessment 2 (Beaver & Carter, 2006), but any quality retell rubric would likely suffice. Finally, to assess his reading prosody, we used the multidimensional fluency scale (Zutell & Rasinski, 1991). When he completed his first reading, and the assessments were complete, he plotted his scores on four different graphs: accuracy, words per minute (automaticity), comprehension, and prosody. He then reread the text a second and third time, both times we measured everything but comprehension, and he plotted his scores again on the graph. On the fourth and final reading, we assessed all measures, including comprehension. Then, he could see the visual of his progress in all areas (see Figure 5.1 for an example), which can also be motivating as the student sees himself actually improving as a reader.

Read Two Impress

Emilio did show some progress from repeated readings, but he still struggled, particularly with prosody. We decided to adjust his intervention. We looked back into the 1960s to a one-on-one intervention called the neurological impress method (NIM; Heckelman, 1966, 1969). The idea was

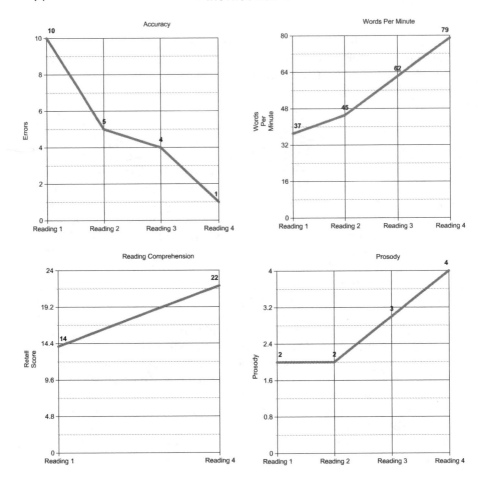

FIGURE 5.1. Graphing students' progress.

to provide assisted readings of text and model fluent oral reading. NIM requires a teacher and a student to begin reading aloud together. Once in unison, the teacher would increase his or her speed slightly, perhaps only reading one syllable ahead of the student. The teacher and student would then continue this for the entire text. Research on NIM revealed promising results (Hollingsworth, 1978; Topping, 1987). While the assisted component was likely the foundation for its success, it lacked the practice component known to be another principle of reading fluency instruction. Thus, we modified NIM to include practice, and called the method Read Two Impress (R2I; Young, Rasinski, & Mohr, 2016).

First, the teacher selects a challenging text for the student. Much like NIM, the teacher and student read aloud in unison, and then the teacher reads slightly ahead of the student with good expression. Instead of continuing on, the teacher stops after a page or paragraph and asks the student to reread the text aloud, and thus students have an immediate opportunity to practice. The teacher and student continue this process throughout the text. Indeed, it is less authentic than other approaches, but remember, this method is reserved for students who struggle greatly in reading, and studies have shown it can positively increase students reading fluency and comprehension after 4 to 10 weeks (Young, Mohr, & Rasinski, 2015; Young et al., 2018).

Read Like Me

In an effort to add a bit more authenticity, we again revised the R2I protocol. Read Like Me (Young, Lagrone, & McCauley, 2020) takes a whole–part–whole approach that includes real reading, and also more practice. First, a teacher selects a challenging text and emphatically reads it aloud to the student. The teacher and student then engage in R2I throughout the text. After working through the entire text using the R2I protocol, the student then reads the entire text back to the teacher, which ideally engages the student in a successful and authentic reading of a challenging text.

Other Examples of Whole-Class Practice

Poetry recitations, song fests, and delivering speeches also incorporate the principle of authentic practice. Poetry, arguably, was written to be read aloud with appropriate pace, pitch, pause, and intonation for purpose of entertainment. Indeed, poets practice these recitations in the form of repeated readings and pay close attention to the meaning and tone they wish to convey to the audience.

Research also shows that reading while singing can improve a reader's fluency, particularly expression and volume, phrasing, and pace (Young, Valadez, & Gandara, 2016) as measured by the multidimensional fluency scale (Zutell & Rasinski, 1991). In the study, second-grade classrooms learned two songs per week. First, the teacher projected the lyrics and read them aloud to the students. Next, the students joined the teacher in a choral reading—an approach also found to improve reading fluency (Rasinski, 2010). After several repeated choral readings, the teacher added the music and the classes rehearsed the song. After 2 days of rehearsal, the students performed. The process was repeated with a new song during the second half of the week. The teachers who planned the reading-while-singing activity used the principle of authentic practice as a foundation for the activity's development.

Moreover, teachers often incorporate speeches into the content areas, such as social studies. Students assume the identity of a prominent figure, choose one of their speeches (or a portion if the speech is long), and rehearse the speech with the goal of performing it for an audience. While teachers might be concerned more with content learning, the process of learning and reciting speeches certainly includes the principle of authentic reading practice. One aspect that is also common across many of the examples we have provided is that the "level" of the text is not of primary concern—the texts are chosen for quality and content. With the proper amount of assistance and practice, often students are able to master their chosen texts, and read them aloud accurately, with automaticity, and with appropriate expression that matches the meaning—all three of the components of fluency. Moreover, with the principle of practice in mind, we encourage teachers to consider additional engaging and authentic ways to help students practice reading to develop their fluency.

Conclusion

A substantial amount of empirical research suggests that practice-based strategies, such as derivations of assisted and repeated readings, can positively affect reading development in a variety of aspects, including the components of reading fluency. Teachers should trust the principle of authentic reading practice and incorporate it into their reading instruction. Furthermore, and good news for teachers, there is a strong relationship between reading fluency and reading comprehension (Sabatini, Wang, & O'Reilly, 2019), and thus activities targeting reading fluency development will likely translate into improved reading comprehension, the main goal of reading. Of course, in order to become great comprehenders of texts, students need to develop the foundational skills, such as fluency. Although there are many existing activities based on assisted and repeated readings, there is a constant need for improvement, further development, and refining to meet the needs of all learners in contemporary classrooms. Thus, we encourage teachers to think carefully about how the principle of practice (adding authenticity is a big bonus) can be applied flexibly in the classroom.

REFERENCES

Allington, R. (1983). Fluency: The neglected reading goal. *The Reading Teacher, 36*(6), 556–561.

Beaver, J. M., & Carter, M. A. (2006). *The developmental reading assessment–second edition (DRA2)*. Upper Saddle River, NJ: Pearson.

Benjamin, R. G., & Schwanenflugel, P. J. (2010). Text complexity and oral reading prosody in young readers. *Reading Research Quarterly, 45*(4), 388–404.

Clark, R., Morrison, T. G., & Wilcox, B. (2009). Readers' Theater: A process of developing fourth-graders' reading fluency. *Reading Psychology, 30*(4), 359–385.

DiSalle, K., & Rasinski, T. (2017). Impact of short-term fluency instruction on students' reading achievement: A classroom-based, teacher initiated research study. *Journal of Teacher Action Research, 3,* 1–14.

Dowhower, S. L. (1991). Speaking of prosody: Fluency's unattended bedfellow. *Theory Into Practice, 30*(3), 165–175.

Flood, J. D., Lapp, D., & Fisher, D. (2005). Neurological Impress Method PLUS. *Reading Psychology, 26*(2), 147–160.

Griffith, L. W., & Rasinski, T. V. (2004). A focus on fluency: How one teacher incorporated fluency with her reading curriculum. *The Reading Teacher, 58*(2), 126–137.

Heckelman, R. G. (1966). Using the neurological impress remedial reading method. *Academic Therapy, 1,* 235–239.

Heckelman, R. G. (1969). A neurological-impress method of remedial-reading instruction. *Academic Therapy, 4*(5), 277–282.

Hollingsworth, P. M. (1978). An experimental approach to the impress method of teaching reading. *The Reading Teacher, 31,* 624–626.

LaBerge, D., & Samuels, S. J. (1974). Toward a theory of automatic information processing in reading. *Cognitive Psychology, 6*(2), 293–323.

Miller, J., & Schwanenflugel, P. (2008). A longitudinal study of the development of reading prosody as a dimension of oral reading fluency in early elementary school children. *Reading Research Quarterly, 43*(4), 336–354.

Mohr, K. A. J., Dixon, K., & Young, C. J. (2012). Effective and efficient: Maximizing literacy assessment and instruction. In E. T. Ortlieb & E. H. Cheek, Jr. (Eds.), *Literacy research, practice, and evaluation: Vol. 1. Using informative assessments for effective literacy practices* (pp. 293–324). Bingley, UK: Emerald Group.

National Institute of Child Health and Human Development. (2000). *Report of the national reading panel. Teaching children to read: An evidence-based assessment of the scientific research literature on reading and its implications for reading instruction* (NIH Publication No. 00-4769). Washington, DC: U.S. Government Printing Office.

Rasinski, T. (2000). Speed does matter in reading. *The Reading Teacher, 54*(2), 146–151.

Rasinski, T. V. (2010). *The fluent reader: Oral reading strategies for building word recognition, fluency, and comprehension* (2nd ed.). New York: Scholastic.

Rasinski, T. V., Rikli, A., & Johnston, S. (2009). Reading fluency: More than automaticity?: More than a concern for the primary grades? *Literacy Research and Instruction, 48*(4), 350–361.

Rinehart, S. (1999). Don't think for a minute that I'm getting up there: Opportunities for Readers' Theater in a tutorial for children with reading problems. *Journal of Reading Psychology, 20,* 71–89.

Sabatini, J., Wang, Z., & O'Reilly, T. (2019). Relating reading comprehension to oral reading performance in the NAEP fourth-grade special study of oral reading. *Reading Research Quarterly, 54*(2), 253–271.

Samuels, S. J. (1979). The method of repeated readings. *The Reading Teacher, 41,* 756–760.

Samuels, S. J. (2002). Reading fluency: Its development and assessment. In A. E. Farstrup & S. J. Samuels (Eds.), *What research has to say about reading instruction* (3rd ed., pp. 166–183). Newark, DE: International Reading Association.

Schreiber, P. A. (1980). On the acquisition of reading fluency. *Journal of Reading Behavior, 7,* 177–186.

Snowling, M. J., & Hulme, C. (2005). *The science of reading: A handbook.* Malden, MA: Blackwell.

Topping, K. (1987). Paired reading: A powerful technique for parent use. *The Reading Teacher, 40,* 608–614.

Tyler, B., & Chard, D. (2000). Using Readers Theatre to foster fluency in struggling readers: A twist on the repeated reading strategy. *Reading and Writing Quarterly, 16*(2), 163–168.

Worthy, J., & Prater, K. (2002). "I thought about it all night": Readers Theatre for reading fluency and motivation. *Reading Teacher, 56*(3), 294–297.

Young, C., Durham, P., Miller, M., Rasinski, T., & Lane, F. (2019). Improving reading comprehension with Readers Theater. *Journal of Educational Research, 112*(5), 615–626.

Young, C., Lagrone, S., & McCauley, J. (2020). Read Like Me: An intervention for struggling readers. *Education Sciences, 10*(3), 57.

Young, C., Mohr, K. A. J., & Rasinski, T. (2015). Reading together: A successful reading fluency intervention. *Literacy Research and Instruction, 54*(1), 67–81.

Young, C., Pearce, D., Gomez, J., Christensen, R., Pletcher, B., & Fleming, K. (2018). Examining the effects of Read Two Impress and the neurological impress method. *Journal of Educational Research, 111*(6), 657–665.

Young, C., & Rasinski, T. (2009). Implementing Readers Theatre as an approach to classroom fluency instruction. *The Reading Teacher, 63*(1), 4–13.

Young, C., & Rasinski, T. (2018). Readers Theatre: Effects on word recognition automaticity and reading prosody. *Journal of Research in Reading, 41*(3), 475–485.

Young, C., Rasinski, T., & Mohr, K. A. J. (2016). Read Two Impress: An intervention for disfluent readers. *The Reading Teacher, 69*(6), 633–636.

Young, C., Stokes, F., & Rasinski, T. (2017). Readers Theater plus comprehension and word study. *The Reading Teacher, 71*(3), 351–355.

Young, C., Valadez, C., & Gandara, C. (2016). Using performance methods to enhance students' reading fluency. *Journal of Educational Research, 109*(6), 624–630.

Zimmerman, B. S., Rasinski, T. V., Kruse, S. D., Was, C. A., Rawson, K. A., Dunlosky, J., & Nikbakht, E. (2019). Enhancing outcomes for struggling readers: Empirical analysis of the fluency development lesson. *Reading Psychology, 40*(1), 70–94.

Zutell, J., & Rasinski, T. (1991). Training teachers to attend to their students' oral reading fluency. *Theory Into Practice, 30*(3), 211–217.

6

. . . .

Comprehension and Vocabulary

Douglas Fisher, Nancy Frey, and Rachelle Savitz

The students in Raymond Ortega's fourth-grade class have been studying inventors. They are working to answer these essential questions: *What drives people to create something different? Why explore the unknown?* They have read a great deal of information, including several chapters from the book *Toys: Amazing Stories behind Some Great Inventions* (Wulffson, 2000). This investigation required students to develop specialized vocabulary, such as the differences between *needs* and *wants* as these terms apply to *supply* and *demand*. They also learned a range of technical terminology including *characteristics, consumer,* and *capitalism*. Further, they had to summarize information, ask questions, infer meanings, and clarify concepts, all of which are good reading comprehension practices.

Mr. Ortega's students know they will write in response to the unit questions in an essay in which they share their thinking, using evidence from the texts they have read. Mr. Ortega knows his students need to write reports of information, arguments, and narratives on a regular basis if they are to develop their literacy prowess. When students write, they use their understandings and vocabulary to convey information. Mr. Ortega understands the crucial connection between reading and writing, and therefore both must be the focus of instruction if students are to develop their working vocabulary and comprehension skills. Limiting instruction to reading alone will not ensure students develop strong literacy skills (e.g., Graham et al., 2018).

In addition to writing their essays, the students in Mr. Ortega's class know they will be provided an opportunity to complete another task, this one in response to the question "What did these texts inspire you to do?" In this case, students have a great deal of choice in what they will do and produce. Some might want to organize a debate, others might conduct research, while still others could develop presentations. Mr. Ortega's focus is shifting reading from a passive experience in which students consume texts to an active experience in which student produce and share, based on their understanding of the texts they read. As Mr. Ortega says, "The point of comprehension is to do something that matters." In other words, the point of comprehension is not to simply comprehend. It is to understand deeply and be moved by that understanding to take action in the world. This leads us to the key principle for this chapter: *Comprehension and vocabulary are taught in service of something greater.*

The Skills Required to Comprehend

As Thorndike (1917) noted, comprehension requires the cooperation of many forces. Students must decode the words, ascribe meaning to those words, read fast enough to focus on meaning, and engage in reasoning. Each of the forces is critical if students are to comprehend a text. Some of these forces have a ceiling, meaning that once they develop, there is no more room for additional growth. For example, once a reader knows the names of the letters in a given language, there is no more learning of letters that needs to occur. Other forces continue to develop across the readers' life. For example, vocabulary continues to expand; we learn new words and phrases on a regular basis. Paris (2005) described this difference as constrained and unconstrained skills. Figure 6.1 contains a list of constrained and unconstrained skills in reading.

Note the two areas of focus for this chapter (i.e., vocabulary and comprehension) are identified as unconstrained skills. The students in Mr. Ortega's class were expanding their vocabulary and applying their thinking and reasoning to a range of texts. They will continue to do so over

Constrained Skills	Unconstrained Skills
Phonemic awareness Phonics Reading fluency	Vocabulary Comprehension

FIGURE 6.1. Constrained and unconstrained skills.

their lifetimes. Having said that, it is important to note that vocabulary and comprehension learning should not be relegated to the upper grades. Word learning and working to understand the text begin as soon as students start reading (and listening to) texts.

In fact, early vocabulary knowledge is a predictor of later reading success. Nagy (2005) notes that "of the many benefits of having a large vocabulary, none is more valuable than the positive contribution that vocabulary size makes on reading comprehension" (p. 27). It is clear there is a strong relationship between vocabulary and comprehension. That is, although vocabulary and comprehension are equally important and valuable, understanding their connection is vital. They do not operate in silos, nor should they be taught in a way that uncouples the two in the minds of students. The better a student knows the meanings of the words in a text, the better the student will be able to comprehend the text.

Knowledge is a key component of both comprehension and vocabulary. Knowledge fuels reading and listening comprehension: the more you know about a topic, the more likely you are to understand a new text on that topic. And one of the best ways to build a strong knowledge base is through wide reading. This leads to one of our essential factors that allow teachers to implement the key principle of this chapter.

Essential Factor 1: Students Need Expansive Opportunities for Reading

Expansive opportunities for reading may be delivered in the form of whole-class read-alouds, shared readings, or close readings. During read-alouds, teachers read from a text that students do not see. The focus is on listening comprehension and vocabulary development. In shared readings, the teacher reads from a text while the students follow along. The focus is on comprehension, vocabulary, and speech-to-print. During close readings, students read and discuss a complex text with their peers based on text-dependent questions. The focus is on applying what you have learned to a complex piece of text.

Extended reading opportunities can also happen through independent reading, at home and at school. It can occur in literature circles and book clubs, or any other form of reading lots of narrative and informational texts across the curriculum. By providing opportunities for students to surround themselves with words, information, and stories, students build background knowledge and strengthen their vocabulary (Beck, McKeown, & Kucan, 2002; Graves, 2006). But simply reading a lot is not, in and of itself, going to ensure that students develop strong vocabulary and reasoning skills. Students need instruction, not just practice, which brings us to our second essential factor.

Essential Factor 2: Students Need Strategic, Intentional Instruction

Instruction matters. And some types of instruction are better than others in terms of developing students' vocabulary knowledge and comprehension skills. For example, we have known for decades that there is no evidence that round-robin reading will improve students' understanding of texts, much less their fluency (Opitz & Rasinski, 1998). Alternatively, there is evidence that discussions about texts are valuable. When students engage in meaningful and authentic discussions about a text with others, they are not only further developing their own interpretations but also forming unique connections with multiple perspectives. Students may then turn back to the text to justify their interpretations using textual evidence (Graves, Juel, Graves, & Dewitz, 2010).

Graves (2006) developed a four-part vocabulary instruction framework that consists of the following components: (a) providing rich and varied language experiences, (b) teaching individual words, (c) teaching word-learning strategies, and (d) developing word consciousness. Each component of this framework is essential if vocabulary learning is going to occur. Importantly, Graves notes that some words need to be taught. This can occur through direct instruction. Hopefully, gone are the days of students "learning" through rote memorization that included activities such as looking up definitions in the dictionary and completing fill-in-the-blank assignments (Zutell, 2008). Rather, students need to be taught the meanings of the targeted terms and be provided multiple opportunities to practice these words. In addition, students need to develop word learning strategies including morphology and the use of context clues. Modeling word solving is one way that teachers can ensure students develop these habits for analyzing unfamiliar terms.

In addition, students need rich and varied language experiences so they use the words. For example, word sorting engages students in actively comparing and contrasting words, searching for patterns, and forming conclusions they can apply to new words (Williams, Phillips Birdsong, Hufnagel, Hungler, & Lundstrom, 2009). Reading aloud to students and following up with interactive discussion about the text supports vocabulary development for young children (e.g., Blachowicz & Fisher, 2015).

Further, strategic teacher-led think-alouds scaffold vocabulary processing while graphic organizers such as semantic maps make vocabulary learning visible. A think-aloud is when teachers verbally share what they are doing and thinking while modeling a new skill or strategy. There is no one right way to teach vocabulary, but there are many evidence-based practices that have been shown to be useful in students learning new vocabulary.

In terms of comprehension, it is important to remember that readers interpret texts and words based on their own prior knowledge, background, and experiences as well as cultural, personal, and social histories. This was highlighted by Rosenblatt's (1995) reader response theory, which emphasizes that the reader's reading and understanding of a text is dependent on the reader's interaction and connections made. Having said that, it is crucial to recognize that Rosenblatt also noted, "The reader must remain faithful to the author's text and must be alert to the potential clues concerning character and motive" (p. 11). Rosenblatt cautioned that readers might ignore elements in a text and fail to realize they are "imputing to the author views unjustified by the text" (p. 11).

Almasi and Hart (2015) contend that decoding, fluency, and content knowledge alone do not ensure comprehension. They argue that comprehension instruction that supports process knowledge through multifaceted strategy instruction is most successful in improving comprehension. It is comprehension instruction that weaves these together. Because successful reading requires using several strategies at once, instruction should reflect the reading process in its entirety, rather than being broken into subskills. Therefore, comprehension strategies should be taught in combination as flexible and interconnected, rather than in isolation. Comprehension instruction should include the use of teacher thinkalouds, open-ended questioning, and discussion of strategies such as constructing mental images, asking questions while reading, making inferences, predicting, and summarizing.

Having said that, we agree with Shanahan (2019), who noted that "a common error in reading education is to treat reading comprehension as if it were a skill or a collection of discrete skills." Asking questions and identifying the main idea—two examples of common comprehension skills—are influenced by a wide range of text features such as vocabulary, sentence structures, text cohesion, organization, graphics, and the use of literary devices, to name a few. Thus, it seems reasonable to suggest that students need to know how to do these things and that they need lots of practice in applying these to different types of texts. As they do so, their teachers should monitor when comprehension breaks down and identify additional areas of instruction or practice. For example, if a student's comprehension was compromised while reading a complex narrative, then additional instruction and practice might help if it were aligned with those types of texts. Additional practice in informational texts, or more comfortable texts, probably would not help. This leads us to our third essential factor: the value of practice.

Essential Factor 3: Students Need Deliberate Practice

Practice does not make perfect, despite the common saying. Instead, practice makes permanent. Students need practice if the instruction they receive is intended to stick—but not just any type of practice. Too often, students are given rote tasks that simply require mindless repetitions. How many times have we seen the three-page worksheet that requires students to read random sentences and identify facts versus opinions? That's not what we're talking about. As Ericsson (2006) described, we are looking for deliberate practice, which has a number of specific components (see Figure 6.2 for a visual developed by Deans for Impact, 2016).

Notice that deliberate practice requires that students push past their comfort zone and that they have goals. In other words, the practice is difficult. In terms of comprehension, the texts used for practice cannot give up their meanings easily. If they do, there is no practice effect. Students need to understand that the practice will push them. If students believe their teacher thinks they should be able to accomplish the task easily, they are likely to become frustrated and to quit the task. When they know it is going to push past their comfort zone, and they accept the challenge of learning, practice becomes powerful.

In addition, students need goals, and a mastery goal orientation is more valuable than a performance goal orientation when it comes to practice. A mastery goal might be to make inferences while reading, whereas a performance goal might be to get 8 out of 10 quiz questions right. Their goal orientation is important, as there is a positive correlation between the use of active learning strategies such as self-generated questions and rereading, and mastery goals. Conversely, students with a performance goal orientation tend to use more superficial learning approaches such as guessing and skipping challenging content (Meece & Miller, 2001). The result of a performance goal orientation is that it undermines the core principle of deliberate practice, which is to engage with difficult concepts. That said, practice does not need to be a slog. When the practice tasks are relevant and engaging, this is easier. Thus, teachers need to identify practice tasks, such as game-based learning, that invite students into the work.

THE FIVE PRINCIPLES OF DELIBERATE PRACTICE

FIGURE 6.2. Deliberate practice. Reprinted by permission from Deans for Impact (2016).

But practice in isolation will not ensure that students learn more or better. They need—no, they deserve—feedback about their efforts and accomplishments. When teachers assign practice, even relevant and interesting practice, but then collect and then ignore it, students come to understand that their efforts are not important. It becomes a compliance task rather than a learning task. Instead, the practice work that students do should drive the type of further instruction and grouping, to ensure instruction is related to students' needs and experiences. If most of the class has committed a similar error, reteaching is in order (not to mention more practice after the additional instruction). If a small group of students have made an error, then targeted support should be provided to those students and the others should not be subjected to that. Rather, they should be engaged in other tasks.

The final aspect of Ericsson's theory of deliberate practice is the development of a mental model. The practice should provide students with opportunities to develop a representation of how that which is being practiced really works in the real world. In terms of reading comprehension, students need to develop mental models of what it means to work to understand a text. They need mental models of what readers do when they don't know what to do or struggle to comprehend. And they need mental models of success, and what deep understanding looks and feels like.

Thus far, we have focused on aspects of vocabulary and comprehension that provide students with skills and concepts they can use to read, analyze, and understand texts. But we believe there is more to comprehension than this. These aspects are important but insufficient to realize the power of the principle introduced at the outset of this chapter. We believe that comprehension should be thrilling and that students need to do something with the ideas and information they gain from the texts they read.

The Thrill of Comprehension

As Mr. Ortega implied, the point of comprehension has been lost. Most curricula available today focus on developing students' ability to comprehend. Again, this is important. But how many students, rightfully so, ask "So what?" after they finish a reading? They are not motivated by the experience. In response, their teachers try to incentivize, reinforce, or even manipulate them into reading. Imagine the increased desire to read, and understand, texts when students are inspired to take action. That's exactly what happened in Mr. Ortega's classroom. Luis wanted to know more about the invention of electricity and read pages and pages so he could develop a presentation for his peers. Carmen wanted to know about "girl inventors," so her teacher ordered her a copy of the book *Wonder Women: 25 Innovators, Inventors, and Trailblazers Who Changed History* (Maggs, 2016). Carmen consumed the book. And then she found the book *Girls Think of Everything: Stories of Ingenious Inventions by Women* (Thimmesh, 2002) in the school library and read it through. Eventually Carmen created a poster titled "Girl Inventors" in which she profiled several of the people she read about and described how the world would be different without each of the inventions. Suzanna, a reluctant reader in Mr. Ortega's class, asked if she could write her own book. As she said, "I wanna tell my story. I invented something to help my mom. Can I write a story about it?" Of course Mr. Ortega was thrilled and told Suzanna that he was very excited to learn about her invention and that he would help her produce her book. David, on the other hand, wanted to write an Amazon.com review of the book so he could share his thinking about inventors with a much larger audience.

As we noted earlier, being inspired to take action is not limited to the upper elementary grades. Young children can do this as well. As part of a listening comprehension lesson, kindergarten students in Eloisa Green's class reviewed the wordless book *Chalk* (Thomson, 2010). As they did so, they identified words for the things they saw. Ms. Green recorded some of the words, specifically decodable words, and displayed them in a pocket chart. For example, Brianna said there was a *boy*, Teddy said they had a *bag*, and Marco said the *sun* was *hot*. In addition to the focus on decodable words, the students discussed what was happening in each illustration. This lesson was designed to expand students' oral vocabularies and listening comprehension. Ms. Green knows that stretching her students' listening comprehension is important. As they learn to read over the next several years, their reading comprehension will begin to catch up with their listening comprehension. However, stunted growth in listening comprehension impedes the development of reading comprehension (Stricht & James, 1984). Without careful attention to the development of listening comprehension, their ability to read for meaning suffers.

But it's what happened afterward that resulted in the thrill of comprehension. While the oral vocabulary and listening comprehension aspects of the lesson are important, Ms. Green did not leave her students there. She deepened their learning by asking them what the text had inspired them to do. This was not the first time that her students had the opportunity to take action based on what they had read. Ms. Green said, "Now it's your turn to show me what you learned. Last week most of us drew and illustrated, so let's all choose something different this time. This book is only illustrations, so how else might you share what you learned?"

Excitedly, the students moved around the room. Several sat at a table that had a digital recorder. They took turns retelling the story with each child being recorded. They focused on the dinosaur and how the children saved the town from the dinosaur by drawing rain.

Others wanted to write. As with most kindergarten classrooms, there is a wide range of reading and writing skills and some students compose multiple sentences, often with transitional spelling. Mia wrote (with corrections to her spelling), "There was rain. The girl made the sun come. But then the dinosaur came. She drew the rain to make it go away."

Still others wanted to work with the words they identified. Hunter and Lilly used the words from the pocket chart to construct new words. For sun, they added *fun, run, gun,* and *bun.* For *boy,* they had *toy, joy,* and *Troy* (the name of a classmate). Another group of students asked Ms. Green if there were other books with only pictures. She said yes, and they asked if they could have one to read. Martin said, "Maybe a different one would be good for us." Justine added, "We want to see if they are alike or different." Ms. Green gave them *Flashlight* (Boyd, 2014). They examined each page and discussed the contents, using rich vocabulary and thinking skills. Thus launched the compare and contrast group that eventually reported to the class that their two books were alike because they had no words and there were boys in both, but they had different stories, different drawings, and different characters. As Martin said, "They are both exciting adventures." Cassidy added, "But this has color only when the flashlight is there. This one [holding the book *Chalk*] is all color."

Revising the Point of Comprehension

Our hope in forwarding this principle is that the point of comprehension is expanded to include taking action as evidence of deep understanding of text. As we have noted, there are a number of forces that must be combined and integrated for textual understanding to occur. As with phonemic awareness, phonics, and fluency, vocabulary stands in service of comprehension. The goal of phonics is not to simply sound out words any more than the goal of fluency is to read fast or the goal of vocabulary to recite definitions of words. These are all in service of comprehension.

But the principle we are forwarding here suggests that comprehension needs to be in service of something else. We want students to be agentic readers so they question what they are reading and learning and relating new information to their own lives. We want students to experience the thrill of comprehending such that they take action and produce something new. We propose that the ultimate measure of textual understanding is not being able to answer recall and reproduction questions but rather to move to the highest levels of Bloom's taxonomy: the ability to evaluate and create. After all, what is the purpose of knowledge building if it is not in service of action? The purpose of education is not to build students as walking warehouses of stored information. The purpose is to foster the means for the next generation to use that knowledge to improve the physical, biological, and social worlds they inhabit. Written and spoken texts are the channels we as humans have relied on to hand down knowledge for thousands of years. But it is up to us educators to light a path for how they can use that knowledge to create new possibilities. Imagine the difference we can make when students are inspired by the texts they read. Who knows what might happen next?

REFERENCES

Almasi, J. F., & Hart, S. J. (2015). Best practices in narrative text comprehension instruction. In L. B. Gambrell & L. M. Morrow (Eds.), *Best practices in literacy instruction* (5th ed., pp. 223–248). New York: Guilford Press.

Beck, I. L., McKeown, M., & Kucan L. (2002). *Bringing words to life: Robust vocabulary instruction.* New York: Guilford Press.

Blachowicz, C. L. Z., & Fisher, P. J. (2015). Best practices in vocabulary instruction. In L. B. Gambrell & L. M. Morrow (Eds.), *Best practices in literacy instruction* (5th ed., pp. 195–222). New York: Guilford Press.

Deans for Impact. (2016). *Practice with purpose: The emerging science of teacher expertise.* Austin, TX: Author.

Ericsson, K. A. (2006). The influence of experience and deliberate practice on the development of superior expert performance. In K. A. Ericsson, N. Charness, P. J. Feltovich, & R. R. Hoffman (Eds.), *The Cambridge handbook of expertise and expert performance* (pp. 683–703). Cambridge, UK: Cambridge University Press.

Graham, S., Liu, X., Aitken, A., Ng, C., Bartlett, B., Harris, K. R., & Holzapfel, J. (2018). Effectiveness of literacy programs balancing reading and writing instruction: A meta-analysis. *Reading Research Quarterly, 53*(3), 279–304.

Graves, M. F. (2006). *The vocabulary book: Learning and instruction.* New York: Teachers College Press.

Graves, M. F., Juel, C. F., Graves, B. B., & Dewitz, P. F. (2010). *Teacher reading in the 21st century: Motivating all learners* (5th ed.). Hoboken, NJ: Pearson.

Meece, J. L., & Miller, S. D. (2001). A longitudinal analysis of elementary school students' achievement goals in literacy activities. *Contemporary Educational Psychology, 26*(4), 454–480.

Nagy, W. F. (2005). Why vocabulary instruction needs to be long-term and comprehensive. In E. H. Hiebert & M. L. Kamil (Eds.), *Teaching and learning vocabulary: Bringing research to practice* (pp. 27–44). Mahwah, NJ: Erlbaum.

Opitz, M. F., & Rasinski, T. V. (1998). *Good-bye round robin: 25 effective oral reading strategies.* Portsmouth, NH: Heinemann.

Paris, S. G. (2005). Reinterpreting the development of reading skills. *Reading Research Quarterly, 40*(2), 184–202.

Rosenblatt, L. M. (1995). *Literature as exploration* (5th ed.). New York: Modern Language Association.

Shanahan, T. (2019, November 9). How to analyze or assess reading comprehension. Retrieved from *www.shanahanonliteracy.com/blog/how-to-analyze-or-assess-reading-comprehension*.

Stricht, T. G., & James, J. H. (1984). Listening and reading. In P. D. Pearson, R. Barr, M. L. Kamil, & P. Mosenthal (Eds.), *Handbook of reading research* (Vol. 1, pp. 293–317). White Plains, NY: Longman.

Thorndike, E. L. (1917). Reading as reasoning: A study of mistakes in paragraph reading. *Journal of Educational Psychology, 8,* 323–332.

Williams, C., Phillips Birdsong, C., Hufnagel, K., Hungler, D., & Lundstrom, R. P. (2009). Word study instruction in the K–2 classroom. *The Reading Teacher, 62*(7), 570–578.

Zutell, J. (2008). Changing perspectives on word knowledge: Spelling and vocabulary. In M. J. Fresch (Ed.), *An essential history of current reading practices* (pp. 186–206). Newark, DE: International Reading Association.

CHILDREN'S LITERATURE

Boyd, L. (2014). *Flashlight*. San Francisco: Chronicle Books.

Maggs, S. (2016). *Wonder women: 25 innovators, inventors, and trailblazers who changed history*. Philadelphia: Quirk Books.

Thimmesh, C. (2002). *Girls think of everything: Stories of ingenious inventions by women*. New York: Houghton Mifflin Harcourt.

Thomson, B. (2010). *Chalk*. Singapore: Marshall Cavendish Children's Books.

Wulffson, D. (2000). *Toys: Amazing stories behind some great inventions*. New York: Henry Holt.

7

• • • •

Assessment

Dixie D. Massey

In 1941, the United States was on the brink of a world war and still suffering an economic depression. In one family farming on the plains of Nebraska, it continued to be a challenge to survive. The father struggled with ongoing health issues, so two teen boys were busy going to school and taking care of the corn, oats, hogs, and milk cows. During the spring of 1941, the older boy took an exam. Not just any exam. The eighth-grade exam. The results? He missed the cutoff score by less than a point. The outcome? My dad didn't go to high school because he didn't pass the test. Instead, he stayed at home and handpicked corn by the wagonload.

More than half a century later, I found the teacher's guide for the eighth-grade examinations in Nebraska and South Dakota. Dad doesn't recall ever seeing his teacher with one of those guides. The guide itself is wide ranging, covering topics from agriculture to literature, mathematics to art. While my father certainly wasn't the only one of his generation to end his education at the eighth grade, his experience is one more example of the long-trending importance and impact attached to a single score on a test. Yet the story highlights an important point: a person is more than a single assessment score. Thus, the guiding principle for this chapter is as follows: *Effective literacy assessment is more than a single score on a test. Effective literacy assessment seeks to create a complex profile of the student, relying on multiple data sources, while also considering the child's background, strengths, and interests in order to help determine effective instruction for the teacher and give productive feedback to the student.*

To understand the principle, it is helpful to clarify how assessment is defined in this chapter. For this chapter, the terms *assessment* and *testing* will be used to refer to different things. *Assessment* will be used to refer to the overarching framework of how we learn about and evaluate another's development and performance (see Figure 7.1). *Testing* is one component of assessment. It typically involves answering specific questions, and may be attached to a variety of consequences. It may or may not inform pedagogy.

In addition to defining how assessment will be used for this chapter, we must also consider how we are using the term *effective*. What makes assessment effective versus ineffective? Evaluating effectiveness is determined by the purpose. If the purpose of assessment is to compare one school with another, then the assessments that are used will be different than when the purpose of assessment is to inform classroom pedagogy (Black & Wiliam, 1998). For this chapter, we will be considering the classroom level of assessment. The purpose of these assessments is to inform the teacher, his or her students, and the families of the students about the content, skills, and strategies a student has demonstrated, as well as next steps of learning. That is, assessment forms a feedback loop with pedagogy when it informs our understanding of the students (Black & Wiliam, 2018; OECD, 2008), and we are able to use that understanding to shape instruction (Black & Wiliam, 1998; Neuman, 2016).

Why Is Assessment a Principle of Effective Literacy Instruction?

Defining Literacy

Effective assessment is dependent upon how we view literacy (DeVries, 2017). The International Literacy Association (2018) defined literacy as reading, writing, speaking, listening, viewing, and composing. Within that broad definition, we will focus more specifically on reading as an exemplar for the challenges within the broader scope of the additional areas of literacy. Is reading an amalgamation of smaller skills? Valencia and Pearson (1987) wrote that reading has frequently been described as "an aggregation—not even an integration—of all these skills" (p. 729). If reading is viewed as a list of skills to be placed into a scope and sequence, then students must master each skill before they move forward. Students are viewed as having a deficit if they have not mastered the skills that are linked to their particular grade-level expectations.

Some of these reading skills are constrained (alphabet, reading rate), and some, like comprehension, are unconstrained (Stahl & García, 2017). Consider reading rate, which is commonly tested in schools, starting in

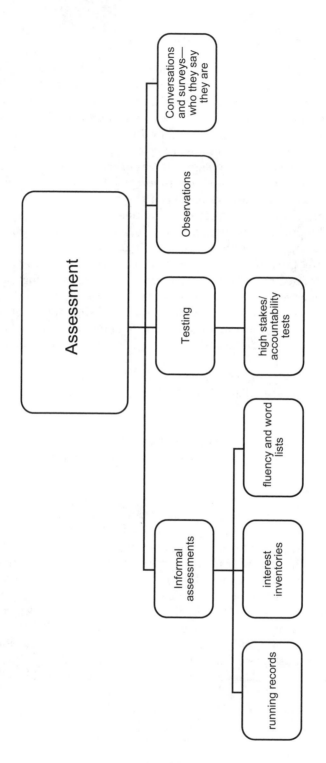

FIGURE 7.1. Components of assessment.

kindergarten or first grade and continuing into middle school. The students are given a list of words or a passage and asked to read. They receive a score for the number of words read correctly in a minute. This number of words per minute is compared to a range of numbers that is deemed to be "acceptable" for the grade level. If students fall below this acceptable level, they are frequently given some kind of intervention, including multiple practices reading and rereading passages. And with enough practice, their scores on reading rate generally go up.

However, what happens to students' comprehension if there is a strong emphasis on raising reading rate? Perhaps they don't attend to meaning because all the assessment considered was rate. They may not learn that efficient readers vary their rate based on a variety of factors, including their purpose for reading and the depth of understanding they wish to gain from the task. Perhaps they begin to divorce "reading" from "meaning making" because of the complexity of assessing some literacy components. Further, these discrete skills isolated from larger context may not remain the same ones needed by the time a student reaches adulthood (Johnston, 2005).

Deficit versus Strength View of Assessment

A deficit view of assessment looks for what students cannot do and then provides targeted instruction in that component or skill in order to move the student forward. Moving forward typically means acquiring a specific skill such as decoding and comprehending particular passages.

This approach can be unintentionally detrimental to children. For example, educators frequently describe students as a "level 4" or a "letter G" as if these designations have some inherent meaning. Students begin to take on these labels as their identities, translating scores into "I'm a bad reader." This often neglects what the student already knows, does, and can leverage to learn new skills. It fails to recognize that assessment practices affect teaching and represent children in particular ways and can result in avoidance of punishment or penalty rather than approaching learning (Johnston, 2005). Alvermann (2001) described this phenomenon as follows:

> Literacy education is less skill development and more about access to cultural resources and to understanding of how schools that promote certain normative ways of reading texts may be disabling some of the very students they are trying to help. (p. 679)

A further detriment comes from the often unending cycle, or web, of disability. As Johnston and Costello (2005) described,

Once "identified," children remain caught in the problematic discursive web, partly because the problem is represented as a trait of the child rather than as in the instructional environment, partly because the identification process groups children together who share common identifications, and partly because the child is moved to a system that specializes in children's problems that often emphasizes different understandings about literacy learning. (p. 261)

A view of their strengths means reading as more than a collection of composite skills. Instead, students are viewed as sense makers (Aukerman, 2008) who use the funds of knowledge they have from their backgrounds and experiences in order to interpret their current world (González, Moll, & Amanti, 2006). This complex view of what it means to read holds that reading is localized. That is, people in different settings engage in literacy practices differently, and performance of a task in a testing context is not and should not be representative of performances in all contexts (Baker, 2007; Johnston, 2005). For example, students may summarize a text differently when describing a self-selected story that they read with a grandparent versus a school-assigned text.

If reading is viewed from this complex, strengths-based approach, then we need assessments that do more than analyze discrete skills (Johnston, 2005; Johnston & Costello, 2005). The challenge of this broader view of assessment is that it is complex and hard to measure. As Sarroub and Pearson (1998) noted, we can assess only the "residue" of the reading acts as opposed to the actual processes.

What Does Assessment Look Like When Applied Flexibly in the Classroom?

If we are to have a complex view of literacy assessment, then many questions follow. Teachers ask questions such as The school wants scores; when do I have time to collect all of this other data? What do I collect? What do I do with what I collect? How do I apply assessment flexibly? The following assessment guidelines address these important questions.

Observe, Test, and Talk

Many districts, principals, and teachers claim that their instruction is data driven. As Neuman (2016) found after studying nine New York City schools, data driven meant considering information from only test scores and item analyses. Students were identified as needing work in specific skills and then given additional instruction—usually worksheets or computer work that focused on those skills. In Neuman's study, the students who received this type of instruction were often students of color or poverty, while students who were not in those categories received more open-ended instruction. Neuman reflected, "We've concluded that data-driven instruction can distort the way reading is taught, harming the students who need high-quality instruction the most" (p. 25). She then called for a broader definition of data, as well as instruction that was data informed versus data driven.

Effective literacy assessment that is data informed seeks to build a profile of individual readers that is complex, as opposed to (over)simplifying the reader. Creating a profile requires considering not just multiple assessments but also varying the kinds of assessments that are used through observations, tests, and opportunities for talk (formal interviews, think-aloud protocols, and informal conversations). A complex view of assessment seeks to understand who the child is, both in school and outside of school. Essentially, every interaction with that student and the student's family adds to the profile and thus to the understanding about the student. In the research world, this is referred to as triangulating data.

To describe these points of data, I use an analogy borrowed from painting. When painting a portrait, some artists first sketch the person, using very rough sketches. There are typically features missing, even important features such as hair or a mouth. As the artist continues, the portrait begins to look more and more realistic with details added to complete the picture.

In this way, students are similar. Tests provide one type of information. Formal tests help us evaluate students against set criteria. They also suggest other information beyond what is tested, such as students' stamina for longer passages and how students perform in pressurized situations. These tests are analogous to the rough sketch that an artist uses to begin to find the proportions and vague outline of the portrait. Informal tests, such as reading inventories, can provide a general picture of students' prior knowledge, decoding and word recognition, fluency, and comprehension in a relatively short amount of time. These inventories begin to add detail, as if an artist were adding more features to the sketch.

Observations offer critical information about students, not unlike when an artist begins to add color to a sketch. The teacher as observer, also called kid watcher (Goodman, 1978, 1985) or sensitive observer (Clay, 1993), is critical to assessment that is adaptive. As Johnston and Costello (2005) wrote, the observer notices details of literate behavior, "imagining what they mean from the child's perspective, knowing what the child knows and can do, and knowing how to arrange for that knowledge and competence to be displayed, engaged, and extended" (p. 262). When we watch an artist, we sometimes say they are bringing the painting to life. Similarly, as we watch, we begin to represent the individual life of the student. It is here that we move from scores that can be reported about numerous students into nuanced observations that are student specific.

Finally, student talk is an important part of triangulating data. It is analogous to an artist adding the shading and small details that finish a portrait. Seeking the student's words challenges or confirms our observations but adds the details of why they are doing what they are doing. Student talk comes from formal conversations as part of discussion groups, book clubs, or one-on-one interviews. The think-aloud is another important data point for creating a complex profile of students. Ericsson, Chase, and Faloon (1980) popularized the use of think-alouds to understand the thinking that went with people playing chess. Gradually, the think-aloud became an assessment tool to understand why students made the choices that they made. For example, Pressley and Afflerbach (1995) used a form of student think-alouds to identify more than 90 strategies that students used as they were reading. More recent research has paired think-alouds with screenshot technologies to identify how students use search engines to find information on the Internet (Coiro & Dobler, 2007). By asking students to think aloud, we gain access into their processes of thinking, rather than just the outcomes of their thinking.

Informal conversations are also critical. They give us insights into how students talk when they do not feel the same pressure to give a "correct" answer. Consider Batu. When I first met Batu, he was referred to me by school personnel because of his low scores on literacy assessments. He initially did not want to read or do any work. He kept his hood up and barely made eye contact. One of my colleagues began initiating conversations with him and discovered that Batu had a haircut that he hated. He wanted his mom to pay for a haircut that she thought was too expensive for their budget. Instead, she cut his hair. Batu was embarrassed by his haircut, so he shaved his head. His hood was up to cover his head. The discomfort he felt over his hair and his immigrant family's inability to pay for a haircut was intense. This knowledge did not mean that Batu's literacy scores went up. However, knowing some of Batu's background helped us understand Batu. He wanted to fit in, and yet at every turn his language, family, social status, test scores, and more created barriers that kept him from fitting in to the community of school.

Batu's story emphasizes why triangulating data is key and why a part of that triangle should be interviewing or talking with students, whenever possible, just as an artist takes multiple passes at a portrait. Scores can suggest lack of understanding. Observations can suggest lack of caring. But interviews and conversations can suggest a whole new way to interpret the scores and observations. These new interpretations open the way to different paths for instruction. For Batu, finding a way for him to fit into a small group within the larger class showed us a different side of him—one that was much more animated and allowed him to attempt interpretations of text that he avoided previously.

In sum, we can't assume that if a student scores poorly on a test that they need additional modeling or practice on discrete skills. Being flexible in our assessment means we need to dig deeper and collect evidence from multiple kinds of data in order.

What's There? What's Missing?

If you view assessment as one or multiple additional things to add to an already-busy day, the reality is that you will probably abandon that assessment. Instead, before you try to add new data points, carefully consider assessments that are already in place. Consider the assessment list from a second-grade teacher in Figure 7.2.

After compiling a list of assessments, think about what the assessments measure. By focusing on the "What It Measures" cell, you recognize that you have testing evidence for constrained skills such as rate, alphabet, and phonemic knowledge (Stahl & García, 2017). You have limited information about comprehension, an unconstrained literacy skill. You might also recognize that while the STAR test claims to measure comprehension, that information requires students to answer questions about what words complete a sentence with multiple-choice answers. Thus, you want to gather additional information about how a student comprehends under different conditions. Further, as Figure 7.3 shows, you have two tests but not any talk or observational data, so you think about assessments that will allow you to add those data points. Figure 7.4 shows additional assessments that you might include to address the deficits you found.

It is good to review this information regularly, such as each quarter or semester, and adjust as needed. For example, literacy achievement is strongly influenced by a learner's metacognitive abilities, motivation, self-regulatory tools, and social interactions (Afflerbach, 2007). By reviewing Figure 7.4 later in the year, you might notice that you are not collecting any

Assessment	Data Type	What It Measures
DIBELS	Test	Words read in a minute
STAR	Test	Instructional reading level through comprehension questions

FIGURE 7.2. A second-grade teacher's assessment list.

Assessment	Data Type	What It Measures
DIBELS	Test	Words read in a minute
STAR	Test	Instructional reading level through comprehension questions
What's Missing?		
	Talk Observation	Comprehension

FIGURE 7.3. Adding assessments for talk and observational data.

information about students' motivation. One way to start is with observations, specifically by observing a focal student or group during the week and making notes about when the student appears to be motivated to read and when the student appears unmotivated to read, as shown in Figure 7.5.

With that information, pull the student aside for a short conversation that begins with something like "I noticed that when you were reading the story from our anthology, you didn't look very interested, but when I let people read their library books, you seemed very interested. Can you tell me more about when you are interested in reading and when you aren't very interested in reading?" You can add a rating scale of 1–5 and ask them to rate how motivated they are to read various things, or you can simply take notes. Recording observations and having short conferences can take 5 minutes or less. Not everything needs to be collected from individual students. Consider holding a short conference with a reading group and asking them to answer a single question.

Assessment	Data Type	What It Measures
DIBELS	Test	Words read in a minute
STAR	Test	Instructional reading level through comprehension questions
What's Missing?		
1. One-on-one reading conference 2. Think-aloud 3. Book club discussions	Talk Observation	Comprehension

FIGURE 7.4. Finding additional assessments to address deficits.

Student: José	
Observation	**Conference**
9/25 José looks around the room and avoids reading the anthology. He could not answer questions from the text. During the same week, he hurried to the library to check out a book about soccer, one that he said he had read before.	José said he likes to read books about soccer. He also said he knows all the words in his library book and that makes him want to read it.

FIGURE 7.5. Observation notes on students' motivation.

If these things are to be integrated into your routine, you will need to keep them very short but consistent. You will also need a system. You might use a binder with a page or section for each student or spreadsheet on the computer or a note-taking app. Ultimately you will have to find the system that you will stick with and that provides the biggest payoff in terms of learning about students and using that information to shape instruction.

Assessment Should Benefit Students

Students can easily feel as if schools are places where they do a lot of work for no reason. As someone who is in many different classrooms in my role of teacher educator and in my role as a parent, I have seen children go weeks without receiving any kind of score or feedback. Teachers show me folders stuffed with student work that may or may not be graded, but students never see it or only see a score.

Test scores are often reported to parents and administrators. These test scores are highly valued by many principals and districts as the basis of "data-driven" instruction. Feedback that students receive may be limited to hearing they read 60 words a minute, they are a level G, or they scored a 2 on the end of grade test. In reality, this isn't feedback; it's a label. While labels may be helpful for teachers when it comes to making some decisions about what students need next, we need to avoid giving labels to students as if they have inherent value. A "level G" or "2" does not describe what students can do in a way that helps them improve or take pride in what they know. Worse, it confirms a deficit perspective and becomes an identity that the student accepts (e.g., "I'm bad at reading; I'm a level 1").

A complex view of assessment means that students should receive feedback, and it should be helpful to them (Afflerbach & Cho, 2011). It should be frequent and specific. It should identify what the student did well. When possible, it should identify a next step. There are many athletic coaches who put this principle into practice effectively. For example, I recently heard a swim coach say, "Tianna, you're reaching further than you did 2 weeks ago. Now, I want you to make sure that as you pull your arm out of the water, you're pulling it out right by your ear. Let me see you do that." In this feedback, the coach labels how the student has improved and what to work on next, and then offers a short amount of time for practice before the coach moves on.

Literacy assessment can be similarly focused. For example, Ben may be good at using his background knowledge to make inferences. Feedback to Ben might sound like "Ben, you used your experiences with your own pets to help you infer how our character was feeling. That is an excellent use of background knowledge to make inferences that help you understand the text. The next thing I want you to check is if that inference makes sense with what the text says next. Go back and check the text to make sure that your experiences aren't different than this character's."

What Else Is Needed: Teacher Knowledge and Decision Making

Teacher knowledge and decision making are critical to effective literacy assessment. A report issued by the Center for Study of Reading (García & Pearson, 1991) noted, "Our basic thesis in this report is that the keys to meeting the assessment needs of a diverse student population are a flexible approach to assessment and a dramatically improved knowledge base" (p. 2).

There is a long-standing link among teaching, assessment, and decision making. In 1973, Shavelson wrote, "Any teaching act is a result of a decision, either conscious or unconscious," and "the basic teaching skill is decision making" (p. 144). Griffith and Lacina (2018) wrote, "Teaching is decision-making" (p. 506). Teachers make multiple decisions each day about the nature of learners and learning. Prior research on teaching has noted that the most effective teachers adapt based on students' needs rather than to a particular context (Hoffman & Pearson, 2000).

Unfortunately, some teachers think that information from standardized tests or tests prepared by outside companies are more valuable and reliable than the information observed in the classroom. In other situations, the power to make these decisions about assessment and instruction is taken away and teachers become merely managers of students and data. Valencia and Pearson (1987) wrote, "The price we pay for such a lesson is high; it reduces the likelihood that teachers will use their own data for decision making" (p. 729).

In order to make informed decisions, you will need deep knowledge, including knowledge of language, literacy practices, culturally relevant pedagogies, assessment practices, and more, in order to make thoughtful adaptations for your students (Parsons, 2012; Parsons & Vaughn, 2013; Xu & Brown, 2016). According to Valencia and Pearson (1987),

> The best assessment of reading would seem to occur when teachers observe and interact with students as they read authentic texts for genuine purposes. As teachers interact with students, they would evaluate the way in which the students orchestrate resources to construct meaning, intervening to provide support or suggestions when the students appear on the verge of faltering in their attempt to build a reasonable model of the meaning of the text. . . . There is no difference between reading instruction and assessment, and in which both teacher and student provide input, is an ideal. (pp. 729–730)

Such decisions come with a price. As researchers have discovered, these instructional decisions often put teachers in conflict with other teachers and administrators in their instructional environment (Massey, 2006; Parsons, Malloy, Vaughn, & La Croix, 2014). This type of decision making has been described as "going rogue" (Parsons et al., 2014, p. 144) or a "tactical recontextualization and creative adaptation of discourse" (Handsfield, Crumpler, & Dean, 2010, p. 405).

How have teachers come to these decisions that contrast with the status quo of their context? Research suggests that decisions to adapt are rooted in a teacher's professional knowledge, vision, and sense of agency. Further, the decisions are rooted in an intense focus on students in that the teacher monitors the students' understandings and modify instruction for and to the students (Duffy, 2003).

Conclusion

Assessment is an important part of effective literacy instruction. Assessment communicates and validates our understanding of what literacy is and should be (DeVries, 2017). It informs our understanding of the students, including cognitive, metacognitive, motivational, self-regulatory, and social components (Afflerbach, 2007). It provides the blueprint for our instruction (Black & Wiliam, 1998; Neuman, 2016). In order for literacy assessment to be effective, it needs to consider the good of the student. Finally, effective literacy assessment must be based on knowledgeable teachers using assessment in flexible ways that build on specific knowledge of students and literacy practices (Xu & Brown, 2016).

REFERENCES

Afflerbach, P., & Cho, B. Y. (2011). The classroom assessment of reading. In M. Kamil, P. D. Pearson, E. Moje, & P. Afflerbach (Eds.), *Handbook of reading research, IV* (pp. 487–514). New York: Routledge.

Alvermann, D. E. (2001). Reading adolescents' reading identities: Looking back to see ahead. *Journal of Adolescent and Adult Literacy, 44*(8), 676–690.

Aukerman, M. (2008). In praise of wiggle room: Locating comprehension in unlikely places. *Language Arts, 86*(1), 52–60.

Baker, E. L. (2007). 2007 presidential address: The end(s) of testing. *Educational Researcher, 36*(6), 309–317.

Black, P., & Wiliam, D. (1998). Assessment and classroom learning. *Assessment in Education: Principles, Policy and Practice, 5*(1), 7–74.

Black, P., & Wiliam, D. (2018). Classroom assessment and pedagogy. *Assessment in Education: Principles, Policy and Practice, 25*(6), 551–575.

Clay, M. M. (1993). *An observation survey of early literacy achievement.* Portsmouth, NH: Heinemann.

Coiro, J., & Dobler, E. (2007). Exploring the online comprehension strategies used by sixth-grade skilled readers to search for and locate information on the Internet. *Reading Research Quarterly, 42,* 214–257.

DeVries, B. (2017). *Literacy assessment and intervention for classroom* teachers (4th ed.). New York: Taylor & Francis.

Duffy, G. G. (2003). *Explaining reading: A resource for teaching concepts, skills, and strategies.* New York: Guilford Press.

Ericsson, K. A., Chase, W. G., & Faloon, S. (1980). Acquisition of a memory skill. *Science, 208*(4448), 1181–1182.

García, G. E., & Pearson, P. D. (1991). Literacy assessment in a diverse society (Center for the Study of Reading Technical Report No. 525). Retrieved from *www.ideals.illinois.edu/handle/2142/17927.*

González, N., Moll, L. C., & Amanti, C. (Eds.). (2006). *Funds of knowledge: Theorizing practices in households, communities, and classrooms.* New York: Routledge.

Goodman, Y. M. (1978). Kid watching: An alternative to testing. *National Elementary Principal, 57*(4), 41–45.

Goodman, Y. (1985). Kidwatching: Observing children in the classroom. In A. Jaggar & M. T. Smith-Burke (Eds.), *Observing the language learner* (pp. 9–18). Urbana, IL: National Council of Teachers of English.

Griffith, R., & Lacina, J. (2018). Teacher as decision maker: A framework to guide teaching decisions in reading. *The Reading Teacher, 71*(4), 501–507.

Handsfield, L. J., Crumpler, T. P., & Dean, T. R. (2010). Tactical negotiations and creative adaptations: The discursive production of literacy curriculum and teacher identities across space-times. *Reading Research Quarterly, 45*(4), 405–431.

Hoffman, J., & Pearson, P. D. (2000). Reading teacher education in the next millennium: What your grandmother's teacher didn't know that your granddaughter's teacher should. *Reading Research Quarterly, 35*(1), 28–44.

International Literacy Association. (2018). *Standards for the preparation of literacy professionals 2017.* Newark, DE: Author.

Johnston, P. (2005). Literacy assessment and the future. *The Reading Teacher, 58*(7), 684–686.

Johnston, P., & Costello, P. (2005). Principles for literacy assessment. *Reading Research Quarterly, 40*(2), 256–267.

Massey, D. D. (2006). "You teach for me: I've had it!": A first year teacher's cry for help. *Action in Teacher Education, 28,* 73–85.

Neuman, S. B. (2016). Code red: The danger of data-driven instruction. *Educational Leadership, 74*(3), 24–29.

OECD. (2008). *Assessment for learning formative assessment. Learning in the 21st Century: Research, Innovation and Policy.* Retrieved from *www.oecd.org/site/educeri21st/40600533.pdf.*

Parsons, S. A. (2012). Adaptive teaching in literacy instruction: Case studies of two teachers. *Journal of Literacy Research, 44,* 149–170.

Parsons, S. A., Malloy, J. A., Vaughn, M., & La Croix, L. (2014). A longitudinal study of literacy teacher visioning: Traditional program graduates and Teach for America corps members. *Literacy Research and Instruction, 53*(2), 134–161.

Parsons, S. A., & Vaughn, M. (2013). A multiple case study of two teachers' instructional adaptations. *Alberta Journal of Educational Research, 59*(2), 299–318.

Pressley, M., & Afflerbach, P. (1995). *Verbal protocols of reading: The nature of constructively responsive reading.* Hillsdale, NJ: Erlbaum.

Sarroub, L. K., & Pearson, P. D. (1998). Two steps forward, three steps back: The stormy history of reading comprehension assessment (Faculty Publications: Department of Teaching, Learning and Teacher Education). Retrieved from *https://digitalcommons.unl.edu/teachlearnfacpub/39.*

Shavelson, R. J. (1973). What is the basic teaching skill? *Journal of Teacher Education, 24*(2), 144–151.

Stahl, K., & García, G. E. (2017). Using assessments to map and evaluate the comprehension development of young children. In S. Israel (Ed.), *Handbook of research on reading comprehension* (2nd ed., pp. 241–270). New York: Guilford Press.

Valencia, S., & Pearson, P. D. (1987). Reading assessment: Time for a change. *The Reading Teacher, 40*(8), 726–732.

Xu, Y., & Brown, G. T. L. (2016). Teacher assessment literacy in practice: A reconceptualization. *Teaching and Teacher Education, 58,* 149–162.

8

Appropriate Intervention

Ying Guo and Allison Breit

The literacy skills and needs of students in teachers' classrooms today are diverse. For example, it is not unusual in a third-grade classroom to have students reading and writing at first- through fifth-grade levels. Furthermore, many students may be at various stages of learning the English language. Given these wide ranges, teachers must be able to provide appropriate literacy interventions to support a variety of learners. This chapter describes three fundamental principles of appropriate literacy intervention and explains how teachers can organize their classrooms to support all students' literacy learning in kindergarten through fifth grade.

Three Principles of Appropriate Literacy Intervention

The first principle we discuss in this chapter is that appropriate literacy intervention occurs when teachers use a response-to-intervention model (RTI; Balu et al., 2015). An RTI model is a systematic approach to intervention grounded in collecting assessment data to inform instruction. The second principle involves the need for teachers to target high-leverage literacy domains (i.e., phonological awareness, academic language, text structure) when providing literacy intervention (Nagy & Townsend, 2012; Williams et al., 2005). Third, appropriate literacy intervention includes teachers who scaffold learning for their students (Pearson & Gallagher, 1983). Understanding and implementing these three fundamental principles can help teachers develop the tools and flexibility for realizing the literacy potential of all of their students in the classroom. In the following, we discuss each of these principles in further detail.

Principle 1: Utilize RTI Models

In general, the RTI model provides a framework within which teachers may identify students for intervention in any educational area and design increasingly intensive tiers of interventions. The typical RTI model includes multiple tiers and focuses on the extent to which students respond to scientifically validated instruction. The first tier of instruction is applied on a schoolwide basis, and students who do not respond to first-tier instruction are provided a second tier of intervention. The second tier typically provides additional instruction within small groups to offer more opportunities for students to respond to the instruction. A third tier usually involves more intensive instruction based on individual students' learning needs.

This type of multi-tiered support can be applied specifically to the area of literacy. Literacy intervention in the classroom can be organized using a multi-tiered RTI model. First-tier (Tier 1) and second-tier (Tier 2) interventions are often provided by classroom teachers (Fuchs & Fuchs, 2007) whereas third-tier (Tier 3) interventions are often provided by specialists. In this chapter, we address the first two tiers of intervention, focusing on the area of literacy at the elementary level.

Multi-Tiered Literacy Intervention

Tier 1 literacy instruction occurs within general education classroom settings. The literacy instruction in Tier 1 is designed specifically for meeting the needs of a diverse group of students. Thus, Tier 1 instruction involves teachers' use of research-based core reading/language arts curricula. Of special note here is the term *research-based*. If a curriculum is deemed "research based," it does not necessarily mean that the curriculum has been tested and studied (Foorman et al., 2004). Because of the frequent and somewhat muddy use of this term, teachers and administrators can evaluate whether their curriculum or program aligns with evidence from research studies using a rubric created by Foorman, Smith, and Kosanovich (2016). As shown in Table 8.1, the rubric is organized by content area (e.g., fundamental reading skills, writing) for Grades K–2 and for Grades 3–5 (Foorman, Smith, et al., 2016). Each content area includes a list of criteria for evidence-based instructional practices, which are evaluated and rated as 1 (not met), 2 (partially met), 3 (met), 4 (substantially met), or 5 (completely met) within the curriculum.

TABLE 8.1. Example of Ratings and Comments in the Rubric

Item from Rubric	Rating	Example Comment from Curriculum
Grades K–2		
1D. Phonemic awareness instruction follows a developmental progression (e.g., phoneme isolation [first, final, and medial sounds], blending, segmentation, and phoneme deletion); use with tiles then with letters [FR practice guide, Rec. 2, #1].	1 (not met)	Phonemic awareness was noted on the scope and sequence; however, phonemic awareness activities were not evident within the lessons of the instructional materials.
1E. Graphemes (letters) are gradually integrated into phonemic awareness instruction as students become more skilled [FR practice guide, Rec. 2, #1].	5 (completely met)	There is a gradual and consistent link between phonemic awareness and phonics activities throughout the entire set of materials.
1J. Materials support instruction that teaches students how to decode multisyllabic words by looking for pronounceable word parts within them (e.g., compound words and syllables) [FR practice guide, Rec. 3, #3].	1 (not met)	Materials did not include specific instruction on how to decode multisyllabic words.
Grades 3–5		
2E. Specific texts are included in materials for teaching various text structures (e.g., sequence, comparison, contrast, and cause/effect) to support comprehension and careful reading of narrative and informational text [Adol practice guide, Rec. 2, #1].	4 (substantially met)	There are a considerable number of texts to support comprehension. There are graphic organizers in the back of the teacher editions intended to incorporate this item. However, there is no label on the graphic organizer to indicate the lessons to which they correspond. The addition of where the graphic organizers could be used would be helpful to the teacher for navigation purposes.

(continued)

TABLE 8.1. *(continued)*

Item from Rubric	Rating	Example Comment from Curriculum
2L. Materials support instruction that teaches students to understand and analyze various points of view for narrative text (e.g., author, narrator, and characters) and informational text (e.g., what the author wants to explain and multiple accounts of the same event) with increasing complexity [Adol practice guide, Rec. 3].	2 (partially met)	This is marginally included in the mini lessons of the whole group component. Different genres and the author's purpose are discussed; however, points of view lessons/activities were sparse.
3A. Materials include extensive practice with two short, focused (partially met) research projects that allow students to have multiple experiences with the research process throughout the year and facilitate development of the ability to conduct research independently [EL practice guide, Rec. 3; writing practice guide, Rec. 2a and 2b].	2 (partially met)	There is some evidence of this, mostly found in the ancillary materials (science/social studies connections and the activities recommended for centers). However, those materials are not an expected part of daily or even consistent lessons.

Note. Reprinted from Foorman, Smith, and Kosanovich (2016).

While most students are likely to develop appropriate literacy skills given Tier 1 instruction, a portion of students will require additional instruction. Thus, a critical tenant of the RTI model is universal screening and/or progress monitoring to identify students who require supplemental literacy intervention beyond first-tier instruction (National Association of State Directors of Special Education, 2006). Universal screening and progress monitoring typically occurs at the beginning of the school year and involves assessing all student's skills in reading (e.g., decoding, fluency, comprehension), and writing. Students, whose score on universal screening tools fall below a norm-referenced cutoff point or score (e.g., below the 25th percentile on standard word reading measures) or below a performance benchmark related to poor long-term academic performance (e.g., fewer than 40 words read correctly on an oral reading measure), may be at risk for reading difficulties.

Identifying students for supplemental intervention based on one-time universal screening, however, may overidentify students who require supplemental intervention (Fuchs & Fuchs, 2007). For example, one research study showed that some Grade 1 students identified as at-risk based on universal screening tools made good progress over the course of Tier 1 general education without supplemental intervention (Compton, Fuchs, Fuchs, & Bryant, 2006). As a result, monitoring student's progress over time within the first tier of instruction is an integral component of using an RTI model, in addition to onetime universal screening (Jenkins, Hudson, & Johnson, 2007). Progress-monitoring assessments (e.g., curriculum-based measurements) are administered frequently, often weekly or biweekly, and provide information about both levels of student performance and rate of improvement across time. Fuchs and Fuchs (2007) suggest that teachers use universal screening tools in combination with at least 5 weeks of progress monitoring assessments in response to Tier 1 general education to identify candidates for Tier 2 intervention.

RTI frameworks employ three approaches for providing intervention in Tier 2: (1) use of a standard protocol, (2) use of problem solving, and (3) use of a standard protocol/problem-solving hybrid (Fuchs, Mock, Morgan, & Young, 2003). In a *standard protocol* approach, the research-validated treatment is delivered to all students with similar difficulties in a given domain. For example, teachers might group students who struggle with word reading (i.e., at or below the 15th percentile on standardized word-reading measures) together and provide small-group interventions to these students at workstations in the classroom.

Different from the standard protocol approach, the *problem-solving* approach focuses on designing a student-focused intervention based on individual needs (Fuchs et al., 2003). Accordingly, this approach is more fluid and unique to each individual student (Gresham, VanDerHeyden, & Witt, 2005). Using the problem-solving approach, the classroom teacher often collaborates with the support team including administrators, other teachers, and special education personnel to plan and design the individualized intervention. The teacher then provides the intervention to a particular student and collects weekly progress monitoring data. At the end of intervention, the teacher reports the student's rate of improvement and level of achievement to the support team. The support team and teacher make decisions as to whether this student will return to regular classroom programming or receive a different intervention. The *standard protocol/problem-solving hybrid* approach incorporates features of both the standard and the problem-solving protocol (Reschly, 2005). One way of employing the hybrid model is to start with an intervention using the standard protocol and continue, if needed, with additional individual-student sessions using the problem-solving protocol (Callender, 2007). Another way of using a combined protocol with the standard protocol for addressing literacy difficulties and the problem-solving protocol for addressing obvious behavior problems when dramatic behavior problems occur in combination with literacy difficulties (Fuchs & Fuchs, 2007).

Principle 2: Target Specific Literacy Domains in Intervention

This section outlines specific literacy domains to be targeted in literacy intervention. Specifically, we selected three interrelated domains of literacy to discuss: (1) phonological awareness, (2) academic language, and (3) text structure. We emphasize these domains because, according to research, they are associated with later literacy achievement (e.g., Uccelli, Galloway, Barr, Meneses, & Dobbs, 2015) and are particularly amendable to improvement within the context of systematic and explicit intervention (e.g., Connor et al., 2014; Williams et al., 2007).

Phonological Awareness

Phonological awareness is the ability to recognize and manipulate the segments of sounds in spoken words. Phonological awareness in the early grades is one of the top predictors of literacy achievement (National Reading Panel, 2000). Moreover, early interventions have been shown to be effective in remedying phonological awareness deficits, which have been shown to lead to difficulties in reading words as well as characterize reading disabilities (e.g., Rashotte, MacPhee, & Torgesen, 2001). Therefore, phonological awareness is a major focus of literacy intervention for students in grades K–2.

The most commonly studied paradigm for phonological awareness intervention follows a developmental progression: awareness of words and syllables is taught first, followed by development of smaller units within syllables (e.g., onsets and rimes) and then isolation and manipulation of individual phonemes, and finally development of letter–sound correspondence (e.g., Adams, 1998). The following is the list of phonological awareness learning goals with an illustrative activity for teachers to use in literacy intervention.

- Students identify and manipulate syllables in words.
  - The teacher and students clap out syllables in words and count how many times they clapped.
  - The teacher has students rearrange the order of syllables in a word.
- Students recognize and manipulate onsets and rimes within a syllable.

- The teacher shows pictures of four animals (duck, dog, donkey, sheep) to students and ask the questions "What is this animal's name?" and "What sound does this animal's name start with?" and then asks, "Does it start with the same sound as duck?" Finally, the teacher concludes, "Duck, dog, and donkey all begin with /d/. Sheep does not begin with /d/" (Foorman, Beyler, et al., 2016).
  - The teacher instructs students on manipulating the onsets and rimes of syllables to include different sounds. For example, the teacher asks the question "What would we have if we change the /k/ in /k/ /æt/ to /b/?"
- Students recognize and manipulate individual phonemes.
  - The teacher instructs students on segmenting sounds of a word. For example, the teacher asks, "What sounds do we hear in the word *cat*?" The students answer "/k/ -/æ/ -/t/."
  - The teacher teaches students to manipulate individual phonemes. The teacher gives each student a set of boxes, which match the number of phonemes in the selected words, and places a colored disc over each box. The teacher says the selected word and asks students to repeat words, pulling one disc down into a box for each sound they say. Then students blend the individual sounds together and say the word, running their fingers under the box from the left to right (Foorman, Beyler, et al., 2016).
- Students understand letter–sound correspondence to decode words.
  - The teacher instructs on the phoneme connected to an isolated letter. For example, the teacher asks, "What letter makes the /b/ sound?" Students answer, "*b*."
  - The teacher says a vowel followed by a consonant is a short vowel, unless it has an *e* at the end. The teacher asks, "Do we have a vowel in this word?"; the teacher instructs on the difference between long versus short *a*.
- Students build connections between letter–sound correspondences and their awareness of how words are segmented into sounds.
  - The teacher uses word-building activities to improve students' awareness of how words are composed and how each letter or phoneme contributes to its pronunciation. The teacher gives students magnet letters. Next, students add single missing letters to build words. The activity can start with building CVC (consonant–vowel–consonant) words followed by advanced word-building activities combining sound addition and sound substitution (Rashotte et al., 2001). These activities can help students to begin spelling and decoding words.

Academic Language

Academic language broadly refers to the language of school and school text (Nagy & Townsend, 2012). Research studies support the critical role of academic language skills in literacy and the content areas in elementary school and beyond (Townsend, Filippini, Collins, & Biancarosa, 2012). In particular, above Grade 3, academic language skills play an increasingly dominant role in reading comprehension (Uccelli et al., 2015). Accordingly, current trends in education are encouraging teachers to support academic language development. In fact, the Common Core State Standards have emphasized teaching and using academic language across the grade levels (van Lier & Walqui, 2012) as well as addressing specific goals focused on academic language. Despite the importance of academic language in literacy achievement, teachers provide a relatively low volume of academic language-focused instruction, an important area for advancing students' language and comprehension skills. Here, we discuss two critical components of academic language skills (i.e., academic vocabulary and inferential language) for instruction or intervention and provide strategies for teaching these skills.

Academic Vocabulary. Academic vocabulary refers to "words that appear in a variety of content areas and have different meanings in different academic contexts" (Conley, 2014, p. 9). Academic vocabulary consists of words in a specific subject area such as math, science, or English language arts as well as words that are general and used across multiple areas such as *define, check,* and *estimate* (Barnes, Grifenhagen, & Dickinson, 2016). Academic vocabulary may also include phrases that are not common in conversational language (e.g., "away they went"; Foorman, Beyler, et al., 2016).

Selecting appropriate words is the first step of teaching academic vocabulary. Frequently, teachers are encouraged to select vocabulary words for instruction, which appear frequently throughout the school year and across a variety of academic domains and are unfamiliar to most students (Baumann & Graves, 2010). In addition, students should be taught words that are specialized and essential to comprehending a text. Other words defining the structure of text—particularly informational texts (e.g., figure, glossary)—should be taught as well (Barnes et al., 2016). Finally, words that will promote the size of a student's lexicon (i.e., breadth of vocabulary) as well as depth of understanding (i.e., depth of vocabulary; see Silverman & Hartranft, 2015) are important for teachers to teach. In addition to personally selecting vocabulary words to teach, teachers may draw upon word rating systems such as Words Worth Teaching (Biemiller, 2010), the Academic Vocabulary List (Gardner & Davies, 2013), a New

Academic Word List (Coxhead, 2016), or Word Zone (Hiebert, 2005) to select words for academic vocabulary instruction.

Once selected, rich vocabulary instruction can be used to improve understanding and use of academic vocabulary within the classroom. Rich vocabulary instruction is an approach that features explicit manipulation of word-exposure conditions so that students have repeated opportunities to learn and use novel words in highly informative circumstances. The practices of rich vocabulary instruction include providing a student-friendly definition (e.g., *fragile* means that something can break very easily) when introducing a new academic vocabulary word or phrase and then presenting the new word in a meaning context such as a sentence with the new word (e.g., this vase is *fragile* because it broke so easily; Apthorp et al., 2012).

Rich vocabulary instruction also involves providing extended opportunities for students to use and discuss the academic vocabulary words with the goal of supporting deep understanding of words (Baker et al., 2013). In addition, instruction is organized to provide repeated, informative exposures to new academic vocabulary words in many different contexts, such as read-alouds and classroom discussions in language-arts instruction, hands-on science activities, and math word problems (Apthorp et al., 2012). For students in need of more instruction in academic vocabulary, teachers may provide more concrete learning experiences to learning word meanings. These experiences may include writing the selected words on the whiteboard, having students repeat the words, using manipulatives (e.g., picture card) to support understanding of word meanings, and asking students to use the words in their conversation and writing, all of which may complement the first tier of literacy instruction.

Inferential Language. Inferential language refers to using information in the text plus background knowledge and experiences to discuss topics beyond the immediate context. The ability to understand and use inferential language allows students to think beyond the words in the text to predict, hypothesize, and contrast. Readers rely upon two types of inferences to comprehend text accurately (Kispal, 2008). The first type is *text-connecting inferences* in which the reader relies on linguistic cues present in the text to draw connection within the context. For example, in order to build an understanding of the sentence *Tom gave Sally his coat,* the reader must infer that *his* refers to *Tom* (although this was not explicitly stated).

The second type of inference important for text comprehension is *gap-filling inferences* in which the reader uses background knowledge or experiences to fill in details not explicitly stated in the text. For instance, to comprehend the text *The toy is on fire. Mike grabbed a bucket of water,* one must activate his or her background knowledge that water puts out fire and infer that Mike grabbed the bucket of water because he was trying to put the fire out. Because inferential language requires higher-level thinking skills, it can be difficult for many students to understand, particularly those with comprehension difficulties (Yuill & Oakhill, 1991).

Inferential language skills can be purposefully targeted in systematic and explicit literacy intervention (Foorman, Beyler, et al., 2016). Several techniques can be used to facilitate inferential language skills through classroom-based experiences. Table 8.2 provides examples of some of these techniques. Later, we explain one technique (i.e., asking inferential questions) in detail because it is easily implemented when providing literacy intervention.

Inferential questions can be asked before reading, during reading, and after reading within the context of shared-reading activities (Bradshaw, Hoffman, & Norris, 1998). Inferential questions are used to challenge students to think deeply about what the text means (see examples of inferential questions in Figure 8.1). As students' progress, teachers may ask increasingly complex questions to encourage them to use higher-level thinking skills (e.g., hypothesizing, explaining, predicting) and inferential language. These inferential questions will improve student's comprehension of text as they search for clues in the text they read and activate their background knowledge.

While asking inferential questions is important, supporting students' responses to these questions is even more important. Teachers might support students' responses by encouraging students to elaborate on their

TABLE 8.2. Techniques for Teaching Inferential Language Skills

Instructional Techniques	Grade	Resources
Asking inferential questions	Kindergarten and Grades 4–5	Bradshaw, Hoffman, & Norris (1998); Holmes (1985)
Integration (making connections to texts, experiences, and knowledge)	Kindergarten–Grade 4	Connor et al. (2014); Language and Reading Research Consortium, Jiang, & Davis (2017)
Using key/clue words	Grades 1–3	Yuill & Joscelyne (1988); Yuill & Oakhill (1988)
Highlighting contents	Grade 1–3	Yuill & Oakhill (1988)
Using interpretive cloze	Kindergarten	Bradshaw, Hoffman, & Norris (1998)

Text Clues + Background Knowledge/Experiences to Answer Inferential Questions

- Why did the character _____?
- What do you think _____?
- Predict what will happen if _____?
- If you were the author _____?
- What can you conclude _____?
- What do you think is the most important message in the text?
- What lesson did you learn from the text?
- Do you agree with what _____ said? Why or why not?

FIGURE 8.1. Examples of inferential questions.

answers as well as the text's meaning (Shanahan et al., 2010). Depending on grade level, teachers might also model how to give the reasoned answer that fully addresses the question via explaining his or her critical thinking (Baker et al., 2013). In addition, teachers may prompt students to include more details in their answers and prompt them to interpret the events in the text in light of their experience, background knowledge, or other related texts they have read (Foorman, Beyler, et al., 2016).

Text Structure

Text structure refers to how a written text is organized to convey meaning to the reader (Hogan, Bridges, Justice, & Cain, 2011). When a reader is able to recognize the relationships across and within sentences or larger units of text, he or she is able to build a mental model of what was read and comprehend the text (Langston & Trabasso, 1998). Research studies have suggested that knowledge of text structure is important to reading comprehension (Gersten, Fuchs, Williams, & Baker, 2001). Moreover, intervention research has shown that students who are taught to understand text structure exhibit greater gains in reading comprehension than those who are not taught about text structure (Al Otaiba, Connor, & Crowe, 2018; Williams et al., 2007). Thus, a focus on the knowledge of text structure is essential within literacy intervention.

Text structure is typically described according to two types of written texts: narrative and informational. Knowledge of both types of texts gives a framework in which readers can more readily recognize elements of texts to guide comprehension (Hogan et al., 2011). Next, we discuss narrative text structure and informational text structure and how to teach each structure through literacy intervention.

Narrative Text Structure. A narrative tells a story or a sequence of events. In the elementary grades, examples of narrative texts include historical fiction, fables, and autobiographies. Narrative texts often follow a predictable text structure, often referred to as *story grammar*. Story grammar elements include settings, characters, problems, conflicts, plots, and resolutions (Gersten et al., 2001; Stetter & Hughes, 2010). These components of story grammar are typically strung together in a particular order within a narrative text. In some stories, there are multiple episodes; however, the components maintain the same order across episodes (Hogan et al., 2011).

In implementing literacy intervention at the first tier and second tier, narrative text structure can be taught by classroom teachers using graphic organizers. A story map is one type of graphic organizer and varies in complexity. For example, a simple story map includes the beginning, middle, and end of story, while a more complex map delves into intricacies of the plot. In addition to a story map, other graphic organizers can be used to teach narrative structure. These include (1) a chart that matches the structure to content of the story, (2) a list of pictures of major events that represent the sequence in the story, or (3) a diagram of the plot that connects major action points within the story (Davis, 1994). When using these graphic organizers, teachers should explain why the graphic organizer is useful and how to use it. Teachers should adapt narrative text structure instruction to the abilities of students. For kindergarten students, teachers may focus on the text with simple structure using the basic story map. As students develop, teachers may introduce students to a wider variety of structure elements (e.g., multiple conflicts and subplots; Shanahan et al., 2010).

Informational Text Structure. Informational texts contain information such as facts, explanations, and reasons for true-life phenomenon. Different from narrative texts, informational texts offer a variety of text structures and are not as predictable. The most commonly taught text structures with elementary school students include sequence, which emphasizes a chronological order to describe events; cause/effect, which delineates one or more causes and then describes the ensuing effects; and compare/contrast, which compares and contrasts two or more similar events, topics, or objects (Meyer & Poon, 2004). Table 8.3 describes the structure of informational text. In general, informational text structures apply to paragraph or passages, and the entire text may include different text structures (Williams et al., 2005).

There are several approaches that can be used to teach informational text structure in literacy intervention. One approach is to directly teach clue words (e.g., *first, next, last; same, different; because*) that signal the use

TABLE 8.3. Structures of Informational Texts

Text Structure	Description	Clue Word Examples
Sequence	In what order things happen	*First, second, next, then, later, finally*
Cause and effect	How one event leads to another	*Because, cause, effect, therefore, so*
Compare and contrast	How things are alike and different	*Same, similar, alike, unlike, however*

Note. Based on Shanahan et al. (2010).

of a certain structure (see Table 8.3; Al Otaiba et al., 2018). For example, while sharing an informational text with students, teachers can introduce and teach the clue words associated with the structure. Teachers then provide practices that help students recognize the clue words. Examples include clue-word bingo games and clue-word memory activities. Teachers can also ask students to use these clue words to retell the text. After these activities, teachers can introduce a new informational text and ask students to locate a given clue word and figure out the text structure. Another approach to increase the knowledge of informational text structure is to use graphic organizers to organize information visually from informational texts (Williams et al., 2007). Graphic organizers used for informational texts can include concept maps, Venn diagrams, fishbone charts, and sequence diagrams or flow charts.

Principle 3: Scaffold Literacy Learning

Literacy intervention at the first tier and second tier includes scaffolding in an "I do"–"We do"–"You do" (Pearson & Gallagher, 1983) format. The purpose of "I do" is for the teacher to model for students what it is they are to do. In the "We do," the teacher and students can coparticipate in doing something, which is followed by the "You do," in which students practice what it is they should do either with peers or independently. The teacher may circle back through the gradual release process, as the concept/text becomes more difficult.

An example lesson plan using the scaffolded learning format is provided in Figure 8.2. As shown, the lesson focuses on academic vocabulary and is divided into a focus lesson ("I do"), guided practice ("We do"), collaborative practice ("You do it together"), and independent practice ("You do it alone"). The focus lesson involves the teacher's introduction, explanation, and modeling of using context clues to help determine word meaning. Guided practice includes students' practicing the use of context clues to figure out the meaning of unfamiliar words with the teacher's support. During collaborative practice, the teacher gradually releases the responsibility of using the context clue strategy to the students and moves into the role of facilitator. During independent practice, the teacher requires accurate and flexible use of the context clue strategy in multiple contexts.

Focus Lesson ("I Do")

- Explain the usefulness of context clues.
  - Select five difficult words from a book that the class is reading and show how context can be used to derive meaning.
- Demonstrate the process of using context.
  - Ask the questions such as "What information in the book will help me figure out the meaning of the unknown words?" and "From all the information provided about the unknown word, what does it seem to mean?"
- Try out the tentative meaning of the unknown words.
  - Show students how to try out the tentative meaning of the unknown words (e.g., substitute the meaning of word and read the sentence).
  - Explain if the tentative meaning does not make sense; try to revise it.
- Model the process.
  - Explain the thinking processes that you go through (e.g., using a comparison, searching out synonyms) as you attempt to figure out the meanings of words.
  - Try out these tentative meanings.

Guided Practice ("We Do")

- Select a passage from the book, and ask students to look for unfamiliar words.
- Have students use context clues to figure out the meaning of unfamiliar words, and do two words cooperatively.
- Ask students to try the process on their own.
- Discuss the meaning of the unfamiliar words and the types of clues they used.

Collaborative Practice ("You Do It Together")

- Have students use context clues for an unknown meeting in a reading selection with a partner.
- After reading, students talk about the meanings that they derived and the strategies they used with a partner and revise as needed.
- As students finish, pick one student with a strong response to share his or hers with the class.

Independent Practice ("You Do It Alone")

- Have students apply context clues on their own in written assignments and collaborative projects.

FIGURE 8.2. Example lesson plan.

Conclusion

Appropriate literacy intervention relies on three fundamental principles: using RTI models, targeting specific literacy domains, and scaffolding literacy learning. To be appropriate, implementation of literacy interventions in classrooms must be designed to ensure (1) whole-class or large-group explicit instruction is delivered as a first tier to all students in the classroom, and (2) additional small-group explicit instruction is provided to students who do not respond to the first tier of intervention. Concepts and skills that are explicitly targeted at first and second tiers of instruction include phonological awareness, academic language, and text structure. Finally, literacy learning in intervention must be scaffolded in ways that support and help students build capacity to read and learn independently.

REFERENCES

Adams, M. J. (1998). *Beginning to read: Thinking and learning about print.* Cambridge, MA: MIT Press.

Al Otaiba, S., Connor, C. M., & Crowe, E. (2018). Promise and feasibility of teaching expository text structure: A primary grade pilot study. *Reading and Writing, 31*(9), 1997–2015.

Apthorp, H., Randel, B., Cherasaro, T., Clark, T., McKeown, M., & Beck, I. (2012). Effects of a supplemental vocabulary program on word knowledge and passage comprehension. *Journal of Research on Educational Effectiveness, 5*(2), 160–188.

Baker, S. K., Santoro, L. E., Chard, D. J., Fien, H., Park, Y., & Otterstedt, J. (2013). An evaluation of an explicit read aloud intervention taught in whole-classroom formats in first grade. *The Elementary School Journal, 113*(3), 331–358.

Balu, R., Zhu, P., Doolittle, F., Schiller, E., Jenkins, J., & Gersten, R. (2015). *Evaluation of response to intervention practices for elementary school reading* (NCEE 2016-4000). Washington, DC: National Center for Education Evaluation and Regional Assistance.

Barnes, E. M., Grifenhagen, J. F., & Dickinson, D. K. (2016). Academic language in early childhood Classrooms. *The Reading Teacher, 70*(1), 39–48.

Baumann, J. F., & Graves, M. F. (2010). What is academic vocabulary? *Journal of Adolescent and Adult Literacy, 54*(1), 4–12.

Biemiller, A. (2010). *Words worth teaching: Closing the vocabulary gap.* Columbus, OH: McGraw-Hill SRA.

Bradshaw, M. L., Hoffman, P. R., & Norris, J. A. (1998). Efficacy of expansions and cloze procedures in the development of interpretations by preschool children exhibiting delayed language development. *Language, Speech, and Hearing Services in Schools, 29*(2), 85–95.

Callender, W. A. (2007). The Idaho results-based model: Implementing response to intervention statewide. In S. R. Jimerson, M. K. Burns, & A. M. VanDer-Heyden (Eds.), *Handbook of response to intervention: The science and practice of assessment and intervention* (pp. 331–342). New York: Springer.

Compton, D. L., Fuchs, D., Fuchs, L. S., & Bryant, J. D. (2006). Selecting at-risk readers in first grade for early intervention: A two-year longitudinal study of decision rules and procedures. *Journal of Educational Psychology, 98*(2), 394–409.

Conley, D. T. (2014). Common Core development and substance. *Social Policy Report, 28*(2), 1–15.

Connor, C. M., Phillips, B. M., Kaschak, M., Apel, K., Kim, Y.-S., Al Otaiba, S., . . . Lonigan, C. J. (2014). Comprehension tools for teachers: Reading for understanding from prekindergarten through fourth grade. *Educational Psychology Review, 26*(3), 379–401.

Coxhead, A. (2016). Reflecting on Coxhead (2000), "A New Academic Word List." *TESOL Quarterly, 50*(1), 181–185.

Davis, Z. T. (1994). Effects of prereading story mapping on elementary readers' comprehension. *Journal of Educational Research, 87*(6), 353–360.

Foorman, B., Beyler, N., Borradaile, K., Coyne, M., Denton, C. A., Dimino, J., . . . Wissel, S. (2016). *Foundational skills to support reading for understanding in kindergarten through 3rd grade* (NCEE 2016-4008). Washington, DC: National Center for Education Evaluation and Regional Assistance, Institute of Education Sciences, U.S. Department of Education. Retrieved from *http://whatworks.ed.gov*.

Foorman, B. R., Francis, D. J., Davidson, K. C., Harm, M. W., & Griffin, J. (2004). Variability in text features in six Grade 1 basal reading programs. *Scientific Studies of Reading, 8*(2), 167–197.

Foorman, B., Smith, K., & Kosanovich, M. (2016). *Rubric for evaluation of reading/language arts instructional materials for kindergarten–fifth grade* (REL 2016-137). Washington, DC: U.S. Department of Education, Institute of Education Sciences, National Center for Educational Evaluation & Regional Assistance, Regional Educational Laboratory Southeast.

Fuchs, D., Mock, D., Morgan, P. L., & Young, C. L. (2003). Responsiveness-to-intervention: Definitions, evidence, and implications for the learning disabilities construct. *Learning Disabilities Research and Practice, 18*(3), 157–171.

Fuchs, L. S., & Fuchs, D. (2007). A model for implementing responsiveness to intervention. *Teaching Exceptional Children, 39*(5), 14–20.

Gardner, D., & Davies, M. (2013). A new academic vocabulary list. *Applied Linguistics, 35*(3), 305–327.

Gersten, R., Fuchs, L. S., Williams, J. P., & Baker, S. (2001). Teaching reading comprehension strategies to students with learning disabilities: A review of research. *Review of Educational Research, 71*(2), 279–320.

Gresham, F. M., VanDerHeyden, A., & Witt, J. C. (2005). Response to intervention in the identification of learning disabilities: Empirical support and future challenges. Unpublished manuscript. Retrieved from *www.joewitt.org/Downloads/Response%20to%20Intervention%20MS%20Gresham%20%20Vanderheyden%20Witt.pdf*.

Hiebert, E. H. (2005). State reform policies and the task textbooks pose for first-grade readers. *The Elementary School Journal, 105*(3), 245–266.

Hogan, T. P., Bridges, M. S., Justice, L. M., & Cain, K. (2011). Increasing higher level language skills to improve reading comprehension. *Focus on Exceptional Children, 44*, 1–19.

Jenkins, J. R., Hudson, R. F., & Johnson, E. S. (2007). Screening for at-risk readers in a response to intervention framework. *School Psychology Review, 36*(4), 582–600.

Kispal, A. (2008). *Effective teaching of inference skills for reading* (Research Report DCSF-RR031). Slough, UK: National Foundation for Educational Research.

Langston, M. C., & Trabasso, T. (1998). Identifying causal connections and modeling integration of narrative discourse. In H. van Oostendorp & S. R. Goldman (Eds.), *The construction of mental representations during reading* (pp. 29–69). Mahwah, NJ: Erlbaum.

Language and Reading Research Consortium, Jiang, H., & Davis, D. (2017). Let's know!: Proximal impacts on prekindergarten through grade 3 students' comprehension-related skills. *The Elementary School Journal, 118*(2), 177–206.

Meyer, B. J. F., & Poon, L. W. (2004). Effects of structure strategy training and signaling on recall of text. In R. B. Ruddell & N. J. Unrau (Eds.), *Theoretical models and processes of reading* (5th ed., pp. 810–851). Newark, DE: International Reading Association.

Nagy, W., & Townsend, D. (2012). Words as tools: Learning academic vocabulary as language acquisition. *Reading Research Quarterly, 47*(1), 91–108.

National Association of State Directors of Special Education. (2006). *Response to intervention: Policy considerations and implementation.* Alexandria, VA: Author.

National Reading Panel. (2000, April). *Teaching children to read: An evidence-based assessment of the scientific research literature on reading and its implications for reading instruction* (NIH Publication No. 00-4769). Washington, DC: U.S. Government Printing Office.

Pearson, P. D., & Gallagher, M. C. (1983). The instruction of reading comprehension. *Contemporary Educational Psychology, 8*(3), 317–344.

Rashotte, C. A., MacPhee, K., & Torgesen, J. K. (2001). The effectiveness of a group reading instruction program with poor readers in multiple grades. *Learning Disability Quarterly, 24*(2), 119–134.

Reschly, D. J. (2005). Learning disabilities identification: Primary intervention, secondary intervention, and then what? *Journal of Learning Disabilities, 38*(6), 510–515.

Shanahan, T., Callison, K., Carriere, C., Duke, N. K., Pearson, P. D., Schatschneider, C., & Torgesen, J. (2010). *Improving reading comprehension in kindergarten through 3rd grade: A practice guide* (NCEE 2010-4038). Washington, DC: National Center for Education Evaluation and Regional Assistance, Institute of Education Sciences, U.S. Department of Education. Retrieved from *https://whatworks.ed.gov/publications/practiceguides*.

Silverman, R., & Hartranft, A. M. (2015). *Developing vocabulary and oral language in young children.* New York: Guilford Press.

Stetter, M. E., & Hughes, M. T. (2010). Using story grammar to assist students with learning disabilities and reading difficulties improve their comprehension. *Education and Treatment of Children, 33*(1), 115–151.

Townsend, D., Filippini, A., Collins, P., & Biancarosa, G. (2012). Evidence for the importance of academic word knowledge for the academic achievement of diverse middle school students. *The Elementary School Journal, 112*(3), 497–518.

Uccelli, P., Galloway, E. P., Barr, C. D., Meneses, A., & Dobbs, C. L. (2015). Beyond vocabulary: Exploring cross-disciplinary academic-language proficiency and its association with reading comprehension. *Reading Research Quarterly, 50*(3), 337–356.

van Lier, L., & Walqui, A. (2012). Language and the Common Core State Standards. In *Understanding language: Commissioned papers on language and literacy issues in the Common Core State Standards and Next Generation Science Standards* (pp. 44–51). Stanford, CA: Stanford University.

Williams, J. P., Hall, K. M., Lauer, K. D., Stafford, K. B., DeSisto, L. A., & deCani, J. S. (2005). Expository text comprehension in the primary grade classroom. *Journal of Educational Psychology, 97*, 538–550.

Williams, J. P., Nubla-Kung, A. M., Pollini, S., Stafford, K. B., García, A., & Snyder, A. E. (2007). Teaching cause–effect text structure through social studies content to at-risk second graders. *Journal of Learning Disabilities, 40*(2), 111–120.

Yuill, N., & Joscelyne, T. (1988). Effect of organizational cues and strategies on good and poor comprehenders' story understanding. *Journal of Educational Psychology, 80*(2), 152–158.

Yuill, N., & Oakhill, J. (1988). Effects of inference awareness training on poor reading comprehension. *Applied Cognitive Psychology, 2*(1), 33–45.

Yuill, N., & Oakhill, J. (1991). *Children's problems in text comprehension: An experimental investigation*. Cambridge, UK: Cambridge University Press.

9
· · · ·

Effective Differentiation

Steve Amendum and Kristin Conradi Smith

Mrs. Williams is beginning her 11th year as an elementary school teacher. As she arrives back at school after the summer break, she receives her class list of students for the new year. She is surprised and encouraged by the increasing diversity in the student body at her school. Mrs. Williams notes that, in her class of 23 second-grade students, she has five students with individualized education plans (IEPs) who receive exceptional children's services, seven students who qualify for English learner (EL) services, and three students identified for the school's gifted and talented program. The 23 students come from a range of socioeconomic contexts and identify with a range of racial and ethnic backgrounds. Mrs. Williams looks forward to providing learning opportunities for her students in literacy and supporting them as they progress through the second-grade curriculum standards. Knowing it will be a challenge to accomplish the rigorous goals she sets for all her students, Mrs. Williams attended professional learning during the summer about differentiating literacy instruction.

Mrs. Williams's experience is similar to many teachers as she considers the most effective ways to support her students during literacy instruction. Differentiation is one characteristic of effective instruction that can support students' learning and growth across time. Differentiation, in principle, underscores the notion that students are different, and teachers, by consequence, should adjust their instruction accordingly. Such adjustments to instruction, in theory, create learning experiences that are tailored to students' individual needs and that promote student learning. In this chapter, we focus on the principle of differentiation, addressing how differentiation is conceptualized, why differentiation is a principle of effective literacy instruction, and how differentiation is applied in classroom practice. Here we focus on differentiation related to reading (i.e., differentiating reading instruction). However, we note that the principle of differentiating instruction can be applied across all areas of literacy as well as across content areas.

What Is Differentiation?

The concept of differentiation is noteworthy and recently rated among the most challenging concepts in the annual survey of important topics in literacy teaching and learning (International Literacy Association, 2020). Moreover, the idea of differentiation has been around for more than 65 years (Betts, 1946; Figurel, 1952) and gained popularity through Tomlinson's work (e.g., 2000). Differentiation has been defined as responding to variance among learners by adjusting the content, process, products, or learning environment. Within reading instruction, there are different ways to accomplish effective differentiation; student learning can be supported by differentiating the text, the skill, or the support provided to students (Walpole & McKenna, 2017). For clarity in this chapter, we define differentiation within reading instruction as *modifying instruction to meet the individual needs of readers by adjusting the text, skill, or level of support, as needed.*

Research Evidence Related to Differentiation

The research on differentiation is not as robust as might be expected considering its pervasiveness, with teachers reporting, on average, that they use small groups 3 days a week (Bingham & Hall-Kenyon, 2013). Of the studies that do exist, it is clear that there are considerable benefits to providing differentiated instruction to students. In one study, students made greater reading growth when provided differentiated instruction in addition to a core reading curriculum (e.g., Jefferson, Grant, & Sander, 2017), while other studies have demonstrated greater growth when the core curriculum itself was differentiated (Connor, Morrison, Fishman, Schatschneider, & Underwood, 2007; Connor, Morrison, & Katch, 2004; Connor et al., 2011; Reis, McCoach, Little, Muller, & Kaniskan, 2011). To illustrate, Jefferson and colleagues (2017) reported on the effects of supplementing the Tier 1 core reading curriculum, as part of the first step in the response-to-intervention (RTI) process, with an additional 20 minutes of small-group comprehension instruction and fluency practice in differentiated texts (see Chapter 8 for more on RTI). Results showed a significant advantage on fluency outcomes for students who received the additional instruction when compared with students who received the core curriculum only. Similarly, Connor and colleagues (2004, 2007, 2011) reported on a series of studies in which they investigated the effects of differentiated core instruction matched to students' characteristics on reading achievement. Their results highlighted the significant advantage in reading achievement for students who received differentiated instruction matched to their specific needs and reading development.

Other studies have highlighted case studies of effective differentiation (e.g., Tobin & McInnes, 2008; Watts-Taffe et al., 2012), as well as a framework for providing differentiated instruction based on groups of readers with varying needs (e.g., Jones, Conradi, & Amendum, 2016). For example, Jones and colleagues provided a framework for targeted assessment, guidance for interpreting assessment data, and evidence-based instructional practices matched to students' needs (based on assessment data). Likewise, Watts-Taffe and colleagues described two classrooms that employed effective differentiation. Findings from their study highlighted how teachers in the two classrooms provided effective differentiation through the use of targeted assessment and resultant customized instruction.

Classroom Contexts for Differentiation

Importantly, given that reading instruction typically occurs within a multi-tiered system (Fuchs & Fuchs, 2006), differentiation during reading instruction must be adjusted to the specific tiered context in which it occurs. For example, because Tier 1 instruction is grade-level, standards-driven instruction for all students, and instruction in Tiers 2 and 3 provides increasingly more intensive, smaller-group interventions matched to students' needs, these tiered instructional contexts should inform the most effective ways to differentiate instruction for students. For example, during Tier 1 instruction, grade-level standards typically dictate the appropriate level of text that students should be able to read and comprehend. Consequently, making significant adjustments to the difficulty of the text is likely *not* the best way to provide differentiation; instead, teachers should consider adjusting the level of support provided to students as they engage with a grade-level text that may be challenging for some students, yet is required by grade-level standards.

Conversely, during Tier 2 small-group intervention where instruction is more closely matched to students' needs and development, adjusting the amount of support provided is still an effective method for differentiation. Additionally, a focus on the specific skill(s) needed at a certain point in reading development might be particularly effective for a group of students, knowing that the exact focus skill(s) will vary from group to group, depending on the students. Given that Tier 2 instruction is matched to students' needs and development, this context is where differentiation often occurs. Therefore, much of our following discussion relates to Tier 2 contexts for instruction; however, we also note Tier 1 contexts where differentiation is appropriate.

Why Is Differentiation a Principle of Effective Literacy Instruction?

Given the importance of differentiation (International Literacy Association, 2020), it is important to carefully consider why differentiation is a principle of effective literacy instruction and how differentiation might be enacted during classroom literacy instruction. Because we define differentiation as modifying instruction to meet the individual needs of learners by adjusting the text, skill, or level of support, below we unpack each of these ways to differentiate instruction. To be clear, however, even though we discuss each of these methods of differentiation below, we do not advocate for them equally!

Differentiating the Text

One way that many teachers differentiate their reading instruction is by providing different texts to students (Conradi Smith, Parsons, Vaughn, & Core Yatzeck, 2019). Using a traditional guided reading format (Fountas & Pinnell, 1996, 2012), teachers often select from leveled books matched to students' instructional reading levels to provide instruction in word recognition, fluency, and comprehension during a lesson. Books in the initial levels in the traditional guided reading format typically contain a predictable structure, rather than a decodable format. Later, text levels are assigned based on characteristics such as overall length, lines of text per page, vocabulary difficulty, and plot complexity. Teachers might also differentiate the text level by modifying a grade-level text for different groups of students. For example, a teacher can take a grade-level book or article and replace the text with a version comprising shorter sentence structures or less complex vocabulary. However, as we outline below, modifying grade-level text is not typically a method of differentiation we support.

In our conversations with teachers, we have heard them say that differentiating the difficulty of the text during reading instruction often *feels good*—that teachers feel they are meeting students' needs and development by carefully considering and matching them to an "appropriate" text level. Moreover, teachers prefer this framework because it allows them to apply the same standard, but with different texts. For example, the teacher might have each group work on identifying character traits, or compare/contrast—just with different texts. Although we acknowledge that this might feel right and seems like an easy solution for differentiation, there can be serious negative consequences to consider when differentiating text level (Shanahan, 2011, 2017).

From digging into the research, there are three reasons for concern regarding differentiation by text level. First, when matching texts to students' reading level, there is danger that students who struggle with reading may rarely be exposed to grade-level text, in terms of both word recognition and cognitive complexity. Tatum (2019) described this unfortunate condition by stating that "leveled texts lead to leveled lives." An absence of any regular grade-level text reading will certainly disadvantage students when they are faced with grade-level reading on summative year-end assessments. This practice also systematically excludes students from grade-appropriate academic language/vocabulary and content knowledge. Given that academic language and content knowledge are vital for successful reading comprehension (e.g., Liebfreund & Conradi, 2016; Uccelli, Galloway, Barr, Meneses, & Dobbs, 2015), placing students in lower instructional-level texts could have the unintended consequence of denying them access to important grade-level knowledge and language structures necessary for successful reading comprehension.

Second, although providing students with matched instructional-level text often "feels good," on average, students make less progress when instructed with instructional-level texts than with more difficult grade-level texts (e.g., Morgan, Wilcox, & Eldredge, 2000). For example, Morgan and colleagues demonstrated that students made the greatest reading gains when engaged in daily partner reading with texts two grade levels above their instructional level when compared with a comparison group of students partner reading with instructional-level texts. Of course, working in significantly more difficult texts may necessitate differentiation of the support provided, discussed in a later section.

Finally, differentiating by text level does not ensure that students' needs are actually met. If students are reading below grade level, it is likely that they still struggle with word recognition and fluency. But in matching them to an instructional level with a text deemed appropriate based mainly on their accuracy level, we do not actually address potential underlying word recognition and/or fluency needs. Although time in connected text can, of course, support fluency, it will not provide systematic phonics instruction. Differentiating by text level leads to incidental phonics instruction, at best, and fails to address the actual needs of students who need more.

Because of the many negative consequences associated with adjusting text level, as stated earlier, we typically do not recommend this type of differentiation. However, there may be particular points in students' reading development when adjusting the text may prove advantageous. For example, in students' development of foundational skills it is vital that students learn accurate and automatic decoding (García & Cain, 2014). To support these burgeoning skills, teachers might select particular decodable texts that support and reinforce the specific decoding features and skills recently taught, allowing students to practice those skills with a text designed for that purpose (Foorman et al., 2016). Or, to support comprehension, a teacher might select a particular book or text related to content that a student is interested in or has a great deal of background knowledge about. Note, however, that in these examples, we suggest differentiating the text type or content, not by placing students into leveled text groups.

Classroom Examples

Mr. Armstrong has a group of three first-grade students who are not performing at the midyear benchmark in fluency. After some additional diagnostic assessments, Mr. Armstrong determines that this group of students is struggling with decoding—they have basic decoding skill with regularly spelled three-sound words but struggle to decode words with beginning blends and digraphs. To address this need, Mr. Armstrong plans two small-group reading lessons for his group of three students. The first is a lesson with explicit instruction in *r* blends (*br, cr, dr, fr, gr, pr,* and *tr*) using manipulative letter cards to build words containing blends. Students will build words such as *crop, fret, drip,* and *grim.* Then, students will apply decoding skills with these targeted blends using a decodable text that targets *r* blends, called *Fran Goes to the Prom* (Hartley, n.d.). The second lesson focuses on consonant digraphs and, again, begins with explicit instruction—this time with the digraphs *sh* and *ch.* Students will build words using manipulative letter cards such as *shop, wish, chip,* and *such.* Finally, students will apply decoding skills in two short texts designed to address the targeted digraphs—*Shelly's Shell Shop* (Ryan, n.d.), and *Chip the Chimp* (Charles, n.d.).

In a different classroom, Ms. Frackelton, a fourth-grade teacher, is working hard to integrate more science content into her reading groups. Looking ahead toward her science unit on habitats, Ms. Frackelton finds three different texts on the topic that she can use with her groups for the week. The texts are differently leveled, for a reason: one assumes no background knowledge of habitats, while one of the others jumps right into environmental effects of climate change on regional habitats. The third text is somewhere in the middle, building on knowledge students should have learned in previous grades. To ascertain her students' background knowledge of the topic, Ms. Frackelton gives her students a quick power write (Frey & Fisher, 2006), asking them to list any words or concepts they associate with habitats in one minute. She then differentiates her groups based on the background knowledge assessed.

Differentiating the Skill

A second way to differentiate reading instruction is by differentiating the skill focused on during instruction, especially during Tier 2 instruction (e.g., Jones & Henriksen, 2013; Walpole & McKenna, 2017). This format for differentiation contrasts the prior format (text level) by focusing on a particular skill during small-group instruction, rather than multiple skills while differentiating by text level. For example, Walpole and McKenna (2017) provide a thoughtful framework for differentiating by skill during Tier 2 instruction. In their framework they highlight a developmental sequence for teaching literacy skills during Tier 2 instruction, beginning with phonological awareness and moving through alphabet knowledge, and a systematic series of decoding skills, followed by a focus on fluency, vocabulary, and comprehension (see Figure 9.1).

Teachers use formative assessments to determine students' placements in skill-based groups depicted in Figure 9.1, and as students become proficient with a targeted skill, they move to the next developmental skill. Different from some models of small-group instruction (e.g., Fountas & Pinnell, 1996), Walpole and McKenna (2017) purposely referred to their model as an "unbalanced" model for reading instruction in the first edition of their book (p. 8) because of the focus on discrete skills delivered sequentially. (Notably, their skills-driven framework is for Tier 2 instruction, because Tier 1 instruction will focus instruction on all skill areas of literacy.)

A similar approach was used by Jones and Henriksen (2013), who studied first-grade students receiving skills-focused small-group instruction across a school year. From an initial set of assessments, six skills-based groups (of three to six students) were created to provide skills-driven

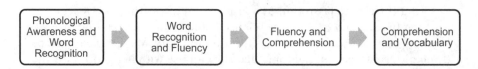

FIGURE 9.1. Sequence for differentiation by skill. Adapted by permission from Walpole and McKenna (2017). Copyright © 2017 The Guilford Press.

instruction. Instruction focused on a range of skills from recognition of individual sounds in words to comprehension strategy instruction. The authors reported that students made noteworthy reading skill growth measured with benchmark testing across the school year.

Differentiation of reading instruction by skill has several affordances for teachers and students. First, skills-driven instruction matched to students' characteristics provides a close match to students' instructional areas of need (Jones & Henriksen, 2013; Walpole & McKenna, 2017). This tight match between students' characteristics and instruction promotes students' learning and growth. Second, as students' skill-based learning and growth occurs, students are better able to profit from Tier 1 grade-level instruction through improved reading skills. Finally, if students are able to progress systematically through a developmental sequence of skills-based instruction, it is more likely that their reading development will be "complete," and they will read at a proficient level. However, we think differentiation of reading instruction can be enhanced by teachers using multiple formats for differentiation, beyond differentiating by text level. Examples include how to conduct individualized assessments, group students accordingly, plan and deliver skills-focused lessons, monitor students' progress and learning, and regroup as needed.

Classroom Example

With 25 students in her third-grade class, Ms. Rowe was used to considerable variety in their reading abilities. She had been trained in differentiating by instructional text level and had grouped her students that way for more than 10 years. While she liked that approach, she had found that it worked better for the students who were already proficient. She could dive into *Because of Winn-Dixie* (DiCamillo, 2000) with a group of her students and engage her students in thoughtful comprehension work. The model had been less successful with her students who struggled. Not only was it difficult to generate the same excitement about the texts for those groups (which the students often perceived to be babyish), but also Ms. Rowe still didn't feel she was actually meeting their needs. Her students in this group often still struggled with decoding—and no amount of time in *Henry and Mudge* books was solving that.

She decided to try a new approach for the school year. At the onset of the year, she gave every student a curriculum-based fluency measure to determine whether they could read grade-level text with appropriate accuracy and automaticity. For students who could, which was approximately 75% of her class, Ms. Rowe placed them into two reading groups based on their interests. Each group would tackle a complex, grade-level novel. For the quarter of her class not on grade level, Ms. Rowe next gave them a decoding inventory in order to pinpoint exactly why they were still struggling with fluency. After determining that most of the students still struggled with similar aspects of word recognition and decoding, Ms. Rowe designed lessons featuring considerable word-level reading, connected-text reading, and writing.

Differentiating the Level of Support

Another way to differentiate reading instruction is by adjusting the level of support provided to students. In the section on differentiating text level above, we noted that students instructed in more difficult texts (i.e., grade level vs. instructional level), on average, make more progress but that working in significantly more difficult texts may necessitate differentiation of the support. If students are simply placed in more difficult grade-level texts, without careful consideration of the necessary support for successful learning, both reading fluency and comprehension will suffer (e.g., Amendum, Conradi, & Hiebert, 2018; Amendum, Conradi, & Liebfreund, 2016; Cramer & Rosenfield, 2008). Therefore, it is vital that appropriate support is provided to students when they read challenging grade-level text (Strong, Amendum, & Conradi Smith, 2018).

In his book about explicitly teaching reading, Duffy (2014) provides multiple lessons. In each, he describes how to provide different levels of support to students, using a gradual release model (Pearson & Gallagher, 1983), which he terms *scaffolded assistance* with three levels: extensive teacher help, less teacher help, and no teacher help. For example, in the provided lesson on determining the main ideas of different sections of an informational text, Duffy provides a lesson introduction, insight for students into how to decide on the main idea, a think-aloud script for modeling the thinking in deciding on a main idea in an example, and then the scaffolded assistance model. In the initial phase of the scaffolded assistance model, extensive teacher help, a script is provided for a second explicit modeling of the strategy. The second phase, less teacher help, provides a script for the teacher to support students as they take on more of the work in determining the main idea of a different section in the text. In the final phase, no teacher help, students are asked to read different sections of the text and determine the main idea(s) independently, keeping track of the process they used for later discussion.

Differentiation of levels of support is useful for both Tier 1 core instruction and Tier 2 instruction. Given that Tier 1 instruction is focused on grade-level standards, text levels, and content, it is important that all students have access. Because some students may be performing below grade level for a variety of reasons, considering how to provide appropriate support to all students to support their success in learning grade-level content is vital. For example, teachers may facilitate echo, choral, or partner reading to provide different levels of support for students while they read. Likewise, in Tier 2 contexts where instruction is matched to students' needs while still considering grade-level content, adjusting support for students is just as important. Using a gradual release model allows for students to move from a supportive context to working independently.

Classroom Example

Ms. Long teaches fifth grade and has three different groups in her reading class. She has chosen the novel *Refugee* (Gratz, 2017) to read with her groups, but based on observations and previous performance, she knows the text will be more challenging for some students than others. She has noticed, over the last few months, that not all of her students are able to track a storyline as well as others, and she anticipates—having read the book ahead of time—that some students are going to particularly struggle with the fact that the chapters in *Refugee* alternate storylines among three different characters. After deciding on the focus for each class lesson, she considers how to support her students differently. She decides all of her students would benefit from a graphic organizer to track what they learn about the three main characters, but she organizes her actual small-group lessons for them differently. For one of her groups, she lets them read on their own before coming to her. In group, they have inferential and critical discussion about the book. Her other two groups need a bit of support, so they read the text while they are at the table with her. For one group, she is particularly focused on providing key stopping points for all students in order to make sure they are making sense of the text as they read. To further facilitate their comprehension, they often read the text together chorally. For the other group, she is worried they will forget to justify their responses in text, so she provides scaffolds to support them.

Centrality of Feedback

In considering the importance of differentiation, we would be remiss if we did not highlight the key role feedback plays. As we underscored at the beginning of this chapter, the very idea of differentiation hinges on the notion that students are different. In adjusting instruction to meet students' needs, of course teachers need to be mindful of how they will differentiate, but additionally, they need to consider how they will provide feedback in order to move students forward. When framing feedback, we mean the moment-to-moment decisions made by teachers *during* instruction (Rodgers, 2004).

Providing effective feedback and responses to students can advance learning and development. Researchers have found that the nature of feedback provided to students affects the particular reading components that are developed (e.g., Ardoin, Morena, Binder, & Foster, 2013; Stevens, Walker, & Vaughn, 2017). But simply providing feedback is not often sufficient; instead, the *type* of feedback provided matters. For example, students in earlier grades often respond best to feedback based on their abilities, while students in upper elementary grades and beyond prefer feedback based on their efforts (Burnett & Mandel, 2010). Most feedback provided by teachers is general and nonspecific (e.g., "good job!"); however, this type of feedback is ineffective because it is not linked to specific student behaviors.

To provide behavior-specific feedback that is effective for student learning, teachers must consider different types of feedback. Rodgers (2004) provides a framework that includes four specific types of feedback for students during reading instruction: telling, demonstrating, directing, and questioning. When telling, teachers simply disclose something to a student by directly telling as the name suggests (e.g., "In this word, *ea* makes the /ē/ sound"). When teachers are demonstrating, they model a process or skill as if they were the students. For example, during a lesson on fluency a teacher might say, "Listen to the way these two sentences sound when I read them fluently," prior to modeling fluent reading. When directing, the teacher tells a student to do something specific (e.g., "Blend the first two sounds in that word"). Finally, when teachers employ questioning, they ask a student questions to prompt thinking or strategy use. For example, they might ask a student, "Does that remind you of something we read before?" or "What sound does that letter make?" Notably, teachers may combine multiple types of feedback in response to a student. For example, when reading a text where a student is having difficulty decoding the word *splash*, a teacher might first direct the student to blend the initial sounds, and then follow up by asking, "What sound comes next, after /sp/? Can you blend all three sounds together?"

Providing useful feedback to students is effective in both Tier 1 and Tier 2 instructional contexts. It is imperative that teachers provide students with behavior-specific feedback related to ability and/or effort. Providing these types of precise feedback to students, rather than general nonspecific feedback, can support students' learning and development.

Conclusion

We began this chapter with a description of Mrs. Williams's experience as she began her school year with 23 diverse second-grade students. As Mrs. Williams wrestled with how to accomplish the rigorous goals she set for all her students, she considered differentiation as an effective principle of literacy instruction. In this chapter, we hope we have laid out a set of ideas that can support Mrs. Williams's teaching and her students' learning across second grade.

We report on differentiation within reading instruction based on the text, skill, and level of support provided, as well as the importance of providing effective feedback. Importantly, we describe how some methods for differentiating instruction may be more effective than others, especially in different instructional contexts. Throughout, we provide descriptions and examples of the principle of differentiation applied in classrooms. Finally, we note the importance of providing support to preservice and inservice teachers to learn about methods for differentiation, particularly those that may be more effective, such as differentiating by skill or level of support when using grade-level text.

REFERENCES

Amendum, S. J., Conradi, K., & Hiebert, E. H. (2018). Does text complexity matter in the elementary grades?: A research synthesis of text difficulty and elementary students' reading fluency and comprehension. *Educational Psychology Review, 31,* 121–151.

Amendum, S. J., Conradi, K., & Liebfreund, M. D. (2016). The push for more challenging texts: An analysis of early readers' rate, accuracy, and comprehension. *Reading Psychology, 37,* 570–600.

Ardoin, S. P., Morena, L. S., Binder, K. S., & Foster, T. E. (2013). Examining the impact of feedback and repeated readings on oral reading fluency: Let's not forget prosody. *School Psychology Quarterly, 28,* 391–404.

Betts, E. A. (1946). *Foundations of reading instruction.* New York: American Book.

Bingham, G. E., & Hall-Kenyon, K. M. (2013). Examining teachers' beliefs about and implementation of a balanced literacy framework. *Journal of Research in Reading, 36*(1), 14–28.

Burnett, P. C., & Mandel, V. (2010). Praise and feedback in the primary classroom: Teachers' and students' perspectives. *Australian Journal of Educational and Developmental Psychology, 10,* 145–154.

Connor, C. M., Morrison, F. J., Fishman, B., Giuliani, S., Luck, M., Underwood, P. S., . . . Schatschneider, C. (2011). Testing the impact of child characteristics × instruction interactions on third graders' reading comprehension by differentiating literacy instruction. *Reading Research Quarterly, 46,* 189–221.

Connor, C. M., Morrison, F. J., Fishman, B. J., Schatschneider, C., & Underwood, P. (2007). Algorithm-guided individualized reading instruction. *Science, 315,* 464–465.

Connor, C. M., Morrison, F. J., & Katch, L. E. (2004). Beyond the reading wars: Exploring the effect of child-instruction interactions on growth in early reading. *Scientific Studies of Reading, 8,* 305–336.

Conradi Smith, K., Parsons, A., Vaughn, M., & Core Yatzeck, J. (2019). *Elementary students' text diets: Results from a national survey.* Paper presented at the annual meeting of the Literacy Research Association, Tampa, FL.

Cramer, K., & Rosenfield, S. (2008). Effect of degree of challenge on reading performance. *Reading and Writing Quarterly, 24,* 119–137.

Duffy, G. G. (2014). *Explaining reading: A resource for explicit teaching of the Common Core Standards* (2nd ed.). New York: Guilford Press.

Figurel, J. A. (1952). What recent research tells us about differentiated instruction in reading. *The Reading Teacher, 6,* 27–44.

Foorman, B. R., Beyler, N., Borradaile, K., Coyne, M., Denton, C. A., Dimino, J., . . . Wissel, S. (2016). *Foundational skills to support reading for understanding in kindergarten through 3rd grade* (NCEE 2016-4008). Washington, DC: National Center for Education Evaluation and Regional Assistance, Institute of Education Sciences, U.S. Department of Education. Retrieved from *http://whatworks.ed.gov.*

Fountas, I. C., & Pinnell, G. S. (1996). *Guided reading: Good first teaching for all children.* Portsmouth, NH: Heinemann.

Fountas, I. C., & Pinnell, G. S. (2012). Guided reading: The romance and the reality. *The Reading Teacher, 66,* 268–284.

Frey, N., & Fisher, D. (2006). *Reading for information in elementary school: Content literacy strategies to build comprehension.* Upper Saddle River, NJ: Pearson.

Fuchs, D., & Fuchs, L. S. (2006). Introduction to response to intervention: What, why, and how valid is it? *Reading Research Quarterly, 41,* 93–99.

García, J. R., & Cain, K. (2014). Decoding and reading comprehension: A meta-analysis to identify which reader and assessment characteristics influence the strength of the relationship in English. *Review of Educational Research, 84,* 74–111.

International Literacy Association. (2020). *What's hot in literacy report.* Newark, DE: Author.

Jefferson, R. E., Grant, C. E., & Sander, J. B. (2017). Effects of Tier I differentiation and reading intervention on reading fluency, comprehension, and high stakes measures. *Reading Psychology, 38,* 97–124.

Jones, C. D., & Henriksen, B. M. (2013). Skills-focused small group literacy instruction in the first grade: An inquiry and insights. *Journal of Reading Education, 38,* 25–30.

Jones, J. S., Conradi, K., & Amendum, S. J. (2016). Matching interventions to reading needs: A case for differentiation. *The Reading Teacher, 70,* 307–316.

Liebfreund, M. D., & Conradi, K. (2016). Component skills affecting elementary students' informational text comprehension. *Reading and Writing, 29,* 1141–1160.

Morgan, A., Wilcox, B. R., & Eldredge, J. L. (2000). Effect of difficulty levels on second-grade delayed readers using dyad reading. *Journal of Educational Research, 94,* 113–119.

Pearson, P. D., & Gallagher, M. C. (1983). The instruction of reading comprehension. *Contemporary Educational Psychology, 8,* 317–344.

Reis, S. M., McCoach, D. B., Little, C. A., Muller, L. M., & Kaniskan, R. B. (2011). The effects of differentiated instruction and enrichment pedagogy on reading achievement in five elementary schools. *American Educational Research Journal, 48,* 462–501.

Rodgers, E. M. (2004). Interactions that scaffold reading performance. *Journal of Literacy Research, 36,* 501–532.

Shanahan, T. (2011). Rejecting instructional level theory. Retrieved from *https:// shanahanonliteracy.com/blog/rejecting-instructional-level-theory.*

Shanahan, T. (2017). The instructional level concept revisited: Teaching with complex text. Retrieved from *https://shanahanonliteracy.com/blog/the-instructional-level-concept-revisited-teaching-with-complex-text.*

Stevens, E. A., Walker, M. A., & Vaughn, S. (2017). The effects of reading fluency interventions on the reading fluency and reading comprehension performance of elementary students with learning disabilities: A synthesis of the research from 2001 to 2014. *Journal of Learning Disabilities, 50,* 576–590.

Strong, J. Z., Amendum, S. J., & Conradi Smith, K. (2018). Supporting elementary students' reading of difficult texts. *The Reading Teacher, 72,* 201–212.

Tatum, A. W. (2019). *Equally probable: Examining the long-term impacts of literacy development for our nation's youth.* Hornsby Distinguished Lecture at William & Mary School of Education, Williamsburg, VA.

Tobin, R., & McInnes, A. (2008). Accommodating differences: Variations in differentiated literacy instruction in Grade 2/3 classrooms. *Literacy, 42,* 3–9.

Tomlinson, C. A. (2000). *Differentiation of instruction in the elementary grades* (ED443572). Champaign, IL: ERIC Clearinghouse on Elementary and Early Childhood Education, Office of Educational Research and Improvement, U.S. Department of Education.

Uccelli, P., Galloway, E. P., Barr, C. D., Meneses, A., & Dobbs, C. L. (2015). Beyond vocabulary: Exploring cross-disciplinary academic-language proficiency and its association with reading comprehension. *Reading Research Quarterly, 50,* 337–356.

Walpole, S., & McKenna, M. C. (2017). *How to plan differentiated reading instruction* (2nd ed.). New York: Guilford Press.

Watts-Taffe, S., Laster, B. P., Broach, L., Marinak, B., McDonald Connor, C., & Walker-Dalhouse, D. (2012). Differentiated instruction: Making informed teacher decisions. *The Reading Teacher, 66,* 303–314.

CHILDREN'S LITERATURE

Charles, R. (n.d.). *Chip the chimp.* Tucson, AZ: Learning A–Z. Retrieved from *www.readinga-z.com/book/decodable.php.*

DiCamillo, K. (2000). *Because of Winn-Dixie.* Somerville, MA: Candlewick.

Gratz, A. (2017). *Refugee.* New York: Scholastic Press.

Hartley, S. (n.d.). *Fran goes to the prom.* Tucson, AZ: Learning A–Z. Retrieved from *www.readinga-z.com/book/decodable.php.*

Ryan, C. (n.d.). *Shelly's shell shop.* Tucson, AZ: Learning A–Z. Retrieved from *www. readinga-z.com/book/decodable.php.*

10

· · · · ·

Explicit Instruction

Dana A. Robertson

Teaching reading, regardless of the students' age, can be an overwhelming endeavor. The students and the teacher comprise a social context featuring a range of academic skills, interests, linguistic and cultural diversity, background knowledge, and family literacy practices. With an understanding that reading is a process of making meaning (Smagorinsky, 2001) *and* building knowledge (Adams, 2011) of/in the world, there is a range of curricular programs and instructional techniques teachers can draw from to teach students to read. Whereas specific curricula and routines can be helpful, a sole reliance on them can deprive students of opportunities to optimally engage in reading and realize its broader potential.

Skillful teachers adapt and respond to both the curricular demands and the students in front of them and, in doing so, draw on a deep knowledge of different approaches to teaching reading grounded in principles of learning. One such high-leverage approach is explicit instruction. In this chapter, I describe the essential characteristics of explicit instruction and provide a rationale for its use as teachers adaptively respond to students' learning needs. I then outline the overall instructional sequence and illustrate the process through a composite example in an upper elementary classroom. Finally, I address possible roadblocks or concerns when using an explicit approach to teaching.

What Does It Mean to Teach Explicitly?

Explicit instruction is intentional teaching. It is a structured and systematic approach to teaching strategies and concepts that is intended to optimize students' engagement and promote specific positive outcomes based on students' assessed needs. The approach is characterized by teachers' use of clear language that connects the strategies or conceptual knowledge to students' real reading purposes, provides explicit demonstration, structures a series of scaffolds that guide and consolidate students' application, provides responsive feedback on students' performance, and prompts and expects independent application in novel reading contexts. As Rosenshine (1986) aptly described, explicit instruction frames an approach teachers use to systematically present new material "in small steps, pausing to check for understanding and eliciting active and successful participation from all students" (p. 60).

Explicit instruction is an unambiguous approach that is meant to provide detailed information to fill in students' experiential gaps or correct misconceptions (Archer & Hughes, 2011; Duffy, 2009). The teacher makes no assumptions about what students already know and can do, and in an effort to optimize engagement in real reading, instruction is not left to chance; instead, the teacher offers as much detail as is needed with a roadmap that helps ensure student success (Robertson, Ford-Connors, & Dougherty, 2017). By making optimal use of instructional time, explicit instruction increases opportunities for students to develop requisite strategies that move them toward achieving not only grade-level expectations but also their own learning goals.

Yet reading is not just the accumulation of isolated skills and strategies or bits of conceptual knowledge. Skilled readers are motivated and able to agentively use their knowledge of reading and the world to successfully read future texts to meet their learning goals (Alexander, 2005; Pressley & Afflerbach, 1995). More than just teaching a strategy, the intended outcome of explicit instruction is to ultimately provide students with a set of procedures and relevant background knowledge for successfully navigating text (Almasi & Fullerton, 2012; Brown, Pressley, Van Meter, & Schuder, 1996; Robertson, Dougherty, Ford-Connors, & Paratore, 2014).

Why Teach Explicitly?

When teachers adaptively use explicit instruction to engage their students with text, they weave together several important elements (see Figure 10.1) of effective instruction: scaffolds, engagement, knowledge building, and

> 1. Provides scaffolded instruction
> 2. Promotes engagement
> 3. Promotes knowledge building and conceptual expertise
> 4. Increases the intensity of instruction

FIGURE 10.1. High-leverage elements of the explicit instruction approach.

intensity through coherence and increased content coverage. Together, these elements promote increased opportunities for success and high levels of achievement.

Scaffolds

Explicit instruction is grounded in the work of Vygotsky (1962), who saw learning as inherently social. Vygotsky argued that children acquire new skills and knowledge through the use of mediational tools. One such tool is language-based interactions with a more "knowledgeable other," for example, a parent or caregiver. In classroom contexts, the teacher, and to a lesser extent a student's peers, serve as that knowledgeable other, providing temporary *scaffolds* (Wood, Bruner, & Ross, 1976) that enable students to engage in challenging tasks that would typically be just out of reach for the student without the assistance.

Providing scaffolded instruction so students can engage in tasks that are appropriately challenging (i.e., not too hard and not too easy) pays big dividends in student outcomes. John Hattie (2009, 2012) in his meta-analyses of hundreds of studies has found that scaffolding of appropriately challenging tasks has positive effects on learning that are more than double what would typically be expected. Through carefully crafted learning opportunities that include instructional scaffolding, as well as the systematic fading of those scaffolds, students are provided just enough support to successfully engage in these more challenging tasks and, thus, move toward more advanced levels of understanding (Robertson et al., 2017).

Engagement

Instruction geared toward engagement—what Guthrie and Wigfield (2000) refer to as *engaged reading*—is also positively associated with improved strategy use and overall reading achievement (Taboada, Tonks, Wigfield, & Guthrie, 2009). Students who are engaged while reading are more likely to persist and actively use strategies to help them monitor their reading, even when tasks are challenging (Guthrie & Humenick,

2004). Thus, while engagement with the task increases strategy use, strategy use also increases engagement.

Explicit instruction of strategies optimizes the amount of time students are able to engage in reading by leaving nothing to chance and letting students in on the "secrets" (Duffy, 2009) needed to successfully access a text. The more time students spend actively reading, the more skilled they become at reading while also developing deeper and broader conceptual expertise (Adams, 2011). With carefully tailored scaffolds, students' interactions with challenging texts are brought within a range where student can experience high levels of success, which supports deeper, cognitive engagement with reading materials and promotes a view of texts as a valuable resource for ongoing learning (Robertson et al., 2017).

Knowledge Building

As mentioned, explicit instruction efficiently provides students with tools to navigate texts and, thus, opportunities to build more conceptual expertise. Teaching explicitly and providing scaffolds that fade over time develops different types of knowledge students can use to apply their strategies to novel reading contexts. Using strategies adaptively requires students to know what the strategy is (i.e., declarative knowledge), how to do it or perform it (i.e., procedural knowledge), and, importantly, when and where the strategy should be used (i.e., conditional knowledge; Archer & Hughes, 2011; Paris, Lipson, & Wixson, 1983). Addressing these different forms of knowledge is essential to build students' capacity for more self-directed learning where they apply these strategies to help them learn.

Yet explicitly teaching strategies alone seems to do little to compensate for a lack of background knowledge. Explicit instruction is also important for developing conceptual knowledge, and developing concepts and strategy knowledge should always be provided within the context of reading for real purposes that matter to students (Duffy, 2009). Since explicit instruction helps to establish the conditions necessary for students to be successful in their reading, students can then read more broadly and deeply on topics of interest. Doing so facilitates students' acquisition of vocabulary, linguistic structures, and concepts (Stahl & Nagy, 2006). Voluminous reading, then, anchors further reading and learning, and the cycle continues. As Adams (2011) notes, "Knowledge truly is the most powerful determinant of reading comprehension" (p. 10).

Intensity

Through scaffolded instruction, engagement, and knowledge building, explicit instruction also increases the intensity of instruction. This is accomplished by optimizing the time students spend in engaged reading, increasing the amount of interaction students participate in with a knowledgeable other, and increasing the amount of content that can be covered more efficiently and effectively. Through spaced practice across days and contexts rather than massed practice all at one time, instructional coherence is established that creates a learning context for students to meaningfully transfer strategies from one situation to another, which, in turn, promotes motivation and engagement and fosters students' confidence in their reading abilities (Bandura, 1997; Guthrie & Humenick, 2004). It is well documented that, especially for those students who find reading challenging, effective instruction must be more intense and coherent than the instruction provided to readers who are developing at a typical pace (Torgeson, 2004; Wharton-McDonald, 2011; Wonder-McDowell, Reutzel, & Smith, 2011).

Looking at the Instructional Approach

To start, explicit instruction is an assessment-driven approach situated within a *gradual release of responsibility model* (Pearson & Gallagher, 1983). Knowing whether explicit instruction is warranted involves learning about who, when, and under what conditions students require it. As Duffy (2009) writes, "You only explain for students who need it" (p. 60), yet this stipulation requires timely and continual observation of students as they respond to instruction. Whereas it can be tempting to follow the explicit instruction approach as a "recipe" of steps as presented, it should not be interpreted as a one-size-fits-all approach to all whole-class lessons. Nor should it be interpreted as only occurring during single lessons.

Within a single lesson and across a unit of study, the entry point into a gradual release of responsibility model varies based on what students need. There are times when all students will benefit from an explicit explanation and modeling of a strategy or concept; there are other times when a teacher may work with a group to provide this level of explicitness after initial instructional activities have already been provided. Once the need for explicit teaching has been established, the instructional sequence within a lesson and across lessons is a four-step approach:

1. Explicit teaching should always be situated in real reading tasks that are relevant to students' lives. Teachers establish relevance and connect to students' lives through the overarching knowledge goal(s) for which the concepts or strategies are needed. For example, when students are reading Louis Sachar's *Holes,* relevant knowledge goals might include, How does understanding *authority* help us understand the relationships between the characters in the story? How does understanding authority

help us understand the relationships between and among individuals in our lives?

2. In service of these knowledge goals, the teacher explains and models a relevant concept (e.g., authority) and/or strategy (e.g., inferring character intentions through dialogue and connecting those intentions to students' experiences) that is needed. Through the teachers' demonstration, the invisible processes of reading become visible for the students as they apply the strategic processing or develop further understanding of the concept.

3. The teacher then facilitates scaffolded practice, prompting students to consider the concept, as in the present example of authority, in a more elaborated fashion through discussion or prompting them to infer and connect to the characters in the text. This process of scaffolding occurs during a single lesson and across lessons as the teacher formatively assesses instructional effectiveness through students' talk and performance and recalibrates instruction as needed.

4. As the teacher provides scaffolded opportunities, they begin to systematically fade those scaffolds over time and prompt students to "take responsibility" for the concepts and strategies in novel contexts (within both the text at hand and other situations), thus increasing their self-efficacy with scaffolds and efficacious feedback. In order for students to take responsibility and apply their knowledge, the importance of relevant and engaging tasks becomes even more paramount. Strategies are flexible tools that students employ when needed, which requires engagement, volition, and metacognitive awareness.

The Importance of Teacher Talk

Explicit instruction is not just about clear teacher talk. Yet, the language choices teachers make are consequential in bringing all of the parts of the explicit instruction model to bear on student learning. These strategic and intentional language choices by the teacher (Johnston, 2004; Robertson, 2013) involve goal-setting talk, explanatory talk, and facilitative talk (including efficacious feedback; e.g., Paratore & Robertson, 2013).

Goal-Setting Talk

When providing explicit instruction, it is important to frame the instruction of strategies or concepts around learning outcomes. Teachers use clear goal-setting talk to help students develop an understanding of each lesson's learning goals and of the connection between the goals and students' lives both inside and outside of school. These goals include both literacy goals and knowledge goals (Paratore & Robertson, 2013). Returning to the earlier example about authority, the teacher had a literacy goal that connected to comprehension (How does understanding *authority* help us understand the relationships between the characters in the story?) and also a knowledge goal that connected comprehension of the text to students' lives (How does understanding authority help us understand the relationships between and among individuals in our lives?).

It is important for teachers to use language that provides clarity about these learning outcomes and the expectations for students. As Duffy (2009) notes, students are better able to learn a strategy or concept when the goal is made visible and relevant. For example, the teacher might say,

> "We have been reading and talking about what is happening in *Holes*. Today, we're going to revisit this last chapter we've read and start talking about *authority*. When someone has authority, it means they have the power or the right to give orders or make decisions. Your parents have the authority to make decisions about what they feel is best for you. Today, we're going to describe how the actions and dialogue of different characters in *Holes* give us important information about who holds authority over others. To do that, we are going to infer information about the characters and use those inferences to describe character relationships. So, you are going to be able to make inferences about characters' actions and talk and use that information to describe the authorial relationship between the characters. I'm going to show you now how to do this."

The teacher's talk in this example uses observable terms (e.g., *describe, make inferences, actions,* and *dialogue*) that connected goals to purposeful reading tasks (i.e., the importance of understanding the relationships between characters in a story). Through these terms, the teacher explicitly explains to students what they should be able to do ("So, you are going to be able to make inferences about characters' actions and talk and use that information to describe the authorial relationship between the characters"). Relatedly, the teacher also uses language that lets students know it should be challenging ("So, you are going to be able to make inferences about characters' actions and talk and use that information to describe the authorial relationship between the characters"). Doing so protects students from embarrassment in front of peers and the teacher and helps students develop the necessary self-efficacy and willingness to persist (Bandura, 1997; Duffy, 2009).

Explanatory Talk

Connected to the goals of the lesson(s), the teacher also uses talk that prompts students to construct meaning and deepen and evaluate their thinking (e.g., about the concept of *authority*), and demonstrates strategic actions (e.g., inferring character relationships). Through explanation, the teacher thoroughly and thoughtfully details each level of strategy knowledge—declarative (what), procedural (how), and conditional (why and when)—and models through think-aloud to make the process visible (Paratore & Robertson, 2013). What is important to note is that the strategies being taught are not introduced in a way that is disconnected from overall text comprehension. Explicit instruction is not about teaching strategies for strategy sake.

Continuing with the example of *authority,* the teacher might then say,

> "We have already talked yesterday about Stanley and how he has been treated by X-Ray since he arrived at Camp Green Lake. When we read stories, it is important to pay close attention to how characters are acting, what they are saying, and how other characters are responding to them. As a reader, I can use this information to think more about the relationships between the characters. Let's look at this page [reads section of text aloud]. To build the meaning about authority among the characters, I need to look at the words on the page and connect those words to my own experiences. My experience tells me that X-Ray has a lot of authority because he is always telling people what to do and other campers seem to listen to him. [The modeling continues to talk about the relationship between X-Ray and Stanley.]"

Here, we see how the teacher is using explicit language to show students how ("To build the meaning about authority among the characters, I need to look at the words on the page and connect those words to my own experiences") and why ("When we read stories, it is important to pay close attention to how characters are acting. . . . I can use this information to think more about the relationships between the characters") to infer information about the characters. As the modeling continues from this excerpt to detail the relationship between X-Ray and Stanley, the teacher is able to elaborate on students' understanding of the concept of authority while showing the relevance of paying close attention to characters' actions, dialogue, and thoughts.

Facilitative Talk

Once the teacher has demonstrated explicitly a particular strategic action or concept, the teacher uses facilitative talk, including efficacious and timely feedback, to apprentice students into real reading. Facilitative talk prompts student talk so they can construct meaning and evaluate their thinking, and can then try on particular strategies within a supportive environment where the teacher (or other students) can step in to create conditions for success for the students. It draws on open-ended questions, elaborates or clarifies student thinking, prompts students to elaborate or clarify, prompts application of strategic actions, and cues students to focus on resources and support, for example, a word wall, anchor chart, or particular text page (Ford-Connors & Robertson, 2017; Paratore & Robertson, 2013).

Facilitative talk also alerts students to how they are doing as they engage in the work with the teacher's help. Efficacious and timely feedback audits and informs (Wiggins, 1993) student attempts and progress toward meeting their learning goals. The teacher notices and names (Johnston, 2004) what the students have done or contributed to the conversation and the outcomes of those actions. Feedback often overlaps with explanatory talk as it helps the students see how to move forward from their current performance (Paratore & Robertson, 2013).

After modeling about the relationship between X-Ray and Stanley on a page or two, the first level of scaffolding occurs as students help the teacher. That is, the teacher is still providing extensive help. The teacher might say,

> "Now it's your turn to help me infer about the relationship between the Warden and the campers. When we think about the idea of authority, how do we know that the Warden has authority over the campers? Let's look together at the next paragraph. What do we notice about what Mr. Pendanski is saying here: 'Don't upset the Warden.' What does that make us think?"

Notice that the teacher is pointing to particular examples in the text to help students locate relevant character actions or dialogue. Notice also that the teacher's initial questions are more open-ended (i.e., "What does that make us think?"). Starting with questioning and prompts that are more open-ended provides students with space to engage in the cognitive work while the teacher is present to support. Based on how the students respond, the teacher can then provide more targeted questions or prompts to help students engage in the work successfully.

After the initial scaffolded task with more teacher help, and if students demonstrated emerging understanding of how to engage in strategic work, the teacher would then prompt students to try to use the strategy or strategies again, yet this time with less teacher help. The teacher might prompt with "Now let's look at the next two paragraphs and decide what the author would like us to think about the relationship between the characters. What do we need to do first?" Again, notice that the teacher's question prompts the students to engage in the cognitive work. Only if the students respond with misconceptions about the procedural knowledge would the teacher step in and reexplain and model how to engage in the reading task or provide more targeted prompts or questions. As the students apply the thinking to the next section, the teacher would again prompt with questions that elicit elaboration and evidence (e.g., "How do you know?" "What clues told you that the campers understand and respect the authority of Mr. Pendanski?").

Finally, maybe the same day as well as over subsequent lessons, the teacher would continue to scaffold students' strategic actions and thinking as necessary. Based on these student attempts, the teacher would prompt students to apply the actions with no teacher help by directing them to read the next pages or chapters inferring the relationships among the characters based on the concept of authority. At this point, the students would be doing the thinking independently of the teacher, connecting the strategic actions of closely examining the characters' actions and dialogue to more deeply comprehend the text while also explaining their reasoning for their inferences. The talk that occurs during these exchanges between the teacher and students is primarily focused on comprehending the text and the knowledge goals that were established so that students see how the strategies are used in service of building knowledge.

Application in Reading

This example describes how a text—in this case, *Holes,* by Louis Sachar—can be read first to share initial ideas about what was read and then revisited to learn a particular strategy and/or concept that is pertinent to students to deepen their understanding about what was read. In this situation (written for an upper elementary classroom), application of the strategies and conceptual understanding will occur as the teacher and students continue to read *Holes* and discuss the ideas of authority, the relationships among characters, and how those relationships and sense of authority might shift over the remainder of the story. Students will also continue to engage in discussions and reflections related to the overarching knowledge goals: How does understanding *authority* help us understand the relationships between the characters in the story? How does understanding authority help us understand the relationships between and among individuals in our lives?

As the students move to other texts read independently or with the teacher, the teacher will ensure that students continue to infer relationships among characters and central ideas in the stories by paying close attention to dialogue and actions and following how those relationships might shift over time as the story progresses.

The composite vignette highlights what is possible when providing explicit instruction and linking formative assessment with explicit explanations and models to carefully sequenced scaffolds provided with facilitative teacher talk. Yet, enactment of these practices in a coordinated fashion is not always as straightforward as it might seem. Several roadblocks or concerns may arise that need to be considered when providing explicit instruction.

Addressing Potential Roadblocks to Providing Explicit Instruction

• *Roadblock 1: A lack of awareness of one's own reading processes because the process has become so automatic as a skilled reader.* Providing explicit explanations of how to read is difficult because it requires an awareness of processes that most teachers engage in with relative automaticity. That is, it is hard to let students in on the "secret" (Duffy, 2009) of reading processes that are not seen by students.

Coupled with this need to redevelop awareness of reading processes, many teachers were never provided training on how to provide explicit instruction during their teacher preparation programs or in professional development from their school districts. Just as students benefit from scaffolded opportunities for active engagement in learning, so too do teachers. Professional learning opportunities (e.g., coaching, book studies, professional learning communities) can help teachers target the explicit instruction of comprehension strategies so they are aware of the types of knowledge that constitute more complete strategy knowledge (e.g., declarative, procedural, and conditional knowledge). These opportunities can also target *how* to effectively model and think aloud about the use of strategic processing to actively comprehend text.

• *Roadblock 2: Explicitly teaching a sequence of strategies without maintaining a focus on knowledge building through active comprehension.* As Duffy (2009) points out, teachers don't want to lose sight of the forest for the trees. Teaching students to use strategies does not mean teaching them to follow a lock-step sequence of strategies, especially if we want students to see purpose and relevance in their learning and transfer their strategy knowledge across contexts. In other words, strategies are *not* the end goal of instruction. Rather, strategies are vital tools that enable readers to access textual information, accomplish learning goals, and acquire knowledge about the world around them. If teachers want students to be able to flexibly and adaptively use their strategy knowledge, then they need to make explicit links for students, explaining how strategies are supportive of knowledge building. In other words, the processes of learning (reading, writing, discussing, using strategies) should never be separate from the "products" of learning.

• *Roadblock 3: Providing scaffolded instruction yet fading those scaffolds too quickly.* While explanations and models are needed to help students "see" what reading processes look like, scaffolds are maybe even more essential for students to actually appropriate these processes and knowledge and bring them to fruition in their own reading. Many times, explicit instruction does not work simply because teachers fade their scaffolds away too quickly. Doing so puts the onus on students to continue to fill in experiential and knowledge gaps before they are ready to do so. Probably the hardest part of the explicit instruction approach, carefully sequenced scaffolds require a balance of keen observations of student behaviors, facilitative prompts and questions, and timely and efficacious feedback that fosters students' self-efficacy and reduces their fear of failure.

The instructional sequence—teacher explains and models, students apply with extensive teacher help, students apply with less teacher help, and students apply with no teacher help—provides a quick reminder for instructional planning. Application of strategies and conceptual knowledge is essential to consolidate learning, yet changing the learning context (e.g., text, genre, topic) sometimes requires teachers to step back again and show students how the strategies or concepts apply to this new context. Just as a great basketball player benefits from repeated practice spaced over time with targeted pointers coming from the coach, so, too, do students benefit from repeated coaching from a teacher.

Conclusion

There is no "silver bullet" that magically increases students' abilities to read and comprehend text. In today's classrooms, with students who represent myriad linguistic, cultural, and experiential backgrounds, the task of supporting everyone's reading and comprehension abilities can seem daunting, indeed. However, teachers have substantial control over this process, with multiple tools at their disposal to support and enable students' access to and comprehension of texts. One of these tools—explicit instruction—can optimize student engagement in real reading tasks because it provides students with the tools and support they need to establish conditions for all students to be successful in advancing their reading abilities.

Certainly, explicit instruction is not a "one-size-fits-all" formula that teachers can employ for instant results. Rather, the diversity of our classrooms calls for a diversity of instructional approaches that encourage students to actively and strategically engage with text and content. Moreover, by employing explicit instruction of strategies and concepts, teachers provide students with multiple access points that play to students' strengths and encourage them to intersect with texts and content in productive and varied ways, creating "space" for the diversity of students' backgrounds and experiences by encouraging students to share their understandings and unique perspectives in the knowledge-building process.

REFERENCES

Adams, M. J. (2011, Winter). Advancing our students' language and literacy: The challenge of complex texts. *American Educator,* pp. 3–11.

Alexander, P. A. (2005). A path to competence: A lifespan developmental perspective on reading. *Journal of Literacy Research, 37*(4), 413–436.

Almasi, J. F., & Fullerton, S. K. (2012). *Teaching strategic processes in reading* (2nd ed.). New York: Guilford Press.

Archer, A. L., & Hughes, C. A. (2011). *Explicit instruction: Effective and efficient teaching.* New York: Guilford Press.

Bandura, A. (1997). *Self-efficacy: The exercise of control.* New York: Freeman.

Brown, R., Pressley, M., Van Meter, R., & Schuder, T. (1996). A quasi-experimental validation of transactional strategies instruction with low-achieving second-grade readers. *Journal of Educational Psychology, 88*(1), 18–37.

Duffy, G. G. (2009). *Explaining reading* (2nd ed.). New York: Guilford Press.

Ford-Connors, E., & Robertson, D. A. (2017). What do I say next?: Using the third turn to build productive instructional discussions. *Journal of Adolescent and Adult Literacy, 61*(2), 131–139.

Guthrie, J. T., & Humenick, N. M. (2004). Motivating students to read: Evidence for classroom practices that increase reading motivation and achievement. In P. McCardle & V. Chhabra (Eds.), *The voice of evidence in reading research* (pp. 329–354). Baltimore: Brookes.

Guthrie, J. T., & Wigfield, A. (2000). Engagement and motivation in reading. In M. L. Kamil, P. B. Mosenthal, P. D. Pearson, & R. Barr (Eds.), *Handbook of reading research* (Vol. 3, pp. 403–422). New York: Routledge.

Hattie, J. (2009). *Visible learning: A synthesis of over 800 meta-analyses relating to achievement.* New York: Routledge.

Hattie, J. (2012). *Visible learning for teachers: Maximizing impact on learning.* New York: Routledge.

Johnston, P. H. (2004). *Choice words: How our language affects children's learning.* Portland, ME: Stenhouse.

Paratore, J. R., & Robertson, D. A. (2013). *Talk that teaches: Using strategic talk to help students achieve the Common Core.* New York: Guilford Press.

Paris, S. G., Lipson, M. Y., & Wixson, K. K. (1983). Becoming a strategic reader. *Contemporary Educational Psychology, 8,* 293–316.

Pearson, P. D., & Gallagher, M. (1983). The instruction of reading comprehension. *Contemporary Educational Psychology, 8,* 317–344.

Pressley, M., & Afflerbach, P. (1995). *Verbal protocols of reading: The nature of constructively responsive reading.* Hillsdale, NJ: Erlbaum.

Robertson, D. A. (2013). Teacher talk: One teacher's reflections during comprehension strategies instruction. *Reading Psychology, 34*(6), 523–549.

Robertson, D. A., Dougherty, S., Ford-Connors, E., & Paratore, J. R. (2014). Re-envisioning instruction: Mediating complex text for older readers. *The Reading Teacher, 67*(7), 547–559.

Robertson, D. A., Ford-Connors, E., & Dougherty, S. (2017). *Engaging readers: Supporting all students in knowledge-driven reading, Grades 4–8.* Lanham, MD: Rowman & Littlefield.

Rosenshine, B. (1986, April). Synthesis of research on explicit teaching. *Educational Leadership,* 60–69.

Smagorinsky, P. (2001). If meaning is constructed, what is it made from?: Toward a cultural theory of reading. *Review of Educational Research, 71,* 133–169.

Stahl, S. A., & Nagy, W. E. (2006). *Teaching word meanings.* New York: Routledge.

Taboada, A., Tonks, S. M., Wigfield, A., & Guthrie, J. T. (2009). Effects of motivational and cognitive variables on reading comprehension. *Reading and Writing: An Interdisciplinary Journal, 22*(1), 85–106.

Torgeson, J. K. (2004). Lessons learned from research on interventions for students who have difficulty learning to read. In P. McCardle & V. Chhabra (Eds.), *The voice of evidence in reading research* (pp. 355–382). Baltimore: Brookes.

Vygotsky, L. (1962). *Thought and language.* Cambridge, MA: MIT Press.

Wharton-McDonald, R. (2011). Expert classroom instruction for students with reading disabilities: Explicit, intense, targeted . . . and flexible. In A. McGill-Franzen & R. L. Allington (Eds.), *Handbook of reading disability research* (pp. 265–272). New York: Routledge.

Wiggins, G. (1993). *Assessing student performance: Understanding the purpose and limits of testing.* San Francisco: Jossey-Bass.

Wonder-McDowell, C., Reutzel, D. R., & Smith, J. A. (2011). Does instructional alignment matter?: Effects on struggling second graders' reading achievement. *Elementary School Journal, 112*(2), 259–279.

Wood, D., Bruner, J. S., & Ross, G. (1976). The role of tutoring in problem solving. *Journal of Child Psychology and Psychiatry, 17,* 89–100.

CHILDREN'S LITERATURE

Sachar, L. (2000). *Holes.* New York: Yearling Books.

11

• • • • •

Using Discussion to Support Literacy Learning

Jacquelynn A. Malloy and Leslie D. Roberts

Ms. Huber projects a group of photos onto the whiteboard. She looks thoughtfully at the photos of children from the late 1800s and, after a pause, turns to her third graders and asks, "What do you notice?" She turns back to the display while hands are raising into the air. She turns back to her students.

"Jack, what do you notice?"

"These are old pictures," he offers.

"How do you know?"

"Their clothes are old and there's no color," he adds.

"I see that too! The photos are in black and white. Anything else? Or would you like to invite someone in?" Ms. Huber offers.

Jack looks around and says, "Sari, what do you notice?"

"They're all children," Sari observes.

"They are," Ms. Huber agrees. "Did anyone else notice that?" Heads nod.

"Where do you think they are?"

"It's not a school . . ." offers Jasmine.

"It's a really old building, kind of—" starts Liam.

Shanita interjects, "—like a work, like a place where they . . ."

"Like a machine place?" supplies Madeline.

And so begins a unit of study on child laborers in the Industrial Revolution—more specifically, how the practice of child labor was challenged and the laws changed to protect children. What begins with a "wondering" becomes a "thinking together" that is the prelude to deeper understandings of how the Industrial Revolution affected the lives of children living in working-class families. This first introduction to the topic was an opportunity for Ms. Huber to gauge students' prior knowledge and to explore their initial reactions to child labor during the Industrial Revolution. She then expands and diversifies knowledge of the topic using a carefully designed text set that includes trade books, videos, and Library of Congress resources (see Table 11.1). As students move into smaller peer-discussion groups, they use rich interactions with these multimodal materials to gather information, deliberate concepts, and make assertions about what they are learning.

The practice that makes deep learning possible in this multimodal and collaborative learning environment is *discussion: the meaningful exchange of ideas about a text or a topic.* Discussions can be whole class, small group, or paired, but the speaking and listening skills that are required for effective discussions require explicit teaching, modeling, and maintenance. Ms. Huber incorporates discussion at every level of her unit planning because she understands an important principle of teaching and learning: the discussion principle, that is, when students discuss topics out loud, they are actively constructing and reconstructing

TABLE 11.1. Text Set: Industrial Revolution (Partial List)

Breaker Boys: How a Photograph Helped End Child Labor.
Burgan, M. (2012). Compass Point Books.

Kids on Strike!
Bartoletti, S. C. (2003). HMH Books for Young Readers.

Kids at Work: Lewis Hine and the Crusade against Child Labor
Freedman, R. (1994). Houghton Mifflin.

Say Something!
Reynolds, P. H. (2019). Scholastic.

"The Industrial Revolution: A Boon to Industry, a Bane to Childhood"
www.youtube.com/watch?v=KHmqEqJN59o

"These Photos Ended Child Labor in the US"
www.youtube.com/watch?v=ddiOJLuu2mo

"Industrial Revolution for Kids: A Simple Yet Comprehensive Overview"
www.youtube.com/watch?v=nl_-6WPQ4Sg

Library of Congress National Child Labor Committee Collection
www.loc.gov/pictures/collection/nclc

meanings that represent a change in understanding over time—their learning in action.

Ms. Huber also appreciates the opportunity afforded by whole- and small-group discussions to "see" what students are thinking. Speakers expose their current interpretation of the topic being discussed by organizing it through spoken language. This can be timely for heading off misconceptions that are developing, for supporting the use of new vocabulary or comprehension strategies, or for guiding students in organizing their ideas more advantageously. A whole-class discussion can indicate the need for shoring up background knowledge, creating an anchor chart or graphic organizer to frame concepts, or to find some supplementary visuals to help students latch onto a new concept. Small-group discussions are opportunities for students to try out new vocabulary in context, to compare their interpretations with those of their peers, and to bolster their comprehension skills by building upon the ideas of others. In this chapter, we present teacher-tested practices that will lead to effective and productive whole-class, small-group, and paired discussions in the classroom.

Facilitating Whole-Class Discussions

Whole-class discussions are optimal proving grounds for honing the listening and speaking skills that are essential to productive discussions. In the whole-class discussion, teachers can offer consistent modeling and facilitation of the skills required to create what Almasi, McKeown, and Beck (1996) describe as a *cognitive worktable*. In their research on literature discussions with fourth graders, these researchers noted that in productive discussions, the responses provided by individuals could be manipulated in the group setting as if they were packets of information that could be arranged and rearranged to construct a group interpretation. Bruning, Schraw, and Royce (1995) contend that when this type of dialectical constructivism is supported in classrooms, a reflective learner stance develops that can increase domain, general, and metacognitive knowledge. Similarly, Nystrand (2006) suggests that discussion be promoted as a *method* of instruction that leads to proficiency in reading comprehension.

Malloy and Gambrell (2011) propose that when individual interpretations of a text are brought into the shared workspace of a discussion, they can be organized through the process of listening, evaluating, and building upon the remarks and questions of the multiple viewpoints of others in the group. Figure 11.1 depicts how interpretations were brought into the shared workspace of the discussion of photos in Ms. Huber's class.

As students are introduced to the photos (see examples in Figure 11.2), Ms. Huber uses guiding questions to first ask what they notice about them and then focus the discussion in the direction of key points about the topic: (1) these are children; (2) this happened a long time ago; and (3) the children are not in school but are at a workplace. As the students move closer to the idea that in previous periods in history children worked instead of attending school, Ms. Huber might read a snippet from *Kids at Work: Lewis Hine and the Crusade against Child Labor* (Freedman, 1994) to give them some background about the photos—and the photographer: "Seeing is believing," said Hine. "If people could see for themselves the abuses and injustice of child labor, surely they would demand laws to end those evils" (p. 5). She might even draw a text-to-text connection to her unit on "courageous voices" (Tracy, Menickelli, & Scales, 2016) by recalling the previously read text (and classroom favorite) *Say Something!* (Reynolds, 2019).

With adapted excerpts from selected texts on child labor in the Industrial Revolution, videos about the topic, and the Library of Congress collection of photos and documents from the National Child Labor Committee, Ms. Huber and her students have a variety of sources for thinking through the lives of children during the late 1800s and early 1900s in factories, farms, and coal mines. As she introduces each new source of information, she takes the time to facilitate how students are organizing that information so that the shared workspace is full of ideas that lead to growth in comprehending. To that end, she gives attention to the skills and dispositions that serve as a foundation of the effective discussions that are presented next.

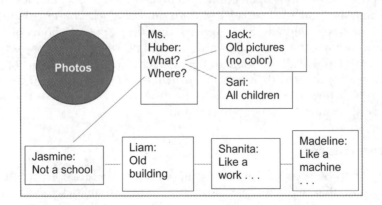

FIGURE 11.1. Interpretations being organized in a shared workspace.

154 • INSTRUCTION •

FIGURE 11.2. Library of Congress photographs by Lewis Hine for initiating discussion. From Library of Congress, Prints and Photographs Division, National Child Labor Committee Collection (the reproduction number for the image on the left is LC-DIG-nclc-01345 and the reproduction number for the image on the right is LC-DIG-nclc-01342).

Inviting In

A discussion is an exchange of ideas about a topic or text and thus requires that multiple ideas—and multiple voices—are included. We have all been in groups where one speaker monopolizes the discussion. When this occurs, the information that is available in the shared workspace can be both limited and redundant. One of the values a teacher can promote in the shared workspace is that we all have ideas to share and these ideas are all welcomed. Of course, this requires that the driving question that leads the discussion is open enough to invite multiple perspectives, such as when Ms. Huber asks, "What do you notice?" Jack's observation that the photos were old and Sari's remark that they were all photos of children were important to interpreting where and when these photos took place. Ms. Huber calls on some students specifically but also allows others to interject as long as their statements help to extend or refine the ideas. She models how we *invite others* into the discussion and suggests that Jack can do the same: "Sari, what do you notice?"

Actively Listening

In order to be successful in extending each other's ideas, it is critically important that students take an active, rather than defensive, listening stance. Discussion is an exchange of ideas, and those ideas must be received and processed so that the exchange can occur. When we listen to someone's statement with a clever rebuttal or denial forming in our minds, we are not truly listening. We have judged the statement and passed a sentence on it that we are forming into a decree. In a classroom where ideas are valued, teachers promote listening to those ideas as a disposition that is essential to the learning power of that community. To support her students in actively listening, Ms. Huber might paraphrase what a student said to show she heard and understood it: "I see that too! All of the photos are in black and white."

Ms. Huber prepares her students for these listening expectations at the beginning of the school year when she models what should happen during *think–pair–share*. In this activity, students talk to an elbow partner about a topic or question posed by the teacher. She prepares her students to have something to offer their partner by emphasizing the "think time" that occurs before the pair–share. This focus on thinking contributes to Ms. Huber's overall class motto: *thinking is learning*, not memorizing, not checking boxes, and not filling in blanks. Rather, we help each other learn by having something thoughtful to say, and thoughtfulness requires think time. She rubs her chin and turns to look at the photo, or to reread the text before putting her thoughts to speech.

Once they have their thoughts together, each student has a brief opportunity to share ideas, but Ms. Huber also requires each listener to paraphrase what was said previously before moving on in the sharing. Paraphrasing serves both speakers and listeners, providing opportunities for listeners to demonstrate their understanding of speakers, and for speakers to clarify what they intended to say, if the paraphrase was not a close approximation of their thinking. The think–pair–share is also an opportunity for students to extend their listening skills as they "follow on" to each other's ideas. At the beginning of the year, Ms. Huber spends a great deal of time thinking aloud and modeling how think–pair–shares should happen in the learning community that she is working to develop. She also demonstrates how this community flourishes when we truly listen to each other's ideas and build upon them.

Following On

Ms. Huber creates a classroom culture where students feel they can contribute to each other's learning. To this end, she promotes the idea that we do not simply pile all of our ideas into our shared workspace but rather follow on to each other's ideas to create a chain of thought that can be extended or elaborated. *Following on* is a way of building on each other's ideas by extending them, as in the "where" thread that occurs on the bottom row in Figure 11.1. In the vignette, Jack elaborates on his observation when he notes that the pictures might be old because they are not in color.

By listening and responding to each other's ideas, students collaborate to understand what they are seeing or reading. Students are supported in using sentence starters such as "I agree with Liam . . ." or "I see what Shanita is saying, but I was also thinking that . . ." or "Do you have some evidence to support what you are thinking?"

Coming to Consensus

As students share their interpretations of texts and visuals in the shared workspace of the discussion, Ms. Huber models and monitors the *inviting in* and *following on* of ideas, looking for voices that have not been shared yet and guiding the reasoning that leads to the extension, substantiating, and contrasting of ideas. If the discussion in our opening vignette had continued, Ms. Huber might have summarized the train of thought and emerging themes that occurred in the discussion as follows:

> "So, we agree that these are photographs taken in a different time, based on the clothing and style of the photos. And we also agree that these are children who are at workplaces rather than at school. Some of you think it would be great to be working instead of at school, because then you'd have money for games. But for the most part, we agree that these children might get an even better job someday if they can go to school, right?"

Better yet, Ms. Huber might have jotted words on the board as students were offering their observations and building on each other's ideas, connecting thoughts with lines, visually separating contrasting ideas, and putting evidence for ideas in parentheses. This provides a visual representation of the Almasi et al. (1996) proposition of the cognitive worktable—one that is concrete enough for students to learn and carry over into their own small-group discussions.

As Ms. Huber releases the responsibility of keeping notes on the discussion, students are encouraged to represent the substance and flow of ideas on an individual whiteboard or notebook paper as the discussion continues. As students become proficient in mapping the discussion, she asks volunteers to help her summarize, noting connections they made that deepened their understanding of the group construction. This final codifying of the manipulation and organization of ideas through creating a summary or consensus prepares these newly developed interpretations to be incorporated into each individual's developing schema.

Whole-class discussions are valuable in exploring what students already know and think about a topic or a text. With a greater availability for teacher facilitation, whole-class discussions become productive spaces for modeling and nurturing the essential skills of thinking, listening, inviting in, following on, and coming to a consensus.

Facilitating Small-Group Discussions

Small-group discussions rely heavily on the discussion skills that are explicitly taught and modeled in whole-class discussions. The expectation that each group member should bring their thoughts and ideas with them, that they should invite each other into the discussion and follow on to each other's ideas, and that they come to a consensus of what was discussed holds true for small groups as well. While the teacher is certainly available to facilitate students in conducting their small-group discussions, she can only listen in on one group at a time, so developing students to the point where they are fairly confident in their discussion skills supports them in being more independent in doing so.

There are several attractive aspects of small-group discussions: the first is that they can be based on choice, such as when students select a book to read together or a topic of interest to study. We know that choice enhances interest and engagement (Taboada, Tonks, Wigfield, & Guthrie, 2009) and the likelihood that students will come to the discussion with ideas to share. Small groups also increase possibilities for students to be heard. With a limited number of contributors to the discussion, students have multiple opportunities to share ideas and build upon them. In K–5 classrooms, small-group discussions can be built around literature or informational texts, and these two types of groups require specific preparation and maintenance by the teacher to promote their effectiveness.

Literature Groups

Book clubs, book discussion groups, and literature circles have been well described in the reading literature (McMahon & Raphael, 1997). Ideally, students are able to choose a book that they will read together, perhaps given a choice by the teacher, and group membership provides a purpose for their independent reading of the text. Book discussions provide spaces for practicing *how* to make sense of what is read by promoting the idea that reading is thinking, and it is the thinking that is exposed in the "out loud" of the discussion. So, a reader's reaction that "I really do *not* like this character!" can be compared with another's assertion that "I don't know—he's kind of nasty, but I think he means well." This might lead to a discussion of how we know a character by what they say and do in the text, directing other members of the group to weigh in on the attributes that the author provides.

In discussions of a particular reading, it is important for the teacher to underscore the primacy of the text in grounding the assertions that are put forth in the discussion. While multiple interpretations can be extracted by group members, it is the responsibility of the group to seek evidence in the text to support those understandings. This is an ideal way to practice comprehension strategies such as identifying an instance of foreshadowing that leads to a prediction, targeting a passage that supports an inference, or making sense of time and place through descriptions of the setting or aspects of the dialogue.

Teachers can support students in using their discussion skills in small literature-based groups by practicing this first in a whole-class book discussion and labeling the essential elements for productive book discussions. Interactive read-alouds are designed to have stopping points for discussion (Fountas & Pinnell, 2006). As the teacher reads, he can model the thinking that is going on by thinking aloud, "Well, does that make sense?" and then maybe rereading a portion to look for clues for understanding.

The pauses are also great for querying students about what they think might, or should, happen next or to weigh in on the actions of a particular character. Following up on each student's response and inviting others in to extend the thinking is a great way to model what should be happening in a small group.

Again, going back and mapping out what was proposed and discussed in consensus-making will help students to label the essential parts of the discussion—that many voices were invited in, that multiple views were welcomed, and that ideas were built upon. Regardless of whether this is kindergarten or fifth grade, students can become independent in their discussion skills when they are regularly identified, labeled, modeled, and given opportunities for practice.

Information Groups

Particularly useful in content learning, students can choose a topic of common interest and become "experts" on that topic. The *expert group* configuration can be used to explore science, social studies, or a language arts topic—for example, planets of the solar system, states and their industries, or types of poetry. Expert groups can "show what they know" through presentations such as movie shorts or information texts or may simply jigsaw with other experts to share multiple views of a common topic. These expert groups serve to deepen content-area learning, such as when expert groups break off to explore inventions during a science unit. Each group selects an invention that was important to advancing society, researches the invention to develop their expertise, and collaborate toward a compelling presentation of the value of their invention to share with their classmates.

Remembering that discussion and intellectual collaboration rely on the inspiration of texts and other sources of information, teachers support students in their discussion and comprehension of the topic by collecting *reliable* and *accessible* sources for research. A text set (Lent, 2012) can be developed for a whole unit of study, with particular resources and materials targeted for each subtopic. Text sets should include a variety of modalities, as text sources are accessible to some but not all, based on text complexity. Tracy, Menickelli, and Scales (2016) highlight the value of a well-constructed text set in supporting learning in ways that reach all students—visually, textually, and through primary sources. Morgan and Rasinski (2012) add that text sets that include multimodal and primary sources promote critical thinking and enlarge students' world knowledge.

Ms. Huber makes use of primary sources quite frequently in introducing and providing background for learning through reading and discussion. The Lewis Hine photographs from the Library of Congress National Child Labor Committee collection, used to initiate the discussion that appears at the beginning of this chapter, transported her third graders to a different time and place, holding constant the experience of being a child, but being a child in a very different circumstance. The primary source and ensuing discussion served to support her students in making sense of the texts they would soon read in trade books and online resources about child laborers and the movement to change their circumstances.

The discussion that occurs in expert groups has a more pragmatic focus than the discussion that occurs in literature-based groups. In expert groups, students should spend some preliminary time reviewing the desired outcome of their research. Some expert groups may meet with members of other groups in jigsaw discussions, which requires that each member have an oral report of the information gathered. Sometimes expert groups prepare a presentation, whether written, oral, or multimodal, to share their learning with their classmates. This requires a clear understanding and reckoning of what the outcome product should involve and how they will ensure that the work gets done. In expert groups, there is ideally some division of labor with members being responsible for adding to the learning by exploring and recording information from whatever source they agree to tackle.

It is in the coming together of this information that the real discussion occurs. As students report what they have learned from their various resources, they can discuss the usability of the information in creating the final product, its relevance and reliability, and make determinations about how best to organize and present what they learned to their classmates.

All of these skills—the preliminary task analysis and assignments, the information gathering and note taking, and the weighing and framing of the information in light of the outcome goal—need to be explicitly modeled and shaped by the classroom teacher.

Flexibly Applying the Discussion Principle

There is considerable evidence in the literature that discussion supports students in learning and comprehending text at all grade and ability levels (see Malloy & Gambrell, 2011). While very young learners require concentrated guidance in sustaining and developing topics, there is evidence that teacher instruction that focuses on listening to and adding on to other's ideas can yield positive results (Maloch, 2002; McIntyre, Kyle, & Moore, 2006; Moses, Ogden, & Kelly, 2015). In the older grades, teachers can move students toward proficiency in sustaining and extending topics (Almasi, O'Flahavan, & Arya, 2001; Fisher & Frey, 2014) and incorporating new information as it becomes available.

Whether in whole-class or small-group discussions, the essential elements for using the discussion principle are similar and well worth teaching and maintaining in the classroom. Whether for language arts teaching or content-area learning, the discussion principle applies to any instructional instance where an active construction and reconstruction of ideas toward deeper and more relevant comprehension is desired. To that end, please consider the following checklist of essential elements of productive discussions when planning your own classroom instruction:

✓ *Provide food for thought* that inspires thinking and discussion, such as passages of text, photos, short videos, or other displays. These should be developmentally appropriate but interesting and challenging as you will be there to support the discussion.

✓ *Carefully balance question types* to promote the exchange of multiple ideas and viewpoints while also guiding the discussion toward particular learning targets using more focused questions. Questions that are asked with a specific answer in mind can direct students' attention to a particular idea but can also be extended by asking "Why do you think that?" or "How do you know?"

✓ *Emphasize think time,* that is, give students a moment to ponder before speaking. You could model this by turning to consider and think about the displayed text or photo before turning back to see the raised hands.

✓ *Invite students in* by addressing students by name and encouraging them to invite each other in as well—"Would you like to invite someone?"

As it becomes apparent that many voices are welcome, students may develop their skills in filling in with each other—offering extensions of each other's thinking without trampling on each other's words, as seen at the end of the discussion in Ms. Huber's class.

✓ *Encourage following on* others' ideas. This is the active and essential element of constructing, deconstructing, and reconstructing an understanding of a topic or text. Students across all grade levels can be supported in first listening to what is being said and then offering something that adds to the discussion. Modeling how to connect or contrast ideas and offering sentence frames for agreeing, challenging, and extending others' thoughts should occur early and often.

✓ *Demonstrate consensus* by intentionally mapping the discussion and representing the themes that emerge, the certainties that are developed, and the questions that remain. While a consensus is not the same as a conclusion, it serves to essentialize the discussion such that it can be stored and later revisited. Students can gradually take over the responsibility of coming to a consensus, which will support them in their small-group discussions.

✓ *Provide models of group types* by showcasing the specific text-dependent discussions that occur in literature groups and the task-focused research sharing that occurs in expert groups. As students develop proficiency in whole-class discussion skills, provide multiple opportunities and support for moving these into smaller-group interactions.

REFERENCES

Almasi, J. F., McKeown, M. G., & Beck, I. L. (1996). The nature of engaged reading in classroom discussions of literature. *Journal of Literacy Research, 28*(1), 107–146.

Almasi, J. F., O'Flahavan, J. F., & Arya, P. (2001). A comparative analysis of student and teacher development in more and less proficient discussions of literature. *Reading Research Quarterly, 36*(2), 96–120.

Bruning, R. H., Schraw, G. J., & Royce, R. R. (1995). Building knowledge and reflective thought. In R. H. Bruning, G. J. Schraw, & R. R. Royce (Eds.), *Cognitive psychology and instruction* (2nd ed., pp. 211–235). Englewood Cliffs, NJ: Prentice Hall.

Fisher, D., & Frey, N. (2014). Speaking and listening in content area learning. *The Reading Teacher, 68*(1), 64–69.

Fountas, I. C., & Pinnell, G. S. (2006). *Teaching for comprehending and fluency: Thinking, talking, and writing about reading, K–8.* Portsmouth, NH: Heinemann Educational Books.

Lent, R. C. (2012). *Overcoming textbook fatigue: 21st century tools to revitalize teaching and learning.* Alexandria, VA: ASCD.

Malloy, J. A., & Gambrell, L. B. (2011). The contribution of discussion to reading comprehension and critical thinking. In R. Allington & A. McGill-Franzen (Eds), *Handbook of reading disabilities research* (pp. 253–262). Mahwah, NJ: Erlbaum.

Maloch, B. (2002). Scaffolding student talk: One teacher's role in literature discussion groups. *Reading Research Quarterly, 37*(1), 94–112.

McIntyre, E., Kyle, D. W., & Moore, G. H. (2006). A primary-grade teacher's guidance toward small-group dialogue. *Reading Research Quarterly, 41*(1), 36–66.

McMahon, S. I., & Raphael, T. E. (Eds.). (1997). *The book club connection: Literacy learning and classroom talk.* New York: Teachers College Press.

Morgan, D. N., & Rasinski, T. V. (2012). The power and potential of primary sources. *The Reading Teacher, 65*(8), 584–594.

Moses, L., Ogden, M., & Kelly, L. B. (2015). Facilitating meaningful discussion groups in the primary grades. *The Reading Teacher, 69*(2), 233–237.

Nystrand, M. (2006, May). Research on the role of classroom discourse as it affects reading comprehension. *Research in the Teaching of English, 40,* 392–412.

Taboada, A., Tonks, S. M., Wigfield, A., & Guthrie, J. T. (2009). Effects of motivational and cognitive variables on reading comprehension. *Reading and Writing, 22*(1), 85–106.

Tracy, K. N., Menickelli, K., Scales, R. Q. (2016). Courageous voices: Using text sets to inspire change. *Journal of Adolescent and Adult Literacy, 60*(5), 527–536.

CHILDREN'S LITERATURE

Freedman, R. (1994). *Kids at work: Lewis Hine and the crusade against child labor.* New York: Clarion Books.

Reynolds, P. H. (2019). *Say something!* New York: Orchard Books.

12

Writing–Reading Integration

Zoi A. Philippakos

Skillful writing involves knowledge of letters, sounds, handwriting, and typing; knowledge of orthographic patterns for accurate spelling of words; knowledge of writing purposes and genres in order to satisfy the needs of the discourse; knowledge of vocabulary, syntax, and grammar to construct a cohesive message to readers; and knowledge of the writing process to navigate the cognitive constraints that writing sets. If writers are challenged by encoding, spelling, handwriting, language, and the writing process, their communication with readers will be impeded. Skillful reading involves phonemic awareness and phonics (see Chapter 4), fluency (see Chapter 5), and comprehension and vocabulary (see Chapter 6; Eunice Kennedy Shriver National Institute of Child Health and Human Development, 2000) and requires the systematic instruction of those elements for initial decoders to become readers. If readers face difficulties at the word-recognition level and cannot accurately and automatically apply the code to read single and multisyllabic words, meaning making will suffer.

The purpose of this chapter is to advocate for instruction that integrates reading and writing. In the following sections, I explain the theoretical rationale for reading and writing relations, identify the conditions for such integration, and provide specific guidelines for classroom application. It should be noted that reading, writing, speaking, and listening are interconnected. However, for the purposes of this chapter, limited comments are made on the connection of writing to oral language.

Writing and Reading: Similar, Yet Not Identical

Reading and writing connections have been pointed out early in the literature (e.g., Fitzgerald & Shanahan, 2000; Tierney & Shanahan, 1991), and recent meta-analyses show that writing interventions support reading comprehension (Graham & Hebert, 2011), reading interventions support writing (Graham et al., 2017), programs that balance reading and writing lead to academic growth (Graham et al., 2018), and writing about content improves learning in social studies, science, and mathematics (Graham, Kiuhara, & MacKay, 2020). The relationship between reading and writing is explained in the following theories: *cognitive, sociocultural,* and *functional.*

Cognitive Theory

Cognitive theory states that reading and writing share cognitive spaces and skills. This relationship is best described by bringing to mind a well with two pails/buckets, where one bucket represents writing and the other represents reading, but they both access water from the same source or by visualizing a common foundation upon which two buildings are constructed (Graham et al., 2016; Shanahan, 2016, 2018). According to Fitzgerald and Shanahan (2000), reading and writing share four categories of knowledge: metaknowledge, domain knowledge, knowledge about universal text attributes, and procedural knowledge.

Metaknowledge refers to an understanding about the function and goals of reading and writing, for example, the understanding that readers and writers have about genre purposes. *Domain* knowledge is specific to prior knowledge about content and is also called *world knowledge. Knowledge about universal attributes* refers to specific knowledge about letters and words, grammar, and syntax within sentences and texts. This knowledge can be illustrated by considering principles of grammar (the past tense of *go* is *went* and not *goed* [something that toddlers often use]) or by principles of directionality in reading and writing (e.g., return sweep [movement from the end of one line to the left/beginning of the next one]) in English that differs from Arabic). Finally, *procedural* knowledge refers to knowledge of strategies to identify, access, use, and create knowledge. This knowledge connects with the use of strategies for summarizing, predicting, and questioning.

Sociocognitive Theory

Sociocognitive theory states that reading and writing serve one purpose, which is to communicate. Therefore, readers read the work of writers to make meaning, and writers write in order to communicate ideas and messages with readers. For such communication to take place, writers need to be aware of the audience and of the purpose of the communication. This is similar for readers who try to extract meaning, construct and deconstruct meanings, and make sense of messages authored by writers.

Functional Theory

Functional theory refers to combined use and supports the idea that both reading and writing are combined to accomplish a specific goal (Langer & Applebee, 1987). For instance, as I write this chapter, I do not rely on information solely from memory but also use information from readings.

The Principle of Writing–Reading Integration: Intentional Connection between the Two

Even though writing and reading share cognitive, pragmatic, and rhetorical spaces, they are different. Shanahan (1988) shared that "reading and writing do not overlap sufficiently to permit complete reading and writing development through an instructional emphasis on one or the other" (p. 637). This realization leads us to the guiding principle for this chapter: *reading and writing should be intentionally integrated*. Therefore, instead of using "boxed" times for the teaching and practice of the two, the "walls" that separate reading and writing should fall.

Integrating Writing and Reading: Teachers' Knowledge

Often at the end of an interactive or shared reading, questions are included that address strategies and content and become points for discussion among teachers and students but could also become writing prompts for students.

When teaching reading, teachers need to have a strong understanding about the development of reading, components of reading, and their relationship to writing. Therefore, they need to understand what phonemes are, how phonological awareness develops, what phonemic awareness is and what tasks within are stronger predictors of reading, what graphemes are, what the alphabetic principle is, and how word recognition develops (Foorman et al., 2016). Further, they need to know how spelling develops, what syllable types are, and how syllable types support both spelling and reading. For instance, when students see printed the word *diner,* they should be able to identify two vowels, two syllables, and break the word after the vowel *i,* reading it as a long-vowel sound. When they spell the word *dinner,* use the syllable types to divide the word and include a double consonant in their spelling to indicate the short-vowel sound in the first syllable (din - ner).

In addition to knowledge about foundational skills, teachers need to know how to support fluency and be aware of the importance of fluent reading in reading comprehension. They should know how to support vocabulary using specific strategies, how to support comprehension by making the process of meaning making audible to students, and how to support them in emulation and internalization of taught strategies. Finally, teachers need to know how to select texts for readers and the importance of grade-level text in teaching grade-level standards without impeding students' growth by only exposing them to instructional-level text or to student-selected text.

When working on writing, teachers need to have a good understanding about foundational skills and not ignore the importance of handwriting fluency on writing development and on writing quality. Further, they should themselves understand the genres of writing and reading and be able to address and comment on those genres while they read and write texts. They should know the writing process and how to flexibly apply different techniques to navigate through it while working on different genres. They should have a good understanding about ways to support a community of learners by being writers themselves and by promoting collaborations in classroom throughout the writing process. They need to know how grammar and syntax support writing quality and incorporate that instruction without overemphasizing it and, finally, how to support the development of handwriting, spelling, and typing fluency as those skills can significantly affect writing quality (Graham et al., 2012).

Across both reading and writing, teachers need to know the importance of self-regulation and influence of self-efficacy beliefs in order to support students' motivation, goal setting, and reflection as readers and writers (Pajares, 1996; Pajares, Johnson, & Usher, 2007; Traga Philippakos, 2020a). Therefore, they should provide feedback on the process used and on students' work, and comment on the use of taught strategies and on students' achieved goals, explaining that learning requires effort but it is attainable. Thus, they may not be able to complete a specific task *yet,* but through structured cycles of goal setting, application, and reflection they will make progress toward their goals.

Writing and Reading Integration: Classroom View

In order to bring this integration to life, this section provides examples from classroom application. Examples are given across grades and disciplines, and some are drawn from research I conducted with colleagues (e.g., Traga Philippakos & MacArthur, under review; Traga Philippakos, Williams, McClurg, Robinson, & Munsel, 2019).

Connecting Letters and Sounds in Sentence Writing

For readers to read, they need to unlock the alphabetic principle and connect sounds (phonemes) with letters (graphemes). Integration of reading and writing in this context would involve teachers working with students on encoding when teaching decoding. For instance, after supporting in small group the tasks of sounding out and blending words with the instruction of high-frequency words, students can apply those skills in reading decodable texts and in writing from dictation sentences. This process of recognizing a letter, connecting it with its sound, and blending sounds together to say the word and understand its meaning can be reversed to segment sounds, connect each phoneme with its grapheme, recall the needed motor stroke to write the letter, record all graphemes that represent phonemes, and reread to confirm the end result and word meaning. Blending and segmenting tasks with segmenting-to-spell approaches can support students' automaticity in learning and applying the code.

Classroom View

Ms. Penn is a first-grade teacher with more than 20 years of teaching experience. In her application of differentiated instruction, she has students grouped and provides support on different levels of need (e.g., word recognition and fluency or vocabulary and comprehension) within a 45-minute block. For the group that works on word recognition and fluency and specifically focuses on blends and digraphs, Ms. Penn has incorporated the following activities:

- Review of what a blend is and what a digraph is
- Sounding and blending of words (10 words)
- Making words (make *pot*; change *pot* to *post,* change *post* to *plot,* etc.)
- Spelling words within sentences from dictation
- Reading text
- Writing sentences

The 15-minute lesson incorporates both the application of reading and writing with students who are listening to from dictation the words to spell and then segmenting to spell in order to record words in given sentences (see Figure 12.1).

```
Do not _____ this!

(Completed for teacher: Do not post this!)

I saw a _____ panther in the _____ of an eye!

(Completed for teacher: I saw a pink panther in the blink of an eye!)

Dictation: Do your best!
```

FIGURE 12.1. Sample fill-in words in sentences and sentence writing from dictation.

Teaching Writing and Reading in the Disciplines

Disciplinary writing according to Shanahan and Shanahan (2008) refers to skills specific to mathematics, science, literature, and history. In disciplinary literacy, the starting point is the content, and the goal is to consider how experts in the fields of science, mathematics, and literature use those strategies. Thus, in disciplinary literacy the learner does not just apply literacy strategies to access the content but also learns to think and act as one would think and act within that discourse. This work in the disciplines is prominent in middle schools.

Students enjoy informational and discipline-related topics that expand their knowledge. Such themes and topics can also function as a motivational tool for their learning (see Mohr, 2006) but would require discussions about text in the disciplines (Massey, 2014). Learning about content can also be achieved by reading such texts in language arts (e.g., using Seymour Simon books as read-alouds to learn about earthquakes when covering natural phenomena in science). Analysis of text structure and discussions about text (e.g., its organization and syntax) can support students' content learning and expand their understanding about genre. Thus, these texts can become a source of knowledge and function as mentor texts for students' own later writing.

Classroom View

Ms. Smith is a fourth-grade elementary teacher with 15 years of experience. She has a degree in biology and a special interest in science and mathematics. She knows that reading and writing complement one another and are tools for learning. When teaching mathematics, she engages in discussions about the ways that the questions are phrased for students to be able to analyze the information provided at the sentence level. Students identify verbs that provide the action for the operation they need to complete or pay attention to the words that indicate more than one operations (e.g., *and*). In addition, she engages students in developing their own problems to apply the operations learned and use any information they learn from other disciplines (e.g., science).

When working in science on life sciences and the structures and functions of life, the class sets up a terrarium and an aquarium. In the process of working on this, Ms. Smith engages students in writing procedural texts that describe the steps of completing a process. They discuss the importance of writing clear steps and the sequential presentation of those steps in science and especially in report writing. Once the terrarium and aquarium are set up, students observe and record their observations through note taking. They read about the life of salamanders, observe, and write reports on those organisms or compare–contrast responses using evidence from information read and from their observational notes. When they write about topics that relate to their organisms, they actively apply strategies they have been taught and use their knowledge about genres to take notes and understand the information. Thus, they actively comment on the structure of a report and look for main ideas/categories and supporting details. For instance, when reading about salamanders and knowing that the text provides information about this organism, they anticipate to learn information about its habitat, diet, life cycle, predators, and so forth.

Pointing Out Strategies That Could Be Used in Writing and in Reading

In *Developing Strategic Writers through Genre Instruction* (Philippakos, MacArthur, & Coker, 2015; see also Philippakos & MacArthur, 2020), students and teachers analyze readings and writing assignments by conducting a rhetorical task analysis to identify the writing purpose and then the genre and its elements. Specifically, they consider the form, topic/title, audience, author, and purpose. The questions asked may slightly differ when examining reading and writing tasks, but the goal is to support students' (a) critical analysis prior to reading for note taking and comprehension, and (b) critical analysis prior to writing for development of ideas, organization, and composition. (See Table 12.1 with information for writing and reading using the task analysis.)

When considering the writing purpose, students and teachers examine whether the purpose is to persuade, inform, entertain, or convey experience (PIECE of the purposes pie; Philippakos, 2018). Next they consider the genres within each purpose (e.g., opinion writing under *persuade,* report writing under *inform,* etc.), and finally the elements for the genre that become the focus of the writing. Students are taught to use those elements as a guide to read and take notes, and as a tool for brainstorming and organizing their ideas (see Figure 12.2 on pp. 172–173).

TABLE 12.1. Task Analysis for Writing and Reading

	Writing	Reading
Form	• Essay, letter, book, etc.	
Topic/title	• What is the topic I am writing about?	• What is the title of the book? • Consider what you know about the topic and if there are vocabulary words you may not know.
Audience	• Who is the reader?	
Author	• What is my perspective? • Am I writing as myself, or do I take someone else's point of view? • What are the implications on my vocabulary, tone, and grammar?	• Who is the author? • What other readings have I done by the same author? • What genres does this author write about? • Is the author the illustrator? • What are possible biases that this author has?
Purpose	• What is the purpose? ○ Persuade, inform, entertain, or convey experience?	
Genre	• What is the genre for that purpose? • What are the organizational features for that genre?	

Once teachers have taught representative genres within each purpose, they can support students' expansion of genre knowledge by identifying the genres in read-alouds and discussing similarities and differences with the ones that students have been taught. To support discussions to internalize genres and their elements and characteristics, teachers can develop a table to record information about each reading and to discuss with students about the genres and their unique structural and linguistic characteristics (see Table 12.2 on p. 174).

Classroom View

Ms. Knox is a fifth-grade teacher. She is in her fourth year of teaching, and her goal is to support students' understanding about text features. Thus, prior to the reading of a text, Ms. Knox examines the *form* and type of text (article, book, letter, etc.), the *topic*, the *audience*, the *author*, and the *purpose* of the text (FTAAP; Philippakos & MacArthur, 2019).

When considering the topic, Ms. Knox examines with students vocabulary words that may support or inhibit understanding and seek clarifications. For instance, when reading the book *Exoplanets* by Seymour Simon, she discusses and explains the meaning of *exo-* (out), connects the meaning of *exo-* with other words (e.g., *exoskeleton*), and reviews with students the planets in the cosmos. This review supports activation of relevant background knowledge that can stimulate ideas for meaning making. When commenting on the author, she considers information she knows about the author and his work. This supports the activation of relevant knowledge about who Seymour Simon is and the genres in which he writes. For this text, the purpose would be to *inform* and the genre would be *report*, potentially with information on compare–contrast. Thus, learners will anticipate learning what an exoplanet it, why humans are interested in exoplanets, and so forth.

Teaching Features and Organizational Elements of Text

It is not possible for students to learn all genres of writing through writing instruction. However, teachers conduct numerous readings during interactive and shared reading and during science and social studies. Instruction on the genres and on the features of those can be beneficial as students learn the elements of genres and use them to comprehend text and to plan and write. If teachers point out the genres, their organizational features, syntax, and linguistic characteristics (McCutchen, 1986), comparisons can be made among those, and students can learn to flexibly think about genres and to anticipate the structure of texts that share a similar purpose and develop them when writing (see Table 12.2 on p. 174).

Analyzing samples and their organizational elements and features can support students' understanding about the genre and about the specific features that make a sample better than another. Teachers may identify the features of genres and discuss with students how the presence of those supports the purpose of a paper. For instance, they may review a sample opinion paper and discuss how the presence of a clear opinion and reasons supports the reader's understanding about what the writer thinks about the topic. While discussing the features of texts, teachers may also review well-written and less clearly written examples, engaging students in identifying the elements of the genre that are present and understanding better how the absence of those and/or lack of organization can affect comprehension. Students may engage in reading those texts, locating and labeling the elements (color-coding may be an option besides underlining), and reflecting on their understanding about the features of a genre (e.g., importance of a position, reasons and evidence/examples, and a restatement of position in an opinion paper). When discussing text, teachers can develop and discuss visuals that represent the

Ideas

Brainstorm	Similarities between Topics	Reading AND Note Taking
Topic A:		Topic B:

Graphic Organizer for Compare–Contrast Writing

Beginning	**Topic:**			
	Purpose:			
Middle	On what are they **similar?**	**Similarities**		
	On what are they **different?**	**Differences**		
		Topic A:		**Topic B:**
End	**Restate Purpose:**			
	Leave a Message to the Reader:			

FIGURE 12.2. Sample brainstorm and graphic organizer for compare–contrast writing. Graphic organizer reprinted by permission from Philippakos, MacArthur, and Coker (2015). Copyright © 2015 The Guilford Press.

• 173 •

TABLE 12.2. Sample Recording of Information during Read-Alouds with Sample Information

Author	Title	Purpose	Genre	Type	Unique Characteristics
Aesop	*Zeus and Frogs*	Entertain	Fable	Fiction	• Moral • Animals talk like humans
Doreen Cronin	*Click Clack Moo*	Entertain	Fantasy	Fiction	• Animals have human attributes
Seymour Simon	*Mars*	Inform	Report	Nonfiction	• Categories of information • Real pictures

Note. Reprinted by permission from Traga Philippakos, Munsel, and Robinson (2018). Copyright © 2018 *The Language and Literacy Spectrum.*

different features of texts to support students' generalization and transfer of knowledge from writing to reading and vice versa (see Table 12.3).

Self-regulated strategy development (Harris & Graham, 2009) provides instruction on text structure for teaching writing. Studies have also examined the use of text structure for reading comprehension with upper elementary students (see Hebert, Bohaty, Nelson, & Roehling, 2018). Studies with first and second graders that incorporated the instruction of text structure as a guide for planning, writing, and revision also found benefits on writing quality (Traga Philippakos, 2019; Traga Philippakos &

TABLE 12.3. Features of Sample Genres

Genre	Purpose	Elements
Opinion	Persuade	*Beginning:* Topic and opinion *Middle:* Reasons, evidence *End:* Restatement and message to reader
Report	Inform	*Beginning:* Topic and purpose *Middle:* Categories (main ideas/points) and evidence *End:* Restatement of purpose and message to reader
Procedural	Inform	*Beginning:* Topic, purpose, materials–skills *Middle:* Steps and explanations *End:* Evaluation, restatement of purpose, message to reader
Story	Entertain	*Beginning:* Character(s), setting, problem *Middle:* Events and complications *End:* Solution and emotions

MacArthur, 2020; Traga Philippakos, MacArthur, & Munsel, 2018). Furthermore, using genre-specific evaluation criteria as a guide for critical review of papers in revision supports students' revisions and overall quality of writing (Philippakos, 2017; Philippakos & MacArthur, 2016). Therefore, the process of identifying the features of a genre and evaluating examples that may lack elements and affect comprehension and overall quality can strengthen learners' critical reading and evaluation as well as written production (MacArthur, 2018; Philippakos, 2017).

Classroom View

Mr. Mocha is a fourth-grade teacher in his fourth year of teaching. He is in the process of teaching a unit on procedural writing, and prior to his modeling, he presents a sample paper that is a good representative of the genre. He then proceeds to discuss with students what the features of text are that make the paper clear and appealing to them as readers, and what they can learn as writers. Once they identify the elements of the genre and other features and evaluate the quality and presentation of those elements using a rubric (e.g., Philippakos & MacArthur, 2019), Mr. Mocha displays a second example that is not as clearly written and that also misses genre elements. He discusses with students their initial impressions about the paper, beyond length (which can be a consequence of missing features or underdeveloped ideas); he discusses and evaluates the paper; and he draws conclusions about the features that support their comprehension and understanding about what they, as writers, should include in their work.

Application of Sentence Starters across Disciplines

Knowledge of sentence starters can support students' development of stylistic diversity and ease in expression of ideas. Further, understanding the function of sentence frames can support learners in anticipating the content of readings. For instance, after reading the beginning of the sentence *One reason* _____, a reader understands that what follows is an answer to why a specific position is true (or not). Graham, Bollinger, and colleagues (2012) provide sentence frames, as well as sentence-expansion and sentence-combining suggestions as ways to support writing competence. Sentence-combining tasks can indeed support students' reading comprehension (Graham & Hebert, 2011; Wilkinson & Patty, 1993) as they help students better understand relationships between ideas. When working with sentence frames, if students are aware of them, they can apply them in oral language and their interpersonal interactions, and in their responses to text across the instructional day. This constant application and repetition can help them internalize those sentence frames and also make them more aware of their function so they can detect them in reading and use them to make meaning.

Classroom View

Mr. Hannan is a second-grade teacher in his second year of teaching. He is working on opinion writing and has already discussed with students the elements and features of opinion writing and sentence frames that are used to present those elements. Mr. Hannan explained to students that they will work on reading a text and identify the position of the character, the reasons the character provides to support that position, and the relevant evidence. The book they would read is *The Pigeon Wants a Puppy* by Mo Willems. Prior to reading the book, Mr. Hannan analyzed the task (using the rhetorical task analysis [FTAAP]) and discussed with students how the purpose of the book is to entertain. Therefore, the text would include narrative features (see Table 12.3), but their purpose as readers is to identify the position of the character and the reasons and evidence that are used to support that position; thus they would use the elements of opinion writing to keep track of the presented ideas (see Table 12.3).

While reading, Mr. Hannan engages with students in collaborative reasoning and proceeds to play the role of the facilitator as students argue with the character about what the character wants ("Pigeon wants a puppy") and the reasons/evidence he provides ("He will take care of it by feeding it once a month"). In the process of responding, Mr. Hannan asks questions: "Do you think Pigeon should have a puppy?" As students respond, he scaffolds the use of sentence frames: *One reason I think Pigeon should not have a puppy is* _____. By supporting the use of sentence frames, students incorporate them in their verbal responses. Later, when they work on their own papers, they include them (with scaffolded support), and finally, they transfer them in their own writing. When working in mathematics, Mr. Hannan reminds students to use their sentence frames to develop their response to questions and provide evidence by visually representing their answer and by recording their answer using words in sentences. This continued practice and application supports students' understanding about ways to represent their responses with clarity for their readers to make meaning.

Writing about Reading

Answering questions about text and developing questions to respond about text are tasks that support reading comprehension (Graham & Hebert, 2011). In responding to questions about texts read, students must not only understand the content but also apply their critical skills to understand the function of features of text. For instance, after reading a selection, they may discuss with the teacher specific personality traits that a character had and answer in writing how the author made those traits identifiable in the text. Answering questions about text supports reading comprehension, but comprehension is further aided when students provide extended responses about text and incorporate personal reactions and responses to text read.

Students may also work on writing summaries of text read. Summarization of text strongly supports reading comprehension, and it can take place across subject areas (English language arts, social studies, and science). For this to take place, students should be able to identify the main ideas within the provided text (Shanahan, 2016, 2018). The use of text structure could also aid students' retelling and identification of main ideas (Shanahan et al., 2010).

Classroom View

Mr. Nichols is a fourth-grade teacher with 2 years of teaching experience. In his writing instruction he makes sure to identify the genre and elements, and use appropriate techniques for planning and revision. In reading, he also considers the elements and text structure to take notes and retell. This is a process he uses primarily for fiction, but as the class expands its knowledge of nonfiction, he applies it across the curriculum. With students he develops a prediction, monitors meaning making by supporting with students the answering of questions about characters, setting, problem, actions, solution, and theme (see Table 12.2), and supports summarization by providing sentence frames: *In this story written by* _____ *and illustrated by* _____ *the characters are* _____. Having this frame and the guidance of the genre elements (see Table 12.3) as an organizer for thinking and meaning making, students can better recall the information and write about it.

Pedagogical Implications and Responsibilities

For writing and reading to be integrated, teachers would need to provide a gradual release of responsibility and to scaffold students' application of taught strategies in reading (Shanahan et al., 2010), in writing (Graham et al., 2012), and in integrated reading and writing tasks. Teacher think-alouds with discussion about goal setting and explanation about *why* specific processes are used and *how* their use supports learning are necessary; the goal is for students not only to learn content and cognitive strategies but also to develop self-regulation and effective ways to manage time, effort, and strategy selection to achieve their goals. Integration of writing and reading should be made explicit in authentic and meaningful contexts.

The role of teacher education programs in achieving an integrated view of writing and reading is a crucial one. Schools of education need to include in their course of study not only instruction on reading but also instruction on writing and on disciplinary literacy for elementary majors. Also, the role of professional development at the school and district levels is critical (Traga Philippakos, 2020b). Teachers need to know how writing and reading develops, what the similarities and differences between the two are, and how to systematically provide opportunities for integration in daily instruction. This does not mean simply asking students to provide responses to reading (although this is a good approach). The goal is for students to see the connections between reading and writing, and how the two combine to facilitate learning and critical thinking.

REFERENCES

Eunice Kennedy Shriver National Institute of Child Health and Human Development, NIH, DHHS. (2000). *Report of the National Reading Panel: Teaching children to read: Reports of the subgroups* (00-4754). Washington, DC: U.S. Government Printing Office.

Fitzgerald, J., & Shanahan, T. (2000). Reading and writing relations and their development. *Educational Psychologist, 35*(1), 39–50.

Foorman, B., Beyler, N., Borradaile, K., Coyne, M., Denton, C. A., Dimino, J., . . . Wissel, S. (2016). *Foundational skills to support reading for understanding in kindergarten through 3rd grade* (NCEE 2016-4008). Washington, DC: National Center for Education Evaluation and Regional Assistance (NCEE), Institute of Education Sciences, U.S. Department of Education. Retrieved from *http://whatworks.ed.gov.*

Graham, S., Bollinger, A., Olson, C., D'Aoust, C., MacArthur, C., McCutchen, D., & Olinghouse, N. (2012). Teaching elementary school students to be effective writers. Retrieved from *https://ies.ed.gov/ncee/wwc/PracticeGuide/17.*

Graham, S., Bruch, J., Fitzgerald, J., Friedrich, L., Furgeson, J., Greene, K., . . . Smither Wulsin, C. (2016). *Teaching secondary students to write effectively* (NCEE 2017-4002). Washington, DC: National Center for Education Evaluation and Regional Assistance, Institute of Education Sciences, U.S. Department of Education. Retrieved from *http://whatworks.ed.gov.*

Graham, S., & Hebert, M. (2011). Writing to read: A meta-analysis of the impact of writing and writing instruction on reading (Report). *Harvard Educational Review, 81*(4), 710–744.

Graham, S., Kiuhara, S., & MacKay, M. (2020). The effects of writing on learning in science, social studies, and mathematics: A meta-analysis. *Review of Educational Research, 90*(2), 003465432091474.

Graham, S., Liu, X., Aitken, A., Ng, C., Bartlett, B., Harris, K., & Holzapfel, J. (2018). Effectiveness of literacy programs balancing reading and writing instruction: A meta-analysis. *Reading Research Quarterly, 53*(3), 279–304.

Graham, S., Liu, X., Bartlett, B., Ng, C., Harris, K., Aitken, A., . . . Talukdar, J. (2017). Reading for writing: A meta-analysis of the impact of reading interventions on writing. *Review of Educational Research, 88*(2), 243–284.

Hebert, M., Bohaty, J., Nelson, J., & Roehling, J. (2018). Writing informational text using provided information and text structures: An intervention for upper elementary struggling writers. *Reading and Writing, 31*(9), 2165–2190.

Langer, J. A., & Applebee, A. N. (1987). *How writing shapes thinking*. Urbana, IL: National Council of Teachers of English.

MacArthur, C. A. (2018). Evaluation and revisions. In C. A. MacArthur, S. Graham, & J. Fitzgerald (Eds.), *Best practices in writing instruction* (3rd ed., pp. 287–308). New York: Guilford Press.

Massey, S. (2014). Making the case for using informational text in preschool classrooms. *Creative Education, 5*(6), 396–401.

McCutchen, D. (1986). Domain knowledge and linguistic knowledge in the development of writing ability. *Journal of Memory and Language, 25*(4), 431–444.

Mohr, K. (2006). Children's choices for recreational reading: A three-part investigation of selection preferences, rationales, and processes. *Journal of Literacy Research, 38*(1), 81–104.

Pajares, F. (1996). Self-efficacy beliefs in academic settings. *Review of Educational Research, 66*(1), 543–578.

Pajares, F., Johnson, M. J., & Usher, E. L. (2007). Sources of writing self-efficacy beliefs of elementary, middle, and high school students. *Research in the Teaching of English, 42*(1), 104–120.

Philippakos, Z. (2018). Using a task analysis process for reading and writing assignments. *Reading Teacher, 72*(1), 107–114.

Philippakos, Z. A. (2017). Giving feedback: Preparing students for peer review and self-evaluation. *The Reading Teacher, 71*(1), 13–22.

Philippakos, Z. A., & MacArthur, C. A. (2016). The effects of giving feedback on the persuasive writing of fourth- and fifth-grade students. *Reading Research Quarterly, 51*(4), 419–433.

Philippakos, Z. A., & MacArthur, C. A. (2020). *Developing strategic young writers through genre instruction: Resources for grades K–2*. New York: Guilford Press.

Philippakos, Z. A., MacArthur, C. A., & Coker, D. L. (2015). *Developing strategic writers through genre instruction: Resources for Grades 3–5*. New York: Guilford Press.

Shanahan, T. (1988). The Reading–Writing Relationship: Seven Instructional Principles. *The Reading Teacher, 41*(7), 636–647.

Shanahan, T. (2016). Relationships between reading and writing development. In C. A. MacArthur, S. Graham, & J. Fitzgerald (Eds.), *Handbook of writing research* (2nd ed., pp. 194–207). New York: Guilford Press.

Shanahan, T. (2018). Reading–writing connections. In S. Graham., C. A. MacArthur, & M. Hebert (Eds.), *Best practices in writing instruction* (3rd ed., pp. 309–332). New York: Guilford Press.

Shanahan, T., Callison, K., Carriere, C., Duke, N. K., Pearson, P. D., Schatschneider,

C., & Torgesen, J. (2010). *Improving reading comprehension in kindergarten through 3rd grade: A practice guide* (NCEE 2010-4038). Washington, DC: National Center for Education Evaluation and Regional Assistance, Institute of Education Sciences, U.S. Department of Education. Retrieved from *https://whatworks.ed.gov/publications/practice guides*.

Shanahan, T., & Shanahan, C. (2008). Teaching disciplinary literacy to adolescents: Rethinking content-area literacy. *Harvard Educational Review, 78*(1), 40–59.

Tierney, R., & Shanahan, T. (1991). Research on the reading-writing relationship: Interactions, transactions, and outcomes. In R. Barr, M. Kamil, P. Mosenthal, & D. Pearson (Eds.), *The handbook of reading research* (Vol. 2, pp. 246–280). New York: Longman.

Traga Philippakos, Z. (2019). Effects of strategy instruction with an emphasis on oral language and dramatization on the quality of first graders' procedural writing. *Reading and Writing Quarterly, 35*(5), 409–426.

Traga Philippakos, Z., Macarthur, C., & Munsell, S. (2018). Collaborative reasoning with strategy instruction for opinion writing in primary grades: Two cycles of design research. *Reading and Writing Quarterly, 34*(6), 485–504.

Traga Philippakos, Z. A. (2020a). Developing strategic learners: Supporting self-efficacy through goal setting and reflection. *Language and Literacy Spectrum, 30*(1), 1–24.

Traga Philippakos, Z. A. (2020b). A yearlong, professional development model on genre-based strategy instruction on writing. *Journal of Educational Research, 113*(3), 177–190.

Traga Philippakos, Z. A., & MacArthur, C. A. (2020). Integrating collaborative reasoning and strategy instruction to improve second graders' opinion writing. *Reading and Writing Quarterly, 36*(4), 379–395.

Traga Philippakos, Z. A., & MacArthur, C. A. (under review). *Examination of genre-based strategy instruction in middle school English language arts and science: First cycle of design-based research.*

Traga Philippakos, Z. A., Munsel, S., & Robinson, L. (2018). Supporting primary students' story writing by including retellings, talk, and drama with strategy instruction. *Language and Literacy Spectrum, 1*(28), 1–22.

Traga Philippakos, Z. A., Williams, L., McLurg, G., Robinson, L., & Munsell, S. (2019). Writing in science: Integrating writing strategy instruction across the curriculum. *Association of Literacy Educators and Researchers Yearbook: Educating for a Just Society, 41*(1), 353–374.

Wilkinson, P., & Patty, D. (1993). The effects of sentence combining on the reading comprehension of fourth grade students. *Research in the Teaching of English, 27*(1), 104–125.

CHILDREN'S LITERATURE

Simon, S. (2018). *Exoplanets.* New York: Harper Collins.

Willems, M. (2008). *The pigeon wants a puppy.* New York: Hyperion.

13

·····

Literacy in the Disciplines

Cynthia H. Brock, Vassiliki (Vicky) I. Zygouris-Coe,
Andrea Hayden, Joshua Montgomery, Kathleen Kniss,
and Katherine Muir Welsh

If you are like us, you have heard elementary teachers lament lacking time in their busy schedules to teach social studies or science. In fact, some of us have expressed similar concerns. There may, however, be additional reasons that elementary teachers struggle to accommodate science and social studies instruction. For example, due to state or local mandates, teachers may prioritize reading and mathematics instruction, causing social studies and science to recede as priorities. Some elementary teachers may also feel they lack the requisite subject-matter knowledge to effectively teach in different content areas (Davis, Petish, & Smithey, 2006; Pressley, Duke, & Boling, 2004; Trygstad, 2013; VanFossen, 2005; Zembal-Saul, 2009).

These challenges notwithstanding, there are myriad reasons elementary teachers *should* systematically teach social studies and science starting in kindergarten. For example, (1) many children are interested in social studies and science topics (Duke, Pearson, Strachan, & Billman, 2011); (2) without strong social studies and science instruction throughout elementary school, students are ill prepared for subject matter instruction in middle school, high school, and beyond (Duke & Martin, 2015; Zembal-Saul, 2009); and (3) literacy can be used as a tool to engage in meaningful social studies and science instruction (National Research Council [NRC], 2012; Yore, Bisanz, & Hand, 2003). Literacy instruction is especially meaningful when it is embedded in purposeful content instruction;

moreover, by effectively using literacy as a tool in content-area instruction, students develop and use literacy skills and strategies (Duke et al., 2011; NRC, 2012; Zembal-Saul, 2009).

We advocate for the regular and explicit teaching of social studies and science in elementary classrooms. Here, we present a flexible framework for using literacy (which includes reading, writing, speaking, listening, and viewing) to engage in explicit, meaningful, and regular social studies and science instruction. The practice of using literacy as an adaptive tool in unique ways in different disciplines is referred to as *disciplinary literacy*. The ideas in this chapter rest on the following principle: Literacy skills and strategies should (and can) be *meaningfully and uniquely used within different academic disciplines* across the grades in elementary school.

As we unpack this principle throughout the remainder of the chapter, we will demonstrate how and why the aforementioned challenges to disciplinary instruction in elementary school can be productively mitigated. In particular, we feature two teachers who exhibit adaptive expertise as they reflect on and adapt their pedagogical practices to meet the dynamic needs of their students (see Chapter 20 for more information on teacher adaptability; Darling-Hammond & Bransford, 2005).

In this chapter, we first elaborate on what we mean by disciplinary literacy, and we explain why disciplinary literacy matters in the elementary grades. Next, we present a framework for enacting our central principle. In order to illustrate how the framework and principle can be flexibly applied and adapted to different grade levels and content areas, we share examples from a fifth-grade history unit and a second-grade science unit.

What Is Disciplinary Literacy, and Why Does It Matter in the Elementary Grades?

Disciplinary literacy refers to the unique ways that reading, writing, talking, listening, and viewing are used within different disciplines (Moje, 2015; Zygouris-Coe, 2012). A disciplinary literacy perspective calls for teachers and students to explore and assume the beliefs, values, norms, and dispositions of disciplinary experts (see the National Governors Association Center for Best Practices & Council of Chief State School Officers' [NGA & CCSSO, 2010] Common Core State Standards [CCSS]; the Next Generation Science Standards [NGSS Lead States, 2013]; and the National Council for the Social Studies' [NCSS, 2010] National Curriculum Standards for Social Studies). For example, historians use literacy tools to corroborate evidence across multiple sources (NCSS, 2017), while scientists use literacy tools to evaluate evidence to support claims about a phenomenon (NRC, 2012).

Disciplinary literacy contrasts with a long-standing dichotomy (i.e., learn to read/read to learn) still evident in some elementary schools today. According to this dichotomy, teachers in Grades K–3 should teach children to *learn to read,* and around fourth grade, teachers should teach children to *read to learn* (Duke, Bennett-Armistead, & Roberts, 2003). Not only is this dichotomy contrary to research (see Duke et al., 2003), but also it robs early elementary children of opportunities to meaningfully engage with disciplinary learning (Gee, 2015). Paradoxically, as children focus on literacy skills devoid of meaningful, integrated content, they are less likely to develop the knowledge that supports all aspects of literacy development (Cervetti & Hiebert, 2015).

Another important reason for teachers to engage in disciplinary literacy instruction in the elementary grades is the recent attention educational standards (e.g., NCSS, 2010; NGA & CCSSO, 2010; NGSS Lead States, 2013) place on the use of literacy tools to support students' content knowledge development (International Literacy Association [ILA], 2017; Moje, 2010; Shanahan & Shanahan, 2012; Zygouris-Coe, 2012). Meeting these standards requires that students develop more sophisticated literacy skills and strategies as they advance through the grade levels. Without developing disciplinary knowledge and skills in elementary grades, students will not be adequately prepared for specialized literacy demands of content learning in later grades and beyond (ILA, 2019).

Elementary teachers can provide even very young students with scaffolded opportunities to participate in disciplinary ways of reading, writing, listening, viewing, communicating, doing, and thinking (Brock, Goatley, Raphael, Trost-Shahata, & Weber, 2014; Welsh, Brock, Robertson, & Thrailkill, 2020). For example, in the context of science, this includes engaging young students in reading scientific texts, using the norms and conventions of science, learning how to form scientific explanations, and using evidence from inquiry activities, texts, academic discussions with peers, and so forth, to support claims (Grysko & Zygouris-Coe, 2020). Meaningfully embedding literacy skills and strategies in disciplinary instruction means that elementary students have opportunities to develop both their literacy skills and their disciplinary content knowledge.

An Adaptive Framework for Enacting Disciplinary Literacy Inquiry in Elementary Classrooms

In this section, we present a framework—borrowed from Spires, Kerkhoff, and Paul (2020), and adapted for elementary grades—to instantiate and enact the central principle of this chapter. A unique feature of the Spires et al. (2020) framework is its focus on disciplinary literacy instruction through inquiry. Inquiry learning is important because it "focuses on students' construction of knowledge" as they engage in the inquiry process (Spires et al., 2020, p. 3).

Indeed, Spires et al. (2020) articulate the following goal for the meaningful, effective, and adaptive implementation of their disciplinary literacy inquiry framework: to construct conditions for students to experience deep content learning through creating and fostering their own learning. In this chapter, we present the components of the framework we have adapted from Spires et al. (2020), illustrating how this modified framework can be meaningfully implemented and adapted in two different elementary grades: one focusing on fifth-grade history and one on second-grade science.

In the remainder of this section, we first introduce the two contexts whereby we flexibly used and adapted our disciplinary literacy inquiry framework. Next, we discuss how the teachers designed each unit and spent time building students' background knowledge at the beginning of each unit. Then, we demonstrate how the teachers taught students to ask compelling questions; gather and analyze sources; synthesize claims and evidence; critically evaluate and revise; and share, publish, and act. As we discuss these components of the disciplinary literacy inquiry framework in the context of elementary grades, we provide concrete examples from a history and a science unit to illustrate what adaptive implementation of each component might look like across content areas and grade levels. Finally, as we provide concrete examples from the two sample units, we present a critique of ways the teachers could adapt and improve them for future use.

Contexts for the Fifth-Grade History Unit and the Second-Grade Science Unit

The Fifth-Grade History Unit

The images in Figure 13.1 and 13.2 represent the culminating event of a 2-week intensive Wyoming Coaching Laboratory (WYCOLA) inquiry project with fifth graders in summer 2019. Wyoming's 2.2-million-acre Wind River Reservation is home to the Northern Arapaho and the Eastern Shoshone. In response to 2018 Wyoming state legislation, the state's social studies standards were revised "to ensure the cultural heritage, history and contemporary contributions" of American Indians of the region are addressed (Wyoming House Bill HB0076, 2017). Thus, because of its importance in Wyoming and beyond, our 2019 summer inquiry unit centered on the following question: What historical events and cultural

FIGURE 13.1. WYCOLA community participants listen to history inquiry presentations.

FIGURE 13.2. WYCOLA fifth graders present their history inquiry projects.

practices have shaped relationships among the Northern Arapaho, the Eastern Shoshone, and other Wyoming citizens?

The 2-week intensive summer inquiry project was part of the larger WYCOLA program. The foundational component of WYCOLA is a laboratory classroom in which a teacher (in this case, the first author of this chapter, Cynthia Brock) teaches fifth-grade learners while WYCOLA participants observe remotely. This allows participants to explore core aspects of instructional practice, instructional coaching, and mentoring, grounded directly in classroom experiences. In this chapter, we foreground the WYCOLA laboratory classroom, wherein the teacher implemented a 2-week history disciplinary literacy inquiry unit with a group of 24 fifth graders from seven different elementary schools in a Wyoming school district. Approximately half of the students were boys and half were girls. Most of the students were of European American descent, but some children were Latinx and African American.

The Second-Grade Science Unit

Our second example is a disciplinary literacy inquiry science unit focused on environmental stewardship, conducted in Miss McKay's second-grade classroom in a western-state Title I school. There were 32 students in Miss McKay's classroom; approximately half of her students were girls and half were boys, and the children were of European American, Latinx, African American, and Pacific Islander descent.

The unit's driving inquiry question was, Why, and how, do we need to care for our air, water, and land? Using this overarching inquiry question, Miss McKay sought to have her students become aware of their own environments, transition from identifying and describing to considering problems and solutions, and finally, to become environmental stewards. Miss McKay chose to focus on community-based environmental stewardship because (1) some science scholars (e.g., Sobel, 1996) emphasize beginning instruction with young children focusing on their own local communities, and (2) Miss McKay strives to teach her students to live and act responsively in their own local community (for a detailed discussion of Miss McKay's science unit, see Welsh et al., 2020).

Adaptive Framework for Enacting
Elementary Disciplinary Literacy Inquiry

Key components of the disciplinary inquiry framework featured in this chapter include (1) choosing a focus area of study and building students' background knowledge, and teaching students to (2) ask compelling questions, (3) gather and analyze sources, (4) creatively synthesize claims and evidence, (5) critically evaluate and revise, and (6) share, publish, and act. While this model can be flexibly adapted to different content areas and grade levels, we focus here on the content areas of social studies and science, two content areas crucial for children's school success that may, unnecessarily, be omitted in busy elementary classrooms (Brock et al., 2014; Shanahan & Shanahan, 2014).

Choose a Focus Area of Study and Build Students' Background Knowledge

As teachers, we are responsible for knowing standards, curriculum guidelines, and expectations in our districts and schools. Thus, we are best equipped to make decisions about curriculum foci. Accordingly, both teachers featured in this chapter chose the focus areas for the units they implemented.

Scholars in the field of literacy (e.g., Bartlett, 1932) have long known that the background knowledge readers bring to texts affects comprehension. In fact, building background knowledge is important for myriad reasons: (1) readers' abilities to make inferences about texts (including visual and auditory texts) depend on their background knowledge, and (2) readers' understandings of informational texts (whether multimodal or traditional) depend on their background knowledge about topic(s) and text structures (Neuman, Kaefer, & Pinkham, 2014).

Fifth-Grade History Unit. Building background knowledge refers to the process of scaffolding students' initial understandings of topics and issues (Lupo, Strong, Lewis, Walpole, & McKenna, 2018). For example, in the fifth-grade history unit, the teacher did a preassessment with her 24 students. She learned that most had little knowledge about their Northern Arapaho and Eastern Shoshone neighbors in Wyoming. Consequently, she began the unit by scaffolding students' collective background knowledge, placing a large 12′ × 12′ plastic Wyoming map (see *www.uwyo.edu/ wga/giant-floor-maps/index.html* for more information) on the classroom floor and showing the students where they lived in relation to the Wind River Reservation (WRR). She also used Wikki Stix to outline the WRR so students could see its size, compared to the overall state.

Moreover, she showed the students short video clips created by the Wind River Education Project (*http://windriveredu.org*) featuring the Northern Arapaho and Eastern Shoshone people talking about their lives and history. Because the use of primary sources is a disciplinary practice integral to social studies, students also viewed a selection of historical photographs that corresponded to the inquiry unit focus. As students developed shared understandings of content, they moved forward *together* in making meaning about the unit focus.

Second-Grade Science Unit. Miss McKay started by building her students' background knowledge about the concept of "environment." First, she sat in her reading chair with her 32 students sitting around her on the reading rug. The word *environment* was written on a sheet of chart paper. She asked her students to share their ideas about this word. After the group settled on a working definition of *environment,* Miss McKay began reading *On Our Way Home* (Braun, 2009), about a family of bears heading home after a day in the woods. As she read, she asked the children to think about the bears' environment. After reading, Miss McKay and the children co-created a concept map of the bears' environment on a large sheet of chart paper. Miss McKay engaged in similar literacy-related activities to build students' background knowledge in the unit on environmental stewardship.

Building Background Knowledge. For disciplinary literacy inquiry at the elementary level, spending time building students' background knowledge is a crucial first step in the inquiry process. It is not possible for students to develop meaningful inquiry questions if they do not know enough about a topic to be interested in it and pose questions about it.

Teach Students to Ask Compelling Questions

Once teachers have spent time building students' background knowledge, it is time to teach students to ask compelling questions. Compelling questions drive the disciplinary inquiry process; however, students need explicit instruction (see Chapter 10) on developing compelling inquiry questions. The following insights, adapted from Spires et al. (2020), scaffold students in developing compelling questions:

1. Teachers should provide examples of high-quality inquiry questions, explaining what makes questions high quality.
2. Teachers should model the process of creating compelling inquiry questions.
3. Teachers should model the process of making mediocre inquiry questions into high-quality inquiry questions.
4. Teachers should encourage students to develop inquiry questions relevant to their interests and lives.
5. Teachers can remind students that compelling questions often begin with the words *how* or *why.*
6. Teachers can then ask students to work in groups to develop their unique questions.
7. Teachers can group students by interest to explore their questions.

Fifth-Grade History Unit. This unit focused on an inquiry topic relevant to students in Wyoming that was chosen based on its importance in the state. As well, the teacher thought aloud about how to create high-quality inquiry questions. She showed students examples of high-quality inquiry questions, and the teacher and students co-constructed a list of attributes of high-quality questions. Additionally, the teacher modeled transforming a mediocre inquiry question into a higher-quality inquiry question.

After the teacher had modeled the process of creating and revising high-quality inquiry questions, she asked the students to identify key subtopics about the Northern Arapaho and Eastern Shoshone. Students were grouped by their interests and provided scaffolding to develop inquiry questions in their small groups (Memory, Yoder, Bolinger, & Warren, 2004). Students' inquiry questions included the following (notice that most, but not all, of these questions started with *how* or *why*):

1. Why do the Northern Arapaho/Eastern Shoshone live on the Wind River Reservation?
2. How did the two tribes come together to govern?
3. Why were schools for American Indians started, and who taught in them?
4. What was the school experience like for Northern Arapaho and Eastern Shoshone students?

Second-Grade Science Unit. Miss McKay developed an overarching unit inquiry question (i.e., why, and how, do we need to care for our air, water, and land?), and she focused on that overarching inquiry question for all of the work in the unit, but she did not work with her second graders to create their own subinquiry questions. For future iterations of this unit, Miss McKay could draw on ideas in this section to help her students develop their own inquiry questions. This would allow for increased student engagement and ownership in the unit and help to develop the disciplinary skill of asking questions, a key science and engineering practice in the Next Generation Science Standards (NGSS Lead States, 2013).

Teach Students to Gather and Analyze Sources

Once students have crafted thoughtful and compelling inquiry questions—or in the case of our second-grade unit example, the teacher crafted the compelling unit inquiry question—the next step of the disciplinary literacy inquiry process is to gather and analyze sources. At this point, teachers must address two crucial concerns: identifying credible resources and close reading, skills which require time to develop and refine (Spires et al., 2020). First, teachers need to help their students learn to find and evaluate online resources for their inquiry projects. Examples of ways to teach students to find and scrutinize sources include (1) modeling how to brainstorm keywords that students can use to search online; (2) providing mini-lessons on which search engines to use and how to use them effectively; and (3) teaching students to be discerning about the sources they find (see Coiro [2003], for ways to work with elementary students regarding this latter issue).

Second, teachers should teach their students to engage in close reading of sources, focusing intensively on the text and striving to interpret precisely what the author is saying. This includes noting the author's word choices and choices of text structure in printed texts as well as image content and placement in multimodal texts (Fisher & Frey, 2012). One of many possible ways teachers can model this process is by engaging in practices such as *think-alouds* whereby teachers read an excerpt of text aloud and, while doing so, identify (aloud) the ideas they are considering as they interpret the text (Fisher & Frey, 2012). Annotating texts is another common strategy for helping students to read challenging texts and engage with them at a deep level (Fisher & Frey, 2015).

Fifth-Grade History Unit. With respect to the fifth-grade inquiry unit, collecting sources is an area where the teacher could make considerable adaptations. Unfortunately, due to summer program time constraints, the teacher only had 16 hours across 2 weeks to implement the unit. Because of this time limit—in conjunction with students' inexperience in conducting online searches—the teacher gathered credible sources for the students from such venues as the American Heritage Center at the University of Wyoming and the Wyoming Historical Society. An important adaptation of this unit would include drawing on the ideas in this section of the chapter to teach students to find their own credible sources.

Since primary sources are a key element in historical inquiry (Monte-Sano, 2011; Muetterties, Slocum, & Masterson, 2019; NCSS, 2017), the teacher provided students with a collection of relevant primary and secondary sources (e.g., photographs, maps, historic documents), and coached students to act as historians by engaging in close reading within and across the sources. For example, she taught students to (1) carefully analyze each source in order to make viable claims as they answered their inquiry questions, (2) corroborate aspects of historical events using their sources, and (3) compile evidence across a variety of credible sources (Levstik & Barton, 2015).

Second-Grade Science Unit. Some work in the second-grade science unit involved having students gather sources; other work involved the teacher gathering sources for students. For example, after Miss McKay taught her students about key vocabulary/concepts, such as *environment,* she asked her students to gather information pertaining to their own school environment. First, Miss McKay divided the students into four groups. Then, each group went to a different area in the school (e.g., the cafeteria, the playground, the school library) while one group stayed in the classroom. Next, taking their science notebooks (Gilbert & Kotelman, 2005) with them, children then drew and labeled at least three things that they noticed in their environments. Finally, returning to the classroom, the students discussed their observations in small groups, and Miss McKay facilitated the creation of concept maps of various locations in the school environment.

Sometimes during her unit, however, Miss McKay collected sources for the students to analyze. For example, for one set of activities, Miss McKay engaged the children in a 5E (i.e., **E**ngage, **E**xplore, **E**xplain, **E**laborate, and **E**valuate) science lesson (Bybee, 2015) to explore the difference between biotic and abiotic items in an environment (see Bybee [2015] for a detailed overview of the 5E science lesson model). Using environment tubs (see Figure 13.3), the children explored the tub contents and created lists in their science notebooks of biotic and abiotic items within the tubs.

Miss McKay then introduced pollution in the form of litter and air pollution (e.g., smoke in baby food jars) into the environment, and the

FIGURE 13.3. Children exploring biotic and abiotic items within environment tubs.

children observed and noted the impact of pollution on the environment. While engaged in this exploration, Miss McKay reviewed "kid-friendly" definitions of academic words such as *environment* and *observe*. Moreover, Miss McKay introduced problems with pollution that can occur in environments. Thus, in this unit, students planned and carried out scientific investigations through making observations to collect and/or analyze data that can be used to make comparisons (NGSS Lead States, 2013).

Teach Students to Creatively Synthesize Claims and Evidence

After students have collected and analyzed sources, they need to synthesize information across sources to answer their inquiry questions and demonstrate knowledge (Spires et al., 2020). Synthesis is particularly important because it invites students to extend beyond summarizing information; when students synthesize information, they identify, prioritize, and merge ideas based on importance.

Teachers can teach synthesis in a variety of ways. For example, students can structure write-ups in terms of claims and evidence rather than a series of paragraphs. Students can also create multimodal visuals to illustrate how they use evidence to make claims (see Figure 13.2 for an example of this idea). Structures such as these provide scaffolding for students as they work to understand challenging primary and secondary sources, to relate information back to inquiry questions, and to synthesize new understandings of ways to use evidence to make and support claims.

Fifth-Grade History Unit. Historians interpret sources by making claims and supporting their claims with evidence (De La Paz, 2005). Seeking to emulate the work of historians, the teacher determined that the end goal for the fifth-grade students' projects would be a combination of short informational writing pieces (an analysis of each primary or secondary source) paired with an argumentative writing piece that made a claim answering their inquiry questions, drawing from primary and secondary sources for evidence. Figure 13.2 provides an overview of the evidence that one group drew on to analyze sources and make claims to address their inquiry questions.

Second-Grade Science Unit. After engaging in a host of activities that included learning about and caring for the environment, Miss McKay and her students reviewed their learning about environmental stewardship. They then engaged in two synthesis activities: creating a Readers' Theater script and creating a class book. Using a shared writing approach (Routman, 2005), Miss McKay and her students synthesized information and ideas from their unit by co-creating a Readers' Theater (Martinez, Roser, & Strecker, 1999) script focused on environmental stewardship.

The second synthesis-related activity culminated in a class book on environmental stewardship. At the end of the unit, Miss McKay prompted her students to identify key ideas from the unit on environmental steward-ship that illuminated ways to take care of the environment. As they talked (both as a whole group and during think–pair–share opportunities), Miss McKay focused the students' attention on information that helped answer their unit inquiry question. After the children decided which aspects of the unit were most significant, Miss McKay asked them to write their ideas in their science notebooks.

Teach Students to Critically Evaluate and Revise

In our own work as teachers, we find it difficult to get students to *want* to critically revise and evaluate their work. However, when students cre-ate final products for authentic audiences, they are *more likely* to want to revise their work since it will be shared with others (Wiggins, 2009). Spires and her colleagues (2020) present a three-tiered evaluation system (i.e., self, peer, and teacher or other outside expert) that teachers can use to (1) help students learn to receive and provide feedback, (2) collab-oratively co-construct knowledge, and (3) plan for further instruction. In the following examples, the teachers strove to provide effective modeling, scaffolding, and targeted feedback to apprentice students in the process of constructing historical and scientific knowledge.

Fifth-Grade History Unit. Students worked in groups of four to cre-ate the display boards depicted in Figures 13.1 and 13.2. Each student took primary responsibility to complete the written analysis for one or two primary or secondary sources on the display chart. Students discussed possible content and then completed the write-up(s) they had negotiated with their teams. Team members took turns reading and editing the com-pleted write-ups, and the teacher also provided feedback.

After the teacher modeled synthesizing individual analyses to make claims to answer research questions, each student group discussed pos-sible synthesis claims to make across their write-ups of each data source. Once students had negotiated their claim, one student in the group took responsibility for writing it. Then, group members and the teacher pro-vided feedback on the writing of the claim. A student in each group typed and printed the group's claim to be pasted on their display boards. Stu-dents also ensured that their argumentative writing piece (claim and evi-dence) was valid by using Wikki Stix to physically connect passages within the writing to the source of the evidence on their boards.

After completing their display boards (see Figure 13.2), students worked collaboratively within their groups to make decisions about sharing their learning with audience members. They decided what each team member would say about their learning, and then created note cards. The teams then practiced their presentations several times before their final presentations.

Second-Grade Science Unit. Miss McKay's second graders critically evaluated and revised their thinking and learning regarding the synthesis activities in two ways. As *communicating information* is an important component of one of the science and engineering practices and the CCSS for English language arts (NGA & CCSSO, 2010; NGSS Lead States, 2013), clear communication of ideas through fluent reading and speaking skills was a performance goal of the Readers' Theater. To support this goal, Miss McKay made copies of the script for each student and modeled reading the script aloud fluently and expressively. Next, she modeled an example of nonfluent reading so the children could see and hear the difference. As well, she modeled a positive example of projecting her voice. Finally, she put the students in small groups to practice reading the script so that they would be prepared to perform it. Thus, Miss McKay modeled the process of giving an oral presentation by providing examples and nonexamples.

Second, students used ideas from their science notebooks to each create a page for a class book. Children wrote about their most significant learning with respect to environmental stewardship and then collaborated with a peer to edit each partner's work. This process of peer editing was a class routine Miss McKay spent considerable time establishing during the writing workshop throughout the year. Once students had written, edited, and received feedback from Miss McKay on their work, they typed and printed their individual pages in the computer lab. Finally, they each illustrated their pages.

Teach Students to Share, Publish, and Act

"When students construct knowledge, create representations of that knowledge, and communicate to an authentic audience, they are no longer imitating experts in a discipline; they are becoming part of the disciplinary community" (Spires et al., 2020, p. 86). Moreover, when students make their work public, they have opportunities to share and discuss what they are learning. When teachers apprentice their students into sharing their work with authentic local (i.e., class, school, or community based) or global audiences, they are acting as agents of social change. Whereas there are many opportunities for students to share their work globally through the Internet, the examples we share from our fifth-grade and second-grade units represent audiences at the classroom, school, and community levels.

Fifth-Grade History Unit. Figure 13.1 illustrates how students engaged in the process of sharing and publishing work for a public community audience. At the end of the inquiry unit, students acted as knowledge creators by creating their own presentation boards whereby they interpreted and synthesized primary and secondary sources to make claims to answer their inquiry questions. Then, they shared their knowledge and expertise with audience members, as parents, friends, and family members gathered for a meal and to view and discuss the students' work.

Second-Grade Science Unit. Miss McKay's students shared, published, and acted on their learning about environmental stewardship in two ways. First, after practicing the reading of their co-created class Readers' Theater script, the students performed their Readers' Theater scripts for their school's kindergarten and first-grade classes. This positioned them as authoritative knowledge brokers about environmental stewardship, which became an important topic of discussion for grades kindergarten through two at Miss McKay's school. Second, children in Miss McKay's class had each written and illustrated one page about environmental stewardship. Miss McKay combined the children's pages into one class book to be shared and enjoyed by all.

Conclusion

We conclude this chapter by returning to its foundational principle: literacy skills and strategies should (and can) be *meaningfully and uniquely used within different disciplines* across the grades in elementary school. Across the chapter, we provided examples of ways two teachers used literacy as an adaptive tool for inquiry-focused instruction in history and science. In particular, we used the fifth-grade history inquiry unit and the second-grade science inquiry unit to demonstrate how teachers can (1) adaptively foster students' use of discipline-specific literacy skills and strategies in the context of inquiry units across different grade levels and content areas, (2) facilitate students' comprehension of multimodal texts, (3) enable students to engage in authentic disciplinary discourse, and (4) support knowledge development in social studies and science.

Moreover, the adaptive examples in this chapter illustrate how the problems we introduced at the beginning of the chapter can be mitigated. For example, disciplinary instruction can (and should) be foregrounded

TABLE 13.1. Key Ideas for Planning Disciplinary Literacy Inquiry Units

Guiding principle for the chapter

Literacy skills and strategies should (and can) be *meaningfully and uniquely used within different disciplines* across the grades in elementary school.

Key components of the disciplinary inquiry framework (adapted from Spires et al., 2020)

1. Choose a focus area of study and build students' background knowledge.
2. Teach students to ask compelling questions.
3. Teach students to gather and analyze sources.
4. Teach students to creatively synthesize claims and evidence.
5. Teach students to critically evaluate and revise.
6. Teach students to share, publish, and act.

Classroom examples of how the guiding principle can be applied during instruction across disciplines in elementary school

1. Build students' content knowledge by reading a wide range of print and digital informational (and other) texts.
2. Use close reading strategies for work with challenging texts.
3. Provide explicit instruction in academic and domain-specific vocabulary.
4. Allow students to generate questions, revise questions, and develop inquiry-based learning experiences related to their questions.
5. Use writing—both formal and informal—as a means of documenting learning.
6. Create opportunities for students to collaborate with peers, share what they are reading and learning, engage in discussions and peer reviews, and present their knowledge about the topic to an authentic audience in ways that are relevant to them.

Classroom examples of how the guiding principle can be applied during literacy/social studies instruction	**Classroom examples of how the guiding principle can be applied during literacy/science instruction**
1. Provide opportunities to practice reading and interpreting primary and secondary sources.	1. Select informational texts that use accurate science language and build students' background knowledge.
2. Utilize graphic organizers that help students to focus on particular aspects of the sources.	2. Use inquiry activities to develop students' ability to plan and conduct experiments and observations.
3. Help students to contextualize resources.	3. Develop science vocabulary and reasoning skills through opportunities to discuss and write about science.
4. Teach the process of making a claim based on evidence gathered from multiple information sources.	4. Use instructional scaffolds (e.g., modeling, sentence starters) to help students construct scientific explanations.
5. Use argumentative writing structures to communicate claims and evidence.	5. Introduce students to texts and phenomena that will spark their curiosity and fuel scientific inquiry.

from the beginning of elementary school; by using literacy as a meaning-ful tool within the disciplines, teachers can efficiently and concurrently foster students' disciplinary learning *and* literacy learning. Addition-ally, the inquiry framework we have provided in this chapter is used in conjunction with disciplinary standards, such as the NGSS (NGSS Lead States, 2013) and the NCSS National Curriculum Standards (NCSS, 2017). Then the standards, the disciplinary literacy inquiry framework, and other important resources, such as Levstik and Barton (2015) and Bybee (2015), can serve as invaluable resources for elementary teachers who may not be content specialists but who recognize that social studies and science must be meaningfully and systematically taught across the elementary grades.

Table 13.1 provides an overview of ways teachers can adapt and apply this chapter's central principle to disciplinary instruction across content areas and grade levels, especially science and social studies. In short, Table 13.1 serves as a useful heuristic for teachers who wish to adaptively plan and reflect on the development and implementation of their own disciplinary literacy inquiry units.

REFERENCES

Bartlett, F. (1932). *Remembering.* London: Cambridge University Press.

Brock, C., Goatley, V., Raphael, T., Trost-Shahata, E., & Weber, K. (2014). *Engaging students in disciplinary literacy, K–6: Reading, writing, and teaching tools for the classroom.* New York: Teachers College Press.

Bybee, R. (2015). *The BSCS 5E instructional model: Creating teachable moments.* Arlington, VA: National Science Teachers Association Press.

Cervetti, G., & Hiebert, E. (2015). Knowledge literacy and the Common Core. *Language Arts, 92*(4), 256–269.

Coiro, J. (2003). Reading comprehension on the Internet: Expanding our under-standing of reading comprehension to encompass new literacies. *The Reading Teacher, 56*(5), 458–464.

Darling-Hammond, L., & Bransford, J. (Eds.). (2005). *Preparing teachers for a changing world: What teachers should learn and be able to do.* San Francisco: Jossey-Bass.

Davis, E., Petish, D., & Smithey, J. (2006). Challenges new science teachers face. *Review of Educational Research, 76*(4), 607–651.

De La Paz, S. (2005). Effects of historical reasoning instruction and writing strategy mastery in culturally and academically diverse middle school class-rooms. *Journal of Educational Psychology, 97*(2), 139–156.

Duke, N. K., Bennett-Armistead, V. S., & Roberts, E. M. (2003). Bridging the gap between learning to read and reading to learn. In D. M. Barone & L. M. Morrow (Eds.), *Literacy and young children: Research-based practices* (pp. 226–242). New York: Guilford Press.

Duke, N. K., & Martin, N. M. (2015). Best practices for comprehension instruction in the elementary classroom. In S. R. Parris & K. Headley (Eds.), *Comprehension instruction: Research-based best practices* (3rd ed., pp. 211–223). New York: Guilford Press.

Duke, N. K., Pearson, P. D., Strachan, S. L., & Billman, A. K. (2011). Essential elements of fostering and teaching reading comprehension. In S. J. Samuels & A. E. Farstrup (Eds.), *What research has to say about reading instruction* (4th ed., pp. 51–93). Newark, DE: International Reading Association.

Fisher, D., & Frey, N. (2012). Close reading in elementary schools. *The Reading Teacher, 66*(3), 179–188.

Fisher, D., & Frey, N. (2015). Improve reading with complex texts. *Phi Delta Kappan, 96*(5), 56–61.

Gee, J. P. (2015). *Social linguistics and literacies: Ideology in discourses*. New York: Routledge.

Gilbert, J., & Kotelman, M. (2005). Five good reasons to use science notebooks: Key to understanding about science notebooks maximizing learning for all students. *Science and Children, 43*(3), 28–32.

Grysko, R., & Zygouris-Coe, V. (2020). Supporting disciplinary literacy and science learning in Grades 3–5. *The Reading Teacher, 73*(4), 485–499.

International Literacy Association (ILA). (2017). *Content area and disciplinary literacy: Strategies and frameworks* (Literacy Leadership Brief). Newark, DE: Author.

International Literacy Association (ILA). (2019). *Children's rights to excellent literacy instruction* (Position Statement). Newark, DE: Author.

Levstik, L., & Barton, K. (2015). *Doing history: Investigating with children in elementary and middle schools*. New York: Routledge.

Lupo, S. M., Strong, J. Z., Lewis, W., Walpole, S., & McKenna, M. C. (2018). Building background knowledge through reading: Rethinking text sets. *Journal of Adolescent and Adult Literacy, 61*(4), 433–444.

Martinez, M., Roser, N., & Strecker, S. (1999). "I never thought I could be a star": A readers theatre ticket to fluency. *The Reading Teacher, 52*(4), 326–334.

Memory, D. M., Yoder, C. Y., Bolinger, K. B., & Warren, W. J. (2004). Creating thinking and inquiry tasks that reflect the concerns and interests of adolescents. *The Social Studies, 95*(4), 147–154.

Moje, E. (2010, March). *Disciplinary literacy: Why it matters and what we should do about it*. Paper presented at the National Writing Project Conference, New Orleans, LA. Retrieved from *www.nwp.org/cs/public/print/resource/3121*.

Moje, E. B. (2015). Doing and teaching disciplinary literacy with adolescent learners: A social and cultural enterprise. *Harvard Educational Review, 85*(2), 254–278.

Monte-Sano, C. (2011). Beyond reading comprehension and summary: Learning to read and write in history by focusing on evidence, perspective, and interpretation. *Curriculum Inquiry, 41*(2), 212–249.

Muetterties, C., Slocum, C., & Masterson, E. (2019). What is a vote worth?: A focused inquiry to scaffold elementary historical thinking. *The Social Studies, 1–10.*

National Council for the Social Studies (NCSS). (2010). *National curriculum standards for social studies: A framework for teaching, learning, and assessment.* Silver Spring, MD: Author.

National Council for the Social Studies (NCSS). (2017). *The college, career, and civic life (C3) framework for social studies state standards: Guidance for enhancing the rigor of K–12 civics, economics, geography, and history.* Silver Spring: MD: Author.

National Governors Association Center for Best Practices & Council of Chief State School Officers. (2010). *Common Core State Standards for English language arts and literacy in history/social studies, science, and technical subjects.* Washington, DC: Author.

National Research Council. (2012). *A framework for K–12 science education: Practices, crosscutting concepts, and core ideas.* Washington, DC: National Academies Press.

Neuman, S., Kaefer, T., & Pinkham, A. (2014). Building background knowledge. *The Reading Teacher, 68*(2), 145–148.

NGSS Lead States. (2013). *Next Generation Science Standards.* Washington, DC: National Academies Press.

Pressley, M., Duke, N. K., & Boling, E. C. (2004). The educational science and scientifically-based instruction we need: Lessons from reading research and policymaking. *Harvard Educational Review, 74*(1), 30–61.

Routman, R. (2005). *Writing essentials: Raising expectations and results while simplifying teaching.* Portsmouth, NH: Heinemann.

Shanahan, C., & Shanahan, T. (2014). Does disciplinary literacy have a place in elementary school? *The Reading Teacher, 67*(8), 636–639.

Shanahan, T., & Shanahan, C. (2012). What is disciplinary literacy and why does it matter? *Topics in Language Disorders, 32*(1), 7–18.

Sobel, D. (1996). *Beyond ecophobia: Reclaiming the heart of nature education.* Great Barrington, MA: Orion Society.

Spires, H. A., Kerkhoff, S. N., & Paul, C. M. (2020). *Read, write, inquire: Disciplinary literacy in Grades 6–12.* New York: Teachers College Press.

Trygstad, P. J. (2013). *2012 National survey of science and mathematics education: Status of elementary school science.* Chapel Hill, NC: Horizon Research.

VanFossen, P. J. (2005). "Reading and math take so much time . . .": An overview of social studies instruction in elementary classrooms in Indiana. *Theory and Research in Social Education, 33*(3), 376–403.

Welsh, K. M., Brock, C. H., Robertson, D. A., & Thrailkill, L. D. (2020). Disciplinary literacy in a 2nd grade classroom: A science inquiry unit. *The Reading Teacher, 73*(6), 723–734.

Wiggins, G. (2009). Real-world writing: Making purpose and audience matter. *English Journal, 98*(5), 29–37.

Wyoming House Bill HB0076 (2017). American Indian education program. Retrieved from *https://wyoleg.gov/2017/Introduced/HB0076.pdf.*

Yore, L., Bisanz, G., & Hand, B. M. (2003). Examining the literacy component of science literacy: 25 years of language and science research. *International Journal of Science Education, 25*(6), 689–725.

Zembal-Saul, C. (2009). Learning to teach elementary school science as argument. *Science Education, 93*(4), 687–719.

Zygouris-Coe, V. (2012). Disciplinary literacy and the Common Core State Standards. *Topics in Language Disorders, 32*(1), 35–50.

CHILDREN'S LITERATURE

Braun, S. (2009). *On our way home.* London: Boser Books.

14

Arranging for Reading Engagement

Gay Ivey and Erika Gray

Imagine two classroom scenarios. In the first, fifth grader Yesenia slams shut her copy of *Love Like Sky* (Youngblood, 2018) and lets out a heavy sigh during a free reading period, prompting nearby classmates to look up from their books. "Peaches is sick!" Yesenia announces. Having gotten her friends' attention, Yesenia explains that the main character's younger sister is ill, and she flips back through the book to show them places that offered clues that had been nagging at her for a few chapters. Her classmate Megan asks to see the cover of the book, and promptly writes down the title and author in a notebook where she keeps a list of books she wants to read. Quentin asks if Peaches has an incurable disease, and Yesenia responds that she will try to figure that out in the next chapter. Latrice mentions that her younger cousin is struggling with a breathing problem, and for the next 5 minutes or so, the group talks about others they know who have health problems, both in real life, and in fiction they have read this year in school.

In a second scenario, first grader Felix is making a book about four-wheelers, and each of the six pages completed so far includes both pictures and words. He is working on a page that features a green vehicle trailed by squiggly lines that appear to indicate motion. With much deliberation, he writes underneath,

KN 4YELS KO FIS. Emilio, his neighboring buddy, leans over and asks, "What does that say?" and Felix responds, "Green four wheelers go fastest." Without hesitation and with great enthusiasm, Emilio suggests, "You should draw us on it going fast through the woods!" Felix immediately begins to draw on the next page as he and Emilio think through the details in the illustrations, including the need for helmets. Felix announces that he will write, "Me and Emilio are riding in the woods." For help with spelling Emilio's name, he consults a sticker on the corner of Emilio's desk where their teacher has printed his name. As he prepares to write "woods," he articulates the /w/ sound, and begins to write *y*, as he wrote previously in his spelling of "four-wheelers," as many emergent readers and writers might do (Morris & Templeton, 1999; Richgels, 1995). Noticing Felix's confusion, Emilio offers, "It starts with a *w*, like Will's name [a classmate], and like *web*," pointing to the *w* accompanied by a picture of a spiderweb on the classroom alphabet/sound chart. Felix gladly accepts the help and adds, "And like *we*, like, 'We are fastest.' I'm gonna write that next." He begins his next sentence with *WE*.

There are important observations to make about these two episodes. The children are motivated to read and write. They are strategic, and they are intentional. They are emotional and animated. They are learning with and from each other. In a nutshell, these children are *engaged* as readers/writers, and they participate in vigorous, student-centered classrooms. The notion of *engagement* becomes even clearer if you contrast these scenarios from those in which children are motivated only to get their literacy assignments finished; when they give up in the face of confusion or difficulty in reading and writing; when their emotions around literacy center on frustration, boredom, anger, or embarrassment; or where they complete assignments in silence and solitude.

You might also notice that no teacher is mentioned in either of these scenarios. Without a doubt, though, a thoughtful, expert teacher has worked to make this kind of engagement possible. Yet clearly, learning is maximized when students have taken up the activities for themselves. How do teachers make this happen? In this chapter, we will make the case for why a focus on engagement with texts and among students is a vital principle of classrooms that expand and accelerate literacy learning, offer some theories about what creates the phenomenon of highly motivated and meaningful literate activity, and describe what teachers can do to arrange for deep engagement and considerable amounts of reading.

Why Are These Principles
of Effective Classroom Environments?

Why should we want an instructional environment in which students are engaged as readers and writers, like Yesenia and Felix and their class-mates, rather than merely compliant? In general, school engagement is consistently associated with positive academic and personal development (Fredricks, Blumenfeld, & Paris, 2004), and engaged reading, specifically, is associated with higher reading achievement and with reducing aca-demic disparities between groups of students (Guthrie, Wigfield, & You, 2012). The list of particular consequences of literacy engagement on chil-dren's development is extensive. For starters, because engagement is likely to contribute to the volume and breadth of reading children accomplish (Ivey & Johnston, 2013), they are also likely to experience what research suggests are additional benefits of extensive contextual reading, includ-ing expanding vocabulary (Duff, Tomblin, & Catts, 2015; Nagy, Ander-son, & Herman, 1987) and improving reading fluency (Allington, 2014).

When students are emotionally and intellectually invested in reading, they are also more likely to persist in their reading and to execute cogni-tive strategies in the face of difficulty (Guthrie et al., 2012). Because high interest in text mitigates the potential negative effects of text difficulty (Fulmer, D'Mello, Strain, & Graesser, 2015; Fulmer & Frijters, 2011), this persistence extends to complex texts that they find personally or socially significant.

Recently, Johnston (2019) theorized an important relationship between literacy engagement and the development of executive function, that is, the ability to manage working memory, cognitive flexibility, and self-control. Juggling and challenging the body's resources simultaneously, Johnston argued, requires activity that is goal oriented, and engagement is similarly goal oriented. Thus, children reading and writing what they care about, and in the process, managing changing cognitive and emo-tional demands of the activity, will expand their executive function. Why would we worry about this possibility? Johnston pointed out research indi-cating that kindergartners with better executive function in the spring of kindergarten also had higher levels of literacy and vocabulary growth, regardless of their beginning-of-year achievement (Blair & Razza, 2007).

If we consider literacy engagement to encompass not only reader–text interactions or time spent actually reading or writing print but also how the children might continue to think about what they read and write when they are away from the text, before, during, and after reading, as well as conversations they have about what they read and write, we real-ize even more benefits. As observed in scenarios we used to open this chapter, when students participate in meaningful literacy tasks, they often recruit each other for conversation or consultation about interesting or puzzling encounters with text. This conversation and problem solving is not a distraction from literacy learning but perhaps the thread that ties it together. Johnston (2019) has argued that classroom talk mediates children's literacy development. Indeed, when children think together, they can experience improvements in comprehension (Rojas-Drummond, Mazón, Littleton, & Veléz, 2014), expressive language and public speaking (Trickey & Topping, 2004), reasoning ability (Mercer, Wegerif, & Dawes, 1999), and ability to provide reasons and evidence (Latawiec, Anderson, Shufeng, & Kim, 2016), to name just a few academic consequences.

These implications of engagement—the development of competence in reading and vocabulary, improvements in executive function, and expansion of classroom talk, with its associated benefits—are no doubt appealing as potential academic goals. But engagement not only offers improvements in reading and writing, it also touches the breadth of human development in positive ways (Ivey & Johnston, 2013). For instance, important emotional and relational work can happen in the context of engaged reading of narratives. When readers encounter texts that matter to them, they enter the social worlds of the narratives, take up the perspectives of characters and experience their emotional lives, and weigh their moral decisions. There is evidence that this is indeed the case for adult readers (Bal & Veltkamp, 2013; Kaufman & Libby, 2012), young children (Lysaker, 2019), and adolescents (Ivey & Johnston, 2013, 2015).

These engagements with the minds of characters and with each other, through the compulsion to talk through and about meaningful texts, leads to an expansion of the social imagination (Johnston, 2012), what some might refer to as theory of mind. Turning back to academic consequences, theory of mind has been shown to explain positive differences in reading comprehension (Atkinson, Slade, Powell, & Levy, 2017; Guajardo & Cartwright, 2016). But also, children with strong social imaginations have more positive social skills (Watson, Nixon, Wilson, & Capage, 1999), healthier and more plentiful positive relationships (Caputi, Lecce, Pagnin, & Banerjee, 2012), and better self-regulation (Carlson, Claxton, & Moses, 2015).

It is likely this latter set of consequences of engagement, those dealing with the personal and social dimensions of human development, is most significant to children. When children are engaged, it is unlikely that their priority is "getting better" as reading and writers; rather, they are trying to take control of their personal and social lives both in and out of school (Ivey, 2019). Classrooms prioritizing engaged reading, for instance, had students that reported making friends over books, reading to understand people unlike them, using conversations about books to ease tensions with family members, and reading to regulate their own emotions and behavior (Ivey & Johnston, 2013, 2015).

What is more, though, is that because they were interested in the social aspects of engagement, they assumed the responsibility of getting other students engaged, served as resources to each other to solve problems around literacy, and helped to shape the curriculum of their English class. In other words, engagement helps to distribute teaching across the classroom. Circling back to Yesenia, Felix, and classmates from the beginning of the chapter, we pointed out that no teacher is mentioned in either scenario, and yet the children appear to be fully engaged, and teaching and supporting each other. In the next section, we suggest theoretical and practical tools teachers can use to create a fertile context for the cognitive, social, emotional, and agentive engagement and consequences we have described here.

What Does This Principle Look Like Being Flexibly Applied in the Classroom?

Teachers play a crucial role in cultivating a classroom environment in which students are engaged. Once we understand the theories that make engagement likely, we can intentionally arrange for it. Self-determination theory, which is key to understanding engagement, suggests that human motivation requires a sense of autonomy, competence, and relatedness (Ryan & Deci, 2000). Autonomy refers to self-direction and following your own purposes (see Chapter 16). Student choice, particularly when the choices available are relevant to children, contributes to a sense of autonomy. But even when good choices are provided, teachers can inadvertently undermine autonomy by interfering with, monitoring, testing, and attaching assignments to student learning (Assor, Kaplan, & Roth, 2002). A sense of competence is acquired when a person feels successful. Like self-efficacy (Bandura, 1986), a sense of competence is most likely experienced within student-centered tasks and with feedback that emphasizes the links between student effort and success (McCabe, 2006). A sense of relatedness is felt when individuals interact and connect meaningfully with others. According to self-determination theory, when all three of these needs—autonomy, competence, and relatedness—are met, students are more likely to be intrinsically motivated.

We typically consider motivation to engage as an individual phenomenon, but teachers can maximize engagement when we conceptualize it as a social phenomenon, fueled by the social activity of the classroom. For instance, meaningful classroom conversation and feeling understood and appreciated by others contributes to a sense of autonomy, competence, and relatedness (Reis, Sheldon, Gable, Roscoe, & Ryan, 2000), so regular opportunities for student-generated talk would expand engagement. Likewise, although the development of interest is often viewed as a solo enterprise, interests often grow out of social influences, such as participation with friends or family in activities that satisfy the need for belonging, vicariously through the interest of others, or through shared cultural values (Bergin, 2016). Theoretically, then, we might optimize engagement not by focusing on one student at a time, per se, but instead by orchestrating social activity so that students are influencing each other in positive ways.

We now turn to two instructional activities in which these theories might be leveraged to support engagement: teacher read-alouds and self-selected reading periods. Woven into and inseparable from each activity is meaningful classroom talk. We focus on student-centered teacher read-alouds and self-selected reading because they are open literacy opportunities in which participation is not limited by level of competence or prior experience, where there is no right or wrong answer, where a range of strategies can be employed, and where there is no ceiling to what can be learned.

Engaging through Teacher Read-Alouds

Teacher read-alouds provide a robust context for inviting children into conversation in which they can think through texts together, problem-solve textual complexity in the open and learn about each other. Although read-alouds are routine in some classrooms, and are frequently used to gear student attention to a particular topic or to teach strategies for comprehension, student engagement in read-alouds will be heightened when children get to determine the course of the conversation and when the goal is not merely to get to the "right" answer or main idea about the text. What does this look like? Consider the following example.

As third-grade teacher Mr. Avery was reading *The Magic Finger* (Dahl, 1999) to his class, he paused along the way and ceded to students the opportunity to talk when events in the book shocked or confused them. For instance, when the main character used her special power to turn her family into geese, the students spontaneously shared their reactions, some delighting and some disagreeing with the character's decision to force her family to experience how it felt to be hunted. The point of allowing the conversation was not to come to agreement, necessarily, but to allow students to share and access a range of perspectives on the matter, with no expectation of a right answer. It is not surprising that oftentimes the parts of stories that catch students' attention and that they want to discuss are those offering ethical dilemmas and questions around the mental activity of the characters. Not coincidentally, as Mr. Avery approached the end of the book, several students decided to read it again on their own. Others selected different books by Dahl that he had highlighted in book talks, anticipating that possibility, and a third group of students decided to read a biography about Roald Dahl.

Earlier in this chapter we referred to research indicating that when students are engaged as readers, they are more likely to execute cognitive strategies when facing difficulty and to persist even in complex texts. In other words, they will do whatever it takes to understand because they want to make sense for their own purposes. The same happens in engaging read-alouds that are supportive of students' sense of autonomy, competence, and relatedness. But in these contexts, the dilemmas are shared openly and become problems for the class to solve. Fourth graders listening to their teacher read *Crenshaw* (Applegate, 2015) were introduced early in the book to the title character, an imaginary large cat who appears in the narrator's life seemingly in times of crisis. When Marcus asked, "Is that cat real?" his classmates were split between yes and no. This student-generated question provided the teacher an opportunity to ask the children how they would resolve their disagreement. Cheyenne suggested a strategy would be to reread and look for hints about whether Crenshaw was real or make-believe. As the teacher revisited several pages, students pointed out clues suggesting the narrator created Crenshaw:

> "He made up a name for him, because he didn't have a name."
> "He made him like purple jelly beans, he said, 'as much as I do.' "
> "He said Crenshaw was a blank slate and he could make him whatever he wanted."

Before moving on, the students mostly agreed that Crenshaw was imaginary, but several said they were still undecided. Although the teacher could have cleared this up the moment the question was asked, this would have not only prevented the children from thinking strategically together but also made it less likely that children would take up this way of problem solving in their own reading.

Engaging through Self-Selected Reading

Drop Everything and Read and sustained silent reading typically refer to the instructional times when students select their own book and read. We worry, though, that these labels limit our imagination for what self-selected reading times can mean for students and their literate development. When students are truly engaged in their reading, they are compelled to talk through and about texts (Ivey & Johnston, 2013). Remember

Yesenia and friends in the opening scenario? To demand silence as students read what matters to them is to limit comprehension, the consideration of multiple perspectives, and the inclination to read more, since students get ideas for their next book from hearing others talk about the characters and scenes that perplex or surprise them. Also, meaningful student-to-student talk is essential to supporting relatedness and sustaining engagement. As evidenced with Yesenia and her classmates, students are eager to enter a conversation and move the discussion beyond the author's words to uncover both personal and literary connections and points of uncertainty. When self-selected reading goes beyond "just letting kids read" and encourages connected talk, students engage at a deeper level because strong feelings of autonomy, competence, and relatedness are fostered.

So, how do teachers nurture such an environment during self-selected reading? Book talks, encouraging and providing space for student to student talk, and using open-ended prompts to expand student discussions are a few examples. For instance, in Mrs. David's fifth-grade class, book talks are used to whet students' appetites for books they may not find on their own. These may be books new to the classroom library, books she believes her students will find relevant and reflect their lives, or books with a common theme or shared author. During one talk about books with main characters trying to solve a dilemma, she read an excerpt from *Bud, Not Buddy* (Curtis, 1999). After Mrs. David read the part of the book in which the students learn Bud's friend, Bugs, got his name after having a cockroach stuck in his ear, Anthony and Michael gesture from across the room that they want to read that book together. This interaction was seen not as off-task behavior but as a result of being part of a class in which it was normal for students to recruit and guide book choice. After a book talk, Anthony and Michael recruited a third student to read the book with them. Again, since they are reading together, silent reading is not an accurate descriptor of this instructional time because the students may read together and should be encouraged to discuss their reactions to the text.

Along with increased social engagement with text, the responsibility for getting students "into" books is distributed. The teacher still has an important role in fostering open discussions during self-selected reading, but this is more of a supporting role instead of a lead role. We can return to Mrs. David to describe what this looks like in the classroom. As she was listening to her students read and talk about their books, she heard Anthony initiate a conversation about his disappointment with Bud's situation at the end of the book. With the intent of expanding the conversation, she asks questions like "How so?" or "Why might Curtis end his book in this way?" These questions keep the conversations among the students and do not interject her opinion. Finding these opportune moments to extend and expand student thinking and talk deepens comprehension and reflects a classroom in which literary experiences are collaborative and social interaction is crucial to engagement.

If students have grown accustomed to "silent" reading times and believe that talking while reading is against the rules, they might need to be nudged to interact. Mrs. David, providing copious amounts of time for students to read is essential, but so is the time students spend thinking and discussing the text. Prioritizing extended opportunities to read and talk about text increases the likelihood students will choose to read voluntarily, seek friends that also enjoy reading, and more readily engage in classroom instruction on the text (Guthrie, Wigfield, Metsala, & Cox, 1999; Stanovich, 2008).

There are several strategies to encourage student–student conversation. For instance, teachers who routinely confer with individual students during self-selected reading might decide to invite a third student to listen in on a conference and then recruit that student's perspectives on what they heard by simply asking, "What are you thinking?" As the teacher walks away, the two students are likely not only to continue to chat but also to chat again on another occasion because of this precedent. A second strategy is to nudge students who have just finished a book to find someone in the class who might like to read that book and share it immediately with that student. Third, teachers might consider setting aside a short time at the end of each reading period to allow any student to say something about their book that is unsettling or interesting. This simple, but powerful strategy helps students to become more aware and interested in the reading experiences of their classmates. The point of all of this is to intentionally turn students toward each other.

Conclusion

Teachers have an essential role in fostering an engaged community of readers that is rich with reading, writing, and student-initiated talk. For instance, teachers can expand their purposes for reading aloud to include exposing students to a variety of genres. Additional engagement is fostered by advertising new text formats, topics, and authors that beg students to become emotionally and intellectually invested. Then, students can "shop" for books in the classroom library. Additionally, teachers can invite students to write and share their own books (see Ray & Cleaveland, 2018). By normalizing student-driven literacy experiences that engage students in peer discussions before, during, and after reading books of their choice, teachers make it more likely that students will be more intrinsically and socially motivated.

REFERENCES

Allington, R. L. (2014). How reading volume affects both reading fluency and reading achievement. *International Electronic Journal of Elementary Education, 7*(1), 95–104.

Assor, A., Kaplan, H., & Roth, G. (2002). Choice is good, but relevance is excellent: Autonomy-enhancing and suppressing teacher behaviours predicting students' engagement in schoolwork. *British Journal of Educational Psychology, 72,* 261–278.

Atkinson, L., Slade, L., Powell, D., & Levy, J. P. (2017). Theory of mind in emerging reading comprehension: A longitudinal study of early indirect and direct effects. *Journal of Experimental Child Psychology, 164,* 225–238.

Bal, P. M., & Veltkamp, M. (2013). How does fiction reading influence empathy?: An experimental investigation on the role of emotional transportation. *PLOS ONE, 8*(1), e55341.

Bandura, A. (1986). The explanatory and predictive scope of self-efficacy theory. *Journal of Clinical and Social Psychology, 4,* 359–373.

Bergin, D. A. (2016). Social influences on interest. *Educational Psychologist, 51,* 7–22.

Blair, C., & Razza, R. P. (2007). Relating effortful control, executive function, and false belief understanding to emerging math and literacy ability in kindergarten. *Child Development, 78,* 647–663.

Caputi, M., Lecce, S., Pagnin, A., & Banerjee, R. (2012). Longitudinal effects of theory of mind on later peer relations: The role of prosocial behavior. *Developmental Psychology, 48,* 257–270.

Carlson, S. M., Claxton, L. J., & Moses, L. J. (2015). The relation between executive function and theory of mind is more than skin deep. *Journal of Cognition and Development, 16,* 186–197.

Duff, D., Tomblin, J. B., & Catts, H. (2015). The influence of reading and vocabulary growth: A case for a Matthew effect. *Journal of Speech, Language, and Hearing Research, 58,* 853–864.

Guajardo, N. R., & Cartwright, K. B. (2016). The contribution of theory of mind, counterfactual reasoning, and executive function to pre-readers' language comprehension and later reading awareness and comprehension in elementary school. *Journal of Experimental Child Psychology, 144,* 27–45.

Guthrie, J. T., Wigfield, A., Metsala, J. L., & Cox, K. E. (1999). Motivational and cognitive predictors of text comprehension and reading amount. *Scientific Studies of Reading, 3*(3), 231–256.

Guthrie, J. T., Wigfield, A., & You, W. (2012). Instructional contexts for engagement and achievement in reading. In S. Christenson, C. Wylie, & A. Reschly (Eds.), *Handbook of research on student engagement* (pp. 675–694). New York: Springer.

Fredricks, J. A., Blumenfeld, P. C., & Paris, A. H. (2004). School engagement: Potential of the concept, state of the evidence. *Review of Educational Research, 74,* 59–109.

Fulmer, S. M., D'Mello, S. K., Strain, A., & Graesser, A. C. (2015). Interest-based text preference moderates the effect of text difficulty on engagement and learning. *Contemporary Educational Psychology, 41,* 98–110.

Fulmer, S. M., & Frijters, J. C. (2011). Motivation during an excessively challenging reading task: The buffering role of relative topic interest. *Journal of Experimental Education, 79,* 185–208.

Ivey, G. (2019). Engaging possibilities: Reinvigorating the call for research on reading. *Literacy Research: Theory, Method, and Practice, 68,* 25–44.

Ivey, G., & Johnston, P. H. (2013). Engagement with young adult literature: Outcomes and processes. *Reading Research Quarterly, 48*(3), 255–275.

Ivey, G., & Johnston, P. H. (2015). Engaged reading as a collaborative transformative practice. *Journal of Literacy Research, 47*(3), 297–327.

Johnston, P. H. (2012). *Opening minds: Using language to change lives.* Portland, ME: Stenhouse.

Johnston, P. H. (2019). Talking children into literacy: Once more, with feeling. *Literacy Research: Theory, Method, and Practice, 68,* 64–85.

Kaufman, G. F., & Libby, L. K. (2012). Changing beliefs and behavior through experience-taking. *Journal of Personality and Social Psychology, 103*(1), 1–19.

Latawiec, B. M., Anderson, R. C., Shufeng, M., & Kim, N.-J. (2016). Influence of collaborative reasoning discussions on metadiscourse in children's essays. *Text and Talk, 36,* 23–46.

Lysaker, J. T. (2019). *Before words: Wordless picture books and the development of reading in young children.* New York: Teachers College Press.

McCabe, P. P. (2006). Convincing students they can learn to read: Crafting self-efficacy prompts. *The Clearing House: A Journal of Educational Strategies, 76*(6), 252–257.

Mercer, N., Wegerif, R., & Dawes, L. (1999). Children's talk and the development of reasoning in the classroom. *British Educational Research Journal, 25*(1), 95–111.

Morris, D., & Templeton, S. (1999). Questions teachers ask about spelling. *Reading Research Quarterly, 34*(1), 102–112.

Nagy, W., Anderson, R., & Herman, P. (1987). Learning word meanings from context during normal reading. *American Educational Research Journal, 24*(2), 237–270.

Ray, K. W., & Cleaveland, L. (2018). *A teacher's guide to getting started with beginning writers.* Portsmouth, NH: Heinemann.

Reis, H. T., Sheldon, K. M., Gable, S. L., Roscoe, J., & Ryan, R. M. (2000). Daily well-being: The role of autonomy, competence, and relatedness. *Personality and Social Psychology Bulletin, 26*(4), 419–435.

Richgels, D. (1995). Invented spelling ability and printed word learning in kindergarten. *Reading Research Quarterly, 30*(1), 96–109.

Rojas-Drummond, S., Mazón, N., Littleton, K., & Veléz, M. (2014). Developing reading comprehension through collaborative learning. *Journal of Research in Reading, 37,* 138–158.

Ryan, R. M., & Deci, E. L. (2000). Self-determination theory and the facilitation of intrinsic motivation, social development, and well-being. *American Psychologist, 55,* 68–78.

Stanovich, K. E. (2008). Matthew effects in reading: Some consequences of individual differences in the acquisition of literacy. *Journal of Education, 189*(1/2), 23–55.

Trickey, S., & Topping, K. J. (2004). Philosophy for children: A systematic review. *Research Papers in Education, 19*(3), 365–380.

Watson, A. C., Nixon, C. L., Wilson, A., & Capage, L. (1999). Social interaction skills and theory of mind in young children. *Developmental Psychology, 35,* 386–391.

CHILDREN'S LITERATURE

Applegate, K. (2015). *Crenshaw.* New York: Feiwel and Friends.

Curtis, C. P. (1999). *Bud, not buddy.* New York: Delacorte Press.

Dahl, R. (1999). *The magic finger* (4th ed.). New York: Scholastic.

Youngblood, L. C. (2018). *Love like sky.* New York: Disney.

15

Authentic, Challenging Tasks

Roya Qualls Scales

What are real-world purposes for literacy, and how do those purposes compare to literacy instruction in schools? First, consider everything you read and everything you wrote in the past 24 hours. Perhaps you read newspapers, books, magazines, posts on social media, your favorite blog, mail (e-mail and USPS), recipes, and nutrition labels. Perhaps you wrote a response to a post on social media or wrote your own posts. Maybe you sent a birthday card to a friend, jotted a to-do list, made a grocery list, and sent e-mails. Next, think about the focus of literacy instruction in schools.

How are we teaching students to be literate, and what messages are we sending them about the real-world purposes of literacy through our assigned tasks? Are we implicitly teaching students that school is a place to conquer tests and has no relevancy to their lives beyond school? Or are we providing students with opportunities to connect their literacy learning with real issues, which requires authentic, challenging tasks? If we strive to teach literacy tapping into students' interests and meaning-ful issues, then we explicitly make connections to learning for authentic purposes and we demonstrate how literacy is a tool for lifelong learning. This chapter explains what is meant by authentic, challenging tasks and explores how such tasks are part of effective literacy instruction and how they are used in the classroom.

What Are Authentic, Challenging Tasks?

In this section, I will first ask you to consider the meaning of *tasks* and reflect on what kinds of tasks you remember from your K–12 literacy experiences. Then we will think about what kinds of literacy tasks are considered authentic and challenging. For the purpose of this chapter, I define tasks as tangible work products.

What does the word *task* mean to you? Maybe you're thinking about your to-do list of items you need to complete. Let's think about what is meant by tasks in a school setting. Doyle (1983) referred to the work students are asked to do in school as academic tasks. Academic tasks were categorized as memorization (recall), procedural (drill and practice using routines), understanding (application), and stating opinions (Doyle, 1983). Think back to when you were a K–12 student. What kinds of tasks do you remember completing as a student? Do you remember literacy tasks such as completing worksheets, writing essays, developing book reports, and responding to literature? Maybe you remember learning how to write poetry, such as acrostics and haikus. Perhaps you remember times when you got to choose what you wanted to write in your journal. Maybe you remember publishing your writing.

Did you have strong feelings about different kinds of literacy tasks you were asked to do? Which literacy tasks did you dread? Why? Which literacy tasks did you enjoy? Why? It's important to remember because I don't want you to be the teacher who assigns seemingly irrelevant tasks just like the ones you dreaded as a student. I remember frequently wondering, "What is the point of this? How will I use this in real life?" It's also important to remember the ones you liked so you can capture the essence of what made them (and school) enjoyable. As a teacher, one of your goals may be to get your students to love learning. If you're having difficulty remembering the kinds of literacy tasks you were asked to do as a student, then perhaps my own journey will help you.

My mom kept my schoolwork from kindergarten through third grade. Mom recently gave me boxes containing all that work, and I was astounded by the sheer number of worksheets I completed. While I realize that some worksheets can promote higher-order thinking, these did not. The worksheets that my 6-year-old self completed required skills such as drawing a line from the CH to the chipmunk, finishing dot-to-dots to demonstrate my knowledge of alphabetical order, coloring sheets that indicated my knowledge of how to read the color words, and circling the singular or plural noun to show which one belonged in the sentence. I know my mom didn't keep everything. The workbooks weren't in there. The book reports weren't in there either. I remember sitting at the kitchen table crying about writing those book reports every week in third grade.

While I have always loved reading, my third-grade homeroom teacher required each student to stand in front of the class every week and read our one-page (handwritten) book reports aloud. I absolutely dreaded those book reports because I was painfully shy and teased about my accent (southeast Texas paired with upstate South Carolina and relocated to rural piedmont North Carolina).

While I suffered through the book reports, one of my most favorite memories about literacy tasks was also from third grade. I was surprised that my mom didn't keep the play based on the book *A Wrinkle in Time* (L'Engle, 1962) I wrote with my four classmates in our academically gifted class. Once we finished writing the play, we created costumes and scenery for it, memorized our roles, practiced, and invited the school to our production. Miss Akers taught my academically gifted class. She left a lasting impression on my view of what school could be. School could be *enjoyable*. Because of Miss Akers, I recognized myself as a good writer who was wildly creative, and I loved attending her class because I knew I was learning about things that were important.

The experiences I shared about my box of tasks can help explain what is meant by authentic, challenging tasks. Building on Doyle's research, Blumenfeld and colleagues (1987) explored how procedures, requirements, and social aspects of tasks influenced students' motivation to complete the work. Further research (Miller, 2003; Miller & Meece, 1999; Parsons & Scales, 2013; Turner, 1995) considered how different types of tasks required higher or lower levels of thought, which related to students' motivation for learning and academic performance. You can tell from my descriptions which tasks required lower levels of thought. One example of that is drawing a line from the CH to the chipmunk. Another example is the dot-to-dot worksheet. In 2008, Parsons developed a rubric (see Figure 15.1) that was based on research about academic tasks and student engagement (Duke, Purcell-Gates, Hall, & Tower, 2007; Miller & Meece, 1999; Turner, 1995) and could be used to rate the openness of tasks.

Parsons's (2008) rubric featured five categories for rating tasks: authenticity, collaboration, challenge, student directed, and sustained. *Authenticity* refers to how closely the task mimics activities we complete in our everyday lives beyond school. For example, writing a letter to my grandmother is something I do in real life, but drawing a line from the CH to the chipmunk is something I would be asked to do only in school. *Collaboration* refers to working alone or working with others on the task. For example, writing and performing the play I wrote with my classmates required extensive collaboration, whereas completing the weekly book report was a solo activity. *Challenge* refers to how much thinking is involved in the completed product, based on the amount of writing is involved. That could range from letter(s) or word(s) to paragraphs. The

Rubric for Rating Openness of Tasks

Describe the task and its product:

Authenticity (Duke, Purcell-Gates, Hall, & Tower, 2007)

1 – The task is limited to tasks that are completed primarily in school.

2 – The task mimics outside-of-school tasks but has features of school-based activities.

3 – The task closely replicates tasks completed in day-to-day lives outside of school.

Collaboration

1 – Students work alone on the task.

2 – Students collaborate minimally in the task.

3 – Students collaborate throughout the task.

Challenge

1 – The task requires letter- or word-level writing.

2 – The task requires sentence-level writing.

3 – The task requires paragraph-level writing.

Student Directed

1 – The students have no input on the task.

2 – The students have input, but the choices have minimal influence on the task.

3 – Students have input into many substantial aspects of the task.

Sustained

1 – The task takes place within one sitting.

2 – The task takes place within one or two days.

3 – The task spans three or more days.

FIGURE 15.1. Parsons's rubric for rating openness of tasks. Adapted by permission from Parsons (2008). Copyright © 2008 International Literacy Association.

worksheet where I was required to circle if a singular or plural noun fit in the sentence required lower levels of markings on the paper, whereas the book reports and the play required more extensive writing. *Student directed* refers to how much choice students have in determining the task itself. Sadly, I had little say in the worksheets I was required to complete because I was told to do them. By contrast, the play I wrote and performed with my classmates was completely driven by students and involved little input from the teacher. What about the book reports? The only choice I had was which book I would read. The book report format was nonnegotiable. *Sustained* refers to how much time the task requires for completion, ranging from one sitting to multiple days. The coloring worksheet was completed in a single sitting, perhaps along with the ABC dot-to-dot sheet. By contrast, the play required multiple days.

Within each category of Parsons's (2008) rubric, a task could be rated as 1, 2, or 3, depending on the amount of thought required. Totaling the scores across categories provides an overall score that reveals the openness of the task. Ratings of 12–15 mean that it is an open task, ratings of 9–11 are moderately open tasks, and ratings of 5–8 are closed tasks. The openness level corresponds with how the task mimics what we do in real life (authenticity) and the level of thinking students are required to do in completing the task (challenge). While I believe there is a need to have a variety of task types in school, I urge you to think carefully about what kinds of tasks you use with your students and consider implementing more authentic, challenging tasks. Let's explore some examples together.

Look at the rubric in Figure 15.1 and think about how the worksheet where I drew a line from the CH to the chipmunk would be rated. For authenticity, it's a score of 1 because that's a task I completed only in school. Collaboration is 1 because it was just me drawing that line. Challenge has to be a 1 because there isn't a rating of 0. Student directed is rated as 1 because I was required to do the worksheet without choices. Sustained is rated as 1 because I can't imagine this task took longer than a couple of minutes. The total across those categories for this worksheet is 5, which means the worksheet where I drew a line from the CH to the chipmunk was rated as a closed task. Closed tasks require little thought, and they do not mimic real life beyond school. That means closed tasks lack authenticity.

Now let's think about how we would rate the weekly book reports. For authenticity, I could make a case for 2 or 3. Because the homeroom teacher required a specific format for the handwritten report, I'm rating it as a 2. The collaboration rating is 1 because the book reports were written by individuals. Challenge is rated as a 3 because the book report had to be at least one handwritten page. For student directed, I'm sticking with a rating of 2 because the only real choice I had was which book I would read. I'm not sure how many days it took me to read the books and I know the reports took forever to write, so I'll go with a rating of 3 for sustained. The total rating for the book report is 10, which means it's considered a moderately open task. Moderately open means the task requires thought and somewhat mimics life beyond school. As an avid reader, I'm always telling my friends, colleagues, and students about books I loved and why I enjoyed reading them, and I try to convince them to read those same books so we'll have a shared experience.

I bet you can independently use the rubric to rate the challenge level of that task requiring my classmates and me to write and perform.

Authenticity could be a 3 because in the real world, some writers create plays, TV shows, and movies based on novels. Collaboration is definitely a 3 because we worked together throughout the entire process. Challenge is rated as a 3 because of the amount of writing and revising involved. Student directed is rated as 3 because our teacher served only as a guide and we (the students) were the decision makers. Sustained is also rated as 3 because this task took more than a few days. The total rating for the play is 15, which means it's considered an open task. Open means the task requires a great deal of thought (challenging) and closely mimics life beyond school (authentic). This literacy task was authentic, challenging, and relates to my life today. My job requires creative thinking, collaborating with others to pursue a common goal, and writing for publication. I also have a deep appreciation for theater.

Most of the teachers and teacher candidates I work with say they want to make learning fun and they want their students to apply learning in meaningful ways. What they mean to say is that they want to incorporate authentic, challenging literacy tasks in their classrooms so their students will see the purpose of learning while enjoying learning, and understand how learning connects to the world beyond school. That's what effective literacy teachers do.

Why Are Authentic, Challenging Tasks Considered a Principle of Effective Literacy Instruction?

Effective teachers strive to use authentic, challenging tasks in their literacy instruction. Indeed, effective literacy teachers build opportunities for students' learning that invite students' active participation in the classroom community, plan instruction and tasks that promote higher levels of thinking, and engage students in inquiry-based learning that taps into students' interests (Guthrie & Barber, 2019; Malloy, Marinak, & Gambrell, 2019). Inviting students' active participation in the classroom community first requires your commitment to building that community of learners. Building a classroom community means you will need to get to know your students as individuals who have hobbies, interests, and lives beyond school.

How can you get to know your students? Think beyond the person-of-the-week activity. Talk with your students throughout the day, invite them to write about their favorite activities and things they want to learn about, and communicate with families to see what they can share about their children's interests. Chances are, groups of students will have similar interests. That will help you plan engaging literacy instruction and accompanying tasks. Additionally, knowing your students will help you choose books for your classroom library because you want students to choose to read. Your students may be obsessed with reading about tsunamis, volcanoes, unsolved mysteries (Bermuda Triangle, Bigfoot, Flight MH370, Loch Ness monster, the Lost Colony), and the *Titanic*. Do you remember being assigned specific novels to read? How does that compare to when you had choices in your reading materials? Beyond the school walls, we make choices about what we read.

While you will have a set curriculum to teach, literacy standards provide you with which skills and strategies to teach. Literacy standards do not tell you *how* to teach. As the teacher, it is up to you to plan and implement engaging instruction that taps into your students' interests. We know from research that students in Finland score among the highest on international comparisons of achievement. When talking with my teacher colleagues in Finland, they shared that their job is not to get students to memorize information for tests. Instead, their purpose for teaching is to teach students how to learn.

The purpose of your teaching is important to consider. The teachers and teacher candidates I work with tell me they want their students to be lifelong learners. Empowering your students to be lifelong learners is an admirable goal that requires a kind of teaching that is more than getting students to pass tests. It requires you to use an inquiry-based learning approach. What does that really look like in everyday classroom instruction? When visiting schools in Finland, I observed inquiry-based learning on topics from the math, science, and social studies curricula and students' interests. This resulted in active learning that was engaging because it was student centered. Engaging instruction requires interaction, which means the students need to have time for explorations with you and with each other as they apply their learning.

Keep in mind that literacy is considered a tool for learning, regardless of the content area. Literacy doesn't happen in a vacuum—it requires a context. Most classrooms have a schedule posted that tells what time each subject is taught during the day. By compartmentalizing instruction in this way, we send the message that literacy instruction occurs only during the literacy block, such as from 9:00 to 10:30. If you are required to post such a schedule, be sure to explain to your students that literacy really happens throughout the school day and in life beyond school.

Incorporating students' interests into your instruction motivates them to want to learn because you're making it relevant. That means the learning experience is authentic. Using an inquiry approach means students design a plan for how they investigate the topic and demonstrate their learning. That means the learning experience (including the task) is challenging. You may be wondering what this looks like in a real class-room. Here's an example from when I taught kindergarten.

One of the kindergarten curriculum units was about nutrition and making healthy food choices. As I was preparing that unit, the PTA board announced that chocolate milk would be removed from the caf-eteria because they believed it had too much sugar. At that time, milk options in our cafeteria included chocolate, strawberry, whole milk, 2% milk, and skim milk. My kindergartners were devastated because they vastly preferred chocolate milk. I told them that they should stop crying and think about how they could take action to save the chocolate milk. They were highly motivated to do this, so we formulated a plan. Even my students who brought their own lunches and never drank milk in the cafeteria were invested. First, students had to learn how to find out about sugar content in the different kinds of milk in the cafeteria. I taught them how to read the nutrition labels and compare the sugar content. Surpris-ingly, chocolate milk wasn't the worst offender because it was chocolate-flavored skim milk!

Next, students had to consider how they wanted to share their find-ings and identify their audience. This required an understanding of how to present facts while persuading the audience. We read several picture books as mentor texts to see how this worked. Students decided to work in small groups to address the issue for a variety of audiences. One group created posters about how much sugar was in each kind of milk to hang in the cafeteria and in the hallways so students from across the school would be aware and make informed choices. That group also created a peti-tion for students across the school to sign, saying they wanted to save the chocolate milk. Another group wrote a persuasive letter to the PTA board that made a case for why chocolate milk should remain as an option in the cafeteria. Every student in the class signed that letter. The third group created a presentation to inform the principal and assistant principal of the issue, including the findings from examining nutrition labels, and appealed to their assistance with saving the chocolate milk.

While this learning experience took about a month, my kindergart-ners were highly motivated to engage in literacy experiences that would result in their saving the chocolate milk. Literacy tasks involved were authentic, challenging, and what Parsons's (2008) rubric described as open and moderately open. More important, they recognized that literacy was for a larger purpose. Literacy was a powerful tool that not only gave them a voice but also helped get their message across to others. Literacy helped them take a stand for a cause that was dear to them. My kinder-gartners saved the chocolate milk while being empowered by learning how to learn, through authentic and challenging literacy experiences.

What Do Authentic, Challenging Tasks Look Like When Applied Flexibly in the Classroom?

You will not have every day of the school year filled with authentic, challenging tasks. There is a need for students to learn skills that are practiced through closed tasks, such as word study activities where students sort words by spelling patterns to better grasp understanding phonics (see Chapter 4 and Bear, Invernizzi, Templeton, & Johnston, 2020). My hope is that you strive to make connections from those closed tasks to the world so students see that what they learn in school is relevant.

If I asked you to go ahead and design a unit of instruction with literacy tasks that would rate as open or moderately open using Parsons's (2008) task rubric, you could do it. However, there's no guarantee that your future students would enjoy or be actively engaged in the unit or with those tasks because you don't know their interests. Every year your students are different, with different personalities, different interests, and different learning needs. That means you must have well-crafted plans that you can draw from each year, but you also need to be ready to be flexible in your approach. Flexibility is key for providing engaging literacy instruction that includes authentic, challenging tasks. If you want your students to learn, then you need to tap into their interests to get them engaged in authentic literacy opportunities (Guthrie & Barber, 2019). Sometimes this happens in unexpected ways. An example from my first year of teaching illustrates this point.

Bobby struggled with reading and writing in first grade, and he barely made it to second grade. At the start of the second-grade school year, Bobby told me that he hated school because he thought he wasn't a good student. This was a powerful message coming from a 7-year-old child. Perhaps you know someone like Bobby. I had a feeling that simply teaching lessons from the basal reader wasn't going to help Bobby, and I wanted to somehow make him want to learn.

I focused on getting to know all my students during the first couple of weeks, and I discovered that Bobby was fascinated with space and rocks. I stocked my bookshelves with as many library books from the school and public library as I could find about the topics my students loved: dinosaurs, *Titanic,* space, rocks, horses, trains, oceans, and so on. I bought books at yard sales and thrift shops. I didn't know the exact reading levels of those books, and I didn't care. The books featured colorful pictures, and some were thick and others were thin. Of course, I taught students strategies for improving their reading, but I did that through their choices of books. Choices in what they read, based on their interests, meant students wanted to read and they were actively engaged with their reading. It wasn't about counting pages they had to read or setting a timer to read a certain number of minutes each day or completing a reading log each day. My second graders were excited to talk about their books because they genuinely wanted to read them and talk about them.

My students had choices in how they represented their understandings of what they read. I provided a menu of authentic, challenging literacy tasks students could pursue in class that would help them represent their learning. Students also had an option of creating their own literacy tasks, with my approval. Task choices included creating posters to indicate their learning through a combination of words and pictures, making a center that would teach their classmates about their topic through an activity, developing a presentation with a hands-on component, and establishing a timeline for their topic to indicate what else was happening in the world.

One of my second graders loved poetry, so she asked if she could create a book of nonfiction poetry about her topic. Task choices I provided in the menu involved plenty of reading and writing, and students had class time to pursue their work. Students chose whether they worked in pairs or in small groups. Note that all tasks were designed and created in class, not for homework. Students provided me with a list of materials they needed, and I supplied them. Bobby blossomed in second grade because he was given a chance to explore his interests while building his reading and writing skills. Bobby became our class expert on space and rocks, and he branched out to learn more about gemstones. Eventually he became interested in volcanoes, the Ring of Fire, and plate tectonics. Most important, Bobby came to love school because he gained confidence in himself as a learner. Bobby recognized that he was smart. By the end of second grade, Bobby was reading at a mid-third-grade level.

Your students will be interested in things that may or may not appear in your school-provided materials for teaching literacy. For example, one of my students wanted to read only about NASCAR. The basal reader materials provided by my school would have required every student to read the same story and complete workbook pages for that story. The basal reader stories and format of tasks did not appeal to me, to the child who loved NASCAR, or to the other students. After 2 weeks of trying to follow along with the basal, I made the decision to stack the basal readers and the workbooks in a cabinet and leave them there. While your teaching situation may be different and you may be required to use the basal readers and other school-provided materials, I urge you to seek ways to incorporate your students' interests into the school day. Create time for exploring topics that appeal to students, and provide opportunities for them to engage in authentic, challenging tasks based on their interests. As a teacher, it's up to you to be flexible and make the most of these kinds of authentic learning opportunities.

Conclusion

One teacher told me that she liked to use worksheets to keep students busy and keep them quiet. What do you think students in that classroom think about the purpose of school? If you ever recognize yourself as that teacher, please think about why you wanted to be a teacher in the first place. Reconnect with your ultimate purpose for teaching. Perhaps your ultimate purpose is to make learning fun, to create lifelong learners, to teach students to be kind people, to somehow make the world a better place through your students, or maybe it's something else.

How we teach students to be literate and the messages we send them about the real-world purposes of literacy appear through our assigned literacy tasks. Are we implicitly teaching students that school is a place to conquer tests and has no relevancy to their lives beyond school? Or are we providing students with opportunities to connect their literacy learning with real issues, which requires authentic, challenging tasks? If we strive to teach literacy by tapping into students' interests and meaningful issues, then we explicitly make connections to learning for authentic purposes and we demonstrate how literacy is a tool for lifelong learning. This chapter explained what is meant by authentic, challenging tasks; explored how such tasks are part of effective literacy instruction; and shared how they are used in the classroom.

REFERENCES

Bear, D. R., Invernizzi, M., Templeton, S., & Johnston, F. (2020). *Words their way: Word study for phonics, vocabulary and spelling instruction* (7th ed.). New York: Pearson.

Blumenfeld, P. C., Mergendoller, J., & Swarthout, D. (1987). Task as a heuristic for understanding student learning and motivation. *Journal of Curriculum Studies, 19*(2), 135–148.

Doyle, W. (1983). Academic work. *Review of Educational Research, 53*(2), 159–199.

Duke, N. K., Purcell-Gates, V., Hall, L. A., & Tower, C. (2007). Authentic literacy activities for developing comprehension and writing. *The Reading Teacher, 60*(4), 344–355.

Guthrie, J. T., & Barber, A. T. (2019). Best practices for motivating students to read. In L. M. Morrow & L. B. Gambrell (Eds.), *Best practices in literacy instruction* (6th ed., pp. 52–72). New York: Guilford Press.

Malloy, J. A., Marinak, B. A., & Gambrell, L. B. (2019). Evidence-based best practices for developing literate communities. In L. M. Morrow & L. B. Gambrell (Eds.), *Best practices in literacy instruction* (6th ed., pp. 3–26). New York: Guilford Press.

Miller, S. D. (2003). How high- and low-challenge tasks affect motivation and learning: Implications for struggling readers. *Reading and Writing Quarterly,* *19,* 39–57.

Miller, S. D., & Meece, J. L. (1999). Third-graders' motivational preferences for reading and writing tasks. *Elementary School Journal, 100*(1), 19–35.

Parsons, S. A. (2008). Providing all students ACCESS to self-regulated literacy learning. *The Reading Teacher, 61*(8), 628–635.

Parsons, S. A., & Scales, R. Q. (2013). What are we asking kids to do?: An investigation of the literacy tasks teachers assign students. *Yearbook of the Association of Literacy Educators and Researchers, 35,* 143–156.

Turner, J. C. (1995). The influence of classroom contexts on young children's motivation for literacy. *Reading Research Quarterly, 30*(3), 410–441.

CHILDREN'S LITERATURE

L'Engle, M. (1962). *A wrinkle in time.* New York: Ariel Books.

16

· · · · ·

Autonomy-Supportive
Classroom Environments

Samantha T. Ives, Madelyn Stephens Wells,
and Seth A. Parsons

Imagine you are observing Mrs. Johnson, a first-grade teacher.
You are there before the students arrive, and as they come in,
Mrs. Johnson puts a finger to her lips, motioning to the children to sit down quietly and read the photocopied story she has
already placed on each student's desk. As the last few students
trickle in, Mrs. Johnson smiles at you, even though her finger is
still up reminding all students to remain silent. She walks over
and whispers, "I've finally perfected the daily entrance. Isn't it
so peaceful in here?" You ask what the story they are reading
is about. "Oh that—it's really not very good. I am just using it
to make sure they are quiet. We won't actually be using it for
anything."

As the day progresses, you notice how this philosophy per-
vades every decision. During the language arts block, all students are required to silently read the same book. Many of the
students groan and complain about the book, saying it is boring,
but quickly put their heads down and fall silent at Mrs. Johnson's threat to make them read instead of going to recess. A few
minutes later, when two students are caught having a conversation about the book, they are asked to stay in the room and
eat silently at their desks during lunch as a punishment for not
adhering to the classroom rules. "Silent reading time does not
mean play time with your friends," Mrs. Johnson says loudly as
she gives the two students a disappointed glare.

Next week, you are observing Mrs. Johri, a first-grade teacher just down the hall from Mrs. Johnson. As the students enter, laughing and chatting, Mrs. Johri directs them to choose one of three work stations. She motions you over and explains, "Students are allowed to choose where to go in the morning, but early on in the year, I explained the benefits of each station. The students are reminded periodically that they should choose a station that meets their goals and needs, not a station their friends are at." When a student enters and seems unsure of where to go, Mrs. Johri asks her a few questions, and then offers a suggestion of where she could spend her time.

During independent reading, Mrs. Johri explains that each student has selected a book genre to focus on during this time. Many have chosen fantasy and fairy-tale stories, a few are reading nonfiction, others are focusing on realistic fiction, and one or two are reading informational texts. "The students are working on writing their own books," Mrs. Johri explains. "We read a book from each genre together and discussed it. Students were asked to pick their favorite genre to read more examples of." You hear two students talking about Halloween next week. They both have their fairy tales closed on the desks in front of them. Mrs. Johri squats between the two girls and tells them about her costume: Lizzy the lizard from *The Magic School Bus*. They giggle. She then starts talking to them about what they notice about the differences between a fairy tale and informational text.

The examples in this vignette illustrate two different types of classrooms: a controlling environment, where the teacher removes all choice and ownership from the classroom and makes all decisions, and an autonomy-supportive classroom, where students have impactful influence in classroom proceedings throughout the day. The two types of classrooms are not mutually exclusive. Indeed, rarely will a classroom be totally controlled or entirely student led. There are variations and degrees. In this chapter, we propose that literacy instruction can be optimized if it is infused with autonomy support. We begin by elaborating on what autonomy support is. We then explain how it is a principle of effective literacy instruction, one that can be applied to various classroom activities. Next, we illustrate what autonomy support looks like in literacy instruction.

What Is Autonomy Support?

Autonomy is a core component of self-determination theory, a leading explanation of human behavior (Ryan & Deci, 2017). According to this theory, people have three basic psychological needs: the need for relatedness or belonging, the need for competence, and the need for autonomy (Ryan & Deci, 2000). When these needs are met, students are better equipped to engage and learn. Student motivation naturally grows when teachers create and maintain classrooms that are autonomy supportive.

Autonomy is a feeling of self-determination in which students experience volition in their actions. Autonomy is often a result of choice, or free will, in activities and goals. Although choice is a key component of autonomy, an even more important feature is that individuals are acting voluntarily. Autonomous activities are ones in which students want to participate because these activities align with their goals, values, or interests.

In autonomy-supportive classrooms, teachers personalize information to include content that is relevant to students, and students have ownership over what and how content is learned. However, as mentioned before, choice is just one part of autonomy. Students must have some desire to engage in at least one of the choices in front of them. Giving students an array of unappealing choices does not support autonomy (Wallace & Sung, 2017). Rather, it may send the signal to students that their teacher either does not know or does not care about their personal interests.

The opposite of an autonomy-supportive context is a controlling environment, where student autonomy is thwarted (Reeve & Jang, 2006; Ryan & Deci, 2017). Controlling classrooms do not take into account students as individuals with independent goals and desires. In settings lacking autonomy support, students have no choice in their learning and do not know how the class is relevant to their lives. In contexts in which autonomy is actively thwarted, instructors disregard student individuality and rely on controlling practices to push their students to comply. These controlling practices can be things like threats or reprimands, evaluation meant to praise or punish instead of providing helpful information about progress, or rewards meant to coerce students into behaving a certain way. What is most important is how students interpret their teachers' actions and their classroom environment. A core aspect of autonomy support is ascertaining students' perspectives, which is how teachers can gather information on whether students feel autonomous in the classroom.

Autonomy is not synonymous with independence. That is, autonomy support does not mean students are given free reign. Instead, student relevance, ownership, and choice can be enacted within the framework of curricular standards and expectations. Furthermore, it is unrealistic to expect teachers to align every lesson with their students' individual interests. Another way to support student autonomy is to provide clear and authentic rationales for instructional decisions or classroom assignments (De Naeghel, Van Keer, Vansteenkiste, Haerens, & Aelterman, 2016; Reeve & Jang, 2006). Even if, as is often the case, teacher autonomy is thwarted through curricular demands that may not align with teachers' goals, explaining the reasoning behind tasks or outwardly recognizing how tasks may or may not align with student interests are two ways to support student autonomy when choice is not an option.

Why Is Autonomy Support a Principle of Effective Literacy Instruction?

Creating autonomy-supportive classroom environments is a principle of effective literacy instruction because autonomy is central to students' motivation to read and write. Even though motivation is often justified based on its clear connection with achievement (Reeve & Jang, 2006; Taboada, Tonks, Wigfield, & Guthrie, 2009), it is worthwhile to note that motivation is valuable on its own. When students are given autonomy in their literacy learning, they become intrinsically motivated to engage in classroom activities and out-of-school literacy contexts. Intrinsic motivation, the most autonomous form of motivation, results in enjoyable experiences and optimal functioning (Ryan & Deci, 2017). When students enjoy what they are doing and how they are learning, classrooms become settings for exploration, discovery, and transformational interactions. Furthermore, when students who are driven by autonomous goals engage in reading and writing, they show a preference for more challenging activities and increase their self-regulated use of strategies to overcome obstacles (Koestner, Otis, Powers, Pelletier, & Gagnon, 2008; Standage, Duda, & Ntoumanis, 2005). Furthermore, when teachers create autonomy-supportive environments, teachers themselves report higher motivation for teaching, greater skill in teaching, and more satisfaction with their teaching practice (Cheon, Reeve, Yu, & Jang, 2014).

If we, as teachers, can support student autonomy, we can optimize student motivation and engagement and thereby enhance literacy achievement and psychological well-being (Andreassen & Bråten, 2011; De Naeghel et al., 2014; Patall, Cooper, & Wynn, 2010; Taboada et al., 2009). We can reach kids who have been disenfranchised in schools: students who do not see themselves in texts in schools; students who are constantly reprimanded, criticized, and punished for being themselves; students who are essentially told to "do what I tell you" all day every day from preschool on. Motivation, agency, ownership, and self-efficacy do not come from "doing what one is told." Those feelings and attributes come from being an autonomous human being who was supported in making decisions that facilitated literacy engagement and learning. Teachers who support their students' autonomy honor their diverse experiences and respect the varied funds of knowledge each student brings to a classroom (Moll, Amanti, Neff, & Gonzalez, 1992).

It is important to note that supporting students' autonomy is a way to reap benefits beyond even the ones outlined above. When teachers provide students with autonomy support, they are helping to fulfill not only students' need for autonomy but also their other psychological needs (Ryan & Deci, 2017). In order to create an autonomy-supportive environment, teachers need to get to know their students by engaging in dialogue with them and listening intently when they speak in class. This effort by the teacher supports students' need for relatedness. In a similar way, when teachers know their students' interests and goals, they can accordingly modify their instruction or interactions with students (Vaughn, Parsons, Gallagher, & Branen, 2016). Consequently, students will feel effective in their environment and will experience success fueled by their intrinsic motivation to engage and scaffolded by the structure provided by their teacher. This supports students' need for competence. Fulfillment of the three basic psychological needs consistently supports students' motivation, engagement, performance, and well-being (Ryan & Deci, 2017), and since autonomy-supportive environments can help fulfill these needs, and thus create positive outcomes, autonomy support is a clear principle of effective literacy instruction.

What Does Autonomy Support Look Like in the Classroom?

Student autonomy is not something to consider every now and then. Rather, autonomy support should be embedded within the school day. Reeve (2016) identified three instructional time points when autonomy can be supported in a lesson: during the initial planning, while introducing the topic or activity, and while responding to obstacles students encounter during the lesson. Below are some characteristics of autonomy support, followed by descriptions and examples of what it looks like in the classroom.

Meaningful Choice

Giving students meaningful choice does not mean that you offer complete free choice, nor does it mean that every aspect of an assignment needs to incorporate choices. Meaningful choice means giving students impactful options in their learning to support their need for autonomy (Rogat, Witham, & Chinn, 2014). For example, perhaps you are studying a unit on volcanoes, and you give students a project where they need to read background information. You may give students a choice between three different informational articles to read. However, there may be a time when it is necessary for all students to read a specific article. Instead of providing choice in text, you may give students a choice on how to display the knowledge they gained from this article. Options could include creating a visual representation of what they learned through a diagram or infographic, writing a short story from a unique perspective (such as the lava's), or recording a mock podcast meant to relay their knowledge of volcanoes. Another example is when students are learning about history. Perhaps you offer students a choice of the type of text you have them read: one group reads a nonfiction explanation of an event and another reads a historical fiction account. A final example of offering choice is in writing. If you are having students write a personal story, perhaps you allow them to write in the form of a poem or a picture book.

You can sometimes give students even more freedom in their learning. This level of choice is often reasonable during independent reading. However, in lessons where students are developing new skills and are navigating unfamiliar territory, students need, and actually often prefer, more structure (Jang, Reeve, & Deci, 2010; Webb, Massey, Goggans, & Flajole, 2019). Furthermore, providing students with structure that they need to be successful is a way of showing that (1) you considered students' perspectives by recognizing the parts of a task that could overwhelm or mislead students, and (2) you want your students to successfully engage with the task so they have the opportunity to construct their learning.

Demonstrating Relevance

Demonstrating relevance means explaining to your students how an activity, lesson, or unit is relevant to their lives. The most basic and necessary way to do this is by providing students with rationales. Providing rationales and highlighting relevance are essential practices to support students' autonomy (Assor, Kaplan, & Roth, 2002; Wallace & Sung, 2017). Verbally articulating the importance of a lesson or activity will go a long way with students because this helps them understand the purpose. This rationale should be authentic. Telling students they are doing an activity to prepare for a standardized test or "for their future" is not authentic or relevant enough to influence their actions. Every class activity should have a rationale that can be explained to students, and these should be provided to students with occasional reminders of the purpose. For example, before asking students to read a nonfiction article, you may explain how adults read nonfiction on a regular basis, describing the nonfiction that you read daily to enhance your life and providing examples of jobs or activities that necessitate nonfiction reading.

Another way to demonstrate relevance is by making connections between reading and writing and the "real world." For example, if students are reading a story about police officers, then you could bring an officer into the classroom for a question-and-answer session. Or if students are studying flowers and pollination, you can have the students go outside and take pictures of flowers and possibly bees. Then they can create an artifact demonstrating their understanding of pollination while incorporating the pictures they took. The more you can bring the "real world" into the classroom, or take the class out into the "real world," the better.

Promotion of Independent Thinking and Ownership

Autonomy-supportive teachers encourage students to be individuals and to think for themselves (Reeve & Jang, 2006; Wallace & Sung, 2017). In other words, autonomy-supportive teachers empower students to have their own opinions and ideas. This autonomy support is demonstrated by both the actions of teachers and the responses of teachers. You may promote independent thinking actively by asking students to share perspectives, make comments, and come up with their own ideas. For example, when reading a story as a class, you could ask students what they think the most important part of the story is and allow them to explain their thinking. One way to ensure all students get a chance to share their own ideas without taking up the majority of instructional time is by having them engage in cooperative small-group discussion. If you have each student share his or her idea with the whole class, only one student's voice is heard at a given time. However, if you organize students in groups of four, for example, and allot time for each group member to share his or her understanding with the small group, then a quarter of the students in your classroom have the opportunity to speak and be heard at a given time.

You may also be responsive in your promotion of independent thinking. One way to do this is when students offer a unique response, teachers may highlight this ingenuity, even if it is not what you were expecting. For example, if a student provides an answer that you were not ready for or do not want to focus on, you can acknowledge the answer and recognize its originality. You may even encourage students to take a minute to discuss this new perspective with a partner before transitioning back to the lesson sequence. Even statements such as "Tell me more" or "Please elaborate on that" honor students' thinking and their contributions to class and content.

Adaptability and Flexibility

Being adaptive and flexible means you are open to ideas and solutions outside of your original plans (Vaughn & Parsons, 2013). In many ways, this characteristic aligns with choice and independent thinking in that students are respected members of the classroom who have genuine input into its processes. Likewise, being adaptive and flexible is not the same as "anything goes." Teachers have the final say and authority in the classroom, and at the end of the day, they must do what they can to ensure students learn specific skills and content. Instead, being adaptive and flexible means being open to different ways for ensuring that students obtain those skills (Parsons, Dodman, & Burrowbridge, 2013).

For example, imagine a scenario where you ask students to write a poem about a time they did something positive for their community. One of your students, Elijah, wants to detail how he helped clean up a road near his house through a spoken word poem performed in front of the class. Being adaptive and flexible in this situation means you could discuss with Elijah how grateful you would be to have him introduce a potentially unfamiliar form of poetry to his classmates. Then you could note how part of this learning task is to practice writing, so even though you understand spoken word poetry goes beyond words on a page, you would like for him to also write out the poem, provide a written rationale for key performance-related choices he made, or allow him to brainstorm a way he can incorporate writing in the assignment.

Responsive and Respectful Feedback

Students feel that their work is valued when teachers give feedback that is individualized, helpful, and respectful (Reeve & Jang, 2006). Admittedly, this can be a challenge considering many current classroom sizes. However, you can focus on a specific skill to comment on in a piece of writing. For example, you may assign students to write a persuasive paragraph convincing their parents to allow them to stay up late to watch a movie on Friday night. You may choose to focus your feedback on only the persuasive features of this paragraph. You give a specific comment for each student about his/her persuasiveness, rather than commenting on all aspects of the writing. Even if it is short, specific feedback shows students that you cared enough to read their work. In addition, highlighting improvement you may see in their persuasive writing is another way of supporting autonomy by recognizing students' growth and effort.

Conclusion

Motivation is an important consideration for teachers' literacy instruction. Motivation and engagement are associated with enhanced reading achievement. One way to heighten student motivation and engagement is by supporting their autonomy. Autonomy is a basic psychological need, and autonomy support is a component of literacy instruction that teachers can control. Teachers can support students' autonomy by providing choices, making content relevant, promoting independent thinking, adapting instruction, and giving responsive feedback. As a principle of effective literacy instruction, autonomy support is something that can be flexibly applied in your instruction. As you plan, as you teach, and as you reflect, we encourage you to thoughtfully consider where you can incorporate the ideas from this chapter that can help you enhance the autonomy students experience in your classroom. These instructional actions will help you optimize students' motivation for and commitment to reading and writing.

REFERENCES

Andreassen, R., & Bråten, I. (2011). Implementation and effects of explicit reading comprehension instruction in fifth-grade classrooms. *Learning and Instruction, 21*(4), 520–537.

Assor, A., Kaplan, H., & Roth, G. (2002). Choice is good, but relevance is excellent: Autonomy-enhancing and suppressing teacher behaviours predicting students' engagement in schoolwork. *British Journal of Educational Psychology, 72*(2), 261–278.

Cheon, S. H., Reeve, J., Yu, T. H., & Jang, H. R. (2014). The teacher benefits from giving autonomy support during physical education instruction. *Journal of Sport and Exercise Psychology, 36*(4), 331–346.

De Naeghel, J., Valcke, M., De Meyer, I., Warlop, N., van Braak, J., & Van Keer, H. (2014). The role of teacher behavior in adolescents' intrinsic reading motivation. *Reading and Writing, 27*(9), 1547–1565.

De Naeghel, J., Van Keer, H., Vansteenkiste, M., Haerens, L., & Aelterman, N. (2016). Promoting elementary school students' autonomous reading motivation: Effects of a teacher professional development workshop. *Journal of Educational Research, 109*(3), 232–252.

Jang, H., Reeve, J., & Deci, E. L. (2010). Engaging students in learning activities: It is not autonomy support or structure but autonomy support and structure. *Journal of Educational Psychology, 102*(3), 588–600.

Koestner, R., Otis, N., Powers, T. A., Pelletier, L., & Gagnon, H. (2008). Autonomous motivation, controlled motivation, and goal progress. *Journal of Personality, 76*(5), 1201–1230.

Moll, L. C., Amanti, C., Neff, D., & Gonzalez, N. (1992). Funds of knowledge for teaching: Using qualitative approach to connect homes and classrooms. *Theory Into Practice, 31,* 132–141.

Parsons, S. A., Dodman, S. L., & Burrowbridge, S. C. (2013). Broadening the view of differentiated instruction. *Phi Delta Kappan, 95*(1), 38–42.

Patall, E. A., Cooper, H., & Wynn, S. R. (2010). The effectiveness and relative importance of choice in the classroom. *Journal of Educational Psychology, 102*(4), 896–915.

Reeve, J. (2016). Autonomy-supportive teaching: What it is, how to do it. In W.

C. Liu, J. C. K. Wang, & R. M. Ryan (Eds.), *Building autonomous learners* (pp. 129–152). Singapore: Springer.

Reeve, J., & Jang, H. (2006). What teachers say and do to support students' autonomy during a learning activity. *Journal of Educational Psychology, 98*(1), 209–218.

Rogat, T. K., Witham, S. A., & Chinn, C. A. (2014). Teachers' autonomy-relevant practices within an inquiry-based science curricular context: Extending the range of academically significant autonomy-supportive practices. *Teachers College Record, 116*(7), 1–46.

Ryan, R. M., & Deci, E. L. (2000). Self-determination theory and the facilitation of intrinsic motivation, social development, and well-being. *American Psychologist, 55*(1), 68–78.

Ryan, R. M., & Deci, E. L. (2017). *Self-determination theory: Basic psychological needs in motivation, development, and wellness.* New York: Guilford Press.

Standage, M., Duda, J. L., & Ntoumanis, N. (2005). A test of self-determination theory in school physical education. *British Journal of Educational Psychology, 75*(3), 411–433.

Taboada, A., Tonks, S. M., Wigfield, A., & Guthrie, J. T. (2009). Effects of motivational and cognitive variables on reading comprehension. *Reading and Writing, 22*(1), 85–106.

Vaughn, M., & Parsons, S. A. (2013). Adaptive teachers as innovators: Instructional adaptations opening spaces for enhanced literacy learning. *Language Arts, 91,* 81–93.

Vaughn, M., Parsons, S. A., Gallagher, M., & Branen, J. (2016). Teachers' adaptive instruction supporting students' literacy learning. *The Reading Teacher, 69,* 539–547.

Wallace, T. L., & Sung, H. C. (2017). Student perceptions of autonomy-supportive instructional interactions in the middle grades. *Journal of Experimental Education, 85*(3), 425–449.

Webb, S., Massey, D., Goggans, M., & Flajole, K. (2019). Thirty-five years of the gradual release of responsibility: Scaffolding toward complex and responsive teaching. *The Reading Teacher, 73*(1), 75–83.

17
. . . . . .
Culturally Relevant Pedagogy
and Multiliteracies

Jennifer Turner, Chrystine Cooper Mitchell, and Olivia Ann Murphy

As literacy teacher educators, we often hear these questions from new and veteran practitioners:

> "How do I teach literacy effectively to students of color?"
> "We've never had this group of diverse kids in our school before, and we don't know how to work with them, so where do we begin?"
> "How can I make literacy meaningful to students who have such different backgrounds?"
> "I know I'm supposed to be supporting students' cultural backgrounds through literacy, but how?"

These are extremely important questions, particularly because student populations are growing increasingly diverse.

In this chapter, we use the term "students of color" to represent children who come from diverse racial and ethnic backgrounds, and/or speak home languages that are not English. We want to acknowledge that while the term "students of color" emphasizes race, ethnicity, and language, classroom literacy teachers should also recognize and affirm the other intersecting dimensions of identity (e.g., gender, sexual orientation, religion, age, and socioeconomic status) that students of color perceive as salient to them. Importantly, students of color now comprise "the new majority" in public schools (Carr, 2016), as African American and Indigenous student populations have grown at moderate rates and Latinx and

Asian American student populations have significantly increased over the past decade. Given that the teacher workforce consists primarily of White, monolingual females (Au, 2011; Turner & Mitchell, 2019), we recognize that culturally relevant pedagogy needs to be built into the common language and practices in schools.

In what follows, we articulate four principles that will help new and practicing literacy teachers implement culturally relevant pedagogies for K–5 classrooms. Defined by Gloria Ladson-Billings (1994, 1995, 2014), culturally relevant pedagogies are instructional approaches and practices for students of color that promote (1) *academic achievement,* or the successful development of literacy knowledge valued by schools; (2) *cultural competence,* as the maintenance of their cultural integrity and authenticity through language and other community-based practices; and (3) *sociocritical consciousness,* which facilitates students' "critique [of] the cultural norms, values, mores, and institutions that produce and maintain social inequities" (Ladson-Billings, 1995, p. 162). Taken together, these principles serve as the foundation of pedagogical practices that sustain "the cultural and linguistic competence of their communities while simultaneously offering access to dominant cultural competence" (Paris, 2012, p. 95).

Culturally relevant pedagogies are essential for teaching racially, ethnically, and linguistically diverse literacy learners because they reframe literacy *achievement gaps* as *opportunity-to-learn* gaps. Achievement gap discourses narrowly define literacy as skills and knowledge assessed in high-stakes testing regimes (Turner & Albro, 2017) and (mis)characterize diversity as a "problem" or "challenge" to overcome in literacy teaching and learning (Au, 2011; McIntyre & Turner, 2013). Moreover, achievement gap discourses reinforce deficit views of students of color by presuming that they are "at risk" for literacy failure because they are unmotivated to learn, don't value education, or come from illiterate families and communities (Au, 2011; Edwards, McMillon, & Turner, 2010).

In contrast, opportunity-to-learn discourses demonstrate that performance gaps between White students and students of color are the result of, and reproduced by, unequal pedagogical practices (e.g., skill and drill literacy curricula), restrictive systems and structures (e.g., reading groups that serve as *de facto* tracking systems and limit student access to higher-level reading materials and instruction), and uncritical teacher mindsets (e.g., color-blind ideologies such as "I don't see race; I treat all children the same"). Informed by opportunity-to-learn frameworks, culturally relevant teachers simultaneously work to interrogate the structures, policies, and systems that mitigate the literacy learning of students of color while enacting new pedagogies that privilege their cultural resources and linguistic repertoires as learning assets in K–5 classrooms.

Our chapter seeks to demonstrate how culturally relevant pedagogies are enacted through and supported by *multiliterate practices* in K–5 classrooms. New London Group (1994) reminds us that multiliterate practices are important because "classroom teaching and curriculum have to engage with students' own experiences and discourses, which are increasingly defined by cultural . . . diversity and the different language backgrounds and practices that come with this diversity" (p. 88). By infusing multiliteracies with principles of culturally relevant teaching, we encourage teachers to enact pedagogies that invite students of color in K–5 classrooms to use multiple modes (e.g., visual images, written languages, aurality, and movement) in print-based and digital texts to assert their cultural and linguistic identities, to communicate their content learning and school knowledge, and to critique sociopolitical realities and take action for social justice (Cappello, Wiseman, & Turner, 2019).

Four Principles for Enacting Culturally Relevant Instruction

We turn now to four principles of culturally relevant literacy instruction that center and support students' multiliterate practices in K–5 classrooms:

1. Build caring relationships with students, families, and communities.
2. Foster learning that sustains students' cultural and linguistic knowledge.
3. Provide access to school literacy by leveraging students' cultural and linguistic funds of knowledge.
4. Cultivate students' sociopolitical consciousness.

In defining each principle, we highlight research-based examples that help teachers to see new possibilities for culturally relevant practice in their own K–5 classrooms.

Principle 1: Build Caring Relationships with Students, Families, and Communities

Our first principle of culturally relevant literacy instruction is building caring relationships with students, families, and communities. Caring is a cornerstone of culturally responsive teaching because "it places teachers in an ethical, emotional, and academic partnership with ethnically diverse students, a partnership that is anchored in respect, honor, integrity, resource sharing, and a deep belief in the possibility of transcendence"

(Gay, 2002, p. 109). All students need caring teachers in schools; however, teachers who care enough to demonstrate deep respect for and affirmation of the identities, histories, knowledges, and literacies of students of color are especially important because schools often perpetuate curricular, psychological, and emotional violence on diverse learners (Johnson, 2018; Nieto, 1999). Culturally relevant teachers transform schools into humanizing spaces by "recogniz[ing] and nurtur[ing] the affective and socioemotional dimensions of students" (Milner, 2017, p. 88); in other words, these teachers understand that they are responsible for *reaching* students of color and ensuring their psychosocial safety before *teaching* them.

In K–5 classrooms, culturally relevant teachers use literacy as a tool for developing caring relationships. Teachers who read aloud high-quality multicultural literature can build trust, empathy, and affirmation among peers in the classroom community. Books such as *The Name Jar* (Choi, 2003) and *René Has Two Last Names/René Tiene Dos Apellidos* (Laínez, 2009) encourage students of color to take pride in the cultural significance of their family names and to resist pressures to adopt more Americanized names. Caring relationships are also the foundation of collective responsibility, which elementary teachers promote through discursive framing (e.g., using "we"), group projects, and positive classroom interactions (Turner & Kim, 2005). Multiliterate activities such as (1) interviewing peers about their lives outside of school, (2) writing and performing scripts for Readers' Theater, and (3) writing and illustrating digital reports about future career aspirations also facilitate empathetic relationships and collaborative learning (Albro & Turner, 2019; Turner & Kim, 2005). These research-based examples demonstrate that caring teachers do not let students of color "get by" with doing shoddy academic work, nor do they hold mediocre expectations for their achievement; rather, culturally relevant "teachers care so much about ethnically diverse students and their achievement that they accept nothing less than high-level success from them and work diligently to accomplish it" (Gay, 2002, p. 109).

Building strong relationships with families and communities are also integral aspects of culturally relevant pedagogies in K–5 classrooms. In her landmark study, Ladson-Billings (1994) asserted that culturally relevant teachers viewed their students as extended family and cultivated relationships beyond the classroom by inviting them to their churches and to their scouting troops, and by attending local community events that showcased students' talents (e.g., sporting events, concerts). Dantas and Coleman (2010) also found that teachers can use sociocultural perspectives alongside ethnographic methods (e.g., observation, interview) to conduct home visits that help them understand and appreciate diverse families' *funds of knowledge* (Moll, Amanti, Neff, & Gonzalez, 1992), or their historically accumulated bodies of cultural knowledge, literacies, and sociolinguistic practices. Home visits are very "delicate spaces" (Dantas & Coleman, 2010, p. 160) because families may feel vulnerable about sharing their personal lives with teachers; therefore, teachers must be careful to check their own assumptions and biases and position themselves as *cultural learners* so that the families serve as experts on their own children, culture, and communities.

For teachers who cannot visit students' homes, the parent story approach (Edwards, Pleasants, & Franklin, 1999) provides opportunities to build trusting and respectful relationships with parents. In the parent story approach, culturally relevant teachers ask a series of questions about diverse parents' child-rearing practices, language practices, home literacies, and cultural experiences, such as:

> "Tell me about a time when your child learned something new. What made it a positive experience? What were some of the challenges your child experienced?"
> "What activities do you and your child enjoy doing together at home?" (Probe: wide range of literacy practices including storybook reading, drawing/writing, playing online games/using computers, reading/cooking with recipes, and reading religious texts)
> "What activities do you and your family enjoy doing in your community?" (Probe: religious services/events, educational/enrichment classes, cultural events)
> "What do you wish teachers knew about raising African American [or Latinx, etc.] children?"

These types of open-ended, nonjudgmental questions open "narrative spaces" (Edwards & Turner, 2010, p. 143) that allow diverse parents to share insightful stories about their home literacy lives. After collecting these powerful narratives from individual or groups of diverse parents of color, culturally relevant teachers use the information to make strategic connections between the literacy curriculum and instruction and students' home literacies (Edwards et al., 1999; Edwards & Turner, 2010).

Principle 2: Foster Learning That Sustains Students' Cultural and Linguistic Knowledge

Our second principle of culturally relevant literacy instruction is fostering learning that sustains students' cultural and linguistic knowledge. Historically, the outward manifestations of cultural identity by students of color—including ways of speaking, dressing, and playing—are devalued both in schools and society in ways that lead to expectations of academic failure. This has forced students of color to choose between proudly maintaining their own diverse cultural identities, which often leaves them alienated at school, or selectively and sometimes entirely suppressing their cultural identities in order to succeed in school by mainstreaming into the dominant culture (Carter, 2005; Gutiérrez, Baquedano-López, & Tejeda, 1999). Culturally relevant literacy instruction removes this forced choice by opening up classrooms as spaces that encourage students of color to sustain their dynamic cultural and linguistic identities in order to "explore, honor, extend, and, at times, problematize their heritage and community practices" (Paris & Alim, 2014, p. 86).

Additionally, as the United States and the larger globalizing world become increasingly culturally and linguistically diverse, having access to power and being able to navigate this world involves an "ability to communicate effectively to more than just 'standard' English monolinguals/monoculturals, who are becoming a shrinking share of the US population" (Paris & Alim, 2014, p. 89). Through this lens, sustaining students' cultural and linguistic knowledge is more than just a (necessary) move toward equity, access, and reducing the opportunity-to-learn gap: it is the only responsible way to foster academic achievement that prepares students of color to succeed in the 21st century.

Many educators' first attempt to implement culturally relevant pedagogy is promoting visibility—for example, reading/listening to/viewing texts that represent a variety of cultural authors and main characters/protagonists. While aspects of visibility are, indeed, important, implementing culturally relevant pedagogy also requires that teachers make space for students to authentically choose which aspects of their own cultures to bring into the classroom in order to explore and extend cultural understandings. There are endless ways to achieve this goal in elementary literacy instruction, and we discuss one significant one—storytelling—here. In the introduction to *The Storytelling Project Curriculum,* Lee Anne Bell and Rosemarie Roberts (2008) define four types of storytelling that are essential to incorporate in literacy instruction: (1) stock stories, (2) concealed stories, (3) resistance stories, and (4) counternarratives. Elementary students can and should incorporate their dynamic and intersecting cultural and linguistic traditions by participating in all four types and are often excited to do so.

Storytelling offers a way for students of color to share aspects of their lives, interests, languages, and experiences in school, thus creating space for these cultural identities in the classroom. For example, one study found that family storytelling was a way for refugee children to learn about and connect to their culture and traditions and was the only place that these children were hearing stories about relatable heroes (Strekalova-Hughes & Wang, 2019). The study also found that these refugee children *wanted* to write and tell their stories in school because they believed their home stories teach history, teach important life lessons, and are funny; however, no student in the study had actually been asked to tell their stories in a classroom setting.

A program called Nuestros Cuentos—a storytelling project designed to highlight the stories and histories of Latinx and Indigenous youth—offers a look at how asking students to tell their stories can be successfully done. The program asks participating youth to write, edit, and publish their own original stories, and then compiles those stories into a book that gets distributed back into the students' own communities (Torrez, Gonzales, Del Hierro, Ramos, & Cuevas, 2019). The program incorporates reading diverse mentor texts and communal storytelling sharing that promote "a creativity and freedom that allowed students to move across their languages and cultures to create stories that represent their identities through their own lenses" (Torrez et al., 2019, p. 99). Although Nuestros Cuentos is an after-school, community program for elementary and early middle school youth, their practices could easily translate into elementary classrooms or even broader school communities. Individual teachers can turn rich, diverse mentor texts into classroom read-alouds or independent reading, and then ask students to use these texts as inspiration for creating their own poems, stories, or artworks. Then individual classes, grades, or even entire school communities can convene for celebratory readings or showcases, and/or volumes of student works can be collected and distributed physically or digitally to parents, families, and community members.

Storytelling is also a place for teachers to break away from the dyadic view of literacy as traditional reading and writing and incorporate more multimodal forms. In an investigation of multimodal picture book making in a third-grade classroom, Zapata and Van Horn (2017) found that diverse mentor texts and a variety of art tools and media created space for students to freely express their cultural and linguistic traditions. After reading a variety of self-selected diverse mentor texts, students were presented with an array of art materials and media options in order to create their own picture books. Students used and remixed physical materials to tell their stories in a way that allowed "material intra-actions [to] emerge and students' lived realities [to] be performed" (Zapata & Van Horn, 2017, p. 298). When allowed to see relatable stories and histories in diverse mentor texts and provided with multimedia and multimodal ways to write, students were able to "perform aspects of their personal histories" and more accurately and completely tell their own stories in the classroom (Zapata & Van Horn, 2017, p. 312).

Finally, with the advent of more affordable and mass-produced technology, digital storytelling has emerged in the past couple decades as a way for students to tell their stories with the assistance of a variety of visual and auditory supports. The roots of storytelling lie in oral traditions, which allowed a storyteller to communicate a narrative to their audience with "intonation, gestures, expressions, and accents . . . [to] convey the emotional significance of the story along with the words" (Davis, 2004, p. 5). The findings from a study of digital storytelling with a group of urban African American youth illustrated that the storytelling process generated both academic and personal cultural growth. Researchers found that "creating the story, the completed story as an object, and subsequent experiences of presenting the story to others and interacting with others about it all served the work of identity construction" (Davis, 2004, p. 17). Research surrounding digital storytelling in Indigenous communities has generated similar findings at both the personal and community levels. For example, a study describing four different storytelling projects with Indigenous communities found that storytelling connected youth and elders and allowed the community to choose the way their knowledge, culture, and stories are told, represented, and preserved (Iseke & Moore, 2011).

With elementary students, digital storytelling can take a variety of forms depending on the available technology. Teachers can choose to employ simple, animation-focused websites where students can create and record the audio for a story and personalize animations to narrate that story (e.g., Voki or Nawmal). A more complex variation would be for students to use video-splicing web-based applications like iMovie that allow students to take several segments of video and combine them with other images, music, and multimedia forms. A variety of free, education-specific storytelling applications are easily accessible—for example, Comic Life, which allows students to create customized comics, and My Story, which allows students to add art, text, and audio to tell their stories—and often intuitive for 21st-century students who have grown up surrounded by technology like smartphones, electronic toys, and tablet computers. Digital storytelling allows students not only to center their cultural and linguistic repertoires through narrative but also to leverage multiple modes that represent and reflect 21st-century students' ways of knowing and communicating.

Principle 3: Provide Access to School Literacy by Leveraging Students' Cultural and Linguistic Funds of Knowledge

Our third principle of culturally relevant literacy instruction is providing access to school literacy by connecting to students' cultural and linguistic funds of knowledge. Culturally relevant teachers access and draw upon students' funds of knowledge from their homes and communities through their literacy pedagogies, thus bridging the home and school connection while promoting trust (Moll et al., 1992). Making purposeful and strategic connections to students' home language, family traditions, household practices, and community knowledge is essential because students of color learn best when their own experiences and background knowledge are valued and affirmed in classroom literacy instruction (Campano, 2005; Moll et al., 1992).

There is no doubt that students of color need access to academic literacy practices, or the power code (Delpit, 1995), in order to successfully navigate societal spaces (e.g., workplaces, schools). However, traditional literacy curricula and pedagogy have often required that students of color assimilate into the dominant culture, giving up their language, their cultural customs, and their community knowledge in order to learn mainstream literacies that will help them become more "American" (Au, 2011; Nieto, 1999). Challenging this dehumanizing and racist logic, culturally relevant teachers recognize that when students of color can draw upon their funds of knowledge as a bridge to school literacy, they expand their range of academic literacies and acquire meaningful literacies from school activities. Culturally relevant teachers also work to enact more critical stances toward literacies, shifting from mechanical literacy practices toward dynamic literacy practices and discourses that emanate from within students' families, communities, popular culture, and peer groups (Luke, 2012). Multiliterate practices, then, have the potential to provide a foundation from which to utilize K–5 students' linguistic and cultural funds of knowledge.

One approach to honoring students' funds of knowledge is providing opportunities for them to use their heritage language to make meaning through reading and writing. This can be accomplished through comprehension activities aimed at students' meaning making through images. For instance, using wordless picture books can help multilingual students create meaning through multimodality. Kress (1997) suggests reading images is not a linear process, and that it is left up to the reader to interpret aspects of the image. Similarly, documented research has illustrated that wordless picture books can not only help students construct complex meanings but also help them develop reading strategy use such as cross-checking and rereading (Lysacker & Hopper, 2015).

There are specific activities with wordless picture books where teachers can promote the use of meaning making through reading and writing. Examples include having the students record the story inspired by the wordless picture book in their heritage language, writing the text in their heritage language, inventing their own wordless picture book, or even making a book with text into their own wordless picture book (Jalongo, Dragich, Conrad, & Zhang, 2002). The images within a wordless picture book like *Journey* (Becker, 2013), *Drawn Together* (Le, 2018), or *I Walk with Vanessa* (Kerascoët, 2018) are colorful and expressive and promote imagination. These books, and most wordless picture books, have an underlying message or theme that students can comprehend and reinforce their understanding using their own connections and cultural funds of knowledge. By using funds of knowledge to help unpack the images in wordless picture books, students can bridge their knowledge about families and communities with their comprehension. Using wordless picture books with multilingual students can create opportunities to enhance literacy and support cultural meaning making.

Culturally relevant teachers who integrate sketch-to-stretch into literacy instruction routines also strengthen connections to students' cultural and linguistic funds of knowledge. Sketch-to-stretch involves having students visualize a passage of text and then interpret it through drawing. The strategy encourages diverse perspectives and fosters open discussion of various interpretations (McLaughlin & Allen, 2002). The strategy can be useful for students trying to make meaning from a text being read aloud or recorded (e.g., audiobooks, YouTube videos). Sketch-to-stretch can be implemented in ways that leverage students' home languages and cultural repertoires; examples include selecting a particular scene or passage, drawing the most important moment in the text, collaboratively working with a partner and orally describing their drawings, or using a writer's notebook.

Students' cultural and linguistic funds of knowledge can also be incorporated into fluency and vocabulary instruction. A fluency-focused activity that also enhances comprehension is Readers' Theater (Worthy & Prater, 2002), where multiple students come together to read their "part" of the story, allowing time for them to have multiple readings to "practice" for the demonstration. Since the repetition of the reading helps to enhance fluency, the activity promotes fluency and is often used in classrooms as a means of fluency practice. Yet, Readers' Theater has also been used to create cultural awareness and reflect students' cultural experiences. For example, Jeffries and Jeffries (2013) described how students' performance of the book *Bintou's Braids* (Diouf, 2001) in Readers' Theater sparked discussions about the cultural power that hair holds for girls, particularly African American girls, providing new spaces for the class to engage and critique female beauty standards.

Culturally relevant teachers can enhance students' vocabulary understanding using multisensory vocabulary activities, ranging from word illustrations to vocabulary charades, even vocabulary music compositions. Since multilingual learners benefit when vocabulary instruction is contextually rich and cognitively demanding (Cummins, 1996), multisensory vocabulary practice opportunities can be an important part of the literacy curriculum. Similarly, Husty and Jackson (2008) reported multilingual students achieved a deeper understanding of vocabulary when they were guided through multisensory explorations that used visual clues as definitions in context. They used visual clues, such as interactive vocabulary word walls, and definitions in context using images to present the material and help connect the science content to multilingual students. The visual aid helped the students to reinforce the science concepts and vocabulary words. In addition, games like vocabulary charades, where words are acted out through physical movements, invite students to employ their personal funds of knowledge to make sense of, and help others make sense of, vocabulary words.

Principle 4: Cultivate Students' Sociopolitical Consciousness

Our fourth principle of culturally relevant literacy instruction is cultivating students' sociopolitical consciousness. Culturally relevant teachers equip students with the literacy knowledge, skills, and discourses to critically analyze inequality within society and take action toward social justice (Ladson-Billings, 2014). More specifically, critical multimodal literacy approaches help children, especially those from diverse backgrounds, to *read the word* and *read the world* (Freire, 1985) through texts with print and images. Drawings, for example, helped Marcella, a Latina third grader, move beyond simplistic understanding of nonfiction texts by highlighting the new science knowledge (e.g., facts) that she acquired, demonstrating complex thinking through multimodal elements (e.g., speech bubbles, arrows), and positioning her as a knowledge producer in the classroom (Cappello et al., 2019). Thus, drawings and other multimodal texts provide opportunities for students of color to reflect critically on their schooling experiences, question power and authority, and take action in/on their world.

Students' sociopolitical consciousness can also be developed in digital spaces where students are taught to understand and question past and current societal movements. For example, Price-Dennis (2016) documented how Ms. Jones, a fifth-grade teacher, designed interdisciplinary social justice units (e.g., gender inequality, the Black Lives Matter movement, identity representation) to help urban students examine our society's sociopolitical and historical literacies and to create a space for them to enact their own critical literacies. The units included digital storytelling, enabling the girls to share their narratives using video production apps and through the creation of podcasts. As an exemplar of culturally relevant pedagogy, Price-Dennis (2016) found that the social justice units that Ms. Jones implemented allowed the African American fifth-grade girls to make sense of, and critique, dominant societal narratives as well as their own stories, illustrating that their critical digital inquiries "functioned as conduits for circulating counternarratives to a global audience" (p. 358).

Students' sociopolitical consciousness can also be promoted through multimodal images that convey meanings about social injustice and inequalities. Kuby (2012) demonstrated how five- and six-year-old children can comprehend and compose multimodal images related to racial bus segregation. Kuby helped the students make meaning of racial bus segregation during the civil rights movement through the images and words in a Rosa Parks biography and other nonfiction texts. Then, based on the structure of *Voices in the Park* (Browne, 2001) in which a single event is illustrated from four different characters' perspectives, Kuby divided her students into four character groups: Rosa Parks, African American bus riders, White bus riders, and the White bus driver. After discussing these different characters' perspectives regarding Rosa Parks and her bus arrest, the class composed an illustrated book that represented their critical understandings about racial bus segregation. Through these watercolor illustrations, students gave "voice to people who were oppressed" (Kuby, 2012, p. 289) by racial segregation using particular multimodal design elements (e.g., speech bubbles, color) and imagery that depicted individual and collective struggle (e.g., nonviolent protests). Kuby's (2012) example demonstrates how culturally relevant teachers connect difficult social topics to students' schema as well as to emotions people may have felt during the historical events.

Similarly, using social justice literature for read-alouds nurtures students' sociopolitical consciousness by engaging them in conversations about the oppression and discrimination that people of color have faced, and the individual and collective actions that people of color have taken to fight against injustice. Historical fiction such as *Esperanza Rising* (Muñoz Ryan, 2000), *The Watsons Go to Birmingham–1963* (Curtis, 1995), and *Baseball Saved Us* (Mochizuki, 1993) is particularly engaging for elementary students. Realistic fiction should also be featured in K–5 classrooms. Contemporary works such as *Layla's Headscarf* (Cohen, 2009), *Desmond and the Very Mean Word* (Tutu, 2012), and *First Day in Grapes* (Perez, 2002) might facilitate discussions about how racism influences bullying behavior (Wiseman, Vehabovic, & Jones, 2019), while books like *Too Many Tamales* (Soto, 1996), *Those Shoes* (Boelts, 2009), and *Year of the Dog* (Lin, 2006) might spark conversations about family and community experiences.

Finally, students' sociopolitical consciousness can be developed through *social justice literature circles*. Social justice literature circles promote critical reading and critical thinking skills and may also foster inquiry about difficult historical and contemporary social issues (Frederick, 2006). Social justice literature circles help students unpack sociopolitical issues through scaffolded questioning such as:

"Who has the power in this situation/relationship? Who is being oppressed?"
"What group or groups are missing from this story?"
"Did the character feel powerful or powerless? Why or why not?"
"What is the connection between the conflict in this story and your own community?"
"What does it mean to be discriminated against?"
"What does equality look like, and how is it portrayed or not portrayed in this book?"

By engaging in discussions through social justice circles, students critically comprehend and make meaning of these texts, become more cognizant of the injustices facing their communities, and learn how they can begin to stand up against inequality and speak truth to those in power.

Conclusion

This chapter outlines four principles that literacy teachers can use to enact culturally relevant pedagogies. Culturally relevant teachers intentionally orchestrate literacy activities and instructional routines that

- Build caring relationships with students, families, and communities;
- Foster learning that sustains students' cultural and linguistic knowledge;
- Provide access to school literacy by leveraging students' funds of knowledge; and
- Cultivate students' sociopolitical consciousness.

Culturally relevant pedagogies are effective for students from all racial, ethnic, and linguistic backgrounds and, in particular, provide students of color with more equitable opportunities to access academic literacies. However, culturally relevant pedagogies are more than just "good teaching" or a list of "best practices"; rather, the four principles featured in this chapter promote a mindset that empowers teachers to enact "humanizing pedagog[ies] that respect and use the reality, history, and perspectives of students as an integral part of educational practice" (Bartolome cited in Ladson-Billings, 1995, p. 160). For young literacy learners in our K–5 classrooms, culturally relevant pedagogies sustain their diverse ethnic, racial, and linguistic identities and (re)affirm the cultural knowledges while supporting their acquisition of the multiliterate practices and the critical thinking skills necessary for productive participation in civic life.

REFERENCES

Albro, J., & Turner, J. D. (2019). Six key principles: Bridging students' career dreams with literacy standards. *The Reading Teacher, 73*(2), 161–172.

Au, K. (2011). *Literacy achievement and diversity: Keys to success for students, teachers, and schools.* New York: Teachers College Press.

Bell, L. A., Roberts, R. A., Irani, K., & Murphy, B. (2008). *The Storytelling Project curriculum: Learning about race and racism through storytelling and the arts.* New York: Barnard College.

Campano, G. (2005). The second class: Providing space in the margins. *Language Arts, 82*(3), 186–193.

Cappello, M., Wiseman, A., & Turner, J. D. (2019). Framing equitable classroom practices: Potentials of critical multimodal literacy research. *Literacy Research: Theory, Methods, and Practice, 69,* 1–21.

Carr, S. (2016, June). Tomorrow's test. Retrieved from *www.slate.com/articles/life/ tomorrows_test/2016/06/american_is_becoming_a_majority_minority_nation_ it_s_already_happened_in.html.*

Carter, P. L. (2005). *Keepin' it real: School success beyond Black and White.* New York: Oxford University Press.

Cummins, J. (1996). *Negotiating identities: Education for empowerment in a diverse society.* Ontario, CA: California Association for Bilingual Education.

Dantas, M. L., & Coleman, M. (2010). Home visits: Learning from students and families. In M. L. Dantas & P. C. Manyak (Eds.), *Home–school connections in a multicultural society* (pp. 156–176). New York: Routledge.

Davis, A. (2004). Co-authoring identity: Digital storytelling in an urban middle school. *THEN: Technology, Humanities, Education, and Narrative, 1*(1), 1–21.

Delpit, L. (1995). *Other people's children.* New York: New Press.

Edwards, P., McMillon, G. T., & Turner, J. D. (2010). *Change is gonna come: Transforming literacy education for African American students.* New York: Teachers College Press.

Edwards, P., Pleasants, H., & Franklin, S. (1999). *A path to follow: Learning to listen to parents.* Portsmouth, NH: Heinemann.

Edwards, P. A., & Turner, J. D. (2010). Do you hear what I hear?: Using the parent story approach to listen to and learn from African American parents. In M. L. Dantas & P. C. Manyak (Eds.), *Home–school connections in a multicultural society* (pp. 137–156). New York: Routledge.

Frederick, T. (2006). Choosing to belong: Increasing adolescent male engagement in the ELA classroom. *Changing English: Studies in Culture and Education, 13*(1), 151–159.

Freire, P. (1985). Reading the world and reading the word: An interview with Paulo. *Language Arts, 62*(1), 15–21.

Gay, G. (2002). Preparing for culturally responsive teaching. *Journal of Teacher Education, 53*(2), 106–116.

Gutiérrez, K. D., Baquedano-López, P., & Tejeda, C. (1999). Rethinking diversity: Hybridity and hybrid language practices in the third space. *Mind, culture, and activity, 6*(4), 286–303.

Husty, S., & Jackson, J. (2008). Multisensory strategies for science vocabulary. *Science and Children, 46*(4), 32–35.

Iseke, J., & Moore, S. (2011). Community-based Indigenous digital storytelling with elders and youth. *American Indian Culture and Research Journal, 35*(4), 19–38.

Jalongo, M. R., Dragich, D., Conrad, N. K., & Zhang, A. (2002). Using wordless picture books to support emergent literacy. *Early Childhood Education Journal, 29*(3), 167–177.

Jeffries, R., & Jeffries, D. (2013). Cultural signification through Reader's Theatre: An analysis of African American girls and their hair. *Multicultural Learning and Teaching, 9*(2), 203–218.

Johnson, L. L. (2018). Where do we go from here?: Toward a critical race English education. *Research in the Teaching of English, 53*(2), 102–124.

Kress, G. (1997). *Before writing: Rethinking the paths to literacy.* New York: Routledge.

Kuby, C. R. (2012). Evoking emotion and unpacking layered histories through young children's illustrations of racial bus segregation. *Journal of Early Childhood Literacy, 13*(2), 271–300.

Ladson-Billings, G. (1994). *The dreamkeepers: Successful teachers of African American children.* San Francisco: Jossey-Bass.

Ladson-Billings, G. (1995). But that's just good teaching: The case for culturally relevant teaching. *Theory Into Practice, 34*(3), 159–165.

Ladson-Billings, G. (2014). Culturally relevant pedagogy 2.0: Aka the remix. *Harvard Educational Review, 84*(1), 74–84.

Luke, A. (2012). Critical literacy: Foundational notes. *Theory Into Practice, 51*(1), 4–11.

Lysacker, J., & Hopper, E. (2015). A kindergartener's emergent strategy use during wordless picture book reading. *The Reading Teacher, 68*(8), 649–657.

McIntyre, E., & Turner, J. D. (2013). Culturally responsive literacy instruction. In B. Taylor & N. Duke (Eds.), *Effective literacy instruction: A handbook of research and practice* (pp. 137–161). New York: Guilford Press.

McLaughlin, M., & Allen, M. B. (2002). *Guided comprehension: A teaching model for grades 3–8.* Newark, DE: International Reading Association.

Milner, H. R. (2017). Race, talk, opportunity gaps, and curricular shifts in (teacher) education. *Literacy Research: Theory, Method, and Practice, 66,* 73–94.

Moll, L., Amanti, C., Neff, D., & Gonzalez, N. (1992). Funds of knowledge for teaching: Using a qualitative approach to connect homes and classrooms. *Theory Into Practice, 31*(2), 132–141.

New London Group. (1996). A pedagogy of multiliteracies: Designing social futures. *Harvard Educational Review, 66*(1), 60–92.

Nieto, S. (1999). *The light in their eyes: Creating multicultural learning communities.* New York: Teachers College Press.

Paris, D. (2012). Culturally sustaining pedagogy: A needed change in stance, terminology, and practice. *Educational Researcher, 41*(3), 93–97.

Paris, D., & Alim, H. S. (2014). What are we seeking to sustain through culturally sustaining pedagogy?: A loving critique forward. *Harvard Educational Review, 84*(1), 85–100.

Price-Dennis, D. (2016). Developing curriculum to support Black girls' literacies in digital spaces. *English Education, 48*(4), 337–361.

Strekalova-Hughes, E., & Wang, X. C. (2019). Perspectives of children from refugee backgrounds on their family storytelling as a culturally sustaining practice. *Journal of Research in Childhood Education, 33*(1), 6–21.

Torrez, J. E., Gonzales, L., Del Hierro, V., Ramos, S., & Cuevas, E. (2019). Comunidad de cuentistas: Making space for indigenous and Latinx storytellers. *English Journal, 108*(3), 44–50.

Turner, J. D., & Albro, J. J. (2017). When I grow up: Assessing American children's perspectives on college and career readiness through drawings. *Literacy, 51*(2), 94–103.

Turner, J. D., & Kim, Y. (2005). Learning about building literacy communities in multicultural and multilingual communities from effective elementary teachers. *Literacy Teaching and Learning, 10,* 21–42.

Wiseman, A., Vehabovic, N., & Jones, S. (2019). Intersections of race and bullying in children's literature: Transition, racism, and counternarratives. *Early Childhood Education Journal, 47*(4), 465–474.

Worthy, J., & Prater, K. (2002). "I thought about it all night": Readers Theatre for reading fluency and motivation. *The Reading Teacher, 56*(3), 294–297.

Zapata, A., & Van Horn, S. (2017). "Because I'm smooth": Material intra-actions and text productions among young Latino picture book makers. *Research in the Teaching of English, 51*(3), 290–316.

CHILDREN'S LITERATURE

Becker, A. (2013). *Journey.* Somerville, MA: Candlewick Press.

Boelts, M. (2009). *Those shoes.* Somerville, MA: Candlewick Press.

Browne, A. (2001). *Voices in the park.* New York: DK.

Choi, Y. (2003). *The name jar.* New York: Dell Dragonfly Books.

Cohen, M. (2009). *Layla's headscarf.* Long Island City, NY: Star Bright Books.

Curtis, C. P. (1995). *The Watsons go to Birmingham–1963.* New York: Random House.

Diouf, S. A. (2001). *Bintou's braids.* San Francisco: Chronicle Books.

Kerascoët. (2018). *I walk with Vanessa.* New York: Penguin Random House.

Laínez, R. C. (2009). *René has two last names/René tiene dos apellidos.* Houston: Piñata.

Le, M. (2018). *Drawn together.* New York: Hyperion.

Lin, G. (2006). *Year of the dog.* New York: Little, Brown.

Mochizuki, K. (1993). *Baseball saved us.* New York: Lee and Low Books.

Muñoz Ryan, P. (2000). *Esperanza rising.* New York: Scholastic.

Perez, L. K. (2002). *First day in grapes.* New York: Lee and Low Books.

Soto, G. (1996). *Too many tamales.* London: Puffin Books.

Tutu, D. (2012). *Desmond and the very mean word.* Somerville, MA: Candlewick Press.

18
$\bullet\ \bullet\ \bullet\ \bullet\ \bullet$

Critical Approaches to Text

Grace Enriquez

Just over 30 years ago, the world became privy to a remarkable conversation between literacy educators and theorists Paulo Freire and Donaldo Macedo. That dialogue, published along with their written commentary as *Literacy: Reading the Word and the World* (Freire & Macedo, 1987) and now recognized widely as the seminal treatise on the role of literacy in critical pedagogy, debunked the long-standing view that reading and writing were activities that occurred only in an individual's brain. In fact, Freire and Macedo asserted they are anything but that, arguing that too often the term *literacy* is reduced to the functional abilities of reading and writing and largely focused on economic goals.

We still see that narrow perspective alive today when the term *illiterate* is conflated with deficit and poverty. Freire and Macedo (1987) certainly understood that the inability to read and write marked one as illiterate, but they also knew that the benefits of literacy extend beyond personal ability to social acceptance, cultural savviness, and political potential. To them, literacy was less concerned with functional skills and economic betterment and more with enabling one to use those skills to actively reclaim one's voice, identity, and future. Using the term *literacy* meant using "'the language of possibility,' enabling learners to recognize and understand their voices within a multitude of discourses in which they must deal" (Freire & Macedo, 1987, p. 54). To teach students to be truly literate, therefore, requires an approach to texts that encourages readers to critically consider the voices and representations folded within a page (Leland, Lewison, & Harste, 2017; Thomas, 2016).

In this chapter, I demonstrate why critically approaching text is a cornerstone of effective literacy instruction. I begin by explaining what a critical approach to text is, briefly tracing its roots in critical theory and sociocultural theories of literacy. In the next section, I explain why teaching students to critically approach text matters, diving deeper into its role in understanding what literacy is. In the third section, I outline key elements of this instructional approach, supplemented by brief classroom examples, to illustrate ways it plays out in schools.

Critical Approaches to Text: Locating the World in the Word

Critical approaches to text encompass a wide range of perspectives, but as a whole, those perspectives agree that any given text is constructed with the sociocultural and political influences their authors consciously or subconsciously espouse (Leland et al., 2017). Understanding texts is not just about literal meaning making; it also extends meaning making to unearth those influences and consider how they speak to a greater understanding of the world. To unpack what it means to critically approach a text, I first provide a quick review of text-based and reader-based theories of approaching text. I then review two chief theories that guide readers to approach text critically: critical theory and sociocultural theories of literacy.

From Text-Based to Reader-Based Theories: Variations on Reading Texts Critically

Literary scholars tend to frame critical approaches to text through text-based theory—that is, perspectives that stress the literary qualities of a text and primarily use the text's content and form to interpret meaning. Known as literary criticism, these approaches focus on how the world influenced the creation of a text and how a text comments upon the world. Reader-based theories, on the other hand, emphasize the importance of the reader as interpreter of text. Commonly known as *reader response,* such theories recognize that "all readers bring different experiences to a text and understand the text through their own unique cultural and psychological filters" (Sipe, 2008, p. 50). Because language is always shaped by the author's sociocultural, political, and historical influences, texts are therefore inherently saturated with multiple voices of social meaning that generate an ongoing conversation between text and reader (Bakhtin, 1981). Rosenblatt (1978) articulated a transaction that occurs between reader and text, one in which both are ultimately transformed when they come together. The field of literacy has largely embraced this perspective because it values both reader and text, draws upon social constructivist theories of learning (Vygotsky, 1978), and acknowledges how language and literacy are informed and influenced by the many sociocultural contexts in which we live and learn (Heath, 1983; Street, 1984). Literacy researchers have extended reader response theories to consider culturally situated, embodied, and local factors in readers' transactions with texts (e.g., Brooks & Browne, 2012; Dávila, 2015; Enriquez, 2016; Lewis, 2000; Sipe, 2008). In this way, the field continues to discern how readers use their lived experiences and sociocultural identities to make sense of texts, just as that meaning in turn shapes their lives, experiences, and identities.

From Critical Theory to Critical Discourse Analysis

Critical approaches to text stem from critical theory, a philosophical and political stance that focuses on identifying and questioning the power structures usually taken for granted as "truth" (McLaren, 2006). With this foundation, critical approaches to text aim to foster a robust conversation or use of "language in which one speaks *with* rather than *for* Others" (Giroux, 1993, p. 376). Critical theory has evolved to highlight many historically marginalized cultures and traditions, including feminist critical theory (Robbins, 2019) and critical race theory (CRT; Ladson-Billings & Tate, 1995), as well as its branches of Latinx critical race theory (LatCrit) and Asian critical race theory (Solorzano & Yosso, 2001).

When reading texts, critical theory is often applied through critical discourse analysis (CDA). CDA exists in many variations, but collectively, they share "the assumption that because language is a social practice and because not all social practices are created and treated equally, all analyses of language are inherently critical" (Rogers, 2011, p. 2). Understanding that texts are never neutral, CDA investigates this sociocultural relationship between language and text at the literal level (i.e., What metaphors are used? What kind of syntax?) and the societal level (i.e., How is the text typically used? What worldview is promoted?; Fairclough, 1995). In other words, CDA investigates how discourse and power work to create and maintain "truth."

From Sociocultural Theories of Literacy to Critical Literacy

Sociocultural theories of literacy highlight the richly diverse sociocultural identities, practices, and values among students and teachers (Heath, 1983; Street, 1984). Language and texts have sociocultural influences, as does what we do with them and why. In other words, literacy and literacy learning "are integrated with oral language, social activities, material settings, and distinctively cultural forms of thinking, knowing, valuing, and believing" (Gee, 1999, p. 356). Furthermore, what comprises literacy and literacy learning depends on the sociocultural context. This premise helps explain why the daily literacy practices that occur in a classroom may differ from the daily literacy practices that occur at home, at work, at a party, or at the grocery store. How we approach texts is shaped by cultural, historical, and ideological implications that value some ways of constructing meaning around texts and silence others.

Critical literacy actively embraces this socioculturally situated view of literacy and text (Heath, 1983; Street, 1984). Moreover, it provides educators and students with the opportunity use literacy to question, evaluate, and act to reconsider and reshape what constitutes truth and reality. In addition to CDA, critical literacy work is key to approaching texts critically. Shor (1999) affirms, "When we are critically literate, we examine our ongoing development, to reveal the subjective positions from which we make sense of the world and act in it" (p. 3). This kind of critical consciousness, or *conscientization,* to the social and political realities of one's world is the first step Freire (1970) identifies in critical literacy work.

Rather than pinpointing critical literacy or critical approaches to text as an application, method, or skill, critical literacy is an ongoing stance toward a richer understanding of the world and the efforts to build a more just society. Vasquez (in Miller & Kissel, 2019) expounds on the flexible aspect of critical literacy:

> This way of being and thinking can't be taught traditionally using some scope-and-sequence charts and predetermined curricula. To make this powerful work possible, critical literacies need to unfold in the everyday as we incorporate a critical stance in our everyday lives. When this happens, it becomes much easier to support children in taking up, understanding, and analyzing the social and political issues around them. (p. 75)

Thus, there is no single, universal, or fixed definition or model of critical literacy; rather, critical literacy engages both the local and global spaces of one's world, approaching text in a way that is both individual and collectively concerned (Comber, 2015; Freire, 1970; Luke, 2014).

To approach a text critically means acknowledging that it does not exist in a vacuum; rather, texts present their content from a particular lens and worldview. Likewise, we read texts through the sociocultural experiences, beliefs, and identities we carry with us in all we do. Discerning such stances within text and reader, through critical discourse analysis and critical literacy orientations, forms the mainstay of critical approaches to text.

Critical Approaches to Text: Harnessing the Word for the World

So, why does a critical approach to text matter for effective literacy instruction? Living in the 21st century, we are witnessing society's widespread access to digital tools for creating and sharing text, the propagation of divisive rhetoric via social media and channels, and political leaders crying, "Fake news!" at every turn. At the same time, academic standards are being continuously scrutinized to ensure students are well prepared for college and career. High priority must be given to literacy education to support students through these times, and a richer understanding of literacy is needed to help us navigate this world.

Definitions of literacy and literacy education have evolved in response to advances in technology, shifts in student demographics, and new insights about language and learning (Vasquez, Janks, & Comber, 2019). If being literate means tuning into the sociocultural constructs of reality via reading, writing, speaking, and listening, then literacy is about fully embracing that view, no matter what the "text" is, who the students are, and what linguistic and learning repertoires they have. By investigating the ideological and social uses of texts, critical literacy provides an authentic reason to use the utilitarian skills that are conventionally promoted as literacy. In other words, one cannot be fully literate without critically approaching both the texts they encounter and the world around them (Luke & Freebody, 1999).

Engaging in critical approaches to text is a responsive and versatile component of literacy instruction; it is not merely an "add-on" (Jones & Enriquez, 2009). It requires teachers to be amenable to releasing our sense of control and power: "We must become co-learners on a journey with our students" (Kern, 2007, p. 87). Critical literacy, then, is an essential cornerstone of "doing" literacy because it is firmly rooted in the real, present lives of people. Without it, doing literacy and being truly literate is reduced to automated skills that enable us to function in our day-to-day lives, but without much reason outside of that.

Strengthening Students, Strengthening Society

Critical literacy and critical approaches to text, however, are not just about being critical (Souto-Manning & Yoon, 2018). By questioning what appears as truth and reality in text, this approach views the student as a legitimate source of knowledge who is capable of reshaping what counts as truth, "turning them into inventors of the curriculum, critics and creators of knowledge" (Luke, 2012, p. 7). At its heart, critically approaching text is an initiative toward making the world a better place for all: "to be for critical literacy is to take a moral stand on the kind of just society and democratic education we want" (Shor, 1999, p. 24). Examples of critically approaching text can be found across the world and throughout history, including the early 20th-century organization of African American community education and ongoing worldwide efforts to support the education of girls and women (Luke, 2012; Wetheridge, 2016).

Approaching text critically does not need to involve conflict or strife. It could mean having students survey the titles of picture books in the classroom or school library and then raising funds to add more diverse titles to the collection (Jones, Clarke, & Enriquez, 2010; Wager et al., 2019) or ensuring those diverse titles become fully integrated into classroom teaching by selecting them to be core read-aloud books (Enriquez, 2019). Additionally,

> children might investigate their local wetlands and work out ways of enhancing the quality of the water; in another class, they might study the ways in which cartoons work to portray those in power and those on the margins, then produce their own. How teachers negotiate critical literacy practices depends very much on the affordances of their place and the students in the room. (Vasquez et al., 2019, p. 300)

At its center, a critical approach to text supports the hope that what seems unjust, inequitable, or unsafe does not have to stay that way. It is no wonder, then, that Freire and Macedo (1987) aptly define literacy as reading the word and the world.

Critical Approaches to Text:
Classroom Moves for Pedagogical Integration

Let's now move beyond the theoretical, philosophical, and educational underpinnings of critical approaches to text and explore how we can use it to support students' full literate growth. Critical literacy scholars have offered various ways to approach text. For example, Janks (2000) outlined four ways language and power relate to each other: (1) *domination* (How does a text work to position readers in terms of power?), (2) *access* (How does one provide access to dominant uses of language while promoting diversity and challenging social marginalization?), (3) *diversity* (How does one value different ways of representing and communicating ideas in the classroom?), and (4) *design* (How does one reconstruct and generate new meaning with text?). Jones (2006) proposed a three-pronged approach, consisting of deconstructing, reconstructing, and acting upon the use of language to convey worldviews. No matter the approach, critically reading text often includes the following components: integration of authentic text, integration of diverse text, text deconstruction, text reconstruction, and social action.

Integration of Authentic Text

As previously discussed, the central goal of critically approaching text is to reveal the sociocultural values, assumptions, and worldviews woven into all texts. The integration of authentic text supports this goal by providing materials that serve "real world" audiences and purposes, not just school populations and academic or instructional objectives. The term *authentic text* covers a wide range of material, including trade books, newspaper and magazine articles, websites, blog posts, pamphlets, advertisements, letters and e-mails, and other forms of digital texts. Studies have shown that using authentic text enhances student interest, enthusiasm, motivation, and curiosity (Ciecierski & Bintz, 2015), but the benefits also encompass more traditional literacy goals: vocabulary enrichment, word study, grammatical knowledge, and figurative language understanding (Fang & Wei, 2010; Gareis, Allard, & Saindon, 2009). Additionally, using authentic text to teach disciplinary content engages higher-order thinking skills as students work to make sense of them in light of the discipline (Villano, 2005).

Integrating authentic text does not just mean supplementing curricular material; rather, as much as possible, authentic text should constitute the curriculum. This may mean forgoing standardized curricula and preplanned lessons because of the immediate and pressing need for critically reading a text. With colleagues, I illustrated this case when Mr. Lara encountered visibly and vocally upset emergent bilingual students in his sixth-grade ESL class:

> Socorro said that the previous evening a memorandum had been posted at the school entrance informing all after-school program attendees that, starting the following month, busing would no longer be provided for students in the evenings. Hurt and angry, Miguel said, "They can keep their dumb program!" Around the room, there was a palpable sense of both apathy and anger among the students. Mr. Lara knew that attempting to focus their attention and energy on the lesson he had prepared would be fruitless. Mr. Lara had to make a choice about how he was going to proceed with the day's activities—a balancing act between the curriculum and responding to students' lives—not an easy choice for any teacher. (Wager et al., 2019, p. 123)

The memorandum in question was clearly an example of authentic text, something constructed for the real-world audience of the after-school program's students and families and for the real-world purpose of communicating a halt to the bus services. Faced with the urgency of his students' situation, Mr. Lara weighed his options:

> But there was little chance they could concentrate on any school-provided text when the nonacademic world had thrust another text on them, in the form of the memorandum, that would have serious ramifications on their lives . . . [and] dismissing something that was so consequential in their daily lived experiences in favor of pursuing a disconnected instructional objective could have relayed the message that reading did not play an important role in their lives. (Wager et al., 2019, pp. 123–124)

Ultimately, Mr. Lara chose to stand for critical literacy, using the chance to engage students in text analysis and determine who was empowered, who was marginalized by the memorandum, and why. After discussing the power that language and texts hold, he then guided students to write response letters to the after-school program director in order to help them connect their personal lives to the broader social world reflected in authentic text.

Deciding to integrate authentic text arose as a teachable moment for Mr. Lara, but educators do not need to wait for such urgent opportunities to come their way. Authentic text is everywhere, both inside and outside of school walls, in print and online, written, spoken, and visual, shaping and shaped by the lives students experience each day. Rather than wait for an immediate and intense occasion, teachers can ask students to bring in texts they encounter at home, on the walk to school, at the store, or in any other space that comprises their world. These texts, ranging from children's literature to instruction manuals to popular songs and television shows, are artifacts that use language to reflect social relationships and worldviews (Enriquez & Shulman-Kumin, 2014; Morrell, 2008). To effectively use literacy as a tool for enacting social change, we must make the authentic texts of students' lives a central part of our literacy teaching.

Integration of Diverse Texts

If critical approaches to text aim to contemplate the assumptions and values underpinning the texts in students' lives, it makes sense to apply those approaches to the diverse array of texts surrounding us. Questions about what kinds of texts to examine and how to include different texts converge here, reflecting what Janks (2000) refers to as relationships of diversity and access to language and power around texts. In this respect, *diverse text* can indicate the multiple voices, experiences, and worldviews within society, but it can also describe the multiple genres, structures, formats, and modalities in which texts are produced.

Providing students with texts that showcase diverse voices, experiences, and worldviews attunes them to the complexity of our world. However, it can be challenging to locate diverse texts for students to read. Given the current landscape of children's literature, as well as shifting student demographics, there is an ongoing need to provide readers with culturally authentic representations of diverse people, including their voices, bodies, languages, values, and experiences, in the books children read (Children's Literature Assembly, 2019; National Council of Teachers of English, 2015). Thomas (2016) contends, "If today's children grow up with literature that is multicultural, diverse, and decolonized, we can begin the work of healing our nation and world through humanizing stories" (p. 115). Since children's literature accounts for only some of the texts students read in schools, ensuring diverse representation in textbooks, packaged curriculum materials, and other instructional texts becomes an act of critical literacy.

In this regard, incorporating diverse texts also acknowledges literacy as a multifaceted endeavor and attends to the different strengths and abilities students can display with text, particularly for 21st-century tools and technology. Scholars have often employed a pluralized term—*literacies*—or the inclusive term *multiliteracies* in reference to this complexity (New London Group, 1996). Meanwhile, *multimodality* has also gained prominence to account for the ways different communication and representation modes (e.g., gesture, gaze, image, sound, writing, body posture, music) converge and are interpreted and remixed into meaning (Jewitt & Kress, 2008). Literacy researchers (e.g., Alvermann, Moon, & Hagood, 1999; Morrell, 2008; Schroeter & Wager, 2017) have applied these terms to examine how students engaging with pop culture, the arts, and digital media exhibit intricate critical literacy skills.

Take, for example, 5-year-old Roger, who responded to his kindergarten teacher, Ms. Smith's, read-aloud of the picture book *Oliver Button Is a Sissy* (dePaola, 1979) by giggling and swaying his hips back and forth whenever the main character Oliver was called a "sissy" for enjoying dancing (Enriquez, 2016). Juxtaposed with the picture book, a classic and familiar classroom text often used to promote gender equity, Roger's laughter and movement formed an embodied text that contrasted the ideology underlying the book's plot. In another example, eighth graders David and Tyrone grinned, shuddered, and commented, "Gay!" in response to "Smile" (Ford, 2008), a poem in which the assumed male narrator sentimentally observes a girl kissing a boy (Enriquez, 2016). Here, the traditional language-based text of a poem faced the spoken and embodied text of two adolescent boys noticing expressions of romantic tenderness by a male.

Inviting students to consider what both sets of texts (i.e., picture book and laughing/swaying; poem and grinning/shuddering/verbally commenting) were saying about gendered social norms would be an apt exercise in critical literacy and critical discourse analysis. Cappiello and Dawes (2012) posit that providing students with multimodal, multigenre text sets, or diverse collections of texts on a common theme or issue, nurtures critical approaches to text. Using a narrow definition of text limits students' capacity to critically examine the social world around us and curbs their potential to take part in dialogue that could lead to social change.

Text Deconstruction

Perhaps the cornerstone of critical reading is text deconstruction. At this point, it is hopefully clear that to approach a text critically, one must acknowledge the ideological construction of language, literacy, and texts. Text deconstruction, much like critical discourse analysis, aims to uncover tacit assumptions, values, and worldviews within texts through lenses of power, privilege, and perspective (Jones, 2006). Deconstructing text thus requires teachers to ask students the following questions:

- What does the author think about the topic or people in the text? How do you know? What words or phrases indicate the author's perspective?
- Whose voices have power in this text? Why did the author give power to these voices?
- Whose voices or perspectives aren't heard as much, perhaps because they are marginalized or silenced? Why might the author have diminished or omitted them?
- Where else have you heard these voices? Who shares that same voice in the real world?
- How is this author positioning your individual or cultural perspective on the topic in this text? Does it align with the author's? Is it mentioned but not given much serious consideration? Is it is missing from the text? (Wager et al., 2019, p. 114)

Such questions move the reader among text, self, and society. The objective is not simply to critique the text but also to engage in dialogue toward deeper understanding of how that text positions the reader within the broader world.

An example from Ms. Rosa's multigrade early childhood classroom illuminates how text deconstruction can work even with our youngest, emergent readers:

After reading a Seymour Simon (2001) book titled *Animals Nobody Loves,* [Ms. Rosa] asked students to find the evidence that supported the argument that nobody liked men-of-war. She elaborated: "Clearly, there is all this evidence that is showing that he is presenting this kind of biased perspective on this animal, so what are the things he's saying that are making us feel that way?" (Enriquez & Shulman-Kumin, 2014, p. 21)

Since she had read the text aloud to the class, Ms. Rosa's 4- and 5-year-olds were able to repeat the language they heard from the book as evidence of Simon's orientation toward men-of-war. Concluding her question with "that are making us feel that way?" was a purposeful move to connect the text to her students' realities.

Ms. Rosa also prepared for such text deconstruction work in her teacher education coursework. Using the nonfiction picture book *Can We Save the Tiger?* (Jenkins, 2011), Ms. Rosa co-designed an instructional activity with other elementary school teachers:

Jenkins' statement "Ugly things can be endangered, too" puts readers in the position to view all animals introduced before page 26 as *beautiful*. Pose the questions to students, *What characterizes an animal as beautiful or ugly?* Should the "beauty" of an animal be based on the way it looks or its function within the food chain? Why does Martin Jenkins frame vultures as *ugly*? Do you agree with his statement that "Ugly things can be endangered, too" or would you rewrite this page? If you agree with his statement that vultures are ugly, explain why. If you disagree with his framing of vultures as ugly, then explain why you disagree and rewrite page 26 to frame vultures in a new way. (Enriquez, 2014, p. 33)

Again, in deconstructing text, Ms. Rosa explicitly drew lines between the text and students' lives, helping them consider where each individually stands on this issue in the broader world context.

Text Reconstruction and Counter-Storytelling

Recognizing the creative power of youth of all ages to rewrite and remix the world before them, text deconstruction is but one step in critically approaching text (Morrell, 2008; Souto-Manning & Yoon, 2018). Reconstructing texts or counter-storytelling to acknowledge a multiplicity of voices and perspectives, especially to redistribute power to those that have historically been silenced, capitalizes on that creativity and generative capacity in all of us. Accordingly, one might ask:

- Could there be another way to interpret or understand the facts or events in the text?
- How might we retell or reinterpret the facts or events to hear the voices of those who are marginalized or silenced? (Wager et al., 2019, p. 115)

Such questions move critical approaches to text in a more dynamic and constructive direction. Reconstructing text and counter-storytelling are productive endeavors aimed at social justice.

For example, while reading aloud the picture book *Arturo y Clementina* (Turin & Bosnia, 2012), a story about a female turtle who leaves her husband when she can no longer take his commands to stay at home or his condescending treatment of her hobbies and interests, third-grade dual-language teacher Mr. Dimas noticed that several of his male students were attempting to justify Arturo's abusive actions as a test of Clementina's love. Seeking to interrogate the ideological power that Arturo's character conveyed and give Clementina's voice more power, Mr. Dimas asked not just text deconstruction questions but also reconstructive ones, including, "So can Clementina test Arturo too? Or is she not allowed to do that?" He also engaged students in discussions intended to help his students determine how power could be redistributed more equitably, asking questions along the lines of the following:

- What is another way that Arturo could respond to Clementina?
- What is something you could say to Arturo to help him see things from Clementina's perspective?
- What could happen if Clementina had more power from the start of the story?
- How could Clementina have more power in the story? (Wager et al., 2019, p. 115)

To help students reconstruct the tale, Mr. Dimas then asked them to write an encouraging letter to Clementina. At the story's conclusion, Clementina has left her oppressive situation while Arturo bemoans her ungrateful actions. One student, Carmen, however, asked if she could also write a letter to Arturo, believing he deserved admonishment for his behavior. Others joined in, writing their own letters to Arturo in hopes of reconstructing his outlook to be more compassionate and fair.

Teachers can facilitate text reconstruction by designing activities that require students to rewrite text, just as Mr. Dimas did here and as Ms. Rosa in the previous vignette. They can also support students' individual motivations and efforts to reconstruct their world, such as Carmen's proposal to address Arturo as well. Moreover, reconstructing texts is not limited to language-based media. A range of multimodal activity can showcase students' reconstruction of texts, including drama, music, visual art, and spoken word (Jocson, 2008; Leland et al., 2017; Morrell, 2008; Schroeter & Wager, 2017). As a component of critical literacy, text reconstruction centers on productive, agentive efforts of using text toward social justice.

Social Action

Moving from critically reading text toward social action, from the word to the world, prompted Freire (1970) to see literacy as *praxis,* or "theory-based action/action-based theorizing" (Shor, 1999, p. 16). For him, literacy pedagogy was a call to action. After all, what is the point of learning to read and write, if not to use them to improve conditions in the world around us?

In Ms. Brodsky's kindergarten classroom, a unit on "fairness" was part of the district-mandated social studies curriculum, but she knew it could be too abstract for students if she didn't help them connect it to their own lives (Enriquez, 2020). Throughout the year, Ms. Brodsky had often overheard them talking about birthday and holiday presents. Given the socioeconomic diversity of her students, she also noticed a disparity between what some students requested and what they received for presents. Working toward conscientization, she read aloud two books about children who are shunned by peers because of their limited wardrobe, *The Hundred Dresses* (Estes, 1944/2004) and *Each Kindness* (Woodson, 2012). Class discussions soon turned to the different treatment of people because of their material possessions, but through text deconstruction they also identified assumptions about race and poverty. To foster students' growing critical consciousness, Ms. Brodsky shared videos of toy commercials and asked the school librarian for help finding nonfiction articles for emergent readers about gift-giving traditions around the world.

Wondering if these efforts were making a difference, and knowing she was still fulfilling her district requirements, Ms. Brodsky turned the instructional decisions to the class, asking, "So what should we do with everything we learned about fairness?" A lively brainstorming session ensued, with the idea of holding a toy donation drive emerging as a viable opportunity for 5-year-olds. Ms. Brodsky found a local children's charity that would accept the donations but went one step further, arranging a field trip to the facility to see how the donations were cleaned, sorted, and distributed to local families. Students also decorated gift bags and cards for the children who would receive the toys, using social action to once more connect the word and the world.

Conclusion

• •

If literacy is indeed about "the language of possibility" (Freire & Macedo, 1987, p. 54), then taking critical approaches to text is clearly an important principle of effective literacy instruction. Rooted in critical theory and sociocultural theories of literacy, this principle acknowledges the pivotal role students play in using text to make sense of the world they inhabit. Moreover, critically approaching text gives purpose to literacy learning, thereby being an essential element of what it means to be literate. Thus, literacy not only remains a utilitarian pursuit but also becomes a way to reveal how one participates in the world. Critically approaching text asserts that literacy is full of possibility, for learners of all ages, to ensure we can all participate in more equitable and just ways.

REFERENCES

Alvermann, D., Moon, J., & Hagood, M. (1999). *Popular culture in the classroom: Teaching and researching critical media literacy.* Newark, DE: International Reading Association.

Bakhtin, M. (1981). Discourse in the novel (M. Holquist, Trans.). In M. Holquist & C. Emerson (Eds.), *The dialogical imagination: Four essays* (pp. 259–434). Austin: University of Texas Press.

Brooks, W., & Browne, S. (2012). Towards a culturally situated reader response theory. *Children's Literature in Education, 43,* 74–85.

Cappiello, M. A., & Dawes, E. T. (2012). *Teaching with text sets.* Huntington Beach, CA: Shell Education.

Children's Literature Assembly. (2019). On the importance of critical selection and teaching of diverse children's literature. [Position statement]. Retrieved from *www.childrensliteratureassembly.org/uploads/1/1/8/6/118631535/clapositionstatementontheimportanceofcriticalselectionandteachingofdiversechildrensliterature.pdf.*

Ciecierski, L. M., & Bintz, W. P. (2015). Using authentic literature to develop challenging and integrated curriculum. *Middle School Journal, 46*(5), 17–25.

Comber, B. (2015). Critical literacy and social justice. *Journal of Adolescent and Adult Literacy, 58*(5), 362–367.

Dávila, D. (2015). #WhoNeedsDiverseBooks?: Preservice teachers and religious neutrality with children's literature. *Research in the Teaching of English, 50*(1), 60–83.

Enriquez, G. (2014). Critiquing social justice picturebooks: Teachers' critical literacy reader responses. *New England Reading Association Journal, 50*(1), 27–37.

Enriquez, G. (2016). Reader response and embodied performance: Body-poems as performative response and performativity. In G. Enriquez, E. Johnson, S. Kontovourki, & C. Mallozzi (Eds.), *Literacies, learning, and the body: Putting theory and research into pedagogical practice* (pp. 41–56). New York: Routledge.

Enriquez, G. (2019). Rethinking read-alouds: Toward meaningful integration of diverse books in our classrooms. *Primer Calendar, 48*(1), 30, 40.

Enriquez, G. (2020). *Conscientization through children's literature in and beyond the classroom*. Manuscript submitted for publication.

Enriquez, G., & Shulman-Kumin, A. (2014). Searching for "truth": Using children's nonfiction for social justice and Common Core goals. *Journal of Children's Literature, 40*(2), 16–25.

Fairclough, N. (1995). *Critical discourse analysis: The critical study of language*. New York: Longman.

Fang, Z., & Wei, Y. (2010). Improving middle school students' science literacy through reading infusion. *Journal of Educational Research, 103*(4), 262–273.

Ford, A. (2008). *"Smile": The third fruit is a bird*. Cardiff, Australia: Picaro Press.

Freire, P. (1970). *Pedagogy of the oppressed*. New York: Continuum.

Freire, P., & Macedo, D. (1987). *Literacy: Reading the word and the world*. New York: Bergin & Harvey.

Gareis, E., Allard, M., & Saindon, J. (2009). The novel as textbook. *TESL Canada Journal, 26*(2), 136–147.

Gee, J. P. (1999). Critical issues: Reading and the new literacy studies: Reframing the National Academy of Sciences report on reading. *Journal of Literacy Research, 31*(3), 355–374.

Giroux, H. (1993). Literacy and the politics of difference. In C. Lankshear & P. McLaren (Eds.), *Critical literacy: Politics, praxis, and the postmodern* (pp. 367–378). Albany: State University of New York Press.

Heath, S. B. (1983). *Ways with words: Language, life and work in communities and classrooms*. Cambridge, UK: Cambridge University Press.

Janks, H. (2000). Domination, access, diversity and design: A synthesis for critical literacy education. *Educational Review, 52*(2), 175–186.

Jewitt, C., & Kress, G. R. (2008). *Multimodal literacy*. New York: Peter Lang.

Jocson, K. (2008). Youth poets: Empowering literacies in and out of schools. *Counterpoints, 304*.

Jones, S. (2006). *Girls, social class, and literacy: What teachers can do to make a difference*. Portsmouth, NH: Heinemann.

Jones, S., Clarke, L. W., & Enriquez, G. (2010). *The reading turn-around: A five-part framework for differentiated instruction*. New York: Teachers College Press.

Jones, S., & Enriquez, G. (2009). Engaging the intellectual and the moral in critical literacy education: The four-year journeys of two teachers from teacher education to classroom practice. *Reading Research Quarterly, 44*(2), 145–168.

Kern, D. (2007). Flying with critical literacy wings. *New England Reading Association Journal, 43*(2), 87–89.

Ladson-Billings, G., & Tate, W. (1995). Toward a critical race theory of education. *Teachers College Record, 97*(1), 47–68.

Leland, C., Lewison, M., & Harste, J. (2017). *Teaching children's literature: It's critical!* (2nd ed.). New York: Routledge.

Lewis, C. (2000). Limits of identification: The personal, pleasurable, and critical in reader response. *Journal of Literacy Research, 32*(2), 253–266.

Luke, A. (2012). Critical literacy: Foundational notes. *Theory Into Practice, 51*(1), 4–11.

Luke, A. (2014). Defining critical literacy. In J. Zacher Pandya & J. Avila (Eds.), *Moving critical literacies forward: A new look at praxis across contexts* (pp. 19–31). New York: Routledge.

Luke, A., & Freebody, P. (1999). Further notes on the four resources model. *Reading Online, 3,* 1–6.

McLaren, P. (2006). *Life in schools: An introduction to critical pedagogy in the foundations of education* (5th ed.). Boston: Allyn & Bacon.

Miller, E., & Kissel, B. (2019). Vivian Vasquez, NCTE's 2019 Outstanding Elementary Educator in the English language arts. *Language Arts, 97*(2), 72–77.

Morrell, E. (2008). *Critical literacy and urban youth: Pedagogies of access, dissent, and liberation.* New York: Routledge.

National Council of Teachers of English. (2015). *Resolution on the need for diverse children's and young adult books* [Position statement]. Retrieved from *https://ncte.org/statement/diverse-books.*

New London Group. (1996). A pedagogy of multiliteracies: Designing social futures. *Harvard Educational Review, 66*(1), 60–92.

Robbins, C. K. (2019). (Re)framing student development through critical feminist theories. In E. S. Abes, S. R. Jones, & D.-L. Stewart (Eds.), *Rethinking college student development theory using critical frameworks* (pp. 44–50). Sterling, VA: Stylus.

Rogers, R. (2011). *An introduction to critical discourse analysis in education* (2nd ed.). New York: Routledge.

Rosenblatt, L. (1978). *The reader, the text, the poem: The transactional theory of the literary work.* Carbondale: Southern Illinois Press.

Schroeter, S., & Wager, A. C. (2017). Blurring boundaries: Drama as a critical multimodal literacy for examining 17th-century witch hunts. *Journal of Adolescent and Adult Literacy, 60*(4), 405–413.

Shor, I. (1999). What is critical literacy? In I. Shor & C. Pari (Eds.), *Critical literacy in action: Writing words, changing worlds* (pp. 1–30). Portsmouth, NH: Boynton/Cook-Heinemann.

Sipe, L. R. (2008). *Storytime: Young children's literary understanding in the classroom.* New York: Teachers College Press.

Solorzano, D. G., & Yosso, T. J. (2001). Critical race and LatCrit theory and method: Counter-storytelling. *Qualitative Studies in Education, 14*(4), 471–495.

Souto-Manning, M., & Yoon, H. S. (2018). *Rethinking early literacies: Reading and rewriting worlds.* New York: Routledge.

Street, B. V. (1984). *Literacy in theory and practice.* Cambridge, UK: Cambridge University Press.

Thomas, E. E. (2016). Stories still matter: Rethinking the role of diverse children's literature today. *Language Arts, 94*(2), 112–119.

Vasquez, V. M., Janks, H., & Comber, B. (2019). Critical literacy as a way of being and doing. *Language Arts, 96*(5), 300–311.

Villano, T. L. (2005). Should social studies textbooks become history?: A look at alternative methods to activate schema in the intermediate classroom. *The Reading Teacher, 59*(2), 122–130.

Vygotsky, L. S. (1978). *Mind in society: The development of higher psychological processes.* Cambridge, MA: Harvard University Press.

Wager, A. C., Clarke, L. W., & Enriquez, G., with Garcia, C., Lara, G. P., & Reynolds, R. (2019). *The reading turn-around with emergent bilinguals: A five-part framework for powerful teaching and learning (Grades K–6).* New York: Teachers College Press.

Wetheridge, L. (2016). *Girls' and women's literacy with a lifelong learning perspective: Issues, trends and implications for the sustainable development goals.* Paris: United Nations Educational, Scientific and Cultural Organization.

CHILDREN'S LITERATURE

dePaola, T. (1979). *Oliver Button is a sissy.* New York: Harcourt Brace Jovanovich.

Estes, E. (1944/2004). *The hundred dresses.* New York: HMH Books for Young Readers.

Jenkins, M. (2011). *Can we save the tiger?* Somerville, MA: Candlewick Press.

Turin, A., & Bosnia, N. (2012). *Arturo y Clementina.* Barcelona, Spain: Kalandraka.

Woodson, J. (2012). *Each kindness.* New York: Nancy Paulsen Books.

19

Integrating Digital Technology

Amy C. Hutchison

Did you know that mainstream tablets such as the Apple iPad only became available in 2010? How often do you, your students, or children you know use tablets in their daily lives? If you said "A lot!" then you are not alone. According to a recent poll (Cavanagh, 2015), 78% of elementary school students say they regularly use a tablet. Accordingly, classroom instruction has evolved and continues to evolve as a way to take advantages of the affordances of digital tools such as tablets (Hutchison, Beschorner, & Schmidt-Crawford, 2012). Given these facts, the principle guiding this chapter is *digital texts and tools are an essential, not optional, component of 21st-century literacy instruction.*

This principle goes beyond the fact that technology use is ubiquitous among students inside and outside of school. Rather, digital technology has changed the nature of literacy, and instruction should reflect that change. In the following sections, I describe the numerous reasons that learning with digital technology is an essential component of literacy instruction and then explain how this principle can be flexibly applied in the classroom.

Why This Principle?

Students Are Not Literate Unless They Are Digitally Literate

As new technologies have evolved, so have our dominant forms of communication. No longer are print-based textbooks and periodicals the primary sources of information for students or for society at large. Rather, digital and multimodal texts are now the primary means through which we communicate and learn (Vee, 2017). Readers must be able to make meaning from and construct meaning with alphabetic text, images, sounds, videos, color, or some combination of all of those (Hutchison, Woodward, & Colwell, 2016). Because these are dominant forms of communication, it is the purview of literacy and language arts teachers to teach the skills, norms, and expectations associated with these forms of communication (Hutchison & Reinking, 2011). Accordingly, state and national standards have evolved to reflect the need for students to learn to read, write, and communicate with digital technology.

For example, building in complexity across the grade spans, the Common Core State Standards indicate that students should be able to use technology to produce and publish writing and to interact and collaborate with others (e.g., CCSS.ELA-LITERACY.W.3.6). The Common Core State Standards also indicate that students should recall information from experiences or gather information from print and digital sources (CCSS.ELA-LITERACY.W.3.8). By Grade 5, students are expected to be able to "draw on information from multiple print or digital sources, demonstrating the ability to locate an answer to a question quickly or to solve a problem efficiently" (CCSS.ELA-LITERACY.RI.5.7). By Grade 8, students are expected to "evaluate the advantages and disadvantages of using different mediums (e.g., print or digital text, video, multimedia) to present a particular topic or idea" (CCSS.ELA-LITERACY.RI.8.7). These English language arts (ELA) standards indicate the necessity of learning to communicate with digital tools and to learn from digital resources.

In addition to the Common Core ELA standards on the use of digital technology, many states have additional standards related to technology or digital learning, with many of the standards involving skills related to English language arts instruction, such as being an effective digital communicator. Additionally, states are rapidly adopting computer science standards in addition to their basic technology standards (Code.org, 2019). Currently, 34 states have computer science standards, an increase from only 22 states last year. Many states' standards, such as the Virginia Computer Science Standards of Learning, indicate that computer science should be integrated into content-area learning for elementary students, including literacy instruction. Collectively, all of these standards indicate that students are not literate if they are not digitally literate (Dalton, 2012; Hutchison et al., 2016). In other words, students would not be able to meet the requirements set forth by the standards without understanding how to read, write, and communicate with digital technology. Thus, this is the first reason for the principle, presented in this chapter, that digital texts and tools are an essential, not optional, component of 21st-century literacy instruction.

It Is Inequitable to Deny Some Students
the Opportunity to Become Digitally Literate

Although many students now have access to digital devices within their home, many students do not (KewalRamani et al., 2018). Without access to an Internet-connected device at home, students have fewer opportunities to engage in activities that will support the development of digital literacy skills. Further, even when students do have access to an Internet-connected device outside of school, that does not guarantee they have access to an adult, program, or opportunity that will help them build the skills needed for effectively reading, writing, and communicating with digital technology. In a recent study (Hutchison et al., 2016), preadolescent students reported that they participate in a broader range of online activities while at school than they do outside of school. Further, males reported engaging in digital reading and writing activities more often outside of school than did females, even though males and females had equal access to digital resources. This difference reiterates the concern that even when students have access to Internet-connected devices, they cannot be expected to have the impetus or opportunity to use them to build digital reading and writing skills.

This knowledge is particularly concerning when considering the number of high-paying jobs in the United States that involve digital communication and other computing skills. Without digital literacy skills, students will not have access to these jobs, even when ample jobs are available. In 2015 more than 600,000 high-paying tech jobs across the United States were unfilled (Smith, 2016), and the U.S. Department of Labor estimated that in the year 2020 there would be 1.4 million computing-related jobs unfilled (Bureau of Labor Statistics, U.S. Department of Labor, 2014). Even though it is not necessarily the purview of literacy teachers to prepare students for computing-related fields, it *is* their purview to prepare students with the reading, writing, and communication skills that will be necessary for future success. Currently, those skills must be digital *and* nondigital since a large majority of all jobs involve technology-related skills (Muro, Liu, Whiton, & Kulkarni, 2017).

According to a report published by the Brookings Institute (Muro et al., 2017), 517 of 545 occupations studied require the use of digital tools, and they report that jobs involving digital content tend to pay more. Beyond jobs and out-of-school access to Internet-connected devices, as previously mentioned, national and state standards call for digital literacy skills. Thus, it is inequitable to deprive students of opportunities to learn digital skills, which are mandated by the standards and are necessary for a majority of jobs. This potential inequality provides another reason for the inclusion of the primary principle presented in this chapter.

Digital Tools Help Us Level the Playing Field

Beyond inequitable access to digital communication learning opportunities, digital tools can also help us address learning needs that may be rooted in an early lack of learning opportunities or ongoing insufficiencies in learning opportunities. There are many ways that digital technology can be used to support a range of learning needs, which are outlined in this section.

Building Background and Domain-Specific Knowledge

One way that digital tools support high-quality literacy instruction is that they can help build background and/or domain-specific knowledge by providing access to a broader range of texts that may typically be available to students. Lack of prior knowledge, or lack of activation of that prior knowledge, and insufficient vocabulary knowledge are oft-cited reasons that students have difficulty comprehending what they read (Johnson, 1982). One primary cause of insufficient background knowledge or vocabulary knowledge is lack of exposure to experiences, books, and language outside of school (Christ & Wang, 2011). Digital technology provides easily accessible ways to build general or domain-specific knowledge and vocabulary before, during, and after reading experiences. Examples of how to integrate this practice into your instruction are provided in a subsequent section.

Making Reading and Writing Available to All Students, Regardless of Developmental Level

Another way that digital tools can support students with differing learning needs is by making appropriate text available to all students, regardless of reading ability. Students who have difficulty decoding alphabetic text can still engage with and learn from texts that provide audio recordings to go with a text, have interactive images to enhance and explain any text on the page, have videos to explain a concept or of someone reading the text aloud, and more. Although audio recordings have existed for a long time, and many print-based books have images to support written words, digital tools make it much easier to create and find these resources for students. Additionally, through the Internet, teachers can access a greater range of these resources and text types for students, leading to a greater chance of providing support materials that are of high quality, relevant, current, and interesting. Digital tools also make it easier to provide accessible texts to students with visual impairments, hearing impairments, and learning disabilities.

Making Artifacts and Experiences Available to Students

Digital tools can also create equity by enabling teachers to bring artifacts and experiences into the classroom that would not otherwise be accessible. This type of support could be valuable for many reasons. In some geographic locations, there is no access to artifacts and experiences that would support learning. Even when access to out-of-school learning experiences is geographically possible, such experiences may be costly, may require many parent volunteers to participate, and may take too much time away from in-school learning. Alternately, digital resources are freely and readily available for teachers who choose to make use of them. As examples, Discovery Education offers free literacy-themed virtual field trips that can be used to support literacy instruction in a range of ways. Similarly, sites such as Exploratorium, the website of the children's science museum in San Francisco, and that of the National Aeronautics and Space Administration (NASA), provide opportunities to integrate science into literacy instruction. These examples only begin to allude to the seemingly endless store of virtual artifacts and experiences available online. Teachers can use these resources in the classroom to ensure that all students, regardless of geographic location or socioeconomic status, have access to artifacts and experiences that expand their learning opportunities and prepare them for future learning.

Providing Differentiated Means for Demonstrating Knowledge
and Communicating about Learning

Another essential way that digital technology can be used to provide equitable learning opportunity for students is by using digital tools as a way for students to demonstrate comprehension and knowledge in ways that are appropriate for their individual development. For optimal learning, it is important that students have multiple options for expressing and communicating their understandings (CAST, 2018). There are many reasons for this need. For example, students in a typical classroom will be at different levels or stages of development with their literacy skills and may need differentiated assignments that align with their individual readiness. Students may differ in their levels of language proficiency and require differentiated means of expression for that reason. Some students in inclusive classrooms may have learning disabilities and individualized education plans (IEPs) that require differentiated options for response. Some students may simply have different background knowledge and experiences or different interests that make differing means of expression of their ideas an important lesson feature for them. Regardless of the reason, digital tools offer many ways for students to demonstrate comprehension and knowledge and communicate about their learning in ways that are appropriate for their individual development, interests, and needs. Digitally enabled response options for demonstrating understanding gives students the chance to apply their creativity, problem-solving skills, and digital navigation skills to create original products that require them to apply their knowledge of multimodal texts and create one of their own.

Applying This Principle Flexibly in the Classroom

Although the inclusion of digital technology in literacy instruction is necessary for equity among students, it must be carefully, thoughtfully, and flexibly applied in order to provide the kinds of equitable opportunities described in the aforementioned sections. Too often, digital technology is an afterthought to instruction and is not applied in ways that help students strategically build the digital literacy skills needed to be effective at reading, writing, and communicating with digital tools (Hutchison & Reinking, 2011). There are many strategies that teachers can use to avoid this pitfall. In this section, I explain a planning approach that can be used to consider how to meaningfully integrate digital technology into literacy instruction, and will describe specific ways to apply digital technology in literacy instruction to maximize the benefits and affordances of digital tools, while minimizing possible constraints.

One approach that can be used to consider how digital technology can be flexibly applied in a literacy classroom is the technology integration planning cycle (Hutchison & Woodward, 2014). As can be seen in Figure 19.1, the technology integration planning cycle is a planning tool that helps teachers consider several aspects of instruction and how digital tools may enhance or hinder progress toward an instructional goal. A key component of the technology integration planning cycle is that the planning should always begin with an instructional goal rather than a digital tool. By using this planning tool, teachers can first consider the literacy-related desired outcome of a lesson. Then, the teacher considers the types of digital tools that may support that literacy outcome, as well as the ways that digital technology may create better individualized learning opportunities for students.

After that, teachers consider all the ways that the selected digital tools contribute to the instructional goal and other possible ways that digital tools can be used to maximize the benefits of the tools. Relatedly, teachers then consider the possible constraints of using digital tools and ways that digital tools may detract or distract from the literacy-related

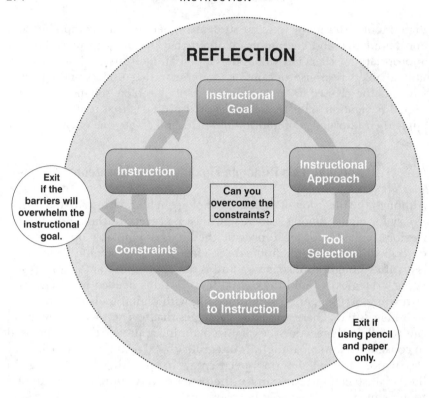

FIGURE 19.1. The technology integration planning cycle. Reprinted by permission from Hutchison and Woodward (2014). Copyright © 2014 International Literacy Association.

instructional goal. Next, the cycle guides the teacher to consider ways to overcome the possible constraints and consider if the constraints outweigh the benefit of using digital tools in the way planned. Finally, teachers consider how aspects of their instruction and instructional environment may need to change as a result of integrating digital technology in the way planned. Examples include planning for the way students will submit their work, rearranging the physical environment, and considering how digital work products will be assessed. A more detailed description of the technology integration planning cycle can be found in the related article by Hutchison and Woodward (2014) or in Hutchison and Colwell's (2015) book *Bridging Technology and Literacy*.

Using the technology integration planning cycle, teachers can consider the ways that digital technology can be flexibly applied to support literacy instruction. As a general guide, I suggest the following categories for considering how to integrate digital tools into literacy instruction: (1) teaching skills for reading, writing, and communicating with digital tools, including understanding how to read and create multimodal texts; (2) making reading accessible for all students; (3) making artifacts and experiences available to students; and (4) providing differentiated means for demonstrating knowledge and communicating about learning. In the following sections, I will provide examples of how these uses of digital technology can be applied to literacy instruction.

In Practice: Building Background and Domain-Specific Knowledge

There are countless ways that digital tools can be used to build background and content-area knowledge, as well as vocabulary knowledge. As previously mentioned, activating and building background knowledge is essential for reading comprehension and for connecting new knowledge to existing knowledge (Johnson, 1982). Thus, in this section I provide a brief example of how the technology integration planning cycle can be used to plan instruction that emphasizes building background and vocabulary knowledge.

Consider this scenario: A teacher is working on the instructional goal of helping students determine the main ideas of an informational text on the American Revolution, particularly focusing on the causes of the American Revolution. However, this teacher has many English learners (ELs) whose English skills are still emerging. Additionally, these students are recent immigrants to the United States and have not had previous instruction on any aspects of American history. Consequently, they are likely to lack background knowledge that is necessary for comprehension. Research indicates that "literacy instruction for [ELs] should heavily focus on the development of background information and cultural schema for reading" (Rance-Roney, 2010, p. 387) and that ELs need intensive and intentional vocabulary instruction to support their comprehension while reading.

This is a scenario in which the technology integration planning cycle can be used to consider how to support these students with digital technology. As shown in Table 19.1, the technology integration planning cycle was applied to determine that Digital Jumpstarts can be used to build background knowledge and domain-specific word knowledge for these students. Additionally, Digital Jumpstarts are likely to be beneficial for all students, regardless of their English-speaking abilities. Digital Jumpstarts are short teacher-created videos with images, audio, and words from a text. They are used to help readers prepare to read a text by scaffolding background information and essential vocabulary prior to reading. They are intended to "lessen the gap between what a student knows and

TABLE 19.1. Using the Technology Integration Planning Cycle to Determine How Digital Tools Can Be Used to Build Background Knowledge

Technology Integration Planning Cycle Component	Instructional Plan
Instructional Goal and/or Standards: What do I want students to know and be able to do?	*Original Instructional Goals:* 1. Students will read an informational text about the American Revolution and determine the two main ideas of the text, providing key details to support their answers. Then they will summarize the text with an emphasis on explaining the primary causes of the American Revolution. 2. Students will use context clues to determine the meaning of unfamiliar words. *Standards Being Addressed:* CCSS.ELA-LITERACY.RI.5.2: Determine two or more main ideas of a text and explain how they are supported by key details; summarize the text. CCSS.ELA-LITERACY.RI.5.4: Determine the meaning of general academic and domain-specific words and phrases in a text relevant to a *Grade 5 topic or subject area.*
Instructional Approach: What instructional approaches do I typically use to teach this content?	*Original Plan:* 1. Students will work with a partner to read the text and determine the main ideas using the "say something" strategy in which Partner 1 reads the text aloud and Partner 2 says something at the end of the page to indicate comprehension or make a connection to the ideas. 2. Students will mark unfamiliar words on the page with sticky notes and try to use context clues to determine the meaning of the word, writing the meaning on the attached sticky note.
Tool Selection: What digital tools will provide students with support for learning this content or enhance the learning experience?	Since many students in the class are immigrants, they may be completely unfamiliar with many aspects of American history that are useful or necessary for understanding the ideas and the domain-specific words. *Revised Plan Using Digital Tools to Provide Background Knowledge:* Digital Jumpstarts (Rance-Roney, 2010), which are short videos with images, audio, and words from the text, can be used to help readers prepare to read the text by scaffolding the background information and essential vocabulary prior to reading.

(continued)

TABLE 19.1. *(continued)*

Technology Integration Planning Cycle Component	Instructional Plan
Contribution to Instruction: How does this use of technology enhance my instruction?	Digital Jumpstarts ensure that all students have sufficient background knowledge to comprehend the text and provide images for vocabulary words that will aid in comprehension.

Potential Constraints: What problems or barriers might I encounter when using this tool in this way? Can I find solutions to overcome the constraints and adhere to my instructional goal?	1. Students may have difficulty accessing the Digital Jumpstarts.
	   Possible Solution: Add them to a shared drive or create a tiny url to make them easy to access.
	2. Digital Jumpstarts won't help some of my students after only one viewing.
	   Possible Solution: Provide access to them outside of school; create a space in the classroom where they can view them independently as needed.

Instructional Considerations: What aspects of my instruction or classroom do I need to change or consider when using digital technology in this way?	Consider which students may benefit for watching the Digital Jumpstarts multiple times, and determine how you will configure your instructional space or materials to provide multiple exposures.

what he or she must learn" (Echevarría, Vogt, & Short, 2008, p. 32). They provide students with exposure to the language and ideas that they will encounter in a text. By planning this instruction with the technology integration planning cycle, teachers can consider the potential benefits and constraints of using Digital Jumpstarts, plan how to overcome potential constraints, and consider how the digital tool can be flexibly applied to meet the needs of individual students.

In Practice: Making Reading and Writing Available for All Students

As previously described, another way that digital tools can enhance literacy instruction is by reading and writing available to students at all developmental levels. One way of individualizing text to make it appropriate for individual students is by using apps and websites that reword text or adapt content to different reading levels. For example, sites such as *http://rewordify.com* can simplify complex sentences and words into easier-to-read text and provides simple definitions for words. Teachers could use tools such as this judiciously to individualize student learning. Relatedly, sites such as *https://newsela.com* provide texts at five different reading levels. Teachers can assign different text levels to each student.

Other ways that digital tools make text available to all students is through audio recordings, interactive features, and videos, and animations that are only available through digital technology. There are many examples of how these tools and features can be used in instruction. Some specific ways that are likely to be of benefit to teachers are as follows:

1. The teacher can record a video or audio recording tool on a table to record themselves reading a book aloud. During independent work time, students can watch or listen as they read along in the book. After listening several times, students can record themselves reading the book.

2. Students hear text read aloud using text-to-speech apps and websites, such as the Voice Dream Reader app. This app enables the user to upload any text and change backgrounds, languages, and text layout. Tools such as this may be useful for students who are not yet fluent readers and for EL students.

3. Students can create their own picture books and read books created by other students using a simple storybook creation app such as Storybook Creator. Depending on students' individual reading and writing skills, they can add words and sentences to their stories.

4. Students can record their voices and turn their audio recordings into text using speech-to-text apps, such as Voice Dream Writer. Additionally, users can have their written text read aloud to them. Tools such as these may be useful for students who have difficulty with letter formation and who are not yet able to write sentences but can orally compose stories.

These suggested uses are only the beginning of how digital tools can be used to make reading and writing more accessible and developmentally appropriate for all students. By planning with the technology integration planning cycle, teachers can consider how to most beneficially apply these tools.

In Practice: Providing Differentiated Means for Demonstrating Knowledge and Communicating about Learning

As mentioned previously, there are many reasons that students may need differentiated means or multiple options for expressing their understanding communicating about their learning. Digital tools enable teachers to provide flexible options for students to meet individual needs. Here are some of the ways digital tools can be applied to help students demonstrate knowledge and communicate about their learning.

1. Students can explain their understanding through a combination of drawing, speaking, images, and screencasting. Sites such as *https://explaineverything.com* and *www.educreations.com* enable students to use any combination of these modes of communication (drawing, speaking, images, screencasting) to explain their ideas and even create media products to teach others about their topic.

2. Students can explain their thinking through an interactive narrated presentation that allows viewers to provide audio comments and written feedback directly into the presentation. One popular site that enables this kind of learning is *https://voicethread.com*. Tools such as this may also help students practice their oral language and conversation skills.

3. Students can simply create digital animations or representations of their ideas by using digital tools such as Scratch or Scratch Jr. (*https://scratch.mit.edu*). Scratch and Scratch Jr. were created as a means of helping children creatively express themselves with a computer, while also learning early coding and problem-solving skills. This tool enables students to share their ideas by creating interactive stories or animations.

4. Another important way that students can use digital tools to express themselves is by using digital graphic organizers that support them in organizing their ideas but go beyond a paper-based graphic organizer by also permitting them to insert images, weblinks, and audio clips to communicate their ideas. Tools such as Popplet (*www.popplet.com*) help students capture thoughts and images in one place and then consider and show the relationship among their thoughts by graphically organizing them. This option can be useful for students who are not yet ready to write their ideas in paragraph form. This can be way to scaffold students' progress toward a larger writing goal.

Conclusion

As was described throughout this chapter, digital tools broaden the repertoire of strategies and approaches that can be used to ensure that all students are able to read, write, and communicate at a level that is appropriate for their individual development. There is tremendous flexibility in how digital tools can be applied to support students for different purposes and goals. However, digital technology should always be used thoughtfully as a means of strategically advanced literacy goals rather than as an add-on to instruction or out of a misguided obligation for providing students with access to technology. Digital technologies are essential tools for building students' ever-expansive literacy skills. In other words, digital texts and tools are an essential, not optional, component of 21st-century literacy instruction.

REFERENCES

Bureau of Labor Statistics, U.S. Department of Labor. (2014). Occupational outlook handbook, 2014–15 edition: Computer and information research scientists. Retrieved from *www.bls.gov/ooh/computer-andinformationtechnology/ computerandinformationresearch-scientists.htm*.

CAST. (2018). Universal design for learning guidelines version 2.2. Retrieved from *http://udlguidelines.cast.org*.

Cavanagh, S. (2015, September 24). Students' tablet, smartphone usage climbs, with strong appetite for apps. Retrieved from *https://marketbrief.edweek.org/ marketplace-k   12/student_tablet_smartphone_usage_climbs_with_strong_appetite_for_apps*.

Christ, T., & Wang, C. (2011) Closing the vocabulary gap?: A review of research on early childhood vocabulary practices. *Reading Psychology, 32*(5), 426–458.

Code.org. (2019, July 11). 33 states expand access to K–12 computer science education in 2019. Retrieved from *https://medium.com/@codeorg/32-states-expand-access-to-k-12-computer-science-education-in-2019-7d2357fe6f3d*.

Dalton, B. (2012). Digital literacies in the classroom: Multimodal composition and the Common Core State Standards. *The Reading Teacher, 66*(4), 333–349.

Echevarría, J., Vogt, M., & Short, D. J. (2008). *Making content comprehensible for English learners: The SIOP® model* (3rd ed.). Boston: Allyn & Bacon.

Hutchison, A., Beschorner, B., & Schmidt-Crawford, D. (2012). Exploring the use of the iPad for literacy learning. *The Reading Teacher, 66*(1), 15–23.

Hutchison, A. C., & Colwell, J. (2015). *Bridging technology and literacy: Developing digital reading and writing practices in Grades K–6.* Lanham, MD: Rowman & Littlefield.

Hutchison, A., & Reinking, D. (2011). Teachers' perceptions of integrating information and communication technologies into literacy instruction: A national survey in the U.S. *Reading Research Quarterly, 46*(4), 308–329.

Hutchison, A., & Woodward, L. (2014). A planning cycle for integrating digital technology into literacy instruction. *The Reading Teacher, 67*(6), 455–466.

Hutchison, A. C., Woodward, L., & Colwell, J. (2016). What are preadolescent readers doing online?: An examination of upper elementary students' reading, writing, and communication in digital spaces. *Reading Research Quarterly, 51*(4), 435–454.

Johnson, P. (1982). Effects on reading comprehension of building background knowledge. *TESOL Quarterly, 16,* 503–516.

KewalRamani, A., Zhang, J., Wang, X., Rathbun, A., Corcoran, L., Diliberti, M., & Zhang, J. (2018). *Student access to digital learning resources outside of the classroom* (NCES 2017-098). Washington, DC: National Center for Education Statistics, U.S. Department of Education. Retrieved from *https://nces.ed.gov/ pubsearch/pubsinfo.asp?pubid=2017098*.

Muro, M., Liu, S., Whiton, J., & Kulkarni, S. (2017). Digitalization and the American workforce. Retrieved from *www.brookings.edu/wp-content/uploads/2017/11/mpp_2017nov15_digitalization_full_report.pdf*.

Rance-Roney, J. (2010). Jump-starting language and schema for English-language learners: Teacher-composed Digital Jumpstarts for academic reading. *Journal of Adolescent and Adult Literacy, 53*(5), 386–395.

Smith, M. (2016, January). Computer science for all. Retrieved from *https://obamawhitehouse.archives.gov/blog/2016/01/30/computer-science-all*.

Vee, A. (2017). *Coding literacy*. Cambridge, MA: MIT Press.

20

Adaptive Teaching

Margaret Vaughn

Across the literature, scholars describe effective literacy teachers as adaptive (Duffy, 2005; Gambrell, Malloy, & Mazzoni, 2011; Snow, Griffin, & Burns, 2005). The concept of adaptability is not new in the field of education. Scholars dating back to John Dewey (1910) emphasized the need for teachers to adopt an adaptive and flexible perspective toward instruction. Schön (1983) highlighted how teachers must engage in adaptive instruction to navigate the complexities of teaching and to engage in classrooms that are the "swampy lowland where situations are confusing 'messes' incapable of a technical solution" (p. 42). Borko and Livingston (1989) suggested that adaptive teachers must draw upon an extensive repertoire of routines and patterns of action while reflecting to incorporate responsive and new instructional moves.

More recently, scholars and researchers have examined, theorized, and explored adaptability as a necessary dimension of classroom literacy instruction (Johnston, Dozier, & Smit, 2016; Parsons, 2012; Vaughn, 2019). These scholars highlight that successful teachers are adaptive and acknowledge the unpredictability of the classroom, see multiple perspectives, and apply knowledge and instructional actions situationally, depending on what is needed in the moment and with the individual students with whom they teach.

While scholars contend that adaptive instruction is an integral dimension of effective literacy instruction, given recent high-stakes accountability reform mandates in the United States (e.g., No Child Left Behind, Race to the Top), teachers have faced increased pressures to standardize their literacy instruction. These reform efforts have pressured teachers to teach literacy using a prescriptive literacy curricula without deviation. This approach has been characterized as "skill and drill" or one where teachers teach isolated skills to prepare for state-mandated literacy assessments. Although this type of instruction was meant to support students, a "skill and drill" approach to instruction is rarely adaptive and fails to meet the needs of all students, particularly students with high needs who face difficulty learning (Aukerman, Belfatti, & Santori, 2008).

Students are so vastly different and complex—in that they come to school with rich cultures, different backgrounds, languages, and abilities—that to effectively build upon these strengths, not one singular approach will fit every student all of the time. Strictly adhering to a teacher's manual or following a pacing guide exactly as it is written rarely meets the needs of all students. To meet students' instructional needs, teachers must be flexible and adaptive in their approach as they creatively develop instructional moves alongside their students to support student learning. Effective literacy teaching requires that teaches are adaptive and reflect-in-action to frame and solve problems in the midst of instruction as they take into account student cues, responses, and other situational variables that they cannot foresee (Schön, 1983; Vaughn, Parsons, Gallagher, & Branen, 2016; Zeichner & Liston, 2013).

Adaptive teachers work alongside their students. During adaptive literacy instruction, teachers make adaptive instructional moves to meet the social, linguistic, cultural, and instructional needs of their students. Students are essential partners during adaptive instruction as they help to shape the direction of the lesson through unanticipated ideas, questions, responses, understandings, and experiences. As a result, adaptive teachers change their instructional practice, weaving knowledge of students' interests, backgrounds, and instructional needs with their knowledge of effective pedagogy to meet students' needs during the lesson (Parsons et al., 2018; Vaughn, 2019).

Adaptive literacy teachers are interpretative, instructive, and metacognitive about their decisions. They approach teaching from a student-generated stance and one that cannot be wholly planned ahead of time. This understanding is not to underestimate the role of instructional planning, but it emphasizes how every moment during instruction is different from the next and cannot be completely planned. For example, during a guided reading lesson, after reading a text about types of trees, a student shares that on the playground there is a grand fir pine tree. Another student shares that during the holidays, his family cuts down a Douglas fir pine tree. Although the next step in the teacher's lesson plan was to focus on word chunks and how to decode words within a text, she puts that activity aside after hearing her students' detailed accounts. She asks students to write about their experiences and to provide as much detail as they can so they can share with others in the class.

During this exchange, the teacher was adaptive, and although she had a well-developed lesson plan, her students' discussions about trees drove her away from her lesson plan. She redirected her instruction to focus on writing personal narratives, thereby adapting what she had originally planned. Opportunities like this are what Sawyer (2004) calls "improvisational" and "interactional and [emphasize the] responsive creativity of a teacher working together with a unique group of students" (p. 13). Teaching adaptively requires this keen ability to be open to opportunities like this during instruction and to harness the ability to improvise and "assemble through blending with existing practices . . . to produce meaningful changes" (Honan, 2004, p. 101). In short, adaptive teachers are innovative in their approach because they make specific instructional moves or adaptations to their instruction on the fly or in the moment that result in enhanced student learning opportunities. These teachers creatively weave together different knowledge (i.e., knowledge of content, teaching, their experiences) and their beliefs and vision for teaching (Vaughn & Parsons, 2013). In doing so, adaptive teachers

- generate instructional adaptations and deliver instructional moves in the moment while teaching;
- co-create authentic learning experiences with students anchored in their interests, questions, and understandings; and
- expertly modify and adapt their knowledge to situational factors.

Research on effective teachers supports the need for adaptability when teaching literacy (Allington & Johnston, 2002; Snow et al., 2005; Vaughn, 2015). Pressley, Allington, Wharton-McDonald, Block, and Morrow (2001) in their studies of exemplary first-grade teachers found that teachers who modified and adapted their instructional materials and approaches were more successful than those who did not. Pressley and scholars (2001) found the following about exemplary first-grade teachers:

> Rather than adapt children to a particular method, teachers adapted the methods they used to the children with whom they were working at a particular time. As they became more sensitive to how children learn, they moved away from simply giving children information and toward facilitating children's exploration of children's own theories and interests. (p. 208)

Williams and Baumann (2008) examined expert elementary teachers in their research synthesis of effective literacy teaching and also found that adaptability was a cornerstone of effective instruction. Similarly, in a review of more than 800 research studies, Hattie (2009) found that effective teachers

> possess pedagogical content knowledge that is more flexibly and innovatively employed in instruction; they are more able to improvise and to alter instruction in response to contextual features of the classroom situation . . . they can more easily improvise when things do not run smoothly. (p. 261)

In sum, adaptability has been found across the literature to be a dimension of effective teaching.

A Model of Adaptability

Adaptive teachers have knowledge and an instructional vision (i.e., what it is they wish to accomplish in their teaching), and the sophisticated ability to build and create instructional moves rooted in knowledge of content, their students, and their beliefs and vision about teaching. Teachers apply instructional moves and adaptations in response to their students that results in a collaborative space between teachers and students.

Knowing about Students' Cultural and Linguistic Backgrounds

A cornerstone of adaptive literacy instruction is how teachers support the individual characteristics of the students with whom they work. Adaptive literacy teachers take their knowledge of their students and reflect on how to adjust their teaching and future goals to meet their students' instructional, cultural, and linguistic needs. Given this, culturally responsive teaching is central to adaptive literacy teaching. A guiding principle of culturally responsive teaching is using "cultural knowledge, prior experiences, frames of reference, and performance styles of ethnically diverse students [and incorporating these into instruction] to make learning more relevant and effective" (Gay, 2002, p. 106). Adaptive teachers must use this knowledge to adapt their instruction to meet the needs of the specific student populations with whom they teach.

Adaptive literacy teachers are responsive and notice what and when their students need support. Responsiveness relies on not only noticing students but also possessing an awareness of students' cultural and linguistic experiences and how they learn (Assaf & Lopez, 2012). In doing so, teachers can learn alongside of students and literacy instruction is student centered. Adaptive teaching emphasizes the role of responsiveness and asks teachers to discover who their students are, their strengths, and their knowledge and incorporate this learned knowledge into their instruction.

Possessing a Variety of Knowledge Categories

Adaptive literacy teaching blends together teachers' knowledge about teaching and their beliefs and vision about students, teaching, and themselves as a teacher. Adaptive teachers take their procedural knowledge (what it is—i.e., phonemic awareness, fluency, comprehension); declarative knowledge (how to do it—i.e., how to teach students to comprehend a text); beliefs (what do I believe about my students and teaching?); and vision (what is it that I wish to accomplish in my teaching?) and apply these dimensions conditionally using conditional knowledge (knowing when to teach it—i.e., my students need this concept at this time). Adaptive teachers develop their knowledge throughout their learning trajectories, through their experiences in and out of the classroom, and through reflective practice.

Procedural knowledge is understanding the content. For example, Ms. Kim, a second-grade teacher, has procedural knowledge because she knows what fluency is and the important role it has in her students' reading lives. Ms. Kim also has declarative knowledge, or in the context of fluency, for example, she knows how to teach fluency, the different strategies and skills, and the supports to use when teaching fluency. Ms. Kim uses conditional knowledge, to deliver instructional moves when her students need it, to support student learning. Adaptive teaching requires the use of these different knowledge categories to support student learning.

Possessing a Vision and Beliefs

Adaptive teaching requires reflection of beliefs and for teachers to possess a vision for teaching in addition to possessing these knowledge categories. Consider, for instance, Mr. Kennedy, a third-grade teacher. His vision, or what it is he ultimately wants for his students as a result of his teaching, is to develop a passion for reading and to become lifelong readers. However, his school's recommendation for reading instruction included strictly adhering to a pacing guide and teaching isolated skills from passages on a worksheet with accompanying multiple-choice questions.

Despite this schoolwide directive, he decided to use his knowledge and beliefs about effective literacy teaching to support his vision. Instead of teaching according to pacing guide, which did not fit the instructional needs of his students, Mr. Kennedy decided to use authentic texts that were relevant to his students' lives and engage students in literature circle discussions. During his instruction, he inserts mini-lessons after hearing students' discussions about what they are thinking and provides parallel texts to support a skill that the students need based on their discussions. During his literacy instruction, Mr. Kennedy could have followed what was asked of him in the curriculum manual and the accompanying worksheets, but instead, he used his vision, understanding about his students, and his knowledge and beliefs to guide his instructional actions. Figure 20.1 displays the model of adaptability in practice.

As this figure indicates, adaptive teachers weave these knowledge categories, their understandings about students and teaching, and their beliefs and vision to construct instructional adaptations *in the moment* to enhance student learning.

Adaptive teaching is a principle of effective literacy instruction and an integral dimension of effective teaching as teachers take knowledge and apply adaptations conditionally depending on what is needed in the moment. What is clear in the literature is that adaptive teachers are effective and successful teachers. But what are characteristics of an adaptive literacy teacher?

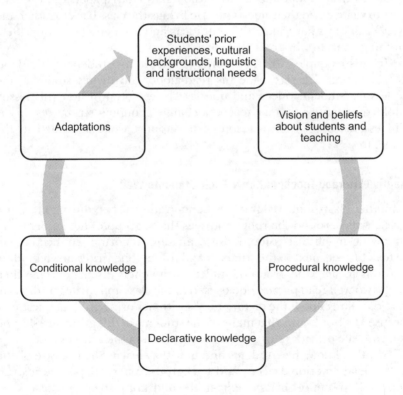

FIGURE 20.1. Model of adaptability in practice.

Characteristics of Adaptive Literacy Teachers

Adaptive Literacy Teachers Listen to Students

Adaptive literacy teachers listen to their students and co-construct the learning outcomes together. They build on their students' agency as they share the floor with their students in a meaningful and authentic manner (Johnston, 2004; Vaughn, 2014, 2018, 2020). In these spaces, students' ideas, inquiries, and interests are central during literacy instruction. Such an approach to teaching requires that teachers and students are co-creators, generating learning outcomes together.

Consider the classroom example of Mr. Riaz, a first-grade teacher who is conducting a read-aloud of a story on space. Before the reading, Mr. Riaz asks students to share and pair with one another and tell what they know about space. Mr. Riaz listens to students and hears several students share their questions. One student says, "How far is it to space?" Another student says, "I want to read about Pluto." Another student says, "I want to draw about aliens." Mr. Riaz takes chart paper and asks students to write down their questions. He brings the class back together and says, "Each of us have such different ideas and such good questions; let's work in groups to work on these ideas."

In this example, Mr. Riaz works alongside his students and adapts his instruction. He sets aside his read-aloud and invites students into the lesson. Students' ideas and queries are essential in how this lesson unfolded. Adaptive literacy teachers change grouping structures, insert mini-lessons, or provide a resource to support what is needed in the moment.

Adaptive Literacy Teachers Know Their Students Well

In another classroom, Ms. Boe, a second-grade teacher, during literature circles, walks around the room and sees that a group of her students are not having much discussion and are missing important connections to the text. She sits next to the students and listens. She writes down guiding questions to help the group of students with their discussion. She then brings two well-read picture books used in the class and invites students to practice talking about the picture books with her using guiding questions. Because Ms. Boe knows that many of the students in this group are shy and reluctant, she provides this scaffold to aid them in their discussion.

Ms. Boe knows her students and how they learn. She is aware of students' social emotional needs and backgrounds and adapts the instructional task to support her students in the midst of instruction.

Adaptive Literacy Teachers Continually Informally Assess Students

During reader's workshop, Ms. Sims, a fourth-grade teacher, conferences with her students. She finds that during her discussion with one of her students, they are missing how to identify the overriding theme in the text they are reading. She pulls a popular text off the shelf, and since she knows that her student has read this text several times, she is well familiar with the plot of the story. Ms. Sims asks the student to write down different events in the story that were important and they discuss the overall theme of the text. Ms. Sims asks the student to do the same in the current story. Given this important scaffold, the student was able to identify the important events and then look back and think broadly about the theme of the story.

As this example illustrates, adaptive teachers continually informally assess students. In this example, Ms. Sims, during her conversation with the student, conducted an informal assessment and found that the student was struggling with identifying theme. She used a resource and provided the necessary support to model how to find the theme. Adaptive literacy teachers continually assess during literacy instruction to understand what their students need and when they need it.

Adaptive Literacy Teachers Reflect on Their Practice

Through the process of knowing students well and observing what is needed in the moment, teachers are able to reflect and create classroom spaces supportive of what their students need. For example, Mr. Jake, a fifth-grade teacher, during a novel study using a variety of graphic novels, asks students to create their own short story. Students share that they want to extend a story about an existing graphic novel they have recently read. Because one of the previous class activities was to expand on a story much like this, Mr. Jake redirects the students and asks them to instead choose a topic for their graphic novel about one of the local issues in their community: whether landowners should sell off their farmland to build or to write about the local debate about the dams. When asked why he decided to restructure this lesson in this way, he shared that his vision for teaching was to develop "problem solvers who have the skills and knowledge to tackle real-world problems. I [made that change] because I wanted them to connect to their own lives and what's really going on in their community so they could take a position either way."

Like Mr. Jake, adaptive teachers reflect on their practice and think about how their instruction supports their vision, using their knowledge of students, pedagogy, and teaching. Reflecting is an essential dimension of adaptive literacy teachers. In order to create spaces like this for students, teachers must engage in reflection to examine how their instructional practices support the diverse needs of their students (Zeichner & Liston, 2013).

Common Rationales and Adaptations during Instruction

Understanding the reasons teachers adapt and the types of adaptations teachers make to support literacy learning is helpful when teaching literacy. Knowing these common adaptations can prepare teachers to teach adaptively. For example, thinking and reflecting about additional resources or supports that students might need during a lesson can be essential in efforts to teach adaptively. Similarly, omitting a planned activity much like the teacher did in the above example with the pine trees is important when teaching adaptively.

Knowing why adaptive literacy teachers adapt is helpful when thinking about how to be ready for opportunities to adapt and modify the curriculum. What are the reasons adaptive literacy teachers adapt? Consider the following classroom vignette where the teacher responded to why she adapted her instruction.

During a third-grade lesson, Ms. Trenk shared that she incorporated a mini-lesson on persuasive writing after two groups of students during literature circles had differing opinions about how schools should react to bullying. She explained:

> "Well, one of the groups was reading *Wishtree,* a realistic fiction story about an immigrant girl and her arrival into a community, and had some really interesting ideas about how students should be in charge of monitoring and changing bullying with other kids. Another group was reading *The Thickedity,* a fantasy story about a girl and her brother who were constantly bullied at school because of their parent's background. This group, too, had some interesting and compelling ideas about what the school and other kids should have done. I decided to incorporate a mini-lesson on persuasive writing so that students could think out their ideas."

This teacher wanted "to challenge, elaborate, or enhance student understanding" to support her students. Ms. Trenk listened to her students and was able to incorporate a lesson on writing a persuasive essay. Like this example, across the research, there are common reasons that adaptive literacy teachers adapt their instruction (see Figure 20.2).

Effective literacy teachers adapt in order to . . .

- Address student misunderstanding
- Challenge, elaborate, or enhance student understanding
- Teach a specific strategy or skill
- Help students make connections
- Use knowledge of student(s) to alter instruction
- Anticipate upcoming difficulty
- Manage time or behavior
- Promote student engagement or involvement
- Follow student interest, curiosity, or inquiry

FIGURE 20.2. Reasons effective literacy teachers adapt.

As this figure illustrates, these are common reasons across the research that teachers adapt their literacy instruction (Parsons & Vaughn, 2013). What are common adaptations that we see during adaptive literacy instruction? As in the above example with Ms. Trenk and her students, she adapted her lesson to insert a mini-lesson on persuasive writing. Figure 20.3 lists common types of adaptations that teachers incorporate into their literacy instruction (Parsons & Vaughn, 2013).

Teachers can be adaptive in all areas of literacy instruction. For example, during a whole-class lesson, teachers can be aware of opportunities where students would be better supported by working in a small group or individually. Similarly, during guided reading, teachers can look for opportunities where they can introduce new content based on either a student inquiry or discussion about a text. Teachers can reflect on the types of rationales and adaptations and reflect on their literacy instruction to notice opportunities when they adapt with these outlined

Adaptations:

- Introduces new content
- Inserts a new activity
- Omits a planned activity
- Provides a resource or example
- Models a skill or inserts a mini-lesson
- Suggests a different perspective to students
- Pulls a small group, conducts an individual conference, or changes grouping structure

FIGURE 20.3. Adaptations found in our previous research.

adaptations in mind. These are just some of the common rationales and adaptations found in the research. There are many more adaptations that teachers can do to support the diverse needs of their students. Through reflective practice, teachers can build and develop an adaptive stance in their teaching.

Conclusion

Adaptive teaching is considered an essential aspect of effective literacy instruction. Adaptability requires teachers to modify their instructional actions based on knowledge of their students' social, cultural, linguistic, and instructional needs. In this chapter, a primary goal was to help uncover what adaptive literacy teaching is and the common adaptations and rationales for teaching adaptively during literacy instruction. Teaching adaptively is indeed a creative and improvisational endeavor and one that effective teachers engage in without hesitation. It is the aim of this chapter to invite you to reflect on your practice and to notice those opportunities during your instruction where students offer questions, insights, and places where they need additional support and to capitalize on them to create enhanced learning opportunities.

REFERENCES

Allington, R. L., & Johnston, P. H. (2002). *Reading to learn: Lessons from exemplary fourth-grade classrooms.* New York: Guilford Press.

Assaf, L. C., & Lopez, M. (2012). Reading rocks: Creating a space for preservice teachers to become responsive teachers. *Journal of Early Childhood Teacher Education, 33*(4), 365–381.

Aukerman, M. S., Belfatti, M. A., & Santori, D. M. (2008). Teaching and learning dialogically organized reading instruction. *English Education, 40*(4), 340–364.

Borko, H., & Livingston, C. (1989). Cognition and improvisation: Differences in mathematics instruction by expert and novice teachers. *American Educational Research Journal, 26*(4), 473–498.

Dewey, J. (1910, 1933). *How we think: A restatement of the relation of reflective thinking to the educative process.* Boston: Heath.

Duffy, G. (2005). Metacognition and the development of reading teachers. In C. Block, S. Israel, K. Kinnucan-Welsch, & K. Bauserman (Eds.), *Metacognition and literacy learning* (pp. 299–314). Mahwah, NJ: Erlbaum.

Duffy, G. G., Miller, S. D., Kear, K., Parsons, S. A., Davis, S., & Williams, B. (2008). Teachers' instructional adaptations during literacy instruction. In Y. Kim, V. Risko, D. L. Compton, D. K. Dickinson, M. K. Hundley, et al. (Eds.), *57th yearbook of the National Reading Conference* (pp. 160–171). Oak Creek, WI: National Reading Conference.

Gambrell, L. B., Malloy, J. A., & Mazzoni, S. A. (2011). Evidence-based best practices for comprehensive literacy instruction. In L. M. Morrow & L. B. Gambrell (Eds.), *Best practices in literacy instruction* (4th ed., pp. 11–36). New York: Guilford Press.

Gay, G. (2002). Preparing for culturally responsive teaching. *Journal of Teacher Education, 53*(2), 106–116.

Hattie, J. (2009). *Visible learning: A synthesis of over 800 meta-analyses relating to achievement.* New York: Routledge.

Honan, E. (2004). Teachers as bricoleurs: Producing possible readings of curriculum documents. *English Teaching: Practice and Critique, 3*(2), 99–112.

Johnston, P. (2004). *Choice words: How our language affects children's learning.* Portland, ME: Stenhouse.

Johnston, P., Dozier, C., & Smit, J. (2016). How language supports adaptive teaching through a responsive learning culture. *Theory Into Practice, 55,* 189–196.

Parsons, S. A. (2012). Adaptive teaching in literacy instruction case studies of two teachers. *Journal of Literacy Research, 44*(2), 149–170.

Parsons, S. A., & Vaughn, M. (2013). Exploring adaptive teaching across contexts: Cross-case analysis of rural and urban educators' instructional adaptations. *Alberta Journal of Educational Research, 59*(2), 299–318.

Parsons, S. A., Vaughn, M., Scales, R., Gallagher, M., Davis, S., & Ward-Parsons, A. (2018). Teachers' instructional adaptations: A research synthesis. *Review of Educational Research, 88*(2), 205–242.

Pressley, M., Allington, R., Wharton-McDonald, R., Block, C., & Morrow, L. (Eds.). (2001). *Learning to read: Lessons from exemplary first-grade classrooms.* New York: Guilford Press.

Sawyer, R. (2004). Creative teaching: Collaborative improvisation. *Educational Researcher, 33*(2), 12–20.

Schön, D. A. (1983). *The reflective practitioner: How professionals think in action.* New York: Basic Books.

Snow, C. E., Griffin, P., & Burns, M. S. (Eds.). (2005). *Knowledge to support the teaching of reading: Preparing teachers for a changing world.* San Francisco: Jossey-Bass.

Vaughn, M. (2014). The role of student agency: Exploring openings during literacy instruction. *Teaching and Learning: The Journal of Natural Inquiry and Reflective Practice, 28*(1), 4–16.

Vaughn, M. (2015). Adaptive teaching: Case studies of two elementary teachers' visions and adaptations during literacy instruction. *Reflective Practice: International and Multidisciplinary Perspectives, 16*(1), 43–60.

Vaughn, M. (2018). Making sense of student agency in the early grades. *Phi Delta Kappan, 99*(7), 62–66.

Vaughn, M. (2019). Adaptive teaching during reading instruction: A multi-case study. *Reading Psychology, 40*(1), 1–33.

Vaughn, M. (2020). What is student agency and why does it matter more now than ever? In Student agency: Theoretical implications for practice [themed journal issue]. *Theory Into Practice, 59*(2), 109–118.

Vaughn, M., & Parsons, S. A. (2013). Teachers as innovators: Instructional adaptations opening spaces for enhanced literacy learning. *Language Arts, 91*(2), 81–93.

Vaughn, M., Parsons, S. A., Gallagher, M., & Branen, J. (2016). Teachers' adaptive instruction supporting students' literacy learning. *The Reading Teacher, 69*(5), 539–547.

Williams, T., & Baumann, J. (2008). Contemporary research on effective elementary literacy teachers. In Y. Kim, V. J. Risko, D. L. Compton, D. K. Dickinson, M. K. Hundley, et al. (Eds.), *57th yearbook of the National Reading Conference* (pp. 357–372). Oak Creek, WI: National Reading Conference.

Zeichner, K. M., & Liston, D. P. (2013). *Reflective teaching: An introduction* (2nd ed.). New York: Routledge.

PART III
. . . .
TEACHERS

21

Reflective Practice

Mary McGriff and Michelle L. Rosen

At our institution, clinical interns take an evening workshop course that allows them time and space to share and reflect on their teaching and observational experiences in local schools. Recently, one of our students, Farah, arrived to class eager to update everyone on the progress of a low-performing fifth-grade student whom we had heard about over the past several class sessions. It happened that Farah's cooperating teacher had just been assigned a team teacher to share planning and teaching responsibilities. According to Farah, the newly arrived team teacher, Mr. Gaines, planned and led his lessons in a different manner, and since his arrival, the struggling student's level of engagement had increased notably.

As Farah explained, rather than "getting through" a stack of papers to be graded, Mr. Gaines used his planning periods to consult websites and a well-respected online teacher forum, seeking supplemental materials and techniques to make their current instructional unit more relevant. She described how Mr. Gaines was a close observer of student work. He was able to notice minor—sometimes infinitesimally small—improvements in this student's work and use these small successes to cultivate continued engagement and essential literacy skill development.

As leaders of the clinical intern seminar, we were thrilled. We were additionally thrilled when, at Mr. Gaines's invitation, we visited his school several times for firsthand observations of his planning, teaching, and collaborations with colleagues. Through Farah's and our own accounts of Mr. Gaines's work, the entire group of interns saw how reflective practice and high expectations are inextricably linked. As the semester progressed, it became clear to us that Mr. Gaines's planning and teaching were consistent with leading research findings on how reflective practice enables teachers to sustain high expectations for their students over time through engagement in an ongoing process of examining the actions, responses, and undergirding beliefs that comprise the practice of teaching. We also noted how Mr. Gaines's practice and that of his colleagues provide valuable exemplars for current and preservice teachers to adapt and apply in their own school settings.

Understanding Reflective Practice

As a principle of effective literacy instruction, reflective practice has been examined and written about by educational researchers and practitioners for decades. This body of research and perspective-taking about reflective practice is useful in helping current teachers consider how and why this principle can be applied in their own professional contexts.

Improving practice through reflection builds upon the work of John Dewey (1933) and his notion that we learn from reflecting on experiences and not merely from the actual experiences. In teaching, Dewey's reflective thought theory highlights the fact that tangible solutions to pedagogical questions and broader conceptual understandings about the questions themselves can emerge from sustained reflection. Effective reflective practice is complex. In order for it to be successful, educators need to be keenly aware of its rigor, intellectual and emotional processes, and time requirements (Rodgers, 2002).

In his book *The Reflective Practitioner*, Donald Schön (1983) presented the idea of "reflective practice" through two forms: *reflection-in-action* and *reflection-on-action*. Through his exploration of these models, Schön showed the difference between the two and the necessity for educators to be able to differentiate. When successful, their reflective processes help reshape what they do in their classrooms, either during instruction (reflection-in-action) or following instruction (reflection-on-action) in an effort to improve their pedagogical thinking (Schön, 1983).

Often referred to as "thinking on our feet," reflection-in-action engages us in the way we look at our own teaching experiences while we associate it with our feelings and focus on our own theories. Reflecting while we are in the act of teaching (reflection-in-action) helps us to inform our actions in the actual situation while it is unfolding in an effort to gain new understandings and grow intellectually. Reflection-in-action is a process that educators bring to their daily teaching, while functioning under complex and tentative conditions (Schön, 1983), and we must be aware it is occurring as we are working.

Reflection-on-action refers to the act of teachers reflecting on their practice after it has been completed. This process also includes the critique of one's own practice. In both types of reflection, emphasis is placed on the significance of the practice and the use of knowledge gained through the reflection on planning and teaching experiences (Schön, 1983).

In later work, Stephen Brookfield (1995) tasked teachers with answering the question of the worthiness of their teaching. In order to answer this question, Brookfield described the need to critically reflect on one's instructional practices. Exemplary teachers who continually refine their authentic voice reveal the value and dignity of their work because they discover its worth. As educators foster this process within themselves, they reap the benefits, which includes inspirational self-assuredness, successfully achieving their teaching goals, and ultimately encouraging their students to be motivated and reflective learners.

Brookfield (1995) recommended four lenses from multiple vantage points to garner increased pedagogical awareness for teachers: (1) autobiographical, (2) the student's eyes, (3) colleagues' experiences, and (4) published research. Teachers ruminate on these perspectives in an effort to provide a foundation for successful pedagogy and the path to successful instruction as they directly correlate to processes of self-reflection, student feedback, peer assessment, and engagement with scholarly literature.

According to Brookfield (2017), the foundation for critical reflection is the autobiographical lens (or self-reflection). Reflecting on previous experiences as both learners and teachers is critical to understanding how one becomes aware of the typical assumptions and inherent reasonings for how teachers' work is framed. Some teachers reveal pedagogical aspects of their own work by exploring teacher journals, peer feedback, evaluations, and personal goals. Others find that creative writing and other forms of aesthetic expression help them to recognize and clarify the underlying dispositions that shape their practice (McGriff, 2017).

While self-reflection is the basis for reflective practice, not stopping there and advancing the process is crucial to effective literacy instruction. Reflective teachers build upon this notion by analyzing student evaluations, assessment results, student journals, or student focus groups. They use these artifacts in an effort to teach more responsively. Brookfield (2017) explained how using both the autobiographical and student lenses, in combination, allows for educators to either endorse or contest existing power relationships in the classroom. An example of the student lens is developing culturally relevant teaching strategies in the classroom. Teachers need to understand the critical importance of learning about students' cultures and communities and actively connecting instructional content to these areas of relevance (Ladson-Billings, 2009). In short, accessing these two lenses, in tandem, allows educators to adjust their instructional practice for the good of student equity and academic achievement.

Reflective teachers engage themselves in these two lenses by looking to peers for mentoring, guidance, and feedback. Collaboration among adult learners is built on a practiced climate of trust where colleagues can share ideas, respectfully talk through differences of opinions, and participate equitably. Additionally, confidence in teaching is gained as a result of interactions with other teachers through the realization that their peers share in some of the same pedagogical obstacles. Motivation, increased levels of collegiality, and successful teaching and learning outcomes are a direct result of teachers participating in purposeful conversations with peers (Brookfield, 2017; Risko & Vogt, 2016).

The fourth and final lens Brookfield (2017) referenced was teachers' interactions with scholarly work or higher education. This connection to the academic world provides a mechanism for teachers to understand the link between their "private" teaching challenges and the larger political processes. A forward-thinking understanding of teaching practices comes from the ability to research, present, or publish scholarly work.

In the vein of using multiple lenses to engage in reflective practice, Risko and Vogt (2016) presented the notion of professional learning through an inquiry process. According to their research, reflective practice is dynamic in that it raises instruction-related questions through various perspectives. Unlike students' out-of-school circumstances as well as school issues such as budget and materials, a teacher's pedagogical approach is one factor within their ability to control. Professional learning has been documented as one of the most important factors in student achievement and may in fact be one of the few indicators of student success that a teacher can regulate (Guskey, 2000; Yoon, Duncan, Lee, Scarloss, & Shapley, 2007). To this end, the Every Student Succeeds Act (U.S. Department of Education, 2015) outlines the ways in which teachers are supported in an effort to help students achieve academically. In certain states, departments of education are committed to using funds provided by this legislation to create programs and policies that support teachers' use of reflective practices throughout the duration of their careers (U.S. Department of Education, 2015).

Reflective practice, according to Mezirow (1997), is the process of making new or revised interpretations of the meaning of experiences, which guides subsequent understanding, appreciation, and action. The implication made here is that learning experiences are grounded in personal experience. From that, educators who are open to feedback and adjustment are more prone to change their learning and ultimately instruction for the better. Much different than educators "receiving" knowledge, this type of practice shifts the focus regarding an educator's vision as it relates to learning. It is built on the assumption that educators actively participate in the continual process of developing and then redeveloping conceptual frameworks, or ways of understanding the nature of their practice (Cochran-Smith & Lytle, 2009).

Why Is Reflective Practice a Principle of Effective Literacy Instruction?

Reflective practice is empowering. It provides literacy educators with a measure of self-directedness in professional learning, and it contributes to a sense of agency in terms of not only what is to be learned but also how it is to be learned (Brookfield, 2017; Mezirow, 1997). As we will illustrate, reflective practice enables teachers to generate knowledge through the systematic examination on their teaching practice, and it places a teacher's work at the core of student learning. Lytle (2006) discusses a concept of teaching literacy that feeds a framework for seeing how educators transform practice by "reading" and "writing" their own practice. A teacher's practice through this framework is seen as a text for them to study. Similar to real "texts," they are open to multiple perspectives in an effort for the practices to generate learning experiences for the educators.

Self-directedness, agency, and knowledge that reflective teaching lies at the heart of student learning have never been more important, particularly in the current educational landscape of prescriptive curricular programs and emphasis on test preparation. Reflective practice brings to the surface the collaborative, inquiring, and human sides of teaching and learning; it sustains and empowers teachers to do the essential work of literacy instruction, and it provides a mechanism for them to carry out this instruction effectively. This was certainly the case in our observation of Mr. Gaines's practice. During our visits to his classroom and school, we had the privilege of witnessing exemplary reflective practice in action.

Reflective Practice during Instruction

You arrive at home to discover an envelope in the mailbox containing a gift card for your favorite store. The envelope has no return address.

Happy Monday! Happy writing!

Sincerely,
Mr. Gaines

During one of our earliest visits to Mr. Gaines's classroom, we immediately took note of the daily creative writing warm-up routine that the students use to start their 90-minute language arts period. As they enter, students retrieve their writing journals and a slip of paper bearing the day's writing prompt. Students then glue the prompt atop a blank page in their journals and spend 5 minutes prewriting a narrative based on the prompt. As they write, Mr. Gaines and his intern—our student, Farah—provide individual assistance to students, helping them to generate ideas or to expand on points in their writing. After this, students spend an additional 10 minutes working either on the day's topic or on a narrative they already started. Lastly, before delving into whatever unit of study the class is currently working on, Mr. Gaines invites two students to share their works in progress. The students appeared clearly familiar with this routine and with Mr. Gaines's consistently reinforced expectation that they remain on task, working as authors to develop their writing pieces.

On this particular day, by the time most students were seated and working, Mr. Gaines noticed Cynthia seated on the other side of the room. Cynthia's journal remained closed, and she was softly talking to Alonzo, the student seated beside her. Rather than publicly call out these students or immediately walk across the room to correct their behavior, Mr. Gaines first assisted two students who wanted his input about how they should develop their respective plots. Moving toward Cynthia and Alonzo, Mr. Gaines checked in with another student. His increasing proximity prompted Alonzo to begin writing. Cynthia, however, continued her furtive whispering. Mr. Gaines then approached Cynthia.

> MR. GAINES: Cynthia, you have your journal out. Good. So (*opening her journal to a blank page and clipping the writing prompt slip to the top*) what store is the gift card from? A clothing store? Music? Is it from one of those ticket sellers where you can get concert or movie tickets?
>
> CYNTHIA: (*Does not respond.*)
>
> MR. GAINES: We listed our favorite music groups and shows and sports on our interest inventories. Remember that we glued them inside the front cover of our journals? Look yours over. I can give you some time to think about which kind of gift card you would really like and some ideas about who might want to surprise you by sending it to you. Think through some options. You already have the information you need to get started right there on your interest inventory. I'll check back with you.

Giving Cynthia a smile, Mr. Gaines moved on to help other students. During this time, Cynthia's journal remained closed. The 5-minute timer sounded, and Mr. Gaines reminded the class that they could either keep working on this topic or go back and work on a narrative they already started. As several students rifled through pages in their journals to find the story they wanted to work on, Mr. Gaines returned to Cynthia.

MR. GAINES: Let's see what's in your interest inventory (*opening Cynthia's journal and scanning her interest inventory responses*). It says here that you like dancing. So, what about a music subscription gift card, like iTunes, so you can get music for your dance routines?

CYNTHIA: I don't really like dancing now.

MR. GAINES: Okay, but you do like some type of music—some group or genre. If this is a music subscription gift card, what music would you spend it on?

CYNTHIA: Either K-pop or hip-hop, probably.

MR. GAINES: You like K-pop. What if you happened to find the gift card mailed to you with enough on it for an album? Let's just say that happened. Who would want to surprise you in a good way like that?

CYNTHIA: My aunt would, probably.

MR. GAINES: Aunt who? What do you call her?

CYNTHIA: Aunt Mia.

MR. GAINES: Okay. In my words, I would write something like (*picking up a pencil and writing on a sticky note*) "Aunt Mia knows I love BTS. I know she did this! I can't believe it." Those are just my words though. You're the one who knows Aunt Mia. How would you say it?

CYNTHIA: (*Begins to write after Mr. Gaines passes her a pencil.*)

Analyzing Reflective Practice during Instruction

Later that day, we had the chance to speak with Mr. Gaines about the lesson. This discussion fully enabled us to appreciate how Brookfield's (1995) concepts of reflection-in-practice and reflection-on-practice intersect. Mr. Gaines informed us that he was a member of an area professional teachers association and explained that this local group of teachers had been examining research literature and considering the diverse interests and concerns of their students—including familial, cultural, and social—in order to optimize engagement in reading and writing during class hours (Brookfield, 1995; Ladson-Billings, 2009). Many national teacher professional associations have a number of local affiliates in each state. See Table 21.1 for related links.

"We're a group that mainly looks at infusing a variety of culturally and contemporarily relevant experiences and texts that will add more choices and greater relevancy to our larger units. The thinking is that the more agency and relevancy students experience, the more they will be invested in their reading and writing. So, those conversations helped me think about off-task behavior in terms of agency and relevancy: *if a student is not doing what I ask, how well do they understand the task as one that is important to them and as one that they ultimately control?* Being a part of this local association has helped me to be more thoughtful and strategic on my feet. We discuss issues like student control and teacher control a lot, and we think about times when a lack of options or connectedness in our own schooling experiences may have limited our literacy development. So, it is less difficult to call those conversations to mind in the moment, like when dealing with a student who is avoiding work."

Mr. Gaines went on to identify relevancy as the central focus of his exchange with Cynthia. As he described it, Cynthia needed help understanding how her own interests could be incorporated into a narrative about finding a gift card. Mr. Gaines explained that he has his students complete interest inventories precisely so that he can make individually relevant suggestions to his students when their writing becomes stalled. He also told us that he learned even more about Cynthia's interest in K-pop music and dancing during an informal conversation with her the prior week, and this interaction helped Mr. Gaines introduce high-interest writing possibilities during their exchange. Then Mr. Gaines shared his thoughts about Cynthia's talking and refusal to follow established procedures prior to his intervention.

"No one likes to see students not following the procedures you worked to prepare, and when I saw Cynthia whispering to Alonzo, I needed to control the urge to go right over there and just tell them both to get to work. I had to remind myself that the goal is for everyone to be engaged writing. So rather than spend energy correcting Cynthia for not following my rules, I thought it better to spend that same energy helping her to get engaged in writing. I first made a point of helping

TABLE 21.1. National Professional Associations and Their Local Affiliates

Professional Association	Website	Resources	Links to Local Affiliates
International Literacy Association	*https://literacyworldwide.org*	Provides an array of professional publications, lesson planning resources, position statements, a daily blog, and other resources for literacy educators.	*https://literacyworldwide.org/get-involved/ila-network/chapters*
National Council of Teachers of English	*https://ncte.org*	Provides professional learning, affiliation, and advocacy resources, including professional journals, books, online learning opportunities, position statements, an online educators' forum, and professional standards.	*https://ncte.org/groups/affiliates*
Council for Exceptional Children	*https://exceptionalchildren.org*	Provides resources for educators of students with special needs. Resources include governmental policy updates, a variety of professional journals, books, a professional learning video series and podcast series, an online member forum, and professional standards.	*https://exceptionalchildren.org/get-involved/units*
National Association for the Education of Young Children	*www.naeyc.org*	Provides resources for educators of children age 8 and below. Resources include in-person and online professional learning, advocacy resources, professional journals, books, an online forum, position statements, and professional standards.	*www.naeyc.org/get-involved/membership/affiliates*

the students who needed my input so that they could remain on-task. Then I focused on getting Cynthia writing. I wanted to point out the choices she had about the narrative details, and I wanted her to realize that she was in the driver's seat when it came to determining how the story got told. I thought that, if I modeled what getting started looked like, but reinforced the idea that *her* words were the ones that mattered, she would be willing to put her thoughts—her words—down on paper and give it a go."

Mr. Gaines's involvement with a professional association enabled him to benefit from research-based, autobiographical, and professional perspectives and experiences of educators in a variety of schools and districts (Brookfield, 1995). And this association's reflections about the concepts of relevancy and agency carried over to support his in-the-moment intervention to prevent disengagement from taking hold and hindering Cynthia's literacy development. His active reliance on interest inventories allowed him to use individually relevant information to keep students engaged in writing. Even more notably, Mr. Gaines's reflective practice afforded him the self-assuredness to be able to prioritize engagement in writing over absolute and immediate compliance with his established routines. Through his involvement in the professional association, he was able to reflect on the role of student agency as a motivator, and rather than engage Cynthia in a struggle over her adherence to classroom rules, he opted to empower her for the purpose of producing an individually meaningful narrative.

Reflective Practice through Professional Learning Discussions

Mr. Gaines met monthly with a small group of his school-based colleagues to reflect on and hone their planning and teaching through the use of professional learning discussion protocols. Professional learning discussion protocols are instructions and guidelines to support collaborative reflection-on-practice (Brookfield, 2017), and they come in a variety of formats. For instance, some protocols include close analysis of student work samples. Others involve the analysis of a specific instructional dilemma about which colleagues work together in sharing perspectives and raising possible resolutions. (The National School Reform faculty website [*https://nsrfharmony.org/protocols*] provides a free repository of discussion protocols.)

During one of our school visits, Mr. Gaines invited us to observe a protocol discussion. At this meeting, second-grade teacher Tracy shared her concerns about five students in her class who were below grade level in reading and who were striving to comprehend the informational articles included within the second-grade curriculum. Tracy shared that she tried adapting materials and instructional approaches for these students to make the texts more accessible to them. She described dividing longer informational texts into smaller sections to prevent these students from becoming overwhelmed by the number of pages. Tracy also described the limited success she has had modeling how to use context clues to make sense of unfamiliar words. She expressed that unfamiliar vocabulary in highly complex, yet mandated informational texts presents the biggest challenge to her students' comprehension.

> "The thing is even with modeling, this is a struggle because of the sheer number of terms they have never heard of before. We need to stop at least twice per paragraph to stretch out a word by its sounds or maybe read the sentences before and after a term to see if we can determine the meaning that way. It is important that this group receive the same materials that the rest of the students have. I know I have to stay on the curriculum pacing schedule. But needing to stop so frequently is making us fall behind. And stopping so frequently is interfering with their comprehension anyway. I'm teaching the materials, but not in a way that they can actively understand what they are reading. So, here's my question for everyone: *What can I do so that my students can understand and engage with the ideas they are reading about?*"

After stating her question, Tracy stopped talking, set a large wall timer to 20 minutes, and silently took notes while her colleagues considered her question. Mr. Gaines and the other teachers present offered thoughtful insights and suggestions in response to Tracy's question. However, the final few minutes of the protocol discussion best highlight the ways in which this mode of reflective practice enables a candid and generative examination of teachers' perspectives.

> JEN: I understand why modeling is so hard. Tracy has to stop too frequently. I wonder what would happen if she pretaught the most important terms with illustrations or even short videos. Then when she reads with her students, she wouldn't need to stop so much.
>
> GINA: The problem is the students are supposed to be learning to apply context clues as they read. Using illustrations and short videos to teach terms works fine for second grade, but they should be learning to become independent with applying context clues. As they move forward, that's really what they need.

JEN: The thing is texts Tracy has to teach are long and the topics aren't ones that students already know about. I can see them getting fatigued with stopping to analyze so many words and figure out how they all fit together. Then, once they get fatigued, there's no point continuing. They're tired, and forcing them to read past that point just makes them dislike reading. That's not going to help them succeed either, so I'm wondering if there's any way to cut the total amount of articles we expect them to read themselves. Are there one or two passages that can efficiently give them practice with different types of context clues? If so, Tracy could take more time to model and let them practice applying context clues with those two. Then she could share the rest of the material as read-alouds or record the rest of the material for students to listen to at the listening center. She may still need to preteach vocabulary for the section she reads or audio records, but the students will still have a realistic amount of text that they can learn to use context clues with.

GINA: That's a possibility. The kids still develop their ability to apply context clues, which they need. Tracy can stay on schedule with the curriculum pacing, but not in a way that is counterproductive. Something else that would help is your idea about pictures and video clips. Maybe Tracy could use those in learning centers. The students could use those to build background knowledge about the topic during center time.

As the timer sounded, Tracy turned it off and thanked everyone for their ideas. She shared that she noted several possible strategies to use. However, before commenting on any of them specifically, she shared that she would need to think some more about how they could be implemented. She ended her remarks this way: "The question I came here with was about helping students understand what they read in the second grade curriculum, but actually, the issue is broader than that. It's that we are setting them up for their long-term success, and this meeting today reminded me that we absolutely can."

Analysis of Reflective Practice
through Professional Learning Discussions

As one example of reflective practice in action, this protocol discussion illustrates how teachers come together to reconcile an apparent misalignment among their school's curriculum pacing requirement, the need to help low-performing students gain meaning from their reading materials, and the need to effectively teach a reading comprehension strategy that the students will need for long-term academic success. Consistent with Risko and Vogt's (2016) assertion that reflective practice is most effective when it centers on the aspects of an issue that are within a teacher's purview, the teachers who were part of this structured conversation wholly avoided discussion of curricular policy or students' out-of-school circumstances. Rather they reflected on the elements of Tracy's dilemma that were squarely within a classroom teacher's ability to control. Additionally, Jen and Gina's segment of the discussion illustrated how the group's established climate of trust enabled them to openly express differing views on how the students' long-term literacy needs would be best served (Risko & Vogt, 2016). As Jen and Gina brought their respective experiences and understandings to the discussion, they were able to create a potential "work-around"—an approach that could enable Tracy to meet their school's curriculum pacing requirement and still effectively teach her group of learners. This teacher-generated knowledge (Cochran-Smith & Lytle, 2009) had clear benefits for Tracy's students. Additionally, by participating in the discussion, all of the teachers affirmed their capacity to take on legitimate instructional dilemmas in a self-directed manner and to create impactful interventions (Brookfield, 2017; Mezirow, 1997). As we saw in Tracy's closing comment, the teachers' reflective practice reinforced their high expectations for their students' academic achievement because it generated tenable approaches and strategies to help bring that success about.

Conclusion

In literacy instruction, reflective practice is a principle that sustains teachers and facilitates student success. At Mr. Gaines's school, reflective practice played a role in positively affecting a fifth grader's attitude about and engagement in writing. It played a role in supporting younger students' reading strategy acquisition. More fundamentally, this principle was enacted in ways that provided teachers with the professional knowledge, confidence, and agency to make these literacy gains possible for the students they serve. Ultimately, that is the value of reflective practice in literacy instruction.

REFERENCES

Brookfield, S. D. (1995). *Becoming a critically reflective teacher.* Hoboken, NJ: Wiley.
Brookfield, S. D. (2017). *Becoming a critically reflective teacher* (2nd ed.). San Francisco: Jossey-Bass.

Cochran-Smith, M., & Lytle, S. L. (2009). *Inquiry as stance: Practitioner research for the next generation*. New York: Teachers College Press.

Dewey, J. (1933). *How we think: A restatement of the relation of reflective thinking to the educative process*. Boston: Heath.

Gusky, T. (2000). *Evaluating professional development*. Thousand Oaks, CA: Corwin Press.

Ladson-Billings, G. (2009). *The dreamkeepers: Successful teachers of African American children*. San Francisco: Jossey-Bass.

Lytle, S. L. (2006). The literacies of teaching urban adolescents in these times. In. D. Alvermann, K. Hinchman, D. Moore, S. Phelps, & D. Waff (Eds.), *Reconceptualizing the literacies in adolescents' lives* (2nd ed., pp. 257–281). Mahwah, NJ: Erlbaum.

McGriff, M. (2017). A teacher's identity and where I'm from. *The Academic Forum, 18*(2), 42–45.

Mezirow, J. (1997). Transformative learning: Theory to practice. *New Directions for Adult and Continuing Education, 74*, 5–12.

Risko, V., & Vogt, M. E. (2016). *Professional learning in action: An inquiry approach for teachers of literacy*. New York: Teachers College Press.

Rodgers, C. R. (2002). Defining reflection: Another look at John Dewey and reflective thinking. *Teachers College Record, 104*(4), 842–866.

Schön, D. A. (1983). *The reflective practitioner: How professionals think in action*. Surrey, UK: Ashgate.

U.S. Department of Education. (2015). Every Student Succeeds Act of 2015 (Public Law No. 114-95). Retrieved from *www2.ed.gov/policy/elsec/leg/essa/index.html*.

Yoon, K. S., Duncan, T., Lee, S. W. Y., Scarloss, B., & Shapley, K. (2007). *Reviewing the evidence on how teacher professional development affects student achievement* (Issues & Answers Report, REL 2007-No. 033). San Antonio, TX: Regional Educational Laboratory Southwest.

22

Teachers as Lifelong Learners

Aimee L. Morewood and Julie W. Ankrum

> There was then, and still is now, a too-common
> belief that if you just had a good undergraduate
> education, you could go and teach. But there's so
> much more to learn.
> —LINDA DARLING-HAMMOND (2019)

Effective teachers of literacy must possess a deep understanding of literacy processes and development in order to meet the needs of all learners in their classrooms. Developing expertise requires time and experience (Collins Block, Oakar, & Hurt, 2011; Fullan & Hargreaves, 2016), and it is unlikely that this can be fully accomplished through an initial educator preparation program (EPP). In fact, many EPPs explain that teachers must be lifelong learners, so they may continue to grow and develop in their expertise. As Darling-Hammond (2019) states in the quote above, we need to continue to challenge the idea that EPPs are able to provide all necessary professional information to teacher candidates. Additional learning must occur for teachers to stay current and relevant and to continue to grow as professionals. Continued effective professional learning opportunities (PLOs) are essential for teachers to develop the expertise necessary to teach all students to read and write. In this chapter, we first summarize research on expert literacy teachers. Then we provide information on teacher change and explain characteristics of effective professional learning opportunities (PLOs). Finally, detailed examples are provided of traditional and emerging PLOs that teachers may choose to build their literacy instructional repertoires.

Expert Literacy Teachers

It is imperative that teachers are lifelong learners. The literature demonstrates well that expert teachers affect student learning (Bean & Morewood, 2011; Fisher, Frey, & Nelson, 2012; Hattie, 2009; Taylor & Pearson, 2002). While EPPs prepare teachers for the profession, novice teachers must continue to learn effective practices so they can strive toward what research tells us that expert literacy teachers do in their instruction. Research in this area shows that expert literacy teachers have a deep understanding of their students' strengths and needs (Pressley et al., 2001), are able to effectively use student assessment data to inform their instruction (Allington & Johnston, 2002; Taylor, Pearson, Peterson, & Rodriguez, 2003), balance word level skill instruction with comprehension instruction (Allington & Johnston, 2002; Pressley & Allington, 2015), and effectively teach in small-group settings (Taylor, Pearson, Clark, & Walpole, 1999; Taylor et al., 2003). Continuing to learn and grow as a professional in these areas allows teachers to capitalize on what research tells us expert teachers do when planning for effective instruction that supports students' individual literacy learning needs.

Knowledge Triad

Teachers must possess and apply various types of knowledge (e.g., content, pedagogy, and curriculum) in order to effectively deliver meaningful instruction (Shulman, 1986). It is essential for teachers to deeply understand literacy content when planning and delivering instruction. This content knowledge includes the complexities of the reading process, the developmental nature of literacy acquisition, and how to determine the competencies held by their learners. In addition, teachers must possess a deep understanding of pedagogical content knowledge (PCK), which is the specialized knowledge of instructional techniques and effective teaching (Shulman, 1986). PCK allows teachers to go beyond simply providing information to students. Hume (2010) further explains PCK as knowledge that grows deeper and wider over time because of teaching and professional learning experiences. The changing needs of students and learning environments make PCK difficult to explicitly describe, and these changing needs support the need for continued learning opportunities for teachers.

Curricular knowledge (CK) is also an important component of teacher knowledge. CK includes teachers' understanding of how instructional content aligns with vertical and horizontal curricula (Shulman, 1986). Vertical curriculum is the content that is taught across grade levels. This type of CK guides teachers' instructional plans because it provides information about what students should know and understand when they come into a particular grade level. It also allows teachers to know and understand the expectation of knowledge for the next grade, so that teachers have a curricular target for their students. On the other hand, horizontal curriculum looks closely at the content that is presented within and across subject areas within a grade level. This type of knowledge allows teachers to better understand how to make connections among the topics they are teaching so that students are able to apply their understanding broadly versus a siloed representation (i.e., students fluidly apply and discuss reading comprehension skills across subject and topic areas versus only focusing on reading comprehension skills during reading class). Because of the high knowledge demands placed on teachers, it is critical to provide ongoing and sustained PLOs in all of these areas.

Metacognition

Effective literacy instruction, like all good teaching, requires informed decision making. Teachers must often adapt their instruction, in the midst of a lesson, in order to meet the needs of their learners (Parsons et al., 2018). The ability to teach responsively in this way depends on deep professional knowledge, which is best developed over time and with support (Hargreaves & Fullan, 2012). Such knowledge progression enhances teachers' ability to adapt instruction, which in turn integrates learned experiences with existing content knowledge. Informed decision making is also dependent upon agency. Teacher agency is the ability to analytically shape instructional responses to various situations (Biesta & Tedder, 2007); in essence, it is connected to multiple decisions and adaptations needed for effective teaching.

Effective PLOs

The purpose of PLOs is to affect teachers' instruction so they can better support student learning. Guskey (2002) developed a model for teacher change within professional development. In his model, Guskey describes three types of change that occur because of the teacher engaging in a PLO. The first type of change involves the teacher; after participating in a PLO, teachers change their teaching practices. The second type of change occurs in student learning outcomes; as a result of the changed teaching practices, student learning is enhanced. The third type of change described by Guskey is a change in teachers' beliefs and attitude. This means that teachers begin to think differently about teaching and learners as a result of successes stemming from their new instructional practices.

When selecting PLOs to enhance teaching, it is important to understand the characteristics of effective PLOs. This has been a focus of research for decades (e.g., Anders, Hoffman, & Duffy, 2000; Guskey, 1986; Showers & Joyce, 1996). A primary characteristic of effective PLOs is that they provide ongoing opportunities for teacher learning (Bean & Morewood, 2011; Desimone, 2009). This means that instead of being limited to one or two sessions, high-quality PLOs are offered in multiple sessions over a long period of time. Effective PLOs are also focused on teachers' specific learning needs (Bean & Morewood, 2011; Parsons, Parsons, Morewood, & Ankrum, 2016). In other words, the topics of study addressed in PLOs are based on instructional areas that need to be refined.

Research also demonstrates that effective PLOs take place in collaborative environments (Bean & Morewood, 2011; Desimone, 2009; Parsons et al., 2016). This means that the participants and the PLO providers collaborate in the process of selecting topics, studying content, and planning the implementation of new practices. Effective PLOs also contain a strong leadership presence (Darling-Hammond, Wei, Andree, Richardson, & Orphanos, 2009; Parsons et al., 2016). For example, the building administrator may participate in the PLO and guides the teachers through implementation of new practices. In addition, effective PLOs guide teachers in the implementation of evidence-based practices and are based on student assessment data to inform instruction.

Effective PLOs support teachers as they extend their knowledge base and improve instructional practices. Literacy instruction is a complex and multilayered process; therefore, it is important to carefully consider the manner in which PLOs aim to develop the knowledge triad (i.e., content, pedagogy, and curriculum). Two contrasting models of PLOs, training and educative, have been described in the research (Duffy, 2004; Hoffman & Pearson, 2000; Richardson & Placier, 2001). Koellner and Jacobs (2015) proposed a third model for effective PLOs, the continuum model. This model is inclusive of elements found in both the training model and the educative model where the elements serve as opposite ends of the spectrum. Table 22.1 summarizes the three different PLO models. These three models provide a framework to use when critically reviewing PLOs. Understanding each of these models allows educators to select PLOs that align with their individual learning objectives and goals.

Training Model

A traditional approach to PLOs, where the learning focus is commonly determined by school administrators, is called the training model of professional development. In this model, new instructional techniques are

TABLE 22.1. PLO Models

	Focused on Teachers' Learning Needs	Structure Promotes Collaborative Environments	Strong Leadership Presence
Training Model Topic determined by administrators Focus on instructional techniques; fidelity of implementation expected		Possibly	Possibly
Educative Model Topic determined by teacher needs Focus on supporting teachers through reflection on existing practices and encouraging experimentation with novel techniques	Specifically address individual teachers' instruction	Co-construction of knowledge	Instructional coaching is often added to provide support for teachers over time.
Continuum Model Balance of both training and educative models Supports teacher learning and instructional change by providing differentiated characteristics based on needs of participants	Offer flexible learning opportunities	Sustained learning opportunities and communication over time	Teacher leaders support teachers throughout the duration of PLO.

often introduced through a workshop, and teachers are expected to integrate them fully them into their repertoires. Quite often the training is limited to one or two provider-led sessions, and the desired outcome is fidelity of the described practices. Since the expected result is typically limited to the implementation of specific routines and structures, the sessions often do not focus on teacher decisions or student learning. For example, after teachers participate in training sessions focused on interactive read-alouds, a teacher may read to students but engage them in low-level discussions (e.g., answering literal questions) during the reading. The training model has been widely implemented across teaching contexts, although they do little to transform practices. Overall, the model contradicts the characteristics of effective PLOs, which were described in the previous section.

Educative Model

In this model, teachers and PLO providers collaborate through inquiry to co-construct knowledge (Hoffman & Pearson, 2000). The educative model is aligned with previously described characteristics of effective PLOs (Anders et al., 2000; Bean & Morewood, 2011; Dillon, O'Brien, Sato, & Kelly, 2011; Duffy, 2004; Morewood, Ankrum, & Bean, 2010; Parsons et al., 2016; Taylor, Pearson, Peterson, & Rodriguez, 2005; Taylor, Raphael, & Au, 2011), because they are embedded in classrooms and extend over the long term. These conditions provide authentic contexts for teachers to engage in informed decision making and in-the-moment problem solving. Educative model PLOs support teachers as they reflect on their existing practices and encourage experimentation with techniques discussed in sessions. Instructional coaching is often added as additional sustained support throughout the professional development plan. In this type of learning experience, teachers become actively engaged in learning, which positively affects their literacy instruction (Desimone, Porter, Garet, Yoon, & Birman, 2002).

Because teacher learning opportunities are sustained over time and guided by collaborative leadership, teachers are afforded opportunities to reflect on the implementation of new practices. Through active engagement in educative PLOs, teachers develop deeper content knowledge, an understanding of how content fits into the school curriculum (e.g., vertical and horizontal), and how PCK influences instructional moves. Teachers also learn to appreciate how the integration of this knowledge directly affects student learning.

Continuum Model

It may not be feasible for some school districts to develop PLOs that are aligned with only the training or educative model (Koellner & Jacobs, 2015). The continuum model aligns with both types of PLOs described by Duffy (2004). Further, a balance of both training and educative models can support teacher learning and instructional change by providing flexible opportunities integrating differentiated characteristics to meet participants' needs.

Past and Emerging PLOs

As previously discussed, effective PLOs have been researched for decades. Besides the characteristics associated with effective PLOs (e.g., ongoing opportunities focused on teachers' learning needs), the type and structure of the PLO are also important pieces of the planning (Anders et al., 2000; Bean & Morewood, 2011; Darling-Hammond et al., 2009; Desimone, 2009; Dillon et al., 2011; Morewood et al., 2010; Parsons et al., 2016; Taylor et al., 2005, 2011). The following types of traditional and emerging PLOs all use the characteristics described in the research. Traditional forms of PLOs can most easily be defined as physically meeting in one common place, at the same time, to learn and grow professionally. These can take place at a school (such as professional learning communities or book study), or the professional learning may occur through graduate coursework at an institution, which extends collaborative connections beyond a school. These types of PLOs have been the source of much of the current research in the field. This is not an exhaustive list, but it is intended to provide examples of different types of traditional PLOs and demonstrates a variety of effective PLOs currently being used in the mainstream to support teacher learning.

In addition to the PLOs that many teachers are familiar with, there are new and emerging ways for teachers to deepen their professional knowledge. Unconferences are one promising new form of a PLO. This collaborative grassroots form of professional development is described as free, informal, and engaging (*www.cultofpedagogy.com/edcamp-teachmeet-unconference*). The Edcamp Foundation advertises unconferences (they call them Edcamps) that are held across the United States and in 41 countries around the world. Based on empowerment and educator learning, these PLOs are participant driven and collaborative in nature. All participants attend Edcamps voluntarily and are free to engage in sessions, or lead a session on an area of interest or strength. While not focused entirely on literacy, the theme of an Edcamp or unconference could be limited to literacy, to allow deep study in this area.

Many of these emerging PLOs use technology to provide teachers with access to many people and topics that they might not otherwise connect with throughout their career. In addition, using technology to learn provides teachers with 24/7 access to learning opportunities; therefore, they do not need to wait for a PLO—they create it. Technology can be used in a variety of ways to grow professionally. Again, the following descriptions are not intended to be exhaustive but do provide examples of ways that technology provides PLOs for teachers.

Twitter

Twitter can be viewed as a place for teachers to engage in PLOs. This type of learning allows teachers to follow a variety of topics from leaders in the field. Research that focuses on the use of Twitter as a PLO suggests that teachers view it as a place to connect with colleagues that support their instructional efforts, share their experiences, and discuss content knowledge that is specific to their current teaching position (Davis, 2013). This type of PLO allows for veteran and novice teachers to join in on the conversation. For example, Angela Curfman, a higher educational instructor (personal communication, December 16, 2019), has her preservice teachers create a professional Twitter account at the beginning of the semester. She calls this assignment "Professional Development in Your Palm." In this assignment, her preservice students follow different content-focused organizations and resources. Then, at the end of the semester, she engages her students in a class conversation where they discuss what they have gained throughout this PLO journey. Another way that Twitter can be used to support PLOs is through professional networking. Sie et al. (2013) suggest that Tweetstorms (e.g., a brainstorming session using Twitter) provide PLOs to teachers through social networking. This research suggests that these networks provide teachers with opportunities to share information, receive feedback from peers, and see value in their work. It is easy to see how these social networking platforms align with the Continuum Model of PLOs.

Podcasts

Podcasts are another platform for teachers to access PLOs. This PLO provides teachers with the opportunity to hear from other professionals in the field on a specific topic. Podcasts typically provide an expert explicitly talking about or describing an event, a topic, or a piece of research. Carlisle, Newman Thomas, and McCathren (2016) found that their preservice teachers who were given podcasts to supplement their required course readings outperformed the group of students that were not provided access to these materials. This demonstrates that podcasts do provide PLOs for preservice teachers to make connections to their required course readings. As preservice teachers become familiar and comfortable with this type of PLO, they can continue to listen to professionals in the field on topics that related to their current teaching position. Graduate courses can also provide direction and access to podcasts that will support inservice teacher learning. For example, graduate literacy courses can use the Voice of Literacy podcasts (*www.voiceofliteracy.org*) to supplement students' reading and understanding of current research in the field. These podcasts allow the authors of articles published in *Reading Research Quarterly* and *Journal of Literacy Research* to further discuss their research. Hearing from authors and literacy researchers in the field often gives practicing and novice teachers more context for how the research was situated and how best to interpret and apply the findings.

Masterminds

A mastermind is a community of learners that meet regularly to discuss their work, solve problems, and improve their practices (*www.cultofpedagogy.com/educator-mastermind*). This type of PLO is most effective if the group is kept small, to allow full participation for all members. While the idea for the mastermind model was developed more than 80 years ago (see Burns, 2013), the collaborative problem-solving group is just beginning to take hold in education. One example of a popular education mastermind was founded by Daniel Bauer. Primarily focused on building leadership, the mastermind is an online global meeting of educators. Teachers, administrators, and instructional coaches participate in the group (*www.betterleadersbetterschools.com/mastermind*). Weekly 1-hour meetings are held to discuss readings and solve problems or challenges faced by group members. Membership requires the submission of an application, followed by an interview; this ensures dedicated and engaged members of the community. Bauer's website provides various resources and a podcast; full access is available to members, while limited access is available to nonmembers.

The emerging PLOs that are highlighted here demonstrate how teachers can take more control over their professional learning. They can be active seekers of knowledge, rather than passive recipients of information.

Conclusion

As Darling-Hammond (2019) states, "If you don't have a strong supply of well-prepared teachers, nothing else in education can work." It is imperative that teachers continue to deepen their knowledge of content, pedagogy, and curriculum and refine their instruction to meet individual needs (Duke, Cervetti, & Wise, 2016; Pearson & Hoffman, 2015). Engaging in effective PLOs can help teachers continue to develop their expertise, which will allow them to successfully meet individual students' learning needs (Collins Block et al., 2011). A variety of options are available for teachers to choose as they continue to learn and grow as literacy professionals. However, it is important understand the characteristics of effective PLOs, so that teachers may be critical consumers and successful lifelong learners.

REFERENCES

Allington, R. L., & Johnston, P. H. (2002). *Reading to learn: Lessons from exemplary fourth grade classrooms.* New York: Guilford Press.

Anders, P., Hoffman, J., & Duffy, G. (2000). Teaching teachers to teach reading: Paradigm shifts, persistent problems, and challenges. In M. Kamil, P. Mosenthal, P. D. Pearson, & R. Barr (Eds.), *Handbook of reading research* (Vol. 3, pp. 719–742). Mahwah, NJ: Erlbaum.

Bean, R. M., & Morewood, A. L. (2011). Best practices in professional development for improving literacy instruction in schools. In L. B. Gambrell & L. Mandel Morrow (Eds.), *Best practices in literacy instruction* (4th ed., pp. 455–478). New York: Guilford Press.

Biesta, G., & Tedder, M. (2007). Agency and learning in the lifecourse: Towards an ecological perspective. *Studies in the Education of Adults, 39,* 132–149.

Burns, S. (2013, October 21). 7 reasons to join a mastermind group. *Forbes.* Retrieved from *www.forbes.com/sites/chicceo/2013/10/21/7-reasons-to-join-a-mastermind-group/#6184a6645deb.*

Carlisle, A., Newman Thomas, C., & McCathren, R. B. (2016). The effectiveness of using a content acquisition podcast to teach phonological awareness, phonemic awareness, and phonics to preservice special education teachers. *Journal of Special Education Technology, 3*(2), 87–98.

Collins Block, C., Oakar, M., & Hurt, N. (2011). The expertise of literacy teachers: A continuum from preschool to Grade 5. *Reading Research Quarterly, 37*(2), 178–206.

Darling-Hammond, L. (2019). Stanford Graduate School of Education: Research stories. Retrieved from *https://ed.stanford.edu/news/if-you-don-t-have-strong-supply-well-prepared teachers-nothing-else-education-can-work.*

Darling-Hammond, L., Wei, R., Andree, A., Richardson, N., & Orphanos, S. (2009). *Professional learning in the learning profession: A status report on teacher development in the United States and abroad.* Palo Alto, CA: School Redesign Network at Stanford University.

Davis, K. (2013). Exploring virtual PLCs: Professional development for the busy practitioner. *Perspectives on School-Based Issues, 14*(2), 28–32.

Desimone, L. (2009). Improving impact studies of teachers' professional development: Toward better conceptualizations and measures. *Educational Researcher, 38,* 181–199.

Desimone, L. M., Porter, A. C., Garet, M. S., Yoon, K. S., & Birman, B. F. (2002). Effects of professional development on teachers' instruction: Results from a three-year longitudinal study. *Educational Evaluation and Policy Analysis, 24,* 81–112.

Dillon, D., O'Brien, D., Sato, M., & Kelly, C. (2011). Professional development and teacher education for reading. In M. Kamil, P. D. Pearson, E. Moje, & P. Afflerbach (Eds.), *Handbook of reading research* (Vol. 4, pp. 629–660). New York: Routledge.

Duffy. G. G. (2004). Teachers who improve reading achievement: What research says about what they do and how to develop them. In D. S. Strickland & M. L.

Kamil (Eds.), *Improving reading achievement through professional development* (pp. 3–22). Norwood, MA: Christopher Gordon.

Duke, N. K., Cervetti, G. N., & Wise, C. N. (2016). The teacher and the classroom. *Journal of Education, 196*(3), 35–43.

Fisher, D., Frey, N., & Nelson, J. (2012). Literacy achievement through sustained professional development. *The Reading Teacher, 65,* 551–563.

Fullan, M., & Hargreaves, A. (2016). *Bringing the profession back in: Call to action.* Oxford, OH: Learning Forward.

Guskey, T. (1986). Staff development and the process of teacher change. *Educational Researcher, 15,* 5–12.

Guskey, T. R. (2002). Professional development and teacher change. *Teachers and Teaching: Theory and Practice, 8,* 381–391.

Hargreaves, A., & Fullan, M. (2012). *Professional capital: Transforming teaching in every school.* New York: Teachers College Press.

Hattie, J. A. C. (2009). *Visible learning: A synthesis of over 800 meta-analyses relating to achievement.* London: Routledge.

Hoffman, J., & Pearson, P. D. (2000). Reading teacher education in the next millennium: What your grandmother's teacher didn't know that your granddaughter's teacher should. *Reading Research Quarterly, 35,* 28–44.

Hume, A. (2010). CoRes and PaP-eRs. *New Zealand Science Teacher, 124,* 38–40.

Koellner, K., & Jacobs, J. (2015). Distinguishing models of professional development: The case of an adaptive model's impact on teachers' knowledge, instruction, and student achievement. *Journal of Teacher Education, 66,* 51–67.

Morewood, A. L., Ankrum, J. W., & Bean, R. M. (2010). Teachers' perceptions of the influence of professional development on their knowledge of content, pedagogy, and curriculum. In S. Szabo, M. B. Sampson, M. Foote, & F. Falk-Ross (Eds.), *31st College Reading Association yearbook* (pp. 201–219). Commerce: Texas A&M University–Commerce.

Parsons, A., Parsons, S., Morewood, A., & Ankrum, J. W. (2016). Barriers to change: Findings from three literacy professional development initiatives. *Literacy Research and Instruction, 35*(4), 331–352.

Parsons, S. A., Vaughn, M., Scales, R. Q., Gallagher, M. A., Parsons, A. W., Davis, S. D., . . . Allen, M. (2018). Teachers' instructional adaptations: A research synthesis. *Review of Educational Research, 88*(2), 205–242.

Pearson, P. D., & Hoffman, J. (2015). Teachers or programs: A historical perspective on where trust is placed in teaching reading. In P. D. Pearson, E. H. Hiebert, & N. K. Duke (Eds.), *Research-based practices for teaching common core literacy* (pp. 237–253.). New York: Teachers College Press.

Pressley, M., & Allington, R. L. (2015). *Reading instruction that works: The case for balanced teaching* (4th ed.). New York: Guilford Press.

Pressley, M., Wharton-McDonald, R., Allington, R., Block, C., Morrow, L., Tracey, D., & Woo, D. (2001). A study of effective first-grade literacy instruction. *Scientific Studies of Reading, 5,* 35–58.

Richardson, V., & Placier, P. (2001). Teacher change. In V. Richardson (Ed.), *Handbook of research on teaching* (4th ed., pp. 905–947). Washington, DC: American Educational Research Association.

Showers, B., & Joyce, B. (1996). The evolution of peer coaching. *Educational Leadership, 53*(6), 12–16.

Shulman, L. S. (1986). Those who understand: Knowledge growth in teaching. *Educational Researcher, 15,* 4–14.

Sie, R., Pataraia, N., Boursinou, E., Rajagopal, K., Margaryan, A., Falconer, I., . . . Sloep, P. (2013). *Educational Technology and Society, 16*(3), 59–75.

Taylor, B. M., & Pearson, P. D. (Eds.). (2002). *Teaching reading: Effective schools, accomplished teachers.* Mahwah, NJ: Erlbaum.

Taylor, B. M., Pearson, P. D., Clark, K. F., & Walpole, S. (1999). Center for the improvement of early reading achievement: Effective schools/accomplished teachers. *The Reading Teacher, 53,* 156–159.

Taylor, B. M., Pearson, P. D., Peterson, D. S., & Rodriguez, M. C. (2003). Reading growth in high-poverty classrooms: The influence of teacher practices that encourage cognitive engagement in literacy learning. *The Elementary School Journal, 104*(1), 3–28.

Taylor, B. M., Pearson, P. D., Peterson, D. S., & Rodriguez, M. C. (2005). The CEIRA school change framework: An evidence-based approach to professional development and school reading improvement. *Reading Research Quarterly, 40,* 40–69.

Taylor, B. M., Raphael, T. E., & Au, K. H. (2011). Reading and school reform. In M. L. Kamil, P. D. Pearson, E. B. Moje, & P. P. Afflerbach (Eds.), *Handbook of reading research* (Vol. 4, pp. 594–628). New York: Routledge.

Index

Deconstruction, text, 260–261
Deliberate practice, 83–85, 84*f*
Design, 256–257
Developmental perspectives, 15, 53, 204
Developmental Reading Assessment 2,
    73
Dictionaries, personal, 10, 70
Differentiation
    adaptive teaching and, 287*f*
    digital literacy and, 272–273, 277–279
    feedback and, 131–132
    overview, 122–125, 132–133
    as a principle of effective literacy
        instruction, 125–131, 128*f*
Digital literacy. *See also* Technology
    classroom applications, 273–279, 274*f*,
        276*t*–277*t*
    overview, 268, 279–280
    principles of effective literacy
        instruction and, 268–273
Digraphs, 53. *See also* Phonemic
    awareness
Disciplinary literacy. *See also* Content
    learning; Instructional practices
    in elementary classrooms, 183–195, 185*f*,
        191*f*
    integrating writing and reading and,
        168–169, 175–176
    overview, 181–183, 195–197, 196*t*
    sentence starters across disciplines and,
        175–176
Discussions. *See also* Conversations as
    assessments
    autonomy support and, 231
    engagement and, 206–207
    flexibly applying, 160–161
    overview, 150–152, 151*f*
    self-selected reading and, 208–209
    small-group discussions, 157–160
    whole-class discussions, 152–157, 153*f*,
        154*f*
Diversity. *See also* Culturally relevant
    instruction; Equity, educational
    adaptive teaching and, 285–286, 287*f*
    critical approaches to text and, 256–257,
        258–260
    text selection and, 258–260

Domain knowledge
    adaptive teaching and, 286
    digital literacy and, 271, 275–277,
        276*t*–277*t*
    integrating writing and reading and,
        164
Domination, 256–257
Drop Everything and Read, 207–209

E

Early Language and Literacy Classroom
    Observation, Pre-K (ELLCO Pre-K),
    18
Early literacy. *See also* First-grade
    instruction; Instructional practices;
    Kindergarten instruction; Literacy
    programs; Second-grade instruction
    advancing word knowledge, 62–65
    assessment and, 91, 92*f*
    comprehension and, 80–85, 80*f*, 84*f*
    overview, 51–52, 65–66
    principles of effective early literacy
        instruction and, 54–61, 58*f*, 60*t*
Educative model of PLO, 315*t*. *See also*
    Professional development
Empowering students, 219, 301
Engagement
    authentic, challenging tasks and,
        219–220, 221–222
    autonomy support and, 228–229,
        232–233
    classroom applications, 205–209
    explicit instruction and, 138–139, 138*f*
    overview, 201–202, 209
    principles of effective classroom
        environments and, 203–205
    whole-class discussions and, 153–155
English learners (ELs), 6, 243–244. *See
    also* Culturally relevant instruction;
    Multiliterate practices
Enhanced alphabetic knowledge (EAK)
    instruction, 58–59, 58*f*, 60*t*
Environment, classroom. *See* Classroom
    environment
Environmental print, 59